JOEL MARCUS is a professor of New Testament
and Christian origins at Duke Divinity School.
His publications include *Jesus and the Holocaust:
Reflections on Suffering and Hope* and *Mark:*

*A New Translation with
Introduction and Commen-
tary.* He taught previously
at Princeton Theological
Seminary, the University
of Glasgow, and Boston
University School of
Theology.

John the Baptist in History and Theology situates
the Baptist within Second Temple Judaism and
compares him to other apocalyptic thinkers from
ancient and modern times. It concludes with
thoughtful reflections on how its revisionist
interpretations might be incorporated into the
Christian faith.

JOHN THE BAPTIST
IN HISTORY AND THEOLOGY

Studies on Personalities of the New Testament
D. Moody Smith, Founding Editor

John the Baptist
in History and Theology

Joel Marcus

THE UNIVERSITY OF SOUTH CAROLINA PRESS

© 2018 University of South Carolina

Published by the University of South Carolina Press
Columbia, South Carolina 29208

www.sc.edu/uscpress

Manufactured in the United States of America

27 26 25 24 23 22 21 20 19 18
10 9 8 7 6 5 4 3 2 1

Library of Congress Cataloging-in-Publication Data
can be found at http://catalog.loc.gov/.

ISBN: 978-1-61117-900-2 (cloth)
ISBN: 978-1-61117-901-9 (ebook)

This book was printed on a recycled stock with 30 percent
postconsumer wasted content.

In memory of Moody Smith
scholar, friend, and man of God

ἐκεῖνος ἦν ὁ λύχνος ὁ καιόμενος καὶ φαίνων,
ὑμεῖς δὲ ἠθελήσατε ἀγαλλιαθῆναι
πρὸς ὥραν ἐν τῷ φωτὶ αὐτοῦ

CONTENTS

PREFACE

Moody Smith, the editor of this series, approached me many years ago—fifteen years? twenty?—about the possibility of writing a book about John the Baptist. I told him that I first had to finish my commentary on Mark but that I might like to do it afterwards. When "afterwards" arrived, however, I found myself writing articles on the parting of the ways between Judaism and Christianity, with the idea of eventually producing a monograph on that subject. Moody very sagely pointed out that John the Baptist was a key figure in the parting of the ways, and I eventually realized that (a) he was right, and (b) I didn't yet know how to make the parting-of-the-ways project gel into a book. So I followed his advice and wrote this book, and I have to say that the experience has turned out to be much more interesting than I had expected. I hope the reader will share my fascination with the task of trying to separate the historical Baptist from the theological interpretations that have encrusted his image, both in the canon and outside of it, and with the task of trying to make sense of that discrepancy.

I wish to thank Moody, in memoriam, for his belief that I was the right person to do the job, and I'm glad that he finally got to see and approve a draft of the manuscript before his final illness. I feel the loss of his friendship and support keenly; he was a wise, good, and godly man, and I will miss him both on and off the tennis court. I also wish to express my deep gratitude to Dale Allison and Mike Winger, who gave me detailed comments on the entire work: greater love hath no man than this, that a man lay down his leisure for his friend's monograph. I also received some very helpful feedback from Al Baumgarten. I am also grateful for the chance to present portions of the work to the New Testament Seminar at Duke University and to the Christianity in Antiquity seminar at the University of North Carolina. And I want to thank Tyler Dunstan and Sinja Küppers, Ph.D. students in the Duke Graduate Program in Religion and Classical Studies Departments, respectively, for help with indexing and copyediting; and Joseph Longarino (see p. 205, n. 88). At the University of South Carolina Press, I have greatly appreciated the help of Pat Callahan, the design and production manager, and especially the forbearance and attentiveness to detail of Bill Adams, the managing editor.

Unless otherwise noted, biblical passages are from the Revised Standard Version (RSV), which tends to be more literal than the newer NRSV; translations of Septuagint passages are from the New English Translation of the Septuagint (NETS); translations of pseudepigrapha are from James H. Charlesworth, ed., *The Old Testament Pseudepigrapha* (OTP); translations of Dead Sea Scrolls material are from Emmanuel Tov, ed., *The Dead Sea Scrolls Electronic Library* (DSSEL); translations of Mishnah passages are from Herbert Danby, *The Mishnah;* translations of Tosefta passages are from Jacob Neusner, *The Tosefta;* translations of passages from the Babylonian Talmud are from Isadore Epstein, ed., *Hebrew-English Edition of the Babylonian Talmud;* translations of classical sources are from the Loeb Classical Library (LCL); translations of apocryphal New Testament materials are from J. K. Elliott, ed., *The Apocryphal New Testament;* translations of the church fathers are from *The Ante-Nicene Fathers* or *The Nicene and Post-Nicene Fathers* (ANF or NPNF). Abbreviations of ancient sources generally follow Billie Jean Collins, ed., *The SBL Handbook of Style,* 2nd ed.

Introduction

THE PROBLEM OF JOHN THE BAPTIST

Who was John the Baptist? According to our earliest sources, the Synoptic Gospels, he was the predecessor of Jesus of Nazareth, the "Stronger One" whom John prophesied would come after him and whose sandal latch he was unworthy to loosen. While John only baptized in water, this "Stronger One" would baptize in the Holy Spirit (Mark 1:7–8) or in the Spirit and fire (Matt. 3:11–12//Luke 3:15–18). John's acknowledgment of his successor's superiority is sharpened in the Fourth Gospel, in which both the author and John himself emphasize that he is *not* the Messiah but only the Messiah's predecessor (John 1:19–23); *not* "the light" but only a witness to the light (1:6–8); *not* the bridegroom but only the best man (3:27–29). This attitude of self-abnegation vis-à-vis Jesus is epitomized by the Baptist's final words in the Fourth Gospel: "He must increase, but I must decrease" (3:30).[1]

But is this picture of John reliable? Knut Backhaus is the latest of many scholars to point out that serious questions arise about the historicity of this Gospel portrait, partly because it is so obvious that it serves Christian interests. As Backhaus puts it: "What has survived may be compared to the Baptist on the Isenheim altarpiece: he is standing under a cross he never saw, in Christian company he never met, with a lamb he never spoke of; and what the Christian painter is mostly interested in is his oversized finger pointing to Christ, whereas his figure clothed in exotic garments steps back into the shadows of history."[2] The dilemma, Backhaus adds, is that we are almost totally dependent on this tendentious Gospel portrait for our knowledge about the history of the Baptist. The only other first-century sources are the book of Acts, written by the author of one of the Gospels (Luke), and the work of the Jewish historian Josephus, who was born a few years after the deaths of John and Jesus (37-38, CE),[3] who died towards the end of the first Christian century, and whose account of the Baptist (*Antiquities* 18.116–119) is itself so terse and tendentious that it does not provide much critical control over the information in the New Testament.[4]

Almost forty years before Backhaus, John Reumann compared these difficulties in an illuminating way with those in the quest for the historical Jesus.[5] Reumann noted that some scholars who in his view had been rightly skeptical about their ability to uncover the historical Jesus had been wrongly sanguine about uncovering the historical John. Reumann warned, however, that the problems involved in trying to reconstruct the life and ministry of the Baptist were at least as difficult as those involved in trying to reconstruct the life and ministry of his famous successor:

> All the hazards of the quest for the historical Jesus exist in the search for the history of John, and then some: conflicting sources, canonical and beyond; tendentiousness in sources; the unsettling role of form and redaction criticism; problems of *religionsgeschichtlich* [history-of-religions] background; the theology of the early Christian church; plus the fact that, if we take seriously the possibility of the Baptist provenance for some of the materials, . . . what we have in the New Testament is *separated* from historical actuality *both by Christian usage and by (earlier) Baptist use.* It is as if we were trying to recover the historical Jesus from traditions filtered through a second, later disciple community of another faith, say Islam (save that the separation in time from the event is shorter).[6] If in the Gospels, to use R. H. Lightfoot's oft misunderstood phrase, we hear, in the case of Jesus "little more than a whisper of his voice," then in the case of the Baptist we have only an echo (or echoes) of his whisper. In short, there is more diversity in modern studies about the Baptist than assumed, more optimism than warranted about recovering knowledge of him historically, and more reason to suspect we cannot throw real light on him than even in the case of Jesus.

Nor are such judgments merely a product of post–World War II skepticism. In a classic work published in 1911, Martin Dibelius, drawing on the 1898 monograph of Wilhelm Baldensperger, saw early Christianity as shot through with polemic against a religious competitor, an independent Baptist movement that continued long after the deaths of John and Jesus and left traces both in the New Testament and in later Christian literature such as the Pseudo-Clementine *Homilies* and *Recognitions*.[7] This layering effect makes it difficult to separate later religious propaganda from the historical kernels about the Baptist in the Gospels.

....

Criteria for Historicity

Dibelius, however, did not think that what we might call "the quest for the historical Baptist" was impossible. He argued, for example, that Matt. 11:11a//Luke 7:28a, in which Jesus praises John as "the greatest of those born from women," was authentic, since it went against the Christian tendency to downgrade John vis-à-vis Jesus.[8] Jesus's praise of John, then, was not a Christian superimposition but reflected the strong personal impression John made upon Jesus.

This is an example of what Jesus scholars have termed the criterion of "dissimilarity": as Backhaus puts it, this criterion tends to identify a tradition or motif as historical when it "does not conform to, or even conflicts with, dominant early Christian tradition interests (for example, the motif 'John baptized Jesus')."[9] Backhaus also lists "the criterion of cross-section" and "the criterion of contextual plausibility" as being relevant for research into the historical Baptist. The former, which is usually termed "multiple attestation," sees historicity as being more likely when "a tradition or motif (however worded) is attested in a multiplicity of texts and/or text types that are clearly independent of each other (e.g. the motif 'John was a popular baptizer')" —a motif that appears independently in Mark, Q, special Luke, John, and Josephus.

The other criterion, that of contextual plausibility, recognizes that John's ministry, like that of Jesus, arose out of first-century Palestinian Judaism and therefore features resembling those common in other early forms of ancient Judaism are more likely to be historical than those that do not (for example, John's eschatological preaching of judgment versus his veneration of Jesus as "the Lamb of God, who takes away the sin of the world" [John 1:29]). This is not to deny that John, like Jesus, could have had original thoughts and that some of these may have been picked up by the early church. But when a thought attributed to either is otherwise unknown in Palestinian Judaism but common in early Christianity (for example, an individual human being attaining equality with God or dying as an atoning sacrifice for humanity), it should probably have to bear the burden of proof of showing that it is *not* a Christian creation.

Recently these criteria have come under heavy criticism,[10] and they should not be applied in a mechanical or heavy-handed way. Still, in trying to separate the historical Baptist from his Christian embellishment, they are useful as general guidelines. We *should* be suspicious of features of the Christian picture of John that seem to serve Christian interests, such as his self-abnegation before Jesus in the Fourth Gospel (which corresponds to the narrator's own attitude) or the Synoptic identification of him as the returned Elijah, clearing a path for the Messiah Jesus. This does not mean that we can automatically throw out such features as unhistorical; indeed, I argue in chapter 3 that the Elijah identification probably *does* go back to John himself, even though later Christians exploited it. All that coherence with Christian thought signifies is that there are grounds for suspicion; it does not necessarily mean the suspicions are justified.

Another, even more important example of the use of the criteria of historicity is this: in the tradition about John, many passages suggest that he was an apocalyptic or eschatological figure, one who prophesied an imminent end of the world, in which God's judgment would be executed by a fiery "Stronger One."[11] This portrayal seems unlikely to have been invented by the early Christians who transmitted it, since it created two problems for them (thus fulfilling the criterion of dissimilarity).[12] These were (a) that the end of the world did not occur in John's days, and indeed has still not occurred nearly two thousand years later; and (b) that Jesus, whom the Christians believed to be the "Stronger One" heralded by John, did not turn out to be the sort of fiery, judgmental figure he prophesied. Other aspects of the Synoptic portrayal of John's ministry fit this sort of apocalyptic setting (thus fulfilling the criterion of coherence): his call for repentance before it is too late; his baptism, which he identifies as the only way to escape from "the wrath to come"; his linkage with scriptures that speak of the eschaton (Mal. 3:1//Isa. 40:3); and even his linkage with Jesus, who himself seems to have been an apocalyptic figure.[13] And John's apocalyptic identity is attested in several different strata of early Christian tradition (Mark, Q, special Matthew, special Luke), including the two earliest ones, Mark and Q, thus fulfilling the criterion of multiple attestation. If we don't know that John was an apocalyptic thinker, we know nothing about him.[14]

....

Sources

I have already mentioned some of the sources this study will mine in trying to use these criteria to get back to the historical Baptist. Understanding their nature is vital to the question of how to use them.

There are three basic first-century sources that speak about John: the Synoptic Gospels (see the glossary), the Fourth Gospel, and the *Jewish Antiquities* by the Jewish historian Josephus.[15] Appendix 3 lists, by source, the pieces of information that we glean from each of these sources about John. All transmit valuable information, but all have an ax to grind, which must be compensated for in evaluating the data they transmit.

All sources, however, are not equal; there is a hierarchy amongst them. Scholars generally recognize, and rightly, that with regard to the Baptist, as with regard to Jesus, the Synoptic Gospels provide the most trustworthy portrait,[16] especially in information that comes from the two main sources of those Gospels, Mark and Q.[17] As noted above, these sources present John as an apocalyptic figure, proclaiming and preparing people for an imminent end of the world.

To be sure, this is not the picture we get from Josephus or, except in a very qualified sense, from the Fourth Gospel. But there are good reasons for these absences. Josephus had a strong antipathy for the sort of apocalyptic expectation that electrified Palestinian Jews in the 60s CE and catalyzed their revolt against the Romans, which in its turn led to the destruction of the Temple in 70 CE and the end of Jewish sovereignty in Palestine. Horrified by the results of the war and wanting to give cultured Greco-Romans an *interpretatio graeca* of Judaism, and to demonstrate that the hotheads who started the revolt had nothing to do with true Judaism, Josephus downplays the role of apocalyptic thinking in Judaism and reinterprets Jewish messianic hopes in a way that removes their subversive political element (see especially *J.W.* 6.312–313). The Fourth Gospel is also averse to futuristic eschatology, since for its author "the End" was accomplished by Jesus's death and resurrection; all hopes for the end, as well as all other human hopes, were achieved in the advent of Jesus. Therefore, instead of being a prophet of the end, John in the Fourth Gospel becomes a prophet of and witness to Jesus, who himself is the End.[18]

Josephus and the Fourth Evangelist are not the only authors with theological interests that affect their description of events; the Synoptic Evangelists have such interests, too, and these will have to be taken into account when trying to separate the historical from the unhistorical in the traditions about John. For example, as already mentioned, all the Synoptics present John as an Elijah-like figure, who comes to prepare the way for Messiah Jesus. This portrayal arouses certain suspicions, since Elijah was supposed to come before the Messiah (cf. Mal. 4:5 [= 3:23 MT]//Mark 9:11),[19] and the portrait of John as Elijah returned from the dead could therefore have been a Christian invention to confirm the messianic status of Jesus.[20] Chapter 3 examines whether or not these doubts are strong enough to make it unlikely that John did see himself as Elijah, as some have claimed, or whether there is countervailing evidence that he did. I conclude that there is.

The identification of John with Elijah does become more explicit in later Christian writings,[21] starting with Matt. 11:14. This is one of two significant additions Matthew makes to a Markan pericope about the Baptist, the other being 3:14–15, where John implicitly confesses his inferiority to Jesus. Both of these additions seem to reflect later Christian interests and therefore can be discounted in reconstructing the historical Baptist. In having John openly proclaim his identity and stress his inferiority to Jesus, they resemble the Fourth Gospel (cf. John 1:19–23, 3:25–30), even though the Matthean Baptist's confession of Elijan identity contradicts what the Johannine Baptist says (John 1:21)—another issue that will be examined in chapter 3.

Most of the special Lukan traditions about John are in the birth narrative in chapter 1, and they include Old Testament allusions, stereotyped pious Jewish characters, and other legendary features that render them historically questionable (for example, the angelic announcement of birth to an old woman, the father's incredulity, his punishment with muteness, and the fetus leaping in its mother's womb when it is brought into the presence of its in utero cousin). It is possible, however, as argued in appendix 4, that many of these stories go back to a Baptist rather than a Christian source. This does not necessarily make them historical, but it does make them important for reconstructing the history of the Baptist movement, which we must try to do if we are to peel away later encrustations around the tradition about John. And it is possible that even this legendary account contains a historical nugget or two, such as John's priestly genealogy and youthful association with the Judean wilderness (Luke 1:80; see again app. 4).

The Fourth Gospel is our latest first-century Christian source about John, and as noted above, in it the traditions about John, like the traditions about Jesus, have been more consistently transfigured by later theology than is the case in the Synoptic Gospels. John the Fourth Evangelist is perhaps contemporary with Josephus, whose account of John is, as noted, also permeated by the author's own interests and ideas. But it would be a mistake to adopt an attitude of unqualified skepticism towards these late first-century sources; they both contain valuable nuggets of historical information that we would not suspect from the Synoptics.

The Fourth Gospel, for example, shows John and Jesus engaging in baptismal ministries at the same time (John 3:23–24; 4:1)—although the Fourth Evangelist immediately corrects himself and says that it was not Jesus who baptized but his disciples (4:2). This looks like an attempt to cover up the embarrassing fact that Jesus, near the beginning of his ministry, was not unique but looked very much like John—which should come as no surprise, since he probably began his career within the Baptist movement (see chap. 5) This portrait of concurrent ministries contradicts the picture in Mark and Matthew, according to which Jesus did not begin his public activity until John had been "handed over" to prison and death (Mark 1:14–15//Matt. 4:12–17). The latter, however, is probably a schematic, theologically motivated portrait, occasioned by the conviction that John's main function was to herald Jesus (cf. Mark 9:9–13//Matt. 17:9–13).

As for Josephus, although he plays down the apocalyptic nature of John's ministry and thus exiles him from his probable theological homeland, he does let us see how deeply threatened Herod Antipas felt by John's appeal to the masses—a threat which was probably, in fact, intertwined with John's apocalyptic message. This picture, as we shall see in chapter 6, provides a plausible motive for Herod's execution of John, and it contrasts with Mark's apologetic presentation, according to which Herod is awed by the holy man (as Pilate is later awed by Jesus) and hesitates to execute him, only doing so when boxed into a corner by his vindictive wife.

There is, then, a hierarchy in terms of overall trustworthiness in the first-century sources about the Baptist, with Mark and Q (our earliest sources) at the top, and John and Josephus (our latest sources) at the bottom. But this does not mean that the later sources are worthless or that the earlier ones are to be trusted uncritically. In the case of each particular tradition under examination, the plausibility of what is related must be weighed against potential ideological motivations for massaging or altering the truth.

Inventory of Traditions about John the Baptist

As a prelude to separating the historical Baptist from his later accretions and to focus the questions that the rest of the study will engage, it is essential to keep in mind the complete inventory of first-century traditions about the Baptist. This I provide in appendix 3, which I invite the reader to peruse now and to revisit as the need arises. Below I summarize the results of this inventory by theme, noting where the sources seem to agree and disagree. To make the outline less messy, I have omitted specific chapter-and-verse or book-and-section number; these can easily be gleaned from appendix 3.

I. Who was John, in terms of Old Testament types and prophecies?
    A. The fulfillment of the "messenger" passages in Exod. 23:20 + Mal. 3:1 (editorial in Mark; from Jesus in Q)
    B. The fulfillment of the "voice crying in the wilderness" passage in Isa. 40:3 (editorial in Mark-Matt.-Luke; self-claim in John)
    C. Elijah?
        1. John wore Elijah-like garb (Mark-Matt.)
        2. Jesus thought of John as Elijah (Mark-Matt)
        3. John thought of himself as neither the Messiah nor Elijah nor "the prophet" (John)
II. What was the purpose of John's baptism?
    A. Forgiveness of sin?
        1. Yes—a baptism of repentance (Mark-Matt.-Luke) for the forgiveness of sins (Mark-Luke)
        2. No

      a.   "For the forgiveness of sins" omitted by Matt, who moves it to the "cup word" at the Last Supper, thus ascribing it to Jesus's death rather than John's baptism

      b.   Josephus specifically denies that John meant his baptism to be used to gain remission of sins—it was merely a washing of the body of those whose souls had already been cleansed by righteousness

  B. To reveal Jesus to Israel (John)

III. Besides baptism, what else did John preach?

  A. Imminent judgment (Q)

  B. Ethical behavior (Luke, Josephus)

  C. Piety towards God (Josephus)

  D. The "Coming One"

      1.   John unworthy to loosen his sandal (Mark, Q, John)

      2.   John contrasted his own baptism in water with the Coming One's baptism in the Spirit (Mark; cf. John) or in the Spirit and fire (Q)

IV. Who came to be baptized by John?

  A. People from Jerusalem and all over Judea (Mark-Matt)

  B. "The whole nation" (Luke)

  C. "Others" = Gentiles? (Josephus)

  D. Tax collectors (Q) and prostitutes (Matthew)

  E. Jesus, who received the Spirit when baptized by John (Mark-Matt-Luke; cf. John)

V. What was John's subsequent relationship to Jesus?

  A. Subordinate to Jesus

      1.   His whole purpose was to bear witness to Jesus, who was the "light" (John)

      2.   John recognized Jesus as "the Lamb of God" (John)

      3.   John recognized Jesus as the one who would baptize with the Spirit (John)

      4.   John recognized Jesus as the one who came "from above," and as the "Son" (John)

      5.   Jesus made and baptized more disciples than John, and John saw this as fitting (John)

      6.   "He must increase, but I must decrease" (John)

  B. Not subordinate to Jesus?

      1.   John himself associated with light (Luke 1)

      2.   John and Jesus had concurrent baptismal ministries (John)

  C. Agnostic about Jesus's messiahship—question from prison (Q)

  D. Jesus's opinion about John

1. On a par with himself
   a. Jesus, when questioned about his authority, replied by asking a question about John's (Mark-Matt.-Luke)
   b. Jesus's parable of children in the marketplace—both John and Jesus are emissaries of Wisdom (Q)
   c. Jesus spoke of John as his predecessor in the way of suffering and death (Mark-Matt.)
2. Laudatory
   a. A burning and shining light (John)
   b. A prophet and more than a prophet (Q)
   c. The greatest of those born of women (Q)
3. Relativizing
   a. Least in the dominion of God is greater than John (Q)
   b. John in era of "Moses and the prophets," Jesus in era of God's dominion (Q)

VI. What was Herod Antipas's relationship to John?
   A. He was in awe of him and tried to protect him (Mark)
   B. He wanted to kill him (Matt., Josephus)
      1. Because John had denounced Herod's marriage (Matt.)
      2. Because he feared that John might start a revolt (Josephus)

....

Approach

The sources about John, then, disagree in some essentials, and even when they all agree, it is still possible that all may be wrong. How can we sift them to determine their truth? To approach this question, I will first argue a key thesis for the remainder of the book: there was serious competition between followers of the Baptist and followers of Jesus from the first century on, and this competition has thoroughly affected the presentation of John in our main source, the Gospels.

Next I will strip away this influence to the extent possible and ask what John thought his own ministry was about.[22] Admittedly, this separation is somewhat artificial. As we have already seen, for example, almost all of our early sources about John are Christian, so (except for Josephus's brief notice) there is no access to "the Jewish John" that does not pass through a Christian checkpoint. Still, it is useful to try to start from the ground up, and that means starting with John's background and role within first-century Judaism. The next two chapters, then, will deal with the theory that John started out as a member of a Jewish sect, the Qumran (Dead Sea Sect) community, and the question of whether or not he saw himself as the Old Testament prophet Elijah, who was expected by Jews to return from the dead before the "great and terrible day of the Lord" (Mal. 4:5).

Then I will move on to topics more directly affected by the competition between early Christianity and the Baptist movement, dealing first with John's baptism. Since this rite was built on previous Jewish water rites and fit within the framework of his apocalyptic Judaism, it might make more sense to include this chapter in the earlier discussion of John within Judaism. But the New Testament treatment of John's baptism is so saturated with Christian theology that the current location seems to be the more logical place. Following this chapter, which includes a consideration of Jesus's baptism by John, I will follow up with an attempt to analyze the subsequent relationship between the two men. Finally, I will deal with John's end: his death at the hands of Herod Antipas. The structure of the study, then, is roughly chronological as well as thematic: first, John's beginnings (apprenticeship at Qumran, prophetic self-consciousness); second, his defining sacrament (baptism) and the defining relationship of his career (Jesus); and, third, his death.

CHAPTER ONE

The Competition Hypothesis

The Gospel of John

The thesis that there was a rivalry between adherents of Jesus and adherents of John the Baptist was first developed by Wilhelm Baldensperger at the end of the nineteenth century on the basis of the Prologue to the Gospel of John,[1] and that Gospel has remained the fulcrum of this thesis ever since. Indeed, even Knut Backhaus, who devoted his doctoral dissertation to refuting the competition hypothesis, had to acknowledge that the Johannine context was an exception[2]—an admission that Ernst Bammel rightly called the Achilles heel of his monograph.[3]

Significantly, polemic against overvaluation of the Baptist appears from the beginning of the Fourth Gospel. The author has copied only ten lines from the preexistent Logos Hymn before he is distracted by the necessity of putting John in his place. Having relayed the hymn's assertion that divine life abode in the Logos and that this life was the light of humanity, the Evangelist comments, in a prose aside, that the Baptist was *not* this light but only a witness to it. Jesus rather than John is the true light that enlightens every person coming into the world (John 1:4–9). The author seems to have inserted both this passage and verse 15 into a preexistent form of the Prologue, since the references to the Baptist break the poetic structure and flow of thought.[4] And both of these passages seem designed to put John in his place, which is under Jesus.

In the continuation of the Gospel, the Evangelist mobilizes the Baptist himself to testify to his own inferiority, making him acknowledge that he is neither the Messiah, nor Elijah, nor even a prophet (1:19–23); that he is unworthy to bend down and untie the sandal of "the Coming One" (1:27); that the whole purpose of his baptismal ministry has been to reveal Jesus to Israel (1:31); and, climactically, that Jesus's influence must increase while his own must decline (3:30). These protestations are emphatic, and all except 1:27 are unparalleled in the Synoptic Gospels. The most logical explanation for them is that the Fourth Evangelist knows followers of the Baptist who are proclaiming the opposite: *John* is the light, perhaps even the Messiah,[5] and the one whose superiority to Jesus was shown by the fact that he preceded him in time (cf. "the one coming after me" in 1:15, 30).[6] Indeed, as Walter Wink points out, the Gospel itself inadvertently testifies to the existence of advocates of John's messiahship when it has John pointedly say to his disciples, "You yourselves bear me witness, that I said, I am not the Christ." (3:28).[7] This pointed "reminder" makes most sense if there were followers of the Baptist in John's environment who maintained the opposite. Probably a large part of the Fourth Evangelist's purpose, both in this passage and in the Gospel as a whole, was either to transfer to Jesus the allegiance of such adherents of the Baptist, as happens in the paradigmatic scene in John 1:35–41, or to counter the arguments of those who remained adamant. One of the ways in which he does so is to demonstrate that while, in one sense, John preceded Jesus, in another sense Jesus preceded John, since Jesus was and is the eternal Word (1:15, 30; cf. 1:1; 8:58).[8]

A similar diminution of the Baptist with regard to Jesus is both implicit and explicit elsewhere in the Fourth Gospel. When Jesus begins his own baptizing ministry, he makes and baptizes more disciples than John (3:26; 4:1). John performs no miracles, whereas Jesus accomplishes a plethora (10:41–42). The point of all this is that Jesus, not John, is the one to follow.

. . . .

Luke-Acts, Matthew

The Fourth Gospel is not the only New Testament document that reflects the attempt of the early Christian movement to prove the superiority of Jesus to the Baptist and thus to absorb or counter erstwhile adherents of the latter. The Third Gospel, along with its companion volume, the Acts of the Apostles, also shows strong signs of confronting a Baptist challenge, especially in Acts 18–19 and Luke 1.

The Acts scenes are set in Ephesus, far from the homeland of the historical Baptist, thus testifying to the long reach of the movement he spawned. They portray the apostle Paul correcting the theology both of followers of John who are ignorant of Jesus (19:1–7) and of a follower of Jesus who knows only the baptism of John (18:24–26). The point is essentially the same as in the Fourth Gospel: John acknowledged the superiority of Jesus, and his latter-day followers should do the same.[9] As in the Fourth Gospel, however, this polemic itself supplies inadvertent evidence to the contrary: some, perhaps many, followers of the Baptist towards the end of the first Christian century[10] did *not* acknowledge Jesus as John's superior.[11]

The first chapter of Luke's Gospel provides additional though indirect testimony to the strength and independence of the Baptist movement. As noted in appendix 4, there is circumstantial evidence that most of the traditions about the Baptist in Luke 1 come from a non-Christian Baptist birth narrative (the exception being the Visitation Scene in 1:36–56, which links the Baptist birth narrative with the birth narrative of Jesus). Not only does the prophecy that John will be Spirit-filled from his mother's womb (1:15) contradict the common Christian view, which Luke himself endorses elsewhere, that the Spirit is an exclusive gift of Jesus (Luke 3:16; Acts 19:1–6), but the whole point of the Baptist birth narrative outside of the Visitation scene is the immense stature of John: he is the greatest human being (cf. Matt. 11:11a// Luke 7:28a) and the forerunner not of any other man but of the Lord himself (Luke 1:16–17, 76). The rhetorical strategy of the Third Gospel, then, seems to be a kinder, gentler form of that of the Fourth: to establish a point of contact with disciples of the Baptist by incorporating as many of their traditions as possible (Luke 1), and then to demonstrate a more perfect way (cf. Acts 18:26) by outlining the link between John and Jesus, and the latter's fulfillment of the former's mission.[12]

Matthew also seems motivated by the need to push back against a claim that the Baptist was Jesus's superior. After mobilizing the familiar passage, paralleled in the other Gospels, emphasizing the opposite—John's unworthiness vis-à-vis the Coming One and the inferiority of his water baptism to Jesus's Spirit baptism (3:11)—Matthew prefaces his description of Jesus's baptism itself with a mini-dialogue in which John tries to stop Jesus from undergoing baptism at his hands: "*I* need to be baptized by *you,* and *you* come to *me*?" (3:14–15, my translation). This invented dialogue is designed to ward off the assumption that the baptizer (John) must be superior to the baptizand (Jesus), since he confers on him a spiritual blessing (cf. Heb. 7:7).[13] Matt. 3:14–15, then, is probably directed at a real threat: people, presumably followers of the Baptist, who say that John's baptism of Jesus showed he was Jesus's superior.

It may be added that both Matthew and Luke, in different ways, put special emphasis on the continuity between John and Jesus. Luke does so by making John a relative of Jesus (through their mothers; see Luke 1:36),[14] Matthew by making John's inaugural proclamation identical to that of Jesus (Matt. 3:2; 4:17). The motivation for these embellishments may in both cases be to balance the memory that the Baptist movement and the early Christian one were sometimes in tension.[15] The Gospels of Matthew, Luke, and John, therefore, provide strong cumulative evidence that, in the latter part of the first century, and in the diverse locales in which those Gospels were written (Antioch? Rome or Asia Minor? Ephesus or Alexandria?),[16] the Baptist movement was a troubling competitor, whose claims needed to be countered by early Christians.

Backhaus argues that the passages in Matthew and Luke do not reflect early Christian competition with Baptist circles, but are merely designed to emphasize the importance of the person of Jesus. The emphasis, according to Backhaus, is Christological rather than polemical: "The NT theologians are not primarily involved in an apologetic/polemical discussion with a competing [Baptist] community, but in a 'protological' discussion within their own community."[17] This thesis is right in what it affirms (that the early Christian writers' overwhelming interest is Christological) but wrong in what it denies (that part of their Christological agenda is to refute excessive claims for the Baptist). As Manuel Vogel has pointed out, Backhaus assumes that the early church developed its Christology in splendid isolation from the jostling groups of first-century Judaism, including Baptist circles—a quasi-docetic and historically unlikely assumption.[18]

. . . .

The Pseudoclementine Literature

The sort of competition we have discerned in the New Testament between followers of the Baptist and followers of Jesus continued in later Christian centuries: the Baptist movement did not die out just because the Jesus movement had appeared on the scene. A crucial piece of evidence is the Pseudo-Clementine literature, now found in the parallel narratives of the Clementine *Homilies,* which date from the early fourth century CE, and the *Recognitions,* which date from the mid-fourth century CE. Both of these works probably depend on earlier Jewish-Christian sources from second- and third-century Syria.[19]

These sources, and later documents that take them up, mount an attack on followers of the Baptist and, in some cases, the Baptist himself. The most important passage is *Rec.* 1.54.8, which goes back to an early source,[20] and which says (in Rufinus's Latin translation), "But some also of the disciples of John, who imagined they were great, separated themselves from the people and proclaimed their master as the Christ."[21] This text concerns a subset of the Baptist group—"*some of* the disciples of John," presumably in comparison with other Baptists who acknowledge the primacy of Jesus. The depiction of the John-exalting group as schismatic, however, is a tendentious attempt to downgrade and discredit it.[22] For this important text (Joseph Thomas called it "un grand prix"[23]) reveals the typical view of the heresiologist: *we* are the original group, and those whom we anathematize have separated themselves from us and thereby from the truth once universally embraced.[24]

As Walter Bauer famously emphasized, however, this sort of denunciation of heretical secessionists can mask a situation in which the opposite is the case: the "orthodox" are an embattled minority, and the "heretics" hold the more primitive and popular theology. As Bauer puts it, "In the picture that the representatives of the church sketch, it is precisely the detail about a great apostasy from the true faith that is seen to be incorrect. . . . It was by no means orthodoxy, but rather heresy, that was present at the beginning."[25] As Bauer points out, for example, the Johannine Elder's paradigmatic denunciation of secessionists in 1 John 2:18–19 is followed by a victory whoop over them in 4:4, but "when in the very next verse we hear his strained admission that 'the world' listens to the others, our confidence that here the 'church' represents the majority and is actually setting the tone evaporates."[26]

The situation is probably similar with the *Recognitions* passage denouncing followers of the Baptist who have "separated themselves from the people": in the author's milieu, it is these "schismatics" who are setting the tone as far as the interpretation of the Baptist's ministry is concerned. This passage repeats language that the author previously, in 1.54.2, had applied to the Sadducees: "The first of these [Jewish sects] then are the ones called Sadducees, who arose in the days of John when they *separated from the people* as righteous ones and *renounced* the resurrection of the dead."[27] But though there are prefigurements of the idea of resurrection in some Old Testament texts (for example, Isa. 26:19; Ezek. 37:1–14), the idea was a late development within Second Temple Judaism, emerging as a (still disputed) dogma in the second century BCE, with Dan. 7–12—that is, the exact time that the Sadducees supposedly split from the rest of the people.[28] The assertion of a secession from the truth, then, is designed to reinterpret what was once a contrary situation on the ground: the Sadducaean position was traditional, while explicit belief in resurrection was innovative. Similarly, the denunciation of separatist Baptists in *Rec.* 1.54.8 is probably designed to cover up the independence of the Baptist movement and allay the suspicion that John's original followers preferred him to Jesus.

A further indication of competition between followers of the Baptist and followers of Jesus comes in *Rec.* 1.60.1: "And behold, one of John's disciples asserted that John was Christ, and not Jesus. 'This is so much the case,' he said, 'that even Jesus himself proclaimed that John is greater than all humans and prophets' [cf. Matt. 11:11a//Luke 7:28a].[29] This is significant not only for its explicit reference to a dispute between partisans of Jesus's messiahship and partisans of John's, but also for the fact that John's supporters could appeal to a saying of Jesus in support of their reverence for John—a circumstance that doubtless strengthened their position.[30]

In these *Recognitions* passages, it is only the followers of the Baptist, not the Baptist himself, who proclaim John as the Messiah and thus in the view of the author mistakenly overvalue him. John himself is free of error. But not in the Pseudoclementine companion piece to the *Recognitions,* the *Homilies* (2.17, 23). This document makes Simon Magus, the arch-heretic of the novel, into a follower of the "Day-Baptist" John—suggesting that John himself was a heretic.[31] Although John is described here as the forerunner of Jesus, some of the details seem to imply that he was reprehensibly trying to outdo his successor: John, we learn, had thirty chief disciples, including a woman named Helena, whereas Jesus had only twelve, all male. Because of the danger posed by the assertion of John's supremacy in the first part of Jesus's saying mentioned in the previous paragraph, moreover, this *Homilies* passage changes the epithet for John from "the *greatest* of those born of women" (ἐν γεννητοῖς γυναικῶν μείζων) to the belittling "*one* born of women" (ὁ ἐν γεννητοῖς γυναικῶν). The passage then goes on to imply that because John was associated with the female side of things ("one born of *women*"), he belonged to an inferior and even demonic order vis-à-vis Jesus,[32] on the principle that the worse (which here is linked with the female) precedes the better (linked with the male).[33]

In a related passage, *Hom.* 3.22–23//*Rec.* 2.8, this theory of paired couples (syzygies), one good and one evil, is used to identify John as the initiator of a heretical sect.[34] As Oscar Cullmann points out, this continues a trajectory already visible within the canonical Gospels: whereas the Synoptics still accord John the title of "prophet," the Fourth Gospel denies it to him (John 1:21), and the *Homilies* go further and make him a *false* prophet.[35] The Pseudo-Clementines, then, provide evidence that competition between Baptist groups and Christian ones did not die out at the end of the first century CE but continued and even intensified in the second, third, and early fourth centuries.[36]

....

Backhaus on the Pseudo-Clementines

Backhaus, aware of these Pseudo-Clementine passages, treats them in some detail.[37] This treatment provides an instructive example of his method, which at times is careful and evenhanded and yet, in the end, unconvincing.

On the one hand, Backhaus acknowledges how serious a challenge the Pseudo-Clementines pose to his thesis that early Christianity was untroubled by competition from independent Baptist circles. Unlike C. H. Dodd, who dismisses the Pseudo-Clementines summarily by saying, "To base a theory upon the evidence of the late and heretical Clementine romance is to build a house upon the sand,"[38] Backhaus thinks they shed considerable light on the image of the Baptist in early Christianity. Backhaus disputes Dodd's adjectives "late" and "heretical" (the source of *Rec.* 1.54, 60 probably goes back to the second century, and to speak of "heresy" at this period is anachronistic) as well as his disparaging noun "romance" (the Pseudo-Clementines are a mixed corpus, and even romances and novels sometimes have historical kernels).[39] And he argues that no one would simply invent a circle devoted to the Baptist if none had existed. The Gospel of John, which Backhaus locates in

Syria, confirms that such a circle did exist in the area that subsequently gave birth to the Pseudo-Clementines.[40]

But Backhaus is not consistent in developing this line of argument. He claims, for example, that although *Rec.* 1.60.1–3 tries to present the Baptist circle in such a way as to emphasize the Baptist's subordination to Jesus, it does so without needing to ("jetzt freilich eindeutig ohne aktuelle Not").[41] If the passage refutes followers of the Baptist who say that their master rather than Jesus is the Messiah, this is not, for Backhaus, a response to the counter-claims of an independent Baptist sect but merely an *inner-Christian* response to a troublesome New Testament text, Jesus's acclamation of the Baptist as the greatest woman-born man.[42] Similarly, the sharp assault on the Baptist in *Hom.* 2.17, 23–24, where he becomes Jesus's evil twin, is a development of the Pseudo-Clementines' dualistic "couples" theory rather than a polemic against contemporary followers of the Baptist.[43] Backhaus asserts that the vitriolic and fantastic nature of the anti-Baptist polemic here is ill-suited to refuting an actual opponent; it is probably intended, rather, to edify insiders.[44]

All of this denial of a tendency, however, itself seems tendentious. *Rec.* 1.60.1–3 *does* deny the claim that John rather than Jesus was the Messiah, just as John 1:6–8 does; as Backhaus himself puts it, the author paints a picture in which John's disciples are separated from their master while John himself stands with Jesus.[45] Why would this be so important to emphasize, except against a contrary position exalting the Baptist over Jesus? Moreover, vehe-ment language such as that in *Hom.* 2.23–24, which makes the Baptist circle, in Backhaus's own words, the germ of all perfidy,[46] requires explanation, and the hypothesis of polemic against a powerful Baptist circle supplies the most plausible one.[47]

On a number of occasions, Backhaus acknowledges that this explanation *is* plausible,[48] but he always circles back to the assertion that it is not the *only* plausible explanation, and indeed that it is in the end neither necessary nor convincing. Other explanations, he insists, such as the necessity of dealing with biblical problems (Jesus's praise of John) or the influence of dualistic, gnostic speculation (the "couples" theory), are equally if not more convinc-ing. But here Backhaus trades in false dichotomies: the polemic against fol-lowers of the Baptist in *Rec.* 1.60.1, for example, could reflect *both* the pressure of a Baptist circle *and* the difficulty created by Matt. 11:11a//Luke 7:28a. More-over, as Thomas already pointed out, the "couples" theory may very well have developed out of the polemic against the Baptist rather than vice versa. Only in the case of John and Jesus, as opposed to the other "couples" (Cain and Abel, Ishmael and Isaac, Esau and Jacob, Aaron and Moses, Simon Magus and Peter), is there a concrete motivation for the theory, namely to respond to the Baptist argument that John was Jesus's superior since he came before Jesus.[49] As noted above, the Fourth Gospel already seems to be responding to this argument (John 1:15, 30).[50]

In the end, Backhaus concedes that a group devoted to the Baptist was probably active in Syria from the end of the first century (as shown by the Fourth Gospel) into the second (as shown by the source of *Rec.* 1.54, 60) and to acknowledge that this group made an impression on later generations of Christians. But he argues that the impression was diffuse and the response nonpolemical, for the threat was weak.[51] This argument, however, was already well answered in 1935 by Thomas, who pointed out that it does not grapple adequately with the persistence and emphasis of the anti-Baptist polemic in the Pseudo-Clementines—fourth-century documents whose sources go back to the second and third centuries. Moreover, the anti-Baptist source now embedded in the *Recognitions* is attested by Ephrem, who died in 373.[52] Over three centuries, then, the critique of the Baptist and his followers remained relevant, and a polemic so constant and widespread is best explained by a concern that remains current.[53] It is significant, moreover, as Thomas notes, that the disparate parts of the picture of John and his disciples in the Pseudo-Clementines cohere as a response to a series of interrelated claims for John by his adherents: "John was greater than Jesus, as shown by his chronological priority to Jesus, and the fact that Jesus himself called him the greatest of those born of woman. Therefore John, rather than Jesus, was the Messiah." In response, the Pseudo-Clementines reframe the saying of Jesus praising John, turning it into a disparagement (he was just one of those born of *women*) and interpreting his chronological priority negatively (in the history of salvation the worse, or even the demonic, precedes the good).[54]

As for Backhaus's point about the fantastic and vitriolic nature of some of the anti-Baptist rhetoric in the Pseudo-Clementines, this is no argument against a real competition between Christians and followers of the Baptist. Ancient and medieval religious polemic, like its modern counterpart, is often vitriolic in the extreme and unmoored to reality, even when dealing with a real competitor.[55] We know, for example, that ancient and medieval Jews were rightly concerned with the Christian threat, which often led to forced and unforced Jewish conversions to Christianity. We also know that ancient and medieval Jews enthusiastically circulated *Toledot Yeshu,* a collection of vitriolic and sometimes fantastic legends about Jesus. Certainly this was, in accordance with Backhaus's analysis, an attempt to strengthen the faith of insiders, that is, fellow members of the Jewish community; but that attempt was made in the face of a real external threat.[56] The sharp distinction Backhaus makes between edification of insiders and defense against outsiders turns out, then, to be a mirage.[57]

....

The Mandean Literature

There is one other piece of evidence in favor of the competition hypothesis: the Mandean literature. The Mandeans are a Gnostic sect (their name means "knowers") that seems to have originated in Transjordanian Syria in the early Christian centuries[58] and still exists in Iraq and a worldwide diaspora. Although the Mandeans were eventually driven by persecution to migrate to southern Babylonia, their religion still shows signs of its origin in the Jordan Valley, above all in the vital place it accords to "Jordan," its term for the flowing water that anchors Mandean ritual life.[59] This water is used in the most important of the Mandean ablutions, which is administered by a priest and referred to as "baptism" *(maṣbūtā)*, and to which mystical significance is ascribed: "Immersion in water is immersion in a life-giving fluid, and gives physical well-being, protection against the powers of death, and promise of everlasting life to the soul."[60]

Mandean literature is relevant for our topic because it praises John as a true prophet[61] and disparages Jesus as a false prophet or even an Antichrist.[62] The strong sense of competition between the two figures surfaces in a text that inverts Matt. 3:13–15: Jesus comes to the Jordan and begs for baptism by John but is initially rejected for his moral failings (lying to the Jews, deceiving the priests, imposing celibacy, and violating the Sabbath). John only relents when a heavenly letter arrives instructing him to baptize the deceiver despite his sins.[63]

It would be logical to see such polemic as a continuation of the sort of exaltation of the Baptist combatted in the Pseudo-Clementines and thus as direct evidence for an early sect of John the Baptist adherents, but there are problems with this thesis. The Mandean baptismal practice, for example, differs from Johannine baptism as described in early sources, since Mandean baptism is neither an initiation nor once and for all but a constantly repeated rite,[64] whereas most ancient sources agree that Johannine baptism was an initiatory, once-and-for-all act.[65] Mandean baptism also has features unknown in any of the sources about Johannine (or Christian) baptism, such as drinking the baptismal water. Such differences help convince most scholars that John the Baptist did not directly found the Mandean movement. Indeed, while the figure of John appears frequently in Mandean texts, and while he was probably present in Mandeanism from the beginning, he never became central to it.[66] The salvific figure in Mandeanism is not John but Manda di-Ḥiyyah ("the Knower of Life").[67] Unlike other human figures such as Adam and his sons, John does not have a heavenly double who visits the underworld or performs other salvific actions.[68] John sometimes appears in Mandean literature, moreover, under the Arabic name *Yahyā*,[69] and he is first termed a prophet in texts that respond to Islamic claims for Muhammad.[70] This suggests that a part of John's status in Mandeanism reflects the rise of Islam.

If the Mandean movement had developed directly out of the Baptist one, moreover, we would expect a stronger connection with the historical Baptist than we find. The depiction of John in Mandean texts seems far removed from history, and it is usually dependent on Christian traditions, often of an apocryphal nature but drifting even further into the realm of fairy tale and myth.[71] There are also some clashes between Mandean practices and reliable ancient evidence about John. We have already noted the differences between Mandean and Johannine baptism. Mandeans also adjure fasting, in contrast to the description of John and his disciples in Matt. 11:18//Luke 7:33 and Mark 2:18. And, reflecting Christian influence, they observe Sunday as their weekly festival day rather than the Jewish Sabbath.[72] All of this renders questionable the way in which an earlier generation of scholars used Mandean literature to fill out the picture of John and his disciples provided by our earliest sources—most famously, the way Rudolf Bultmann mobilized it to support his claim that a form of Gnosticism prevailed among John's disciples in the late first century and that the Fourth Evangelist composed his Gospel to counter this Baptist Gnosticism.[73]

But though there does not seem to be a valid argument for a *direct* connection between the Mandean movement, on the one hand, and John and his earliest followers, on the other, there may still have been an *indirect* connection. It is probably an exaggeration to claim that John only entered the Mandean thought world in the late Byzantine or early Islamic period.[74] Although, as noted above, the Arabic name *Yaḥyā* does occur in Mandean texts, it is not as frequent as the name *Yūhānā*, which is close to the Hebrew/Aramaic form *Yōḥānān*. The *Yaḥyā* texts, moreover, could be a later redaction of pre-Islamic sources.[75] The points of contact with relatively early Christian apocrypha, especially the Protoevangelium of James,[76] suggest an origin for some Mandean traditions about the Baptist long before Islamic times,[77] perhaps in an early Syrian context.[78] Most striking of all, and most relevant here, is the fact that the Mandean texts presuppose intense competition between John and Jesus, and between Jesus's followers and John's. This feature does not reflect the viewpoint either of Islam or of orthodox Christianity, but is, as noted, similar to the Pseudo-Clementine literature, which, like Mandeanism, is rooted in the Syria of the early Christian centuries. All of this suggests that the Mandeans probably, at an early stage in their development, were in contact with, and influenced by, Baptist sectarians in Syria who were in competition with Christians—although the Mandeans themselves are not to be identified with these sectarians.[79]

This reconstruction helps solve the conundrum posed by Edmondo Lupieri: if the Mandeans indeed originated in the Jordan Valley at a relatively early point in the Christian era, they should have come into contact with the Baptist movement, which was located in the same area at the same time; and one might therefore expect that their traditions about John would have historical value. Why do they not do so but appear to be based on Christian traditions, generally of an apocryphal nature? But, on the other hand, if there was no connection between the Baptist movement and the early Mandeans, why did the latter construct such a large legend precisely around John?[80]

In response, we may ask whether Mandean contact with Baptist sectarians would necessarily have produced a treasure trove of knowledge about "the historical John." After all, it is unknown how much historical information later Baptist sectarians themselves preserved about their founder before he metamorphosed into a mythical figure.[81] Moreover, although Baptist adherents seem to have been present in second-century Syria, they were probably not as significant a factor there as Christians were. The early Mandeans, perhaps, had enough contact with these Baptist sectarians to know that they exalted John and opposed Christian claims for Jesus, and this was the chief idea that they incorporated into their own new movement—perhaps partly as a reaction to the growing Christian domination of the area.[82] Despite this embrace of Baptist anti-Christianity, the Mandeans could not help being strongly influenced by the pervasive Christianity of their environment—hence the contact with Christian traditions such as those in the Protevangelium of James.

Again, an analogy may clarify the dynamic: both the Falashas of Ethiopia in the Middle Ages, who claim descent from King Solomon through the Queen of Sheba, and the Crypto-Jews of New Mexico in recent years, who claim descent from Jews persecuted by the Spanish Inquisition, identify with Christianity's predecessor and competitor, Judaism, even though the Crypto-Jews definitely, and the Falashas probably, are themselves of Christian origin. In neither case do members of the group usually show a deep knowledge of Judaism, and much of their knowledge of the parent religion comes from their former adherence to its Christian stepchild. Despite their present distance from and even hostility to that stepchild, it was still formative for their faith.[83] These analogies alert us to the possibility that the Mandeans themselves may have originally been Christians who repudiated Christianity after glancing contact with Christianity's predecessor and competitor, the Baptist movement. If this reconstruction is right, the Mandeans would be another, albeit indirect, witness to the competition between Christians and Baptist adherents in the early centuries of the Christian era. If such competition had not existed, the Mandeans' exaltation of John over Jesus would be difficult to explain.

....

Friendly Competition?

But if there was competition between early Christians and followers of the Baptist, of what sort was it? Manuel Vogel, borrowing a phrase from Johannes Tromp, terms it *friendly* competition and cautions against overemphasizing the bad blood between the two groups.[84] John the Baptist is never designated a false Messiah or false prophet in the New Testament (as he is in the Pseudo-Clementine *Homilies*), even in John 1:8a; it is just that he is not (as some apparently were claiming) the *true* Messiah.[85] Indeed, the Fourth Evangelist acknowledges that John was "sent from God" (1:6; cf. 3:28)—a designation that elsewhere applies only to Jesus (3:17, 34; 5:36, 38, and so on) and the Paraclete (14:26). To be sure, the reference in John 3:31 to "the one who is from the earth," who "speaks from the earth" (my translation), coming as it does immediately after the Baptist's self-abnegating and Jesus-exalting declaration in 3:30, might be taken to range John on the side of earthly beings over against the heavenly Jesus[86] and might even be interpreted as a characteristic Johannine intensification of the Q logion about John as the greatest of those born of woman but inferior to those in the dominion of God (Matt. 11:11//Luke 7:28).[87] But this cannot be the complete story about the image of John in the Fourth Gospel, for he is constantly presented as witnessing to the truth that is Jesus (1:6–8, 19–36; 3:25–30); when he does *that,* he is certainly not speaking "from the earth." Rather than being, in the end, a man whose speech is "earthly," John is, for the Fourth Evangelist, "a burning and shining lamp" (5:35).[88] As Michael Theobald puts it, the Johannine Baptist, in his final discourse (3:31–36) as well as elsewhere in the Gospel, does not talk "in an earthly manner" but speaks only the truth about Jesus.[89]

Many of Vogel's warnings against overemphasizing the polemical nature of the Johannine portrait of the Baptist were anticipated by Walter Wink in his important monograph on the Baptist in the Gospel tradition.[90] Wink argues that both 1:35–39 and 3:28 may reflect historical memory more than polemic: Jesus's first followers *were* adherents of the Baptist, and the Baptist did *not,* in fact, regard himself as the Messiah. He also warns about the dangers of mirror-reading Johannine assertions about the Baptist: "By [this] line of reasoning, John was worshipped as Elijah, prophet, messiah, the Light and the Life of men, a wonderworker, the pre-existent Logos through whom all things were made, indeed, even as the Word made flesh!"[91] Wink's conclusion about the Johannine portrait of the Baptist reflects the ambiguity of the evidence: "Polemic and apologetic directed at contemporary "disciples of John" clearly seem to be present, yet Baptists are not the chief opponents of the Evangelist's church. The prime target is Pharisaical Judaism, with the Baptist community deployed to one side, and somewhat closer to the church than to the emergent 'normative Judaism' of the Jamnian scholars. This is not surprising, since in the eyes of the Pharisees both Baptists and Christians belonged to the heretical sectarian baptist movement, and both paid allegiance to John. Apparently the Fourth Evangelist is still in dialogue with these Baptists, countering their hyper-elevation of John and wooing them to the Christian faith."[92] Though this conclusion may overstate the extent to which "normative Judaism" existed in John's time,[93] Wink's overall thesis seems valid. In the eyes of the Fourth Evangelist, Baptists are not enemies like the Pharisees; they are, rather, a mission field to be cultivated. As Philipp Vielhauer puts it, "The missionary church indeed battled against the Baptist sect, but not against, but rather for, the Baptist, and therefore finally not against, but rather for, his adherents."[94]

Vogel finds this sort of irenicism vis-à-vis Baptist followers to be striking in a first-century Jewish/Christian world in which bitter polemic against religious competitors was the norm,[95] and he cites with approval Vielhauer's assertion that this positive attitude probably reflects two interrelated factors: Jesus's own reverence for the Baptist and the church's history-of-salvation forerunner model, which assigned him a positive valence. We should also factor in the historical memory that Jesus had been baptized by John.

But while Vogel is right to emphasize that the New Testament attitude towards the Baptist and his followers does not break out into open enmity, the term "friendly competition" overemphasizes the comity between the parties involved. "Friendly competition" is still competition, and there may be resentment without overt hostility. Open refutation or abuse is not the only way to deal with a troublesome rival, who may instead be won over—a better result if the competitor is also a predecessor with whom one wishes to assert continuity. Rudolf Bultmann puts it nicely: "The Christian attitude to John the Baptist is a divided one: while some passages make the Baptist appear as a confederate in Christian affairs, others emphasize his inferiority to Jesus. Understandably, for both points of view were occasioned by the anti-Baptist polemic."[96]

. . . .

The Islamic Analogy

We may consider, by way of analogy to early Christianity's way of dealing with the challenge of the Baptist, Muhammad's method of dealing with the challenge of Christianity—a faith from which he drew many of the elements of his new religion. We know from the Qur'ān itself that Muhammad was anxious to convert Christians to Islam, and early on, in the Meccan period (610–622 CE), apparently expected them (as well as the local Jews) to convert when they heard his message preached. But when he migrated in 622 to Medina, which had a much higher concentration of Jews and Christians than Mecca, he was surprised and frustrated at the resistance he encountered from both groups—though more consistently from Jews than Christians.

Muhammad's frustration with the Christians, however, never expressed itself as criticism of Jesus himself. In the Qur'ān, rather, Jesus anticipates and points the way toward Muhammad—just as, in the New Testament, John anticipates and points the way toward Jesus. In the case of Muhammad, this relative irenicism probably reflects both a genuine reverence for Jesus and the fact that Muhammad considered Christians to be still "in play" in a way Jews were not. He was engaged in a struggle with Christian traditionalists for the allegiance of run-of-the-mill Christians—just as, according to the competition theory, New Testament Christians were engaged in a struggle with Baptist traditionalists who revered the Baptist over Jesus for the allegiance of run-of-the-mill Baptists. In the case of Muhammad, this competition did not always remain friendly: there is, in some later Medinan suras, fierce criticism of Christian beliefs such as the Trinity and the divinity of Jesus, and Christians along with Jews are accused of falsifying the scriptures to advance their heretical viewpoints. But there are also positive statements, including the striking promise that godly Christians will be rewarded on Judgment Day (2:2; 5:69). David Marshall's way of explaining this mixture of attitudes is illuminating: "Much or even all of the Medinan material which appears positive about Christians in fact refers specifically to Christians who are at some stage in the process of acknowledging the divine origin of the Qur'ān and joining the community of Muhammad's followers." This argument can appeal to texts such as 5:82–85, which begins with positive comments about Christian priests and monks (5:82), but then continues with this account of their reception of the Qur'ān: "And when they hear what has been sent down to the messenger you see their eyes overflow with tears because of the truth they recognise. They say: 'Our Lord, we believe; so write us down among the witnesses'" (5:83).

One could argue that such passages make explicit what is assumed throughout the Qur'ānic appeal to Christians, namely that the proper response of Christians to the Qur'ān is to acknowledge it as divine revelation and so become part of the Muslim community. This approach suggests that behind the apparently conflicting positive and negative material on Christians there is a coherent Qur'ānic attitude: on the assumption that they are ready to believe in the Qur'ān, Christians are seen positively; where they disappoint that expectation, they are seen negatively.[97] It may be that the relation between the Christians and *their* predecessors, followers of the Baptists, is similar: on the assumption that the latter can be won over to belief in

Jesus, they are viewed positively; when, however, they remain obdurate, they are demonized.

But in the earlier era to which the New Testament belongs, this critical state of affairs had not yet arrived. There was competition—sometimes perhaps rather fierce—between traditional Baptists and Christians for the run-of-the-mill Baptists. But this competition did not lead to John being demonized, but to an attempt to redefine him as a Christian before the fact. John the Baptist in the New Testament, like Jesus in the Qur'ān, has not been demonized but adopted—a process made easier by the memory that there had actually been a personal link between the two men. And we can well imagine that Christians such as the author of the Fourth Gospel hoped for and expected a response such as that described in Qur'ān 5:83: the eyes of Baptist followers overflowing with tears as they recognize the truth that their commitment to their master has led them to a better and living master, the risen Jesus. We can imagine them shedding those tears as they announce, like a former Baptist disciple in the Fourth Gospel, "We have found the Messiah" (John 1:41).

The situation is probably similar with Luke, the other New Testament author who seems particularly preoccupied with the Baptist and his disciples. Here again, there is no direct polemic against the Baptist: he points straightforwardly to Jesus, even from his mother's womb (Luke 1:41–45). Surprisingly, however, some of John's latter-day followers need to be informed about his allegiance to Jesus (Acts 19:4)—an indirect acknowledgment of the competitive situation, as is the over-the-top way in which John's mother and the in utero John himself acknowledges Jesus's superiority.

Such indirectness is characteristic of Luke, as can be seen from the way he treats another divisive movement, the so-called "circumcision party" of aggressively Torah-observant Jewish Christians. Whereas the historical Paul in Galatians 2:11–14 rails against this party and the associated "men from James," accusing Peter of hypocrisy for joining them in Jewish practice, Luke in Acts 10:1–11:18 and Acts 15 prefers to play down the friction to portray the church as, more or less, one big happy family. Any tensions that arise are quickly dealt with to everyone's satisfaction, and Peter and James—contrary to Paul's depiction and probably to historical reality—take the leading role in supporting the Torah-free Pauline mission to Gentiles.[98] Luke's portrait in Acts 18–19 of Baptist followers who are quickly and easily persuaded to become Christians is similarly tendentious, an attempt to smooth over the underlying historical reality of mutual uneasiness and competition. The similarity to the reaction imagined in Qur'ān 5:83 is again striking: the Baptist adherents hear Paul's message about Jesus, recognize its truth, and immediately embrace it. The only thing missing from Acts 19 is the tears of the converts, but reception of the Holy Spirit perhaps makes up for this.

In response to Vogel, then, I suggest that the proper rubric for under-standing the relationship between the New Testament writers and the adher-ents of the Baptist is not "friendly" but "muted" competition—perhaps even the Competition That Dare Not Speak Its Name.[99] The analogy of sibling ri-valry within a family suggests itself. Such rivalry is often denied, even by the sibling experiencing it, but remains a powerful subterranean dynamic.[100]

....

Conclusion

Competition between early Christians and followers of the Baptist is evident throughout early Christian sources. This result must be kept constantly in mind as we move to the subsequent chapters of this study, which rely, for the most part, on those same Christian sources as the raw material for re-constructing the historical Baptist. We must constantly remember what the Christians *wanted* to believe about John—that his most important task was to prepare the way for Jesus, not to claim salvific importance for himself—and, when we encounter texts that seem to mirror that belief, we must be vigilant.

This is not to say that everything that corresponds to that Christian at-titude is necessarily unhistorical. For example, in chapter 3 I will argue that John did see himself as the returning Elijah, and in chapter 5 that he did acknowledge Jesus as in some ways his superior; those points, while con-venient for Christians, were also true. But I will have to make an *argument* for these positions, not simply read them off Christian sources, which are so deeply invested in downgrading John to exalt Jesus. And, in other cases, especially the discussion of John's baptism in chapter 4, I will argue that the Christian tradition has distorted John's message by making his rite strictly preparatory.

Before moving on to these areas that are so deeply enmeshed in Christian history and theology, however, I will take a step back to ask about the roots of John's theology: the possibility that he began his career at Qumran.

CHAPTER TWO

Qumran

As the previous chapter demonstrated, competition between early Christians and adherents of John the Baptist thoroughly affected the New Testament presentation of the Baptist himself. Later I will argue that this competition did not begin in the post-Easter period but started in the lifetimes of John and Jesus themselves. Jesus began his ministry, or at least a significant new phase of it, within the Baptist movement, but he subsequently struck out on his own and found it necessary to distance himself from his former teacher even while acknowledging him as a forerunner and fellow emissary of Wisdom (Matt. 11:7–19).[1] The present chapter proposes that the Baptist himself probably went through a similar progression of belonging followed by distance. The earlier group John belonged to was the Qumran sect, the community that produced the Dead Sea Scrolls.

These documents, hidden away in the late first century CE in caves above Wadi Qumran,[2] near the northwestern corner of the Dead Sea, have revolutionized our understanding of Second Temple Judaism since they were uncovered in the winter of 1946–47 by Bedouin shepherds.[3] The scholarly consensus is that this trove of biblical and postbiblical texts, most of the latter unknown before 1947, is the library of a group related to the Essenes, a sectarian movement described by the Jewish philosopher Philo (c. 30 BCE–45 CE), the Jewish historian Josephus (ca. 38–after 93 CE), and the Roman naturalist Pliny the Elder (23/24–79 CE).[4]

Even before the discovery of the Qumran scrolls, as far back as the beginning of the nineteenth century, Karl Heinrich Georg Venturini, in a novelistic biography of Jesus, had portrayed both Jesus and his friend and cousin, the Baptist, as initiates into the secret order of the Essenes.[5] Later in the century, in 1863, Heinrich Graetz linked John with the Essenes on the basis of their common asceticism, purificatory water rites, and presence in the vicinity of the Dead Sea.[6] Graetz even referred to John as "the Essene Baptist."[7] Shortly thereafter, David Friedrich Strauss, in his second book about Jesus, also drew a strong connection between John and the Essenes.[8] But nothing much came of these suggestions until the discovery of the Dead Sea Scrolls, perhaps partly because J. B. Lightfoot subjected Graetz's thesis to a withering critique.[9] To

be sure, in the year after the publication of Graetz's book, and without showing awareness of it, Christian Ginsburg related the Essenes indirectly to John
but directly to Jesus, though with questionable reasoning: "When Christ pronounced John to be *Elias* [= Elijah] (Matt. xi. 14), he declared that the Baptist
had already attained to that spirit and power which the Essenes strove to
obtain in their highest stage of purity. It will therefore hardly be doubted
that the Saviour himself belonged to this holy brotherhood."[10] This is part of a
pattern in eighteenth- and nineteenth-century works on the origins of Christianity: if they mention the Essenes at all, they generally relate them to Jesus
rather than to John; the main appeal seems to be the idea of Jesus's membership in a secret society with a reputation for mystical knowledge.[11] But it was
more common for scholars to follow Lightfoot's lead and deny any Essene
connection to either John or Jesus.[12] Things did not change much in the early
twentieth century; even Martin Dibelius's groundbreaking 1911 monograph
on the Baptist makes only two incidental references to the Essenes, and Ernst
Lohmeyer's monograph of 1932 only four.[13] What is chiefly striking about the
assertion of a link between John and the Essenes in pre-Qumran scholarship,
therefore, is its rarity.

....

Similarities

With the discovery of the Scrolls, however, things began to change, and since
1948 many scholars have linked John directly or indirectly with the Qumran
sect. The strong form of this claim—which this study shares—is that John
started out as a member of the Qumran community. This is a controversial
assertion,[14] and it is based on circumstantial evidence, but there is a lot of
that, including the following:

- The rite of immersion in water was central both to the ministry of John
  the Baptist, as obvious already from his epithet ὁ βαπτιστής, reported
  by both Josephus and the Gospels, and to the life of the Qumran community. The archaeological remains of Qumran include ten large ritual
  bathing pools, or *miqva'ot*. Although the remains of *miqva'ot* in Palestine are not limited to Qumran but scattered throughout the country,
  and although several are found in the villas of Jerusalem's Jewish Quar-
  ter and Herodian Jericho, the Qumran remains are disproportionately
  large and numerous in relation to the population served.[15]
- Moreover, the water rites practiced by the Baptist and by the Qumran
  sect had a similar meaning, including their connection with repentance
  and forgiveness of sins (Mark 1:4; 1QS 3:4–12). Elsewhere in ancient
  Judaism, washing ceremonies were not connected with repentance
  and atonement but with the recovery of ritual purity.[16]

- The forgiveness spoken of in both cases, moreover, is an *eschatological* remission of sins, directly linked with belief in an approaching crisis in world history, in which the wicked will be judged, the righteous vindicated, and the world transformed.[17] In the Gospels, those who come to John's baptism do so to escape from "the wrath to come" (Matt. 3:7// Luke 3:7), and this baptism is associated with the baptism in the Spirit and fire soon to be accomplished by "the Coming One" (Mark 1:7–8// Matt. 3:11–12//Luke 3:16–17).[18] Among the Qumran scrolls, 1QS 3:4–12 speaks of entering into the purifying waters and thereby becoming united with God's Spirit, and the parallelism with the description of eschatological cleansing in 1QS 4:20–25 makes clear that what is described in 3:4–12 is in some sense an end-time event. The water rites practiced by the Baptist and the Qumran community, then, both perhaps inspired by the imagery of Ezek. 36:25–27,[19] looked forward to or gave a foretaste of the outpouring of God's Spirit that was expected for the end-time.[20] And although immersion and other water rites are attested elsewhere in Second Temple Judaism,[21] there seems to be no evidence for an *eschatologically oriented* immersion rite outside of the Qumran community, the Baptist movement, and early Christianity in the pre-70 CE period.[22]
- In Matt. 3:7–12//Luke 3:7–18, moreover, receiving John's baptism is associated with fleeing from the wrath to come, escaping the fire that will burn up the chaff, and being preserved in God's barn—that is, attaining eternal life. As Antje Labahn notes, bathing is never directly associated with attaining life in the Old Testament,[23] but this association does appear in Second Temple Jewish literature. And all of the pre-Christian references she cites are either from Qumran documents (11QTemple 45:15–46:12; 4QTohorot; 4QMMT; 1QS 3:4–9; 4:21; 5:13–14; CD 10:10–13) or from a sectarian book associated with Qumran (Jub. 21:16).[24]
- The Q saying Matt. 3:11–12//Luke 3:16–17 has John predicting an eschatological baptism by fire, which is linked with the burning of the "chaff" (wicked people) in unquenchable fire. Although fire frequently serves as a symbol of divine judgment in the Old Testament and later Jewish apocalyptic literature[25] and although the idea of unquenchable fire goes back to Isa. 66:24, the specific image of *baptism* by fire suggests an additional idea, that of a *stream* or *river* of fire in which those being judged are submerged. Steve Mason sums up the idea well: "In poignant eschatological reversal the most precious life-supporting systems . . . will be turned to fire!"[26] This idea, too, is rooted in the Old Testament,[27] but it reappears in a first-century Jewish apocalyptic writing that turns up at Qumran (1 En. 14:19),[28] and its most frequent attestation is in the

Qumran Hodayot, which speak of a deluge of fire (1QH[a] 16[8]:18–20) and a "spring of light" whose flames will devour all the "children of injustice" (14[6]:17–19), and compare "the torrents of Belial" to a devouring fire that overflows its banks (1QH[a] 11[3]:29–32).[29]

- John's base of operations, according to the Synoptic Gospels, was "the wilderness of Judea" (Matt. 3:1), particularly the area of that wilderness around the Jordan River (Luke 3:3), in which he baptized those who accepted his message (Mark 1:5//Matt. 3:6). Qumran is in the same Judean Desert, near the point at which the Jordan empties into the Dead Sea. The Fourth Gospel, moreover, has John baptizing at "Aenon near Salim" (John 3:23), and one of the traditional sites for this locality, which is supported by the sixth-century Madaba Map, is just northeast of the Dead Sea, opposite Bethabara—a few miles from Qumran.[30] In any event, John was operating in the same general wilderness area as the Qumran community.

- A very important parallel is that, in the Community Rule, the Dead Sea sect links its presence in the Judean Desert with the biblical prophecy in Isa. 40:3, which speaks of preparing a way for the Lord in the wilderness and straightening his path in the desert (1QS 8:12–14; 9:18–20). The Synoptic Gospels (Mark 1:3–4//Matt. 3:1–3//Luke 3:2–4) associate the Baptist's presence in the same Judean Desert with the same Isaian passage, and John 1:23 renders this biblical allusion as a self-identification by the Baptist. It is probable that the Fourth Gospel is right about this: the Baptist did indeed connect his presence in the Judean wilderness with Isa. 40:3, just as the Qumran sect did.[31]

- Nor do the Qumran connections with Isa. 40:3 stop there. An earlier passage in the Community Rule, 1QS 4:2–3, describes the guardian angel of the sect, the Prince of Light, as working to enlighten the sectarian's heart "and to straighten before him all the ways of true righteousness" (*Dead Sea Scrolls Electronic Library* trans. altered)—the quoted words reflecting the characteristic vocabulary of Isa. 40:3.[32] Moreover, another Qumran text, the Aramaic Levi Document, uses similar vocabulary, partially drawn from Isa. 40:3, to speak of a *lustration:* "And I washed myself entirely in living [= flowing] water, and I *made all my ways straight*" (ALD 2:5, my trans.).[33] John the Baptist, of course, also baptized his adherents in flowing water, and his baptism is linked in the Gospels with the Isaian prophecy about making the Lord's way straight.[34] Thus Isa. 40:3 seems to have been a favorite text of the Qumranites, whereas it is rarely used elsewhere in Second Temple Judaism;[35] and it was used by the sectarians, as by the Gospel tradition about John, to allude to water rites and their own presence in the Judean Desert. If these are coincidences, they are amazing ones.

- According to the Gospels (Matt. 3:7–10//Luke 3:7–14), John warned those who came to his baptism that it would do them no good if unaccompanied by repentance and a reformed life. As chapter 4 explores in more detail, Josephus makes the same point more emphatically in his description of the Baptist's teaching in *Ant.* 18.116–117, where he denies that John thought his baptism cleansed people from sin and claims that he saw it merely as a bodily purification symbolizing that the soul had already been cleansed by righteousness. This point is quite similar to that made in two connected Qumran passages, 1QS 3:4–9 and 5:13–14, which refute the idea that ritual bathing accomplishes any atonement for sins unless it is preceded by the spiritual cleansing of repentance.

  It is, to be sure, a common theme already in the Old Testament (for example, Amos 5:21–25; Isa. 1:11–18; Jer. 2:22), which continues in later Jewish traditions, that ritual acts by themselves do not effect atonement;[36] and Philo (*Unchangeable* 7–8) applies this thought to a criticism of pagan water rituals.[37] For the Mishnah, similarly, the proper intention (כוונה) must be present for immersion to count for anything (see, for example, m. Ḥag. 2:6), and according to a later midrash Yoḥanan ben Zakkai, an important late-first-century sage, said that it was not really the water that purified but the ordinance of God (Pesiq. Rab. Kah. 4:7).[38] But the parallel between 1QS 3:4–9, 5:13–14 and Josephus's description of the Baptist's attitude towards his baptismal ministry is still striking; as Rivka Nir puts it: "Nowhere in Judaism before Qumran, neither in biblical times nor in the Second Temple period, was the notion that one could be made clean in body only if one was pure in heart ever connected to the rite of immersion.[39]

- Josephus's description of John's baptism and 1QS 3:7 also use common vocabulary: both speak of being "united" (ליחד/συνιέναι) through immersion (in the one case with God's truth, in the other case, by implication, with other baptizands).[40]

- In the Q passage alluded to above (Matt. 3:7–10//Luke 3:7–9), the Baptist terms "children of vipers" (γεννήματα ἐχιδνῶν) those unrepentant people who have tried to escape the coming divine wrath by participating in his movement. As Otto Betz pointed out in a 1958 article, the denunciatory terms here echo Isa. 59:5, which berates sinners whose treachery has cut them off from God: "They hatch a viper's eggs (בֵּיצֵי צִפְעוֹנִי בִּקֵּעוּ),[41] they weave the spider's web; he who eats their eggs dies, and from one which is crushed, a poisonous snake is hatched" (וְהַזּוּרֶה תִּבָּקַע אֶפְעֶה).[42] As in the Q passage, we see here a reference not only to a venomous snake but also to its offspring.

Significantly, the only reflections of this Isaian passage in extant ancient Jewish literature seem to be in Qumran documents.[43] As Betz already observed, 1QH^a 11(3):17 echoes the end of the Isaian verse when it speaks of the gates of Sheol opening for מעשי אפעה, a term that Betz translates as "Creatures of the Snake"—a close analogue to the "brood of vipers" of the Gospels.[44] Betz's suggestion has not been much noted in the exegetical literature,[45] but his point can be reinforced by noting that there is also an echo of the Isaian passage in CD 5:11–15. Here the author, speaking of the enemies of the sect, says that "their eggs are the eggs of vipers" (ביצי צפעונים ביציהם) before denouncing them as people incapable of purification (לא ינקה). This is strikingly similar to Matt. 3:7//Luke 3:7, where the Baptist bars the "brood of vipers" from his purificatory rite. Moreover, a later passage in the Damascus Document, CD 19:16–24, links with vipers, and threatens with judgment, people who try to enter God's covenant of repentance but display their insincerity by oppressing their neighbors—again, a striking parallel to the Q passage in its context.[46]

• A further connection lies in the priestly origin and leadership of the Qumran community, on the one hand, and the possible priestly background of John, on the other.[47]

These are striking similarities, not only in theme and setting but also in the combination of such factors, as well as in specific vocabulary and imagery (offspring of vipers, river of fire, usage of Isaiah 40:3). It is difficult, then, to agree with Joachim Gnilka when he claims that the commonalities between John and Qumran reflect their participation in the same general milieu, whereas the differences attest to the independence of John, "whom we should scarcely regard as a refugee from Qumran."[48] Some of the parallels between John and Qumran are too striking to ascribe merely to a common milieu. The denunciation in Isa. 59:5 of those who hatch vipers' eggs, for example, is never echoed in Second Temple Jewish literature outside of the Qumran literature, the tradition about John the Baptist, and two sayings attributed to Jesus in Matt. 12:34 and 23:33, which are probably Matthean compositions that pick up the "brood of vipers" language of the Baptist.[49] Isaiah 40:3, similarly, is rarely used elsewhere but is central to the self-understanding of both John and the Sect; both John and the Sect, moreover, used this verse in relation to ritual immersion—again, a unique combination. Neither do we have evidence for any other Second Temple Jewish group that practiced a water immersion oriented to the eschaton and linked with forgiveness of sins and the eschatological impartation of the Spirit. These *distinctive* characteristics are enough to establish a genetic relationship, just as, in the natural world, organisms that share unusual traits usually do so because of a shared gene-alogy. As Charles Darwin puts it in *On the Origin of Species:* "We have no written pedigrees; we have to make out community of descent by resem-blances of any kind. . . . We may err in this respect in regard to single points of structure, but when several characters, let them be ever so trifling, occur together throughout a large group of beings having different habits, we may feel almost sure . . . that these characters have been inherited from a com-mon ancestor."[50] Neither do we have a written pedigree establishing John's connection with Qumran, but there are enough common characteristics of both, characteristics that distinguish them from other Second Temple Jewish figures, to point toward what Darwin calls a "community of descent." Since, moreover, we know that John and the Qumran sect were operating in the same general area and since there is evidence suggesting that he may have been from the sort of priestly background that was especially important in the sect, it seems more probable than not that he started out as a member of the group.

. . . .

The Differences and Their Significance

There are, of course, differences between John's theology, to the extent that we can reconstruct it, and that of Qumran. If there had not been, John prob-ably would have remained a member of the Sect. The differences, moreover, may have intensified once he departed—just as, to extend the biological meta-phor, organisms with shared genealogies tend to diversify when they move into new environments.[51] The following list summarizes the most important differences.[52]

- John's baptism was administered by a baptizer, John himself,[53] whereas Qumran immersions, like those elsewhere in Judaism, seem to have been self-administered.[54]
- John's baptism seems to have been a once-and-for-all event,[55] whereas Qumran immersions were repeated, perhaps several times daily.[56]
- John proclaimed his message openly to all Israel, calling the Jewish peo-ple in general to repent and be baptized, and did not insist that those who received his baptism leave their occupations to follow him (cf. Luke 3:10–14).[57] Qumran, on the other hand, was a closed community, which hid its most important doctrines from outsiders, and only granted en-trance to its "purifying waters," holy meal, and secret interpretation of the Torah after a lengthy novitiate.[58]
- The public nature of John's ministry is particularly emphasized by the interpretation of Isa. 40:3 in Mark 1:4–5 and parallels; here "the voice of one shouting in the wilderness" invites "all Judea and all the

Jerusalemites" to come out to that wilderness to be baptized by him. The Qumran group, by contrast, interprets Isa. 40:3 with respect to its own *separation* from "the congregation of people of perversity" (my trans.) to study the Torah in a wilderness setting (1QS 8:13–16), and the secrets revealed by such esoteric study are to be kept from the "people of the pit," that is, non-Qumranites, to whom the sect members are to maintain an attitude of "eternal hatred" (1QS 9:19–22; cf. Josephus, *J.W.* 2.139, 141).[59]

• While "the Qumran sect was a coherent community located in a specific locale," John was itinerant; though the Gospels say he had disciples, it is unclear how large or stable that group was.[60]

How significant are such differences? Not as significant, I think, as is implied by those who use them to deny a special relationship between John and the Qumran community. These sorts of differences do nothing to efface the genealogical relation that can be posited on the basis of the shared traits of the two movements—traits that, as shown above, are often rare or unique, as far as we know, within Second Temple Judaism. It is characteristic of religious movements, especially sectarian groups, to preserve evidence of their origin through such peculiarities,[61] even as they elaborate the shared tradition in ways that separate them from their sociological "parents"; indeed, such separation may be part of the point of such changes.[62] The way in which Joan Taylor, then, utilizes the differences between the usage of Isa. 40:3 in 1QS 8–9, on the one hand, and in the Gospel tradition about John the Baptist, on the other, seems misguided. Exaggerating the significance of these differences by saying that the text is used "with a completely different hermeneutical emphasis" in the two bodies of literature, she concludes that "this shows that the two groups were not related."[63] But the hermeneutical emphasis is not "*completely* different"; both, for example, use Isa. 40:3 to speak of God's eschatological action in the Judean Desert, which includes forgiveness of sins and is manifested through human actors and related to water rites. And the differences are precisely the sort of thing we would expect if John had started out as a member of the Qumran community but had subsequently broken away.[64] Indeed, they may go some way towards suggesting *why* he broke away. It may be, as W. H. Brownlee suggests, that "John was not satisfied with the way the Essenes were seeking to fulfill Isa. 40:3. They were preparing only themselves for the Messiah's coming, not the nation. His attention was caught by the reference to the 'voice crying in the wilderness.'[65] As he understood the passage, the Essenes should become a voice calling the nation to repentance. . . . The day came when he turned his back upon them and went out alone to become that voice."[66]

. . . .

Why John Left Qumran

Developing Brownlee's insight further, we may discern other factors that may have led to John's break with the Qumran community and the beginning of his independent ministry.[67] These are reasoned guesses, based partly on differences between John's theology and that of Qumran. It is, to be sure, difficult to know exactly what was cause and what was effect—that is, whether John departed from the Sect (or was kicked out) because he disagreed with them, or whether he developed different ideas after he left them, or whether both factors were involved. The last hypothesis seems likely, but it is difficult to know in any particular case whether the difference was catalyst or consequence.

This problem is complicated by the dearth of evidence about John's teaching and practice, and the development of his thought. For example, was the denunciation of insincere, unrepentant "vipers" part of his message from the beginning, or did it develop only after he encountered opposition such as that reflected in Matt. 11:18//Luke 7:33, where John's audience reacts to his asceticism by accusing him of demonic possession? Similarly, did the openness to non-Jews suggested by Matt. 3:9//Luke 3:8 ("God is able from these stones to raise up children to Abraham") characterize his message from the beginning, or was it perhaps influenced by positive encounters with Gentiles following his departure from the Sect?[68] Perhaps in most cases there was a germ of the idea from the beginning of John's ministry, but it developed as that ministry proceeded.

Despite all this uncertainty, I suggest that the reasons for John's departure from Qumran may have included the following:

1) His developing sense of the salvation-historical importance of his own mission, including, perhaps, his growing conviction that he was the eschatological Elijah (see next chapter) and that he, not the Qumran sect as a whole, was the Isaian "voice shouting in the wilderness." Certainly a sect member holding such an expansive self-estimate would find it difficult to submit to the scrutiny of the *Maskil* (Instructor), the priestly leader of the community, one of whose jobs was to weigh each member's spiritual qualities and accordingly assign him a rank in the sect's hierarchy (see 1QS 9:14–16). The *Maskil* and other sectarians may have found it correspondingly difficult to put up with John.[69] His emerging self-consciousness may also have brought him into direct competition with this leader, since it is possible that the latter, as the successor of the Teacher of Righteousness, was himself viewed, and viewed himself, as the eschatological prophet.[70] If so, the dynamic of competition and

separation was later repeated by the departure of the Baptist's erstwhile disciple, Jesus of Nazareth, from the Baptist movement, because of his conviction of his own centrality in salvation history (see chap. 5).[71]

2) A desire to break loose from the self-enclosed world of Qumran and proclaim the message of repentance to "all Israel." Josephus (*Ant.* 18.117–118) and the Gospels (Mark 1:4–5 and parallels) agree that John addressed multitudes, and that his message called on all Jews to repent before it was too late. There is no suggestion in these sources that he embraced any sort of secret doctrine, or held anything back from the multitudes— unlike the Qumran sect, which, as noted above, jealously guarded its secret interpretation of the Torah from "the people of the pit."[72]

3) A different attitude toward the Gentile world. This difference deserves detailed discussion.

....

The Qumran Attitude toward Gentiles

The Dead Sea Sect did not live in splendid isolation from non-Jews; while Qumran was not on a major trade route,[73] it was connected to its nearer and farther environment by roads, and boat travel on the Dead Sea was frequent and easily available to the Qumranites.[74] Moreover, as Eric Meyers points out, "anyone living at Qumran or nearby could easily have trekked back to Jericho, where they could connect with an important trans-regional route that led to Jerusalem to the west and Amman/Philadelphia to the east."[75] In the environs of Qumran itself, it was possible to encounter non-Jews, whether wayfarers, Roman soldiers, or people associated with the Nabatean Kingdom, which reached its zenith during the long reign of Aretas IV (9 BCE–40 CE) and exerted influence in the Dead Sea area—including Qumran—and on both sides of the Jordan.[76] Encounters with Gentiles appear to have happened at Qumran with some frequency, as is clear from rules in the Damascus Document that forbid employing a Gentile to transact one's business on the Sabbath (11:2), spending the Sabbath near a place of Gentiles (11:14–15), or attacking Gentiles, selling them animals that can be used for sacrifice, or selling them slaves who have "entered into the covenant of Abraham" (12:6–11).[77] This Qumran evidence is supported by Josephus (*J.W.* 2.150), who says that the Essenes immerse themselves (ἀπολούεσθαι) after contact with an alien (ἀλλοφύλῳ).

The Qumran attitude towards the Gentile world, however, was complex. The rules against attacking Gentiles violently in the present age do not extend to what *God* may do them, partly through the instrumentality of the sect, in the coming eschatological era. Here fantasies of revenge predominate. One of the battle banners described in the War Scroll bears the inscription, "God's destruction of every futile people" (4:12; כל גוי הבל), and the scroll later praises God for gathering "the assembly of peoples" (קהל גויים) for "annihilation with no remnant" (14:5). It is important to realize, however, that these fantasies were directed at Gentiles who remained Gentiles and not at those who converted to Judaism, especially the Qumran form of it. The passage quoted above about people who have "entered into the covenant of Abraham" already suggests the possibility of Gentile conversion—a position not shared by all ancient Jews.[78]

The status of these proselytes *(gerim),* however, seems to have been ambiguous.[79] They are included in the enumeration of the classes of community members in the Damascus Document, but in last place (CD 14:3–6). The Nahum Pesher, similarly, adds "the proselyte who is joined to them," an expression based on Isa. 14:1, to its list of groups in Palestinian society,[80] after "kings, princes, priests, and people" (4Q169 2:9)—unless *ger* in this instance retains its older, biblical sense of "resident alien."[81] *Ger* almost certainly means "proselyte" in 11QT[a] (11Q19) 40:5–6, where the *gerim* have access to the outer courtyard in the ideal Temple; their rank there, however, is again an inferior one, since they share this space with Israelite women.[82] Still, it is important that this text seems to include the *gerim* in the category of "children of Israel."[83] This makes it all the more puzzling that the Florilegium (4Q174 1:3–4) seems to ban the *gerim* (but not Israelite women)[84] from entrance into the eschatological Temple[85]—unless, here again, *ger* simply means "resident alien."[86]

Despite such uncertainties and ambiguities, CD 14:6 makes it clear that proselytes were treated as part of the elect community by the law that regulated daily life in the Dead Sea Sect.[87] It is possible then that John, as a member of that sect, got to know such proselytes, and if so he may eventually have begun to wonder about the incongruities of their status. Such contact and reflection may have planted the seeds for a revised view of Gentiles, which germinated through further contacts with such people on both sides of the Jordan after John left Qumran.[88] This hypothesis coheres not only with the Q statement about God raising up children to Abraham from the stones of the Jordan Valley but also with Josephus's assertion that Herod decided to arrest and execute John because "others" in addition to Jews began to join his movement (τῶν ἄλλων συστρεφομένων, *Ant.* 18.118).[89] If, moreover, John thought of himself as Elijah returned from the dead, as I will argue in the next chapter, this identification has implications for the question of his attitude towards Gentiles, because Elijah ministered to a widow from Sidon (1 Kgs. 17:1–16), and this ministry to a Gentile, along with that of his disciple Elisha to Naaman the Syrian (2 Kgs. 5:1–14), were remembered as controversial features of their ministries.[90]

. . . .

Revising the Jewish/Gentile Antinomy

It seems likely, then, that one of the precipitating factors in John's departure from Qumran may have been an interest in, curiosity about, and sympathy towards Gentiles that had begun to develop while he still belonged to the sect.[91] This solicitude for Gentiles seems to have gone along with a revised view of the Jewish/Gentile division. This revisionist thinking comes into view in a passage already mentioned, which shows both an apparent linkage with Qumran thought and a significant departure from it. The passage is a Q saying, quoted here in its Matthean version:

^{7}ἰδὼν δὲ πολλοὺς τῶν Φαρισαίων καὶ Σαδδουκαίων ἐρχομένους ἐπὶ τὸ βάπτισμα αὐτοῦ εἶπεν αὐτοῖς· γεννήματα ἐχιδνῶν, τίς ὑπέδειξεν ὑμῖν φυγεῖν ἀπὸ τῆς μελλούσης ὀργῆς; ^{8}ποιήσατε οὖν καρπὸν ἄξιον τῆς μετανοίας ^{9}καὶ μὴ δόξητε λέγειν ἐν ἑαυτοῖς· πατέρα ἔχομεν τὸν Ἀβραάμ. λέγω γὰρ ὑμῖν ὅτι δύναται ὁ θεὸς ἐκ τῶν λίθων τούτων ἐγεῖραι τέκνα τῷ Ἀβραάμ. ^{10}ἤδη δὲ ἡ ἀξίνη πρὸς τὴν ῥίζαν τῶν δένδρων κεῖται· πᾶν οὖν δένδρον μὴ ποιοῦν καρπὸν καλὸν ἐκκόπτεται καὶ εἰς πῦρ βάλλεται.

^{7}But when he saw many of the Pharisees and Sadducees coming for baptism, he said to them, "You brood of vipers! Who warned you to flee from the coming wrath? ^{8}Bear fruit worthy of repentance, ^{9}and do not presume to say among yourselves, 'We have Abraham as our father'; for I tell you, God is able from these stones to raise up children to Abraham. ^{10}Already the axe is placed at the root of the trees; every tree therefore that does not bear good fruit is cut down and thrown into the fire" (Matt. 3:7–10, Revised Standard Version alt.).

Luke's version (Luke 3:7–9) is nearly identical, except that the Baptist's harsh warning is aimed at the crowds rather than the "Pharisees and Sadducees."[92] In reality, though, Pharisees and Sadducees were rivals, not allies.[93] Luke's version, in which John addresses the crowds, is more plausible,[94] though at first it seems strange that he speaks in such hostile terms, and without distinction, to all those who come out to the Jordan to join his baptism. But this is the kind of apocalyptic anthropological pessimism that is also enshrined in Jesus's characterization of "this generation" as evil in Q (Matt. 12:39, 16:4; Luke 11:29).

This sort of connection between John's teaching and Jesus's probably reflects the fact that Jesus began as a disciple of John and absorbed many of his basic ideas from him (see chap. 5), although Bultmann and Carl R. Kazmierski argue on the contrary that Matt. 3:7–10//Luke 3:7–9 is a retrojection of Christian themes onto the Baptist.[95] This, however, seems unlikely, since the passage contains no reference to Jesus; the audience is called to respond, and threatened for not responding, not to the coming Messiah, whose advent is not prophesied until later (Matt. 3:11–12//Luke 3:15–18), but to the message of John himself.[96]

If Matthew 3:7–10//Luke 3:7–9 preserves a memory of the Baptist's eschatological preaching, an important corollary follows: the target of John's attack may not have been a particular religious group within Israel but the covenantal election of Israel in general. To understand the radical nature of this attack, it is necessary to trace the background of the imagery used in Matt. 3:8–10//Luke 3:8–9. It is particularly significant that Matt. 3:9//Luke 3:8 warns against relying on descent from Abraham and that Matt. 3:10//Luke 3:9 speaks of chopping down trees. Exegetes have struggled to find the line of thought here, and some have given up and concluded that there is none, and that the passage is not an original unity.[97] But the combination of images is far from fortuitous: descent from Abraham is often associated with trees and other plant imagery in biblical and later Second Temple sources—including, notably, the Qumran scrolls. There is thus an intrinsic connection between the theme of Abrahamic descent in Matt. 3:9//Luke 3:8 and the attack on tree roots in Matt. 3:10//Luke 3:9.[98] What is new about John's warning is the idea that the trees of Israel—the physical descendants of Abraham—may be destroyed.

. . . .

Old Testament Background

The image of Israel as a plant is deeply rooted, so to speak, in the Old Testament, and is repeated so often in subsequent Jewish literature that it is safe to call it (with apologies for a second pun) a stock image. In two glorious Deutero-Isaian portrayals of end-time deliverance and moral transformation, for example, the people of Israel, who at the eschaton "will all become righteous," are described as "the shoot of my [God's] planting" (נצר מטעי), "terebinths of righteousness" (אילי הצדק), and "the planting of the Lord" (מטע יהוה; Isa. 60:21; 61:3). As these passages demonstrate, the image is linked with the continuity of God's care for Israel: what he has sown, he will protect and nourish until it develops into the flourishing plant he intends it to be, despite all the threats encountered along the way.[99] As Patrick Tiller points out, the Deutero-Isaian passages are programmatic for later Jewish usages of the plant image, which frequently associate the image with the people's righteousness—as happens negatively in our Q passage—and employ the terms "branch" and "planting."[100]

The Old Testament plant image can be used negatively; in Jer. 11:16 and Isa. 5:1–7, for instance, the plant of Israel is threatened with destruction for its evil deeds, and the former passage warns that the olive tree of Judah will be burnt and its boughs lopped off (cf. Matt. 3:10//Luke 3:9; Rom. 11:16). But later in both Isaiah and Jeremiah, it becomes plain that such acts of agricultural vandalism are not God's last word for Israel. The devastated vineyard in Isa. 5:1–7 yields to the "vineyard of delight" in Isa. 27:2–9, and the burnt and broken-off olive tree of Jer. 11:15–17 gives way to the messianic "branch," in whose days "Judah will be saved and Israel will live in safety" (Jer. 23:5–6), and to the promise that God "will plant them in this land in faithfulness," with all his heart and soul (Jer. 32:41). Perhaps relying on such intertextual connections as well as on an overarching conviction about God's election of Israel, rabbinic traditions, when commenting on Isa. 5:1–7, usually concentrate on the identification of Israel as God's beloved in verse 1 or the statement in the first part of verse 7 that she is the Lord's vineyard—ignoring the fierce denunciations in verses 3–6, 7b.[101] Nor is it surprising that Isa. 60:21, one of the two Deutero-Isaian passages that is programmatic for later Jewish usages of the plant/tree imagery, shows up in a famous Mishnaic text as scriptural support for the proposition that "all Israel have a share in the world to come, as it is said, 'Your people shall all be righteous; they shall possess the land for ever; the shoot of my planting, the work of my hands, that I might be glorified'" (m. Sanh. 10:1, my trans.).[102]

Two other peculiarities of the transmission of Isa. 60:21 should be noted. The manuscript tradition shows a notable variation in the transmission of the phrase נצר מטעי, which is translated above "the shoot of my [God's] planting." This is the *qere* reading of the text, but it could also be interpreted as "the shoot of my plantings," plural. The *ketiv* reads נצר מטעו, "the shoot of his planting," singular (on *qere* and *ketiv*, see the glossary), but the plural interpretation is supported both by Qumran Manuscript B, which reads נצר מטעיו, "the shoot of his plantings," and by Qumran manuscript A, which reads נצר מטעי יהוה, "the shoot of the plantings of the Lord." The manuscript traditions, then, disagree about whether God made one planting or several, but all agree that only one shoot resulted. Moreover, since נצר can denote not only a shoot above ground but also a root below it, the plural form נצר מטעיו can be rendered as "the root of his plantings." This observation brings Isa. 60:21 even closer to Matt. 3:10//Luke 3:9, which threatens many trees, all of which share a common root.

Besides Isa. 60:21, one other Deutero-Isaian text is important for exegesis of the Baptist's warning in Matt. 3:7–10//Luke 3:7–9. This is the famous passage in Isa. 51:1–2, whose connection with the Gospel passage can be seen in the italicized words: "Listen to me, you that *pursue righteousness*, you that seek the Lord. Look to the *rock* from which you were hewn, and to the quarry from which you were dug. Look to *Abraham your father*, and to Sarah who bore you; for he was but one when I called him, but I *blessed him and made him many.*" Here, as in the Q passage, there is an appeal to Abraham as a father. Abraham, moreover, is linked both to a rock or rocks and to the pursuit of righteousness (cf. "bear fruit worthy of repentance").[103] Moreover, as we shall see in the next section, many postbiblical writers associate the numerousness of Abraham's progeny, which is referred to at the end of the passage, with images of fecundity, including tree images. We may thus posit as a working hypothesis that John's exhortation in Matt. 3:7-10//Luke 3:7-9 is intended as a deliberate contrast to another exhortation known to his hearers, which may have gone something like this: "Look to Abraham, the rock from which you were hewn, and the plant from which you have sprouted; take up your residence again in the eternal tree of Israelite identity and devotion to God's Law. In so doing, you will bear fruits worthy of repentance and flee from the coming wrath." As we shall see in the following sections, all of these associations of the plant/tree imagery are developed further in postbiblical Jewish literature.

Pseudepigrapha

As the rabbinic endpoints alluded to above suggest, postbiblical usages of the plant metaphor put even more stress than their biblical sources on God's continuing care for Israel. This is already suggested by the first-century BCE pseudepigraphon, Psalms of Solomon.[104]

1) Faithful is the Lord to those who love him in truth,
   to those who endure his discipline,
2) to those who walk in the righteousness of his ordinances,
   in the law which he commanded us that we might live.
3) The devout of the Lord shall live by it forever;
   the orchard of the Lord, the trees of life, are his devout.
4) Their planting is rooted forever;
   they shall not be pulled up all the days of heaven;
5) for the portion and inheritance of God is Israel.
   (Pss. Sol. 14:1-5, New English Translation of the Septuagint trans.)

The final verse here reveals what has been implicit from the beginning of the psalm: it is *Israel* who is God's holy planting and orchard, his portion and inheritance.

This emphasis on Israel as the eternal plant is even clearer in several passages from a later pseudepigraphon, Pseudo-Philo's Liber Antiquitatum Biblicarum, which frequently uses the image of Israel as a vine or other plant.[105] In 12:8-9, for example, Moses implores God not to uproot the vine he has planted, whose roots he has sunk in the abyss and whose shoots he has stretched out to heaven. Here, as elsewhere in the work (18:10, 28:4–5, 30:4–7, 39:7, 49:6), the possibility that God might uproot his planting is broached but rejected as nonsensical. This is because, as Moses's father Amram puts it: "It will sooner happen that this age will be ended forever or the world will sink into the immeasurable deep or the heart of the abyss will touch the stars than that the race of the sons of Israel will be ended. And there will be fulfilled the covenant that God established with Abraham. . . . For God will not abide in his anger, nor will he forget his people forever, nor will he cast forth the race of Israel in vain upon the earth; nor did he establish a covenant with our fathers in vain; and even when we did not yet exist, God spoke about these matters (LAB 9:3–4)."[106]

Or, as the pagan prophet Balaam says in LAB 18:10, specifically using the image of Israel as God's plant: "It is easier to take away the foundations and the topmost part of the earth and to extinguish the light of the sun and to darken the light of the moon than for anyone to uproot the planting of the Most Powerful or to destroy his vine *(eradicare plantaginem Fortissimi aut exterminare vineam eius)*." The theological underpinning here is what Ed P. Sanders has termed "covenantal nomism": the conviction that God has made an eternal commitment to Israel and has sealed the bargain by giving this people a divine Law in whose paths they may walk and find life. If they stray from this Law, God will punish them, but even such straying cannot ultimately remove the plant he has sown with such loving care.[107]

. . . .

Dead Sea Scrolls and Associated Literature

The Liber Antiquitatum Biblicarum and the Psalms of Solomon are not the only postbiblical Jewish works to use this biblical image of Israel as a firmly rooted plant. Several of the ancient documents that employ it, significantly, either come from or turn up at Qumran, thus suggesting a channel through which John may have been become even more aware of the biblical metaphor. For example, three fragmentary texts from Cave 4, 4Q302 ii 2:2–9, 4Q433a, and 4Q500, seem to attest the image, and if Joseph Baumgarten is right that the latter is a midrash on Isa. 5:1–7,[108] it speaks of Israel, or the righteous remnant thereof, as a plant lovingly tended by God. The first of these passages, moreover, appears to express God's eternal commitment to Israel through a tree parable: "Please discern this, O sages: if a man possesses a good tree that towers to heaven . . . and it produces the best fruit—is it not true that he lo[ves] it [ ] and guards it . . . to increase foliage . . . from its shoot . . . and its branches . . . ?" (*Dead Sea Scrolls Electronic Library* trans. alt.). The next few fragments (4Q302 ii 3, iii 2–3), to be sure, appear to speak of the ravaging of this tree and of parts of it being cut down, a symbol of Israel's sin and God's just judgment upon her—a partial parallel to our Q saying. But in the Qumran tree parable this judgment seems not to be the last word; the climax for the Qumran author, rather, as for the Deuteronomic passage he is echoing (Deut. 32:36), appears to be God's eschatological compassion on Israel (4Q302 3c:1).[109]

Other passages from less fragmentary scrolls explicitly use the construct phrase "eternal planting" (מטעת עולם) for the elect community (1QS 8:5; 11:7–9; 1QHa 6:[14]:15; 1QHa 8[16]:6), thus reappropriating for the Qumran sect the horticultural metaphor employed for Israel in Isa. 60:21, which emphasizes the eternity of God's commitment to this plant by modifying it with עולם. It is also significant for comparison and contrast with our Q saying that the Israel plant, according to 4Q433a, will *not* be torn up by its roots; instead, it is outsiders, who are external to it, who will be exposed to the fiery wrath of God. Several of these themes, plus others with strong connections to our Q passage and its immediate context, occur in 1QHª 14(6):13–19: "The men of Your council . . . **will return** at Your glorious word . . . [ ] blossom as a flo[wer] for ever, to raise up **a shoot to be the branches of an eternal planting.** It will cast shade over all the wor[ld] as far as the heaven[s], and **its roots will reach to the depths.** All the rivers of Eden [shall water] its br[anch]es, and it shall become [for me without] bounds. [ ] over the world without end, and as far as Sheol [ ] The spring of light shall become an everlasting fountain without end. In its brilliant flames **all the child[ren of injustice] shall burn,** [and it shall] become **a fire which burns up all the men of guilt completely**" (*Dead Sea Scrolls Electronic Library* trans. alt.). Here we see, not only the people of God as a rooted plant, but also the themes of repentance and destructive fire. But here again it is not the rooted plant that is threatened by fire (that plant is eternal) but those external to it, the "children of injustice."

The plant image, then, is frequently employed at Qumran to emphasize God's commitment to Israel (or the true Israel) and her heavenly calling. But it is even more relevant for exegesis of the Q passage that, at Qumran, the plant metaphor is linked specifically with *Abraham* and his descendants. This agricultural linkage is, in a way, natural, given the famous divine promise to Abraham about the multitude of his *seed,* which is closely associated with the promise of the land (Gen. 12:7, 13:15–16, 15:3–5, 18, 17:7–9, and so on.).

Similarly, Jubilees and 1 Enoch, fragments of both of which appear at Qumran,[110] use plant imagery to speak of Abraham and his descendants. In *Jubilees* 16:26, for example, we read that Abraham "blessed his Creator who created him in his generation because . . . he perceived that from him there would be a *righteous planting for eternal generations* and a holy seed from him, so that he might be like the one who made everything."[111] The imagery of an eternal plant destined for heaven (cf. Jub. 1:16–18) is similar to what we have seen in the Qumran passages, but here the plant is explicitly linked with Abraham.

First Enoch attests a similar association of Abraham with God's chosen plant. In the Apocalypse of Weeks in 1 En. 93, we hear about a "plant of truth" or "plant of righteousness "(93:2).[112] This plant is more carefully defined in 93:5: at the conclusion of the third "week" of the world "a man will be chosen as the plant of righteous judgment, and after him will go forth the plant of righteousness forever and ever." As Loren Stuckenbruck points out, the fourth week refers to the Sinai theophany, so the choice of the "plant of righteousness" in the third week probably represents the election of Abraham, and the eternal blossoming of this plant symbolizes God's everlasting commitment to Abraham's offspring.[113] This is especially likely in view of the linkage Gen. 15:5–6 makes between Abraham, Abraham's "seed," and righteousness.

The Apocalypse of Weeks does not present the subsequent history of the Abrahamic plant as untroubled. First Enoch 93:8, for example, says that, just before the beginning of the eschaton in the seventh week, "the temple of the kingdom will be burned with fire; and . . . the whole race of the chosen root will be dispersed." Here, in an apparent allusion to the depredations of 587 BCE, and significantly for comparison and contrast with Matt. 3:10//Luke 3:9, the root is all that remains after the rest of the chosen plant has been ravaged. These ravages, moreover, include fire. Yet this bad news does not foreshadow the end of the plant; at the conclusion of the seventh week, we read in 93:10, "the chosen will be chosen, as witnesses of righteousness from the eternal plant of righteousness, to whom will be given sevenfold wisdom and knowledge" (cf. 10:16). In the Apocalypse of Weeks, then, as in Jubilees, the plant "is historical Israel, whose source is Abraham."[114] Although reduced and cut back to the root by the judgment that has fallen on it, this plant still preserves a nucleus of righteous Israelites out of which the eschatological triumph can blossom.

When all this is compared with the Q saying, it is hard to say whether the similarities or the differences are more striking. In both there is a strong association between Abraham and his progeny on the one hand and a plant or tree on the other. In both there is an awareness that divine anger has been or will be unleashed against the plant, and this act of judgment is spoken of in terms of fierce pruning and devastation, including fire.[115] But the Q saying seems to contemplate an eventuality that the other sources take pains to deny: not just unfruitful *branches* of the tree may be cut down and cast into the fire, but the tree itself. Already the axe lies, not at the branches of the tree, nor even at its trunk, but at its very root.[116] Jon Levenson, then, is right to speak of the "supercharged rhetoric" of the Baptist's saying about Abraham's progeny, and Dale Allison is right to view it as a repudiation of what Ed Sanders has called "covenantal nomism."[117]

I should add that the teaching of Jesus, as represented in Matt. 15:13 ("Every plant which my heavenly Father has not planted will be rooted up"), the Parable of the Fig Tree (Luke 13:6–9), and the Parable of the Vineyard (Mark 12:1–9 pars.) move in a direction similar to our Q passage in relativizing the Israelite "plantation."[118] If, then, John the Baptist challenged covenantal nomism by implying that the Israel tree was not necessarily eternal, so did his follower Jesus—and he may well have learned to do so from John.[119]

John the Baptist, then, seems to have revised the inbuilt Jew/Gentile antinomy in a more radical way than was done by the group that trained him, the Qumran sect. What explains this more radical revision? As we have seen, part of the answer may be positive experiences with Gentiles, which may have already started when John still lived at Qumran. But the obverse, rejection by his fellow Jews, may also be part of the answer; certainly such rejection, on a general enough level to be presented as characteristic of "this generation," eventually became part of the tradition about John, as it did of the tradition about Jesus (cf. Matt. 11:16–19//Luke 7:31–35). Such rejection (or the perception of such rejection) can easily give rise to the thought that the rejecting people will themselves be rejected by God (cf. Mark 12:1–12 and parallels, especially Matt. 21:43; also Matt. 23:34–36).

....

Summary: John and Qumran

As shown above, it is likely that the period prior to the Baptist's public ministry was shaped by his membership in the Qumran community. From the members of that community, John learned to hope for an imminent end of the world, even an end that was already beginning to arrive. From them he learned to interpret Isa. 40:3 as a prophecy of developments in the wilderness of Judea that was now being fulfilled. From them he learned to think about Israel as a tree and about a coming judgment by fire, and to identify his enemies as a brood of vipers. And from them he learned to link immersion in water with impartation of the Spirit.

But that same Spirit, John would probably have said, eventually led to his break with Qumran. As noted, many factors seem to have contributed to this break, but one of them was probably his dawning consciousness of his own eschatological role. The exact nature of that role is the subject of the following chapter.

CHAPTER THREE

The Elijah Role

John and Elijah in the Gospel Tradition

What sort of end-time role did John envisage for himself? All three of the Synoptic Gospels identify John the Baptist with Elijah. This identification is made possible by 2 Kings 2:11, according to which Elijah did not die but was taken up to heaven, and was therefore still alive and potentially active (cf. 2 Chr. 21:12) and could be expected to return to earth at any moment. In later Old Testament and Second Temple Jewish traditions, the idea developed that he would return right before the end to prepare for the advent of Yahweh and/or the Messiah (cf. Mal. 3:1, 4:5 [Heb. 3:23]; Sir. 48:9–10).[1]

The earliest of the Synoptics, Mark, consequently alludes to Mal. 3:1 in its second verse (Mark 1:2), which speaks of God's messenger who will prepare the way before him; in the next chapter of Malachi this messenger is identified as "Elijah the prophet" (Mal. 4:5 [= 3:25 MT]). The later Synoptics, Matthew and Luke, make this identification explicit. In the Lukan infancy narrative, the archangel Gabriel prophesies that John will go before the Lord "in the spirit and power of Elijah" (Luke 1:17). In Matt. 11:14 Jesus concludes his testimony to the Baptist by saying, "And if you are willing to accept it, he is Elijah, who is to come," an apparent Matthean addition to a Q passage. And just in case Matthew's readers miss this nudge in the ribs, he delivers another six chapters later, adding an editorial comment to the Markan story in which Jesus mentions "Elijah's" violent death: "Then the disciples understood that he had been speaking to them about John the Baptist" (17:13).

These explicit identifications reinforce an impression that emerges more indirectly elsewhere in the Synoptic tradition. In the Markan version of the discussion of "Elijah's" death, for example, Jesus's three closest disciples, seemingly remembering Peter's recent identification of him as the Messiah (8:29) and the confirmation of this insight through a heavenly voice (9:7), ask Jesus, in effect, where the Messiah's expected forerunner might be (9:11). Jesus responds that Elijah has indeed come but that his task has turned out to be, not universal restoration, but preceding the Messiah in the way of suffering and death (9:12–13)—an obvious allusion to the murder of John, which was narrated a few chapters earlier (6:14–29).[2] In both Mark and Matthew, moreover, John wears a garment made of camel's hair and a leather belt (Mark 1:4//Matt. 3:4), apparel reminiscent of Elijah's in 2 Kings 1:8. Finally, John's status as a forerunner, which dovetails with the description of Elijah in Malachi, is attested not only by the way in which the Gospel writers cite the Malachi passage,[3] but also by the words they attribute to the Baptist himself, who admits his inferiority to the "Stronger One" who will come after him (Mark 1:7–8//Matt. 3:11–12//Luke 3:16–17). This quotation of the Baptist is a Mark/Q overlap, since the Matthean and Lukan versions differ significantly from the Markan one, so John's identification of himself as a forerunner is doubly attested in the Synoptic tradition and probably precedes the written Gospels.[4]

The fact that the Synoptic tradition ascribes these words to the Baptist is no proof that he actually said them; early Christian tradents were perfectly capable of putting theologically convenient words into the mouths of characters in their stories, as the example of Matt. 11:14 cited above shows. But in the present instance, John the Baptist's self-description as a forerunner probably does go back to the man himself. As another John (surnamed Meier) has noted, the block in which the self-identification occurs, Mark 1:7–8//Matt. 3:11–12//Luke 3:16–17, "shows no explicit relation to Jesus or Christians," thus meeting the criterion of dissimilarity.[5] To be sure, the Synoptic evangelists, by placing this block right before the baptism of Jesus by John, imply that Jesus was the "Stronger One" expected by John—but that linkage is the work of the Christian tradition, not John.[6] The words attributed to John, by contrast, are equivocal; it is not even totally clear whether the "stronger one" to which he refers is the Messiah, some other eschatological figure, or God himself, though the Messiah is the best candidate.[7] If the Christian tradition had been making the passage up out of whole cloth, it probably would not have fashioned such an equivocal prophecy but would have created a Grünewaldian scene in which John pointed openly to Jesus.[8] Since the Gospels lack such an explicit identification, the conclusion that John probably *did* say something about preceding the "stronger one," and therefore *did* think of himself as a forerunner, seems safe.

But even if John saw himself as a forerunner, does that necessarily mean that he saw himself as Elijah? Some scholars have expressed skepticism[9] or agnosticism[10] about this, and their objections are worth noting. Even though Luke has been cited above as a witness to John's status as Elijah returned from the dead, the Lukan witness is actually mixed: the acknowledgment of John's Elijan status in the infancy narrative (Luke 1:17) is counterbalanced by passages in which Elijan elements are removed from Markan descriptions of John (see Mark 1:6; 9:13, which have no Lukan counterpart) or ascribed to

Jesus.[11] Moreover, the testimony of the Fourth Gospel is unambiguously negative (John 1:19–21): John did *not* identify himself as Elijah—any more than he identified himself as the Messiah or "the prophet" (probably the eschatological Prophet-like-Moses spoken of in Deut. 18:15–19).[12]

These countercurrents raise the question: was John thought of by his contemporaries as the returning Elijah, or is the picture of him as such a later Christian imposition on "the historical Baptist"? And even if the answer to the first question is yes, and John *was* considered by his contemporaries to be Elijah returned from the dead, does this correspond to his own self-understanding? We are, in other words, asking a question parallel to the famous one about the "messianic self-consciousness of Jesus": did the Baptist have an "Elijan self-consciousness"?

....

The Argument against John's Elijan Self-Consciousness

Let us explore in more detail the argument (with which I disagree) that he did not. Although I have contended above that John saw himself as a forerunner, this does not necessarily mean that he thought of himself as Elijah. He might have identified himself, for example, as the voice crying in the wilderness to prepare the Lord's way (Isa. 40:3) without linking that voice with Elijah.[13] And scholars have raised other objections to the hypothesis that John thought of himself as Elijah, the chief among them being the interest of the Christians in creating such a linkage, which had the advantage both of subordinating a potential rival to Jesus and of silencing a potential Jewish criticism: if Jesus was the Messiah, where was Elijah, who was supposed to precede him?[14] Other arguments against John's Elijan self-consciousness include the assertion that significant aspects of the image of Elijah in the Old Testament and Second Temple Judaism have no counterpart in the ministry of John (for example, miracle working; cf. John 10:41) and that significant aspects of the ministry of John have no counterpart in the story of Elijah (above all his baptism but also his unusual diet). Moreover, as noted, the Gospels themselves are divided on the question of John's Elijan identity: Luke is equivocal, and the Fourth Gospel negative.

Even some of the Synoptic evidence that at first seems to favor the Elijah typology, moreover, can be turned against it. In Mark 9:9–13//Matt. 17:9–13, for example, the disciples seem unaware that John is Elijah until Jesus instructs them about it, and in Matt. 11:14 Jesus's pronouncement, "*If you are willing to accept it,* he is Elijah, who is to come," suggests that special insight is needed to discover the connection. Moreover, in Mark 6:14–15, 8:28, and parallels, Herod and the Jewish populace offer John the Baptist and Elijah as two *different* guesses about the identity of Jesus, suggesting that the image of the Baptist and that of Elijah had not totally merged.[15]

. . . .

Rebuttal

Not all of these arguments are equally weighty, however, and some are weak. For instance, the Johannine Baptist's denial that he is Elijah and the Lukan redaction of Mark probably reflect Johannine and Lukan theology more than they do the intention of the historical Baptist, and in Luke the predominant impression remains that the Baptist is Elijah.[16] While John's baptism per se has no Elijan counterpart, moreover, Mal. 3:1–4 ascribes to the Lord's messenger, the returning Elijah (cf. 4:5), a ministry of purification, and purification is inherent in baptismal symbolism.[17] Nor is it conclusive evidence against John's Elijan self-consciousness that the Elijah analogy in the tradition is imperfect. Indeed, we may well imagine that, if it *were* perfect, some scholars would take this as a sign that it had been constructed by later theology.[18]

As Dale Allison has shown in his acute study of the Moses typology in Matthew, indeed, not *all* aspects of the type need to be present in the antitype for a typology to be present; all that is necessary is a critical mass of parallels.[19] Many instances can be cited of historical figures who came to be linked with biblical prototypes; none fit those prototypes exactly, but some did so well enough that contemporaries identified them with their famous predecessors, and scholars have concluded that some at least intended the identification themselves. And these Messiahs, new Moseses, returning Elijahs, and so on, often revealed their secret identities more through actions and allusive words than through open declarations.[20] A fascinating recent example is the Lubavitcher Rebbe, who was thought by millions of disciples worldwide to be the Messiah and who almost certainly thought so himself. Yet he never openly proclaimed his messianic identity,[21] leaving it to his followers to make the connection on the basis of broad hints based on biblical, Talmudic, and kaballistic allusions.[22]

The strongest point of the skeptics is that the identification of John with Elijah was convenient for Christian theology. But it is also true that sometimes the self-serving tenets of religious groups (for example, that Jesus saw himself as Messiah or that John saw himself as Elijah) are actually based in reality. In fact, it is characteristic of new religious movements to build on existing beliefs rather than to invent everything out of thin air.[23] Similarity to later Christian beliefs, therefore, does not establish that a particular tradition *was* invented by the early Christians, only that it *might* have been invented by them. Further proof one way or the other is required.[24]

. . . .

The Hairiness of Elijah

And I think I can show that, in one particular aspect at least of the Christian tradition about the Baptist, the terse reference to his clothing in Mark 1:6//

Matt. 3:4, the Gospel narratives do enshrine a historical memory, one that probably reflects the Elijan self-image of John himself. As noted before, this description appears to be modeled on that of Elijah in 2 Kings 1:8:

2 Kings 1:8 LXX	Mark 1:6
(a) ἀνὴρ δασύς	(a) ἐνδεδυμένος τρίχας καμήλου
(b) καὶ ζώνην δερματίνην	(b) καὶ ζώνην δερματίνην
(c) περιεζωσμένος τὴν ὀσφὺν αὐτοῦ	(c) περὶ τὴν ὀσφὺν αὐτοῦ
(a) a hairy man	(a) wearing camel's hair
(b) and a leather girdle	(b) and a leather girdle
(c) girded around his waist	(c) around his waist

The terminology and structure of sections (b) and (c) of the two verses are very close,[25] and the images in section (a) of the two verses are similar, though not identical: Elijah is a hairy man, whereas John wears a hairy garment. Despite this difference, the overall structure and meaning of the two verses is so similar that it seems incontestable that the latter is meant to echo the former. In the mind of Mark, then (cf. Matt. 3:4), John's appearance did not just reflect an asceticism like that of the Nazarites (Num. 6:5) or the hermit Bannus described by Josephus (*Life* 11),[26] or a Bedouin-like desert existence,[27] but his status as the returning Elijah.

But is this just *Mark's* conception of John, or does it correspond to John's own self-image? We can approach this question by attending to both the similarity and the difference between 2 Kings 1:8 and Mark 1:6. We have just discussed the similarity, but the difference between a hairy body and a hair garment needs more attention. Elijah's hairiness appears first in 2 Kings 1:1–8, where Ahaziah, the king of Israel, has a serious fall. Suspecting that his wounds may be mortal, he sends messengers to seek an oracle from the Canaanite god Baalzebub as to whether or not he will live. The Hebrew prophet Elijah, informed by an angel of this embassy to a pagan god, intercepts Ahaziah's messengers and tells them to rebuke him for it. When the messengers report this rebuke to the king, describing his denouncer simply as "a man" (אִישׁ), Ahaziah asks what sort of man. They reply, אִישׁ בַּעַל שֵׂעָר וְאֵזוֹר עוֹר אָזוּר בְּמָתְנָיו, "a hairy man with a girdle of leather girded about his waist." Ahaziah, recognizing his old antagonist from the description, responds with exasperation, "It is Elijah the Tishbite."

The Revised Standard Version, however, translates the messengers' response differently: "He wore a garment of haircloth, with a girdle of leather about his loins." Here it is Elijah's garment rather than his body that is hairy.

This translation enshrines an interpretation that has been popular among recent exegetes.[28] Eric and Carol Meyers, for example, assert, "It seems certain that what made Elijah the prophet identifiable was a particular garment, not that he had a hirsute body and wore only a belt." And John Gray, while acknowledging that בַּעַל שֵׂעָר might signify "a 'hairy man,' i.e. with long hair and beard," also opines that it could signify "one clad in a rough, shaggy cloak, which was actually recognized as the insignia of a prophet (Zech. 13.4) and was the mantle of asceticism of John the Baptist (Matt. 3.4) and the Sufis of Islam."[29]

This common interpretation, however, is not backed up by cogent argumentation. The Meyerses, for example, do not tell us why it is "certain" that what made Elijah identifiable was a particular garment rather than a hairy body, coupled with the fact that he wore only a belt. Vielhauer is probably right, rather, to suggest that this interpretation rests mostly on a harmonization of 2 Kings 1:8 with the description of the prophet's hairy cloak in Zech. 13:4, the references to Elijah's cloak (not further described) in 1–2 Kings (1 Kgs. 19:13, 19; 2 Kgs. 2:8, 13–14), and the Gospel descriptions of the hairy garment of the Baptist. It is also possible that this interpretation reflects a certain shyness among the scholars at the thought of an Israelite prophet (especially a hairy one?) walking around in his underwear.

Such modesty, however, seems to reflect modern concerns more than it does the conditions of ninth century BCE Israel; indeed, a later Israelite prophet is described as going around naked and barefoot for three years as a visual prophecy that those who resist God will be led into captivity stripped of everything (see Isa. 20:3). Prophets in general were known for bizarre, parabolic behavior, including strange dress and appearance (see, for example, Ezek. 4:1–4). Moreover, אֵזוֹר, the word that the Meyerses translate as "belt" and that Vielhauer renders as "Lendenschurz" (loincloth), is better rendered as "waist-cloth" or "girdle," and is probably "the type of kilt represented by the soldiers of Lachish in the stele of Senaccherib, that wrapped around the waist."[30] Elijah's אֵזוֹר was, in other words, a substantial undergarment rather than briefs, and easily imaginable as the clothing of a fierce, uncompromising, and dramatic Israelite prophet.

The other pieces of evidence cited for the less hairy interpretation of 2 Kings 1:8 are that Zech. 13:4 refers to a hairy cloak (אַדֶּרֶת שֵׂעָר) as the typical garb of the prophet and that Elijah was known to have worn a cloak (1 Kgs. 19:13), to which magical properties were ascribed (2 Kgs. 2:8, 13, 14).[31] The conclusion drawn is that Elijah's cloak must have been a hairy one and that this hairy cloak is what is being invoked when Elijah is spoken of as אִישׁ בַּעַל שֵׂעָר. This conclusion, however, would be on a surer footing if the Deutero-Zecharian passage, which is the only Old Testament evidence for the hairy cloak of the prophets, were from a similar time and place as the Elijah story in 2 Kings 1, but this is debatable.[32]

But even if the hairy cloak were the typical garb of the prophets, that would by no means be evidence that it was the referent of אִישׁ בַּעַל שֵׂעָר in 2 Kings 1:8. Elsewhere in the Old Testament, בַּעַל in combination with a body part always means the person who possesses that sort of body part,[33] and שֵׂעָר by itself unambiguously means "hair." If the author of 2 Kings 1:8 had wanted to refer to a hairy cloak, he would have spoken of אַדֶּרֶת שֵׂעָר, as in Zech. 13:4 and Gen. 25:25, not of שֵׂעָר alone. The Greek of the Septuagint of 2 Kings 1:8, ἀνὴρ δασύς, is equally unambiguous; δασύς means "hairy or shaggy"[34] and modifies ἀνήρ, "man," not a word for a garment. Again, if the translator had wanted to refer to a garment, he would have added some sort of explanatory word or phrase. Besides, if the hairy cloak *were* the typical garb of the prophets, and if that *were* the referent of אִישׁ בַּעַל שֵׂעָר/ἀνὴρ δασύς in 2 Kings 1:8, we would be faced with a puzzle in the narrative: how does Ahaziah know that the prophet the messengers speak of is Elijah in particular? Something more distinctive than a hairy cloak has to be the referent, since the latter was allegedly common to all prophets. And that distinctive thing can only be Elijah's hairy body.[35]

This hairiness fits into a well-known trope in the Hebrew Bible and the Ancient Near Eastern world in general, as has been shown by Susan Niditch in her fascinating study, *My Brother Esau Is a Hairy Man*.[36] The hairy man is a wild, natural creature with a certain primal quality, as illustrated by the description of Enkidu in the Gilgamesh epic:

> [On the step]pe she created valiant Enkidu,
> Offspring of . . . , essence of Nunurta.
> [Sha]ggy with hair is his whole body,
> He is endowed with head hair like a woman.
> The locks of his hair sprout like Nisaba [goddess of grain].
> He knows neither people nor land;
> Garbed is he like Sumuqan [god of cattle].
> With the gazelles he feeds on the grass,
> With the wild beasts he jostles at the watering-place . . .
> [The passage goes on to describe how Enkidu terrifies a hunter.]
> (*Gilgamesh* 1.2)[37]

This association of hairiness with wildness is made specific in a later development of the Baptist legend, Slavonic Josephus 2.110: "He [John] donned the hair of cattle on the parts of his body which were not covered with his own hair. And he was wild of visage."[38]

This sort of wild shagginess can assume a negative valence, as in the case of the wild hunter, Esau, where it is associated with thoughtlessness, impulsiveness, and potential violence (Gen. 25:25–34, 27:40),[39] or in the case of the murderous prince Absalom, whose abundant locks are linked with his beauty and virility (2 Sam. 14:25–27), as well as with the cleverness that enables him to seduce the Israelites away from their allegiance to his father David (2 Sam. 14:28–15:12). In the end, however, Absalom's hair proves to be his undoing, as it gets caught in a tree, leaving him vulnerable to a spear attack from David's general, Joab (2 Sam. 18:9–15).[40] Untamed hair, then, can be dangerous, but it can also be a powerful witness that a figure is "of the earth, earthy" (cf. 1 Cor. 15:47)[41] and therefore close to God, as in the case of Samson, whose God-given strength resides in his hair (Judg. 13–16),[42] and of Jacob masquerading as hairy Esau, whose smell is like that of a field that the Lord has blessed (Gen. 27:5–29).[43]

Elijah's hairiness, therefore, is an integral part of the biblical depiction of him as a man of God, and in the biblical narrative and later Jewish tradition, it forms a contrast with the baldness of his disciple Elisha (2 Kgs. 2:23). Indeed, Elijah and Elisha were so famous for their hairiness and hairlessness respectively that in a late rabbinic midrash they are both mocked for these features by recalcitrant Israelites.[44]

. . . .

Elijah's Hairiness and John's Hairy Garment

Having established how integral hair is to the image of Elijah, we now return to a comparison between that image and the depiction of the Baptist in Mark 1:6. As noted, despite the difference between the depiction of John and the depiction of Elijah (hairy garment vs. hairy body), the Markan verse is clearly modeled on 2 Kings 1:8. But is this just *Mark's* idea, or does it reflect the self-image of the historical Baptist? Did the latter actually wear a garment of camel's hair and a leather girdle around his waist, thus imitating the biblical Elijah, or was the Elijah typology invented by Mark or the early Christian tradition before him?[45] I think we now have enough data to answer this question positively, precisely because of the intriguing combination of similarity and difference between the biblical type and its New Testament antitype.

Mark obviously wishes to link John with the portrayal of Elijah in 2 Kings 1:8. But if he or the tradition upon which he was drawing were freely inventing the description of John, they probably would have created a Baptist whose appearance was in *total,* not *partial,* agreement with the Old Testament description of Elijah. In other words, they would have given John a hairy *body* rather than merely a hairy *garment.*[46] Why did they not do so? The hypothesis that makes the most sense is that Mark 1:6 preserves a historical memory: John actually *did* model himself on Elijah, and he made his appearance *as much as possible* like that of his biblical prototype; but he himself was *not* hairy, so the best he could do was to imitate Elijah by wearing a hairy *garment*.[47] And camel's hair would have been the natural choice for such a garment in the desert environment of the Jordan Valley.[48]

Such a garment, in combination with John's leather girdle, probably would have been enough to associate John with Elijah, and it does reveal something of his own self-consciousness—especially because there was a strong traditional link, going all the way back to the well-known biblical description of Esau (Gen. 25:25), between a hairy garment and a hairy man.[49] Although other biblical figures besides Elijah are hairy or wear hair garments, none but Elijah combines this with a leather girdle. Thus the aspect of John's appearance that does *not* fit the Elijah typology—hairy garment vs. hairy body—guarantees the trustworthiness of the description; but the aspects that *do* fit it—hair in general, leather girdle—testify to his evident desire to model himself after the Old Testament prophet.

....

The Returning Elijah as a Legal Arbitrator

Besides his hairy overcoat, his leather pants, his self-identification as a forerunner, and his eschatological orientation, there are other elements of our sources' portrayal of John that fit into the Elijah pattern, including his location at the Jordan River.[50] The most important of these is the depiction of John taking definitive and sometimes controversial stands on halakhic issues (see glossary). Here I differ from John Meier, according to whom "the sayings and actions of John preserved in the Gospels and Josephus show a total lack of concern with detailed legal questions."[51] On the contrary, John is depicted in our most consistently reliable source, the Synoptics, as entering into such questions vigorously and authoritatively. And this is consistent with an important aspect of the Jewish hopes for the returning Elijah: he was expected to settle controversial halakhic issues.

Already in the biblical portrait of the "first coming" of Elijah, we see him as a zealot for the Law who rebukes the king of Israel for his violation of it, which is connected with his illicit marriage (see 1 Kgs. 16:31–33, 18:17–18)—a typology that brings Elijah close to the Synoptic portrayal of John (Mark 6:18 pars.). Indeed, the biblical Elijah's denunciation of Ahab, who was married to the idolatrous Sidonian princess Jezebel, may be part of the origin of the Talmudic portrayal of the eschatological Elijah as especially concerned with the purity of the marriage relation.[52] Like the biblical Elijah, the Synoptic Baptist is persecuted for his denunciation of the king's marriage.[53]

This biblical view of Elijah as a zealot for the Law develops further in postbiblical Jewish sources. It is evident in the Mishnah, redacted at the beginning of the third century CE, which portrays certain knotty legal disputes as pending "until Elijah comes" to decide them (m. B. Meṣ. 1:8; 2:8; 3:4–5; m. Šeqal. 2:5, etc.). But there is indirect evidence that the expectation was already present by the end of the second century or the beginning of the first century BCE, when 1 Maccabees was written.[54] The Mishnaic formula "until Elijah comes" is strikingly similar to one that occurs in 1 Maccabees, referring to the need to wait "until a trustworthy prophet comes" to settle legal disputes such as the status of the defiled altar stones of the Temple (1 Macc. 4:46) or the Hasmoneans' assumption of the high priesthood and kingship (1 Macc. 14:41). Although the formula in 1 Maccabees does not identify this eschatological decider as Elijah, he may very well be in mind.[55] Similarly, the Qumran expectation of an "interpreter of the Law" who will arise with the "Branch of David" (4QFlorilegium [4Q174] 1–3.i.11) and "teach righteousness at the End of Days" (CD 6:11) may refer to Elijah.[56] A rabbinic tradition (b. Bek. 24a) apparently interprets Hos 10:12, which is the source of the Qumran phrase "teach righteousness at the end of days,"[57] as a reference to that prophet.[58] If one asks why neither 1 Maccabees nor the Qumran texts specify that the trustworthy prophet or interpreter of the Law is Elijah, it may be suggested that they did not need to do so for their original audience, any more than contemporary Christians, speaking of the expected return of the Messiah, need to specify for their coreligionists that this means Jesus. If so, we may now make more precise a thesis from the previous chapter: one of the reasons why John left the Qumran community may have been his growing conviction that he, rather than the present leader of the group, was the true "Teacher of Righteousness," the eschatological Elijah.

Brenda Shaver, in her dissertation on Elijah in Second Temple Judaism, is leery of identifying Elijah with the eschatological Torah-teacher mentioned in 1 Maccabees and the Qumran literature, since in her opinion this identification principally relies on evidence from later rabbinic traditions, and "it is difficult to accept the identification of Elijah as the eschatological teacher merely on the basis of what appears later in the tradition."[59] But there is one tantalizing hint that the identification was earlier: the Septuagint transposes the last two sentences of the book of Malachi, so that Mal. 4:5–6 (3:23–24 MT), which promises the return of Elijah, precedes Mal. 4:4 (3:22 MT), which calls for "remembering" the Law of Moses.[60] At least part of the reason for this transposition may have been a growing understanding of the returning Elijah as an eschatological Torah decider, even in a way a new Moses.[61] This interpretation has the advantage of presenting the final sentence of Malachi in the LXX, the exhortation to remember the Law of Moses, not as an unrelated addendum to the reference to the eschatological Elijah but as its logical conclusion.[62]

....

John as an Eschatological Halakhic Decider and Enforcer

In light of all this, John the Baptist's propensity to take controversial halakhic positions, and to insist on them in no uncertain terms, fits in with the image of the returning Elijah as an eschatological decider and enforcer. Such a figure became necessary because the Torah itself presented knotty problems to those who desired to use it as a guide for making themselves ready for "the great and terrible day of the Lord" (Mal. 4:5). Sometimes the scripture was too vague to be transparent (for example, as noted below, on the question of whether "brother" includes a half-brother, or on the kashrut of honey and skins made from unclean beasts), and sometimes one scripture appeared to contradict another (for example, as also discussed below, over the kashrut of locusts). At other times, moreover, new historical experiences posed unexpected halakhic dilemmas. The altar stones of the Temple, for example, were holy through being dedicated to God but defiled through being touched by pig carcasses. What was to be done with them? What was to be done, in general, and how were faithful Torah observers to live when reality was so ambiguous and scripture so contradictory? The answer of many Jews was to wait for an Elijah-like figure, a trustworthy prophet who would sort things out properly at the eschaton, as once he had done in days of yore.

Is a Camel's-Hair Coat Kosher?

It is noteworthy that, although we know so little about John the Baptist, much of the little we do know shows him taking controversial positions on such disputed halakhic issues. Sometimes, as with the marriage of Herod Antipas, he does so by making pronouncements, while at other times he makes his stance clear by his actions. Sometimes, he seems to go along with the halakhic positions of his former fellow sectarians at Qumran, sometimes he seems to side against them and with the Pharisees, and sometimes he goes his own way. But in every case he does so in a public, "in your face" sort of way.

For example, the outer garment that John wore to simulate hairiness did so by means of the hair of the *camel,* an unclean animal (see Lev. 11:4). In choosing to wear such a garment, John seems to have been wading into a halakhic debate about whether or not the uncleanness of such an animal extends to the use of its hide. The Pharisees, who were the ideological precursors of the rabbis mentioned in the Mishnah, probably thought that it did not: the Mishnah rules that the purity status of the live animal does not extend to its hide after it has been killed, skinned, and the skin treated (see m. Ḥul. 9:2). John's former fellow-sectarians at Qumran, however, seem to have disagreed. Their working principle was that the cleanness of an animal's hide corresponds to the cleanness of its flesh (11QTemple 47:10, 15).[63] In other words, the animal's skin, even after removal from its carcass, retains the purity status of the original beast.[64] Since the camel was an unclean animal, its hide was also unclean.[65] In this instance, then, the Baptist, by wearing a camel's-hair garment, appears to have been siding with the Pharisaic position against the Qumranian one. This, however, is not a sign that John himself was a Pharisee, nor is it evidence against his having once been a member of the Dead Sea Sect.[66] It merely shows him exercising independent halakhic judgment, even against his former associates, and doing so in a provocative way.

The Diet of Locusts and Wild Honey

A second example of John taking a potentially controversial stance is the fact that his diet included locusts and wild honey (Mark 1:6//Matt. 3:4).[67] Although locusts were probably permissible both to the Pharisees (cf. m. 'Ed. 8:4; m. Ḥul. 3:7; m. 'Abod. Zar. 2:7) and to the Qumran sect (11Q Temple 48:3–5; CD-A 12:11–15), and although the Letter of Aristeas (145) and Philo (Leg. All. 2.105) concur, the Torah itself is actually divided, with one Pentateuchal passage (Lev. 11:21–22) declaring them kosher, and another (Deut. 14:19) declaring them unclean. It is possible, therefore, that in John's time some Jews would have had scruples about eating locusts. Later, in the Mishnah, R. Yose b. Yoezer, who declared a certain kind of locust to be clean, was dubbed "Yose the Permitter" or "Yose the Easy-Going" (יוסי שריא; m. 'Ed. 8:4). As James Kelhoffer says, this nickname "suggests that not everyone was pleased with his interpretation."[68]

It is even more likely that wild honey was a controversial food. It is unclear, to be sure, whether the honey referred to in Mark 1:6//Matt. 3:4 is bee honey or the "honey" derived from trees (figs, dates, or tree sap); both could be called μέλι/דבש, and there is evidence for the consumption of both in ancient Palestine.[69] In either case, the kashrut of this food of the Baptist's may have been questioned by some. If it was bee honey, it might be suspect because the bee is not listed among the clean insects in Lev. 11:20–23 and would therefore seem to be among the things that "are detestable to you" and should not be eaten (Lev. 11:23). Jews in Jesus's time who embraced the later Talmudic principle that "what comes out of the unclean is unclean"[70] might have rejected bee honey as unclean. If it was tree honey, it would still fall under the interdict of Lev. 2:11, which forbids honey from being mixed with grain offerings, perhaps because of the fermenting property of such sweet substances.[71] On the basis of the Levitical references, then, honey might be a suspect food.

This suspicion was not universal. Overall, the rabbis approve of consumption of both tree honey and bee honey. They have more work to do to justify bee honey, because of the Levitical aspersions against bees, but m. Ned. 6:9 implies that bee honey is kosher, and m. 'Abod. Zar. 2:7 says so explicitly (cf. m.

Makš. 6:4; b. Bek. 7b). And this approval appears to have extended beyond Pharisaic/rabbinic circles. At Qumran, the Damascus Document forbids the eating of bee larvae (CD 12:12), but other bee products such as honey are not mentioned and presumably permitted. Similarly, *Hypothetica* 11.8, which Eusebius (*Preparation for the Gospel* 8.11.8) ascribes to Philo, describes the Essenes as beekeepers. This suggests that the Essenes, including the Qumran sect, viewed bee honey (unlike other bee products and the bee itself) as kosher.[72] Similarly, Joseph and Aseneth 16:8–16 presents bee honey as the food of angels, which confers eternal life; it is impossible to imagine that the author of this strange document thought honey nonkosher.

But other Jews seem to have disagreed. Philo of Alexandria, for example, said that God considers honey "unfit to be brought to the altar, . . . perhaps because the bee which collects it is an unclean animal" (Spec. Leg. 1.291–292, Loeb Classical Library trans.). This is close to being a declaration that bee honey is nonkosher, and a taboo of this sort may help explain the paucity of evidence for apiculture in ancient Palestine, in contrast to the rest of the Ancient Near East. There is no similar evidence for ancient Jewish suspicion of tree honey, but since the same word, דבש, was applied to both kinds, rigorists who rejected bee honey may have rejected tree honey as well.[73]

As with locusts, then, so also with honey, the evidence about its kashrut in Second Temple Judaism is mixed; most sources view it favorably, but there are enough dissenting voices (including a biblical one) to suggest that some may have judged John's diet sinful. Once again, then, we find John staking out a halakhic position by publicly embracing a diet that would have been controversial in some circles.

Marrying a Brother's Wife

Similar considerations apply to John's rebuke of Herod Antipas for marrying his sister-in-law Herodias (Mark 6:18; cf. Josephus, *Ant.* 18.109–110), presumably because the marriage violated the Levitical ban on "uncovering the nakedness of your brother's wife" (Lev. 18:16; 20:21).[74] The brother whose wife Antipas stole, however, was only his *half*-brother,[75] the son of Herod the Great by Mariamne II (Antipas himself being Herod's son by Malthace). Does the Levitical taboo apply to *half*-brothers? Josephus, who elsewhere tells us that he was a Pharisee (*Life* 12), thinks so.[76] He says that, in marrying the half-brother of her husband, Herodias was "flout[ing] the ways of our fathers" (*Ant.* 18.136). In *J.W.* 2.114–116 and *Ant.* 17.340–341, similarly, he denounces Glaphyra's marriage to Archelaus, the half-brother of her deceased husband. The later rabbis, the successors of the Pharisees, would have agreed with Josephus that Antipas's marriage to Herodias was illegal (see b. Yebam. 55a). And this was not just a Pharisaic position: the Qumran sect also interpreted the Levitical proscriptions as applying to half-brothers: "A man shall not take his brother's wife, nor shall he uncover his brother's skirt, *be it his father's son or his mother's son,* for this is impurity" (11QTemple 66:12–13). In declaring Herod's marriage to Herodias to be unlawful, therefore, John was siding both with his former co-sectarians at Qumran and with their frequent opponents, the Pharisees.

It is not clear, however, that the view of these sects was generally accepted in the first century CE. Ingrid Moen has argued in her dissertation on Herodian marriages that it probably was not, since the Herodians elsewhere seem to have carefully avoided biblically prohibited unions that would have caused offense to the public. As Moen puts it: "The royal Jews, normally, turned down gentile suitors who refused to convert and avoided establishing unions with incestuous marriage partners. No Herodian males married a mother, step-mother, sister, grand-daughter, aunt, uncle's wife or daughter-in-law, despite their tendency to marry within the biologically related family unit (Lev. 18:7–10, 12–15); they practiced only marriage to half-brothers' wives."[77] Moen also points out that even Josephus, who deems the marriages of Antipas and Archelaus illicit, does not claim that they generated unrest or public protest[78] —aside, I would add, from the protest of John the Baptist, which *may* have been made in public, in a direct verbal assault on the tetrarch.[79]

As with John's wearing of camel's hair and his consumption of locusts and wild honey, then, his condemnation of Antipas's marriage seems to reflect his own particular slant on a matter that was ambiguous in the biblical text and was probably the subject of controversy between different Jewish groups.

We may, then, sum up John's halakhic positions in the table on the next page. From this chart it is evident that, in matters related to the cleanness of animals (diet and use of hides), John staked out a fairly liberal position, eating locusts and wild honey and wearing a camel-hair coat. In the area of marriage law, however, he sided with the rigorists.[80] In this combination, he anticipated his protégé, Jesus of Nazareth, who is presented in the Synoptic tradition as being liberal about food laws (see Mark 7:1–23 pars.) but a rigorist about marriage (see Mark 10:2–12 pars.).

In any event, John's frequent interventions on controversial halakhic issues are compatible with the thesis that he saw himself as the returning Elijah.

. . . .

Conclusion: John as Elijah

John's legalistic pronouncement about Herod Antipas's marriage, his legalistically provocative diet, his Elijah-like but halakhically controversial garb, his association with the Jordan, and the eschatological orientation of his preaching, all mark him out as an Elijah-like figure—one who deliberately modeled

John's halakhic theory and practice	Relevant biblical passages	Agrees with Qumran?	Agrees with Pharisees/rabbis?	Other opinions
John wears a camel-hair coat.	Camel unclean as a food in Lev. 11:4, but cleanness or uncleanness of hide not specified.	No, because for Qumran purity of hide is as purity of flesh.	Yes	
John eats locusts.	Locusts are clean as a food according to Lev. 11:21–22 but unclean according to Deut. 14:19.	Yes	Yes for the most part, but the dubbing of R. Yose as "the Permitter" may suggest that there was some opposition.	Philo and Letter of Aristeas permit eating of locusts.
John eats wild honey.	Lev. 2:11 forbids honey from being mixed with grain offerings, and bee is not listed as a clean insect in Lev. 11:20–23.	Yes	Yes	Joseph & Aseneth: honey is the food of angels, but Philo: honey is unfit to be brought to the altar because the bee is unclean.
John denounces Herod's marriage to Herodias, the wife of his half-brother.	Veto on "uncovering the nakedness of your brother's wife" in Lev. 18:16 and 20:21, but it is not stated whether or not this applies to the wife of a *half*-brother.	Yes	Yes	No evidence exists of popular unrest because of the marriage.

himself on the biblical prophet expected to return before the end. This Elijan self-consciousness may have been part of the reason for his departure from Qumran, which was discussed in the previous chapter: there was not room at Qumran for *two* Teachers of Righteousness at a time.

But John's Elijan self-consciousness is also key to the matters discussed in subsequent chapters of this book. The returning Elijah was expected to have a ministry of eschatological purification, as we have seen (Mal. 3:1), and this purification, as we shall see in chapter 4, was the central theme of John's baptismal ministry. The returning Elijah was expected, moreover, to prepare the way for the coming of the Messiah—an expectation that raises the question, to be explored in detail in chapter 5, of whether or not John acknowledged his onetime associate Jesus as the Lord's Anointed. And John's self-image as the second coming of Elijah, who during his lifetime clashed with an Israelite king and prophetically denounced his marriage, also helps explain his clash with Herod Antipas and eventual execution at his hands, which will be explored in chapter 6.

CHAPTER FOUR

Baptism

The Gospels and Josephus on John's Baptism

Chapters 2 and 3 have outlined John's beginnings, especially his probable membership in the Qumran community, and a core aspect of his identity, his self-identification with the returning Elijah. And appendix 4 associates his membership in the Qumran community, which was led by priests, with the possibility that he himself was from a priestly background, as portrayed in Luke 1. These factors may well be connected in turn with the most distinctive aspect of John's ministry: his practice of immersing in water those who came to identify with his movement. As we have seen, this baptismal ministry is a link between John and the Qumran community, which practiced daily ablutions and interpreted them in ways similar to the interpretation given to John's baptism in the New Testament—as an anticipation of the eschaton and the associated gift of forgiveness of sins. John's baptism also links him with the Elijah image, since according to the Bible Elijah, upon his departure from the earth, crossed the Jordan River, the site of John's baptismal activity, and bequeathed a double portion of his spirit to his successor (2 Kgs. 2:7, 8, 14). And it may relate to John's possible priestly background, since priests were responsible for overseeing the ritual purity of the nation, frequently through washing rituals.

But these links provide only some of the raw material for answering the question addressed in the present chapter: what exactly was the significance of John's baptism? We have two main first-century sources about that baptism, the Gospels (Mark 1:4, 7–8 pars.) and Josephus (*Antiquities* 18.117). Both, however, are somewhat problematic and need to be sifted for reliable information.[1]

Mark summarizes John's mission as κηρύσσων βάπτισμα μετανοίας εἰς ἄφεσιν ἁμαρτιῶν, "proclaiming a baptism of repentance unto forgiveness of sins" (Mark 1:4).[2] This clause seems to be written in a sort of shorthand, transparent perhaps to Mark's first readers but puzzling to us, since it leaves vague the exact relation between the crucial terms "baptism," "repentance," and "forgiveness of sins." Particularly enigmatic is the meaning of the genitival expression βάπτισμα μετανοίας ("baptism of repentance"). Is Mark implying that it was a baptism *consisting* of repentance (genitive of content)? A baptism *resulting from* repentance (genitive of source)? A baptism *issuing in* repentance (objective genitive)? A repentant baptism—that is, perhaps, a baptism involving repentance or repentant people (adjectival genitive)? Any of these is possible, since "a substantive in the genitive limits the meaning of a substantive on which it depends" without exactly defining the nature of the limitation.[3] Another matter that Mark leaves open is whether βάπτισμα ("baptism") or μετάνοια ("repentance") is the noun modified by the adjectival expression εἰς ἄφεσιν ἁμαρτιῶν ("unto forgiveness of sins"). This grammatical question has large theological implications, since depending on the way the phrase is construed, forgiveness results either from baptism or from repentance. But which is it? And when is this forgiveness understood to take place—in the present, when the baptism occurs, or at some point in the future, which the baptism anticipates? The vague word εἰς ("unto") admits both possibilities.

Josephus at least takes a stand on some of the issues Mark leaves vague.[4] He says explicitly that John's baptism itself did not, and was not intended to, cleanse people from their sins. It was the repentance preceding baptism that accomplished purification; baptism itself only washed the body:

(116) For Herod had killed this John, although he was a good man, and had exhorted the Jews to exercise virtue by practicing righteousness towards each other and piety towards God, and thus to be joined together by baptism (βαπτισμῷ συνιέναι). (117) For in his eyes baptism was unacceptable as a way of gaining remission of sins (μὴ ἐπί τινων ἁμαρτάδων παραιτήσει χρωμένων), but [acceptable] as a way of obtaining cleanliness of the body, inasmuch as the soul had already in fact been purified by righteousness (ἀλλ' ἐφ' ἁγνείᾳ τοῦ σώματος ἅτε δὴ καὶ τῆς ψυχῆς δικαιοσύνῃ προεκκεκαθαρμένης. (My trans.)

Josephus's stance is clear: John's baptism did *not* impart forgiveness of sins; only the necessary preliminary of repentance could accomplish that.[5]

....

Josephus on John's Baptism

But is Josephus right about this? That he is not totally misleading is suggested by the overlap between Josephus's account of John and Matt. 3:7–10// Luke 3:7–14, where John warns that his baptism will not avail for those who refuse to repent of their sins. Moreover, Mark himself, as noted above, calls John's rite "a baptism of repentance" (Mark 1:4), and he also tells us that the people who came to John, as they were being baptized, confessed their sins (Mark 1:5). For Mark, then, as for Matthew and Luke, repentance was part of the baptismal gestalt, and to that extent all the Synoptic Gospels confirm Josephus's testimony.

There is an even closer parallel between Josephus's description of John's baptism and two interrelated Qumran passages, which were mentioned briefly in chapter 2 and which of course do not refer specifically to John or his baptism. The first of these, 1QS 3:4–9, speaks of the person who refuses to enter the Qumran community in these terms:

> 4) Ceremonies of atonement cannot restore his innocence, and he will not be purified by cultic waters (ולוא יטהר במי נדה). He cannot be sanctified in oceans 5) and rivers, nor purified by any waters of washing (ולוא יטהר בכול מי רחץ). Unclean, unclean shall he be all the days that he rejects the laws 6) of God. . . . For [only] through the Spirit of the counsel/council of truth (כיא ברוח עצת אמת) pervading all the ways of man will atonement be made (יכופרו) for 7) all his iniquities (כול עוונותו); only thus can he gaze upon the light of life and so be joined to [God's] truth by a Spirit of holiness (ברוח קדושה), purified from all 8) his iniquities (יטהר מכל עוונותו). Through an upright and humble attitude his sin will be covered (תכופר חטתו), and by humbling himself before all God's laws his flesh 9) will be made clean (יטהר בשרו). Only thus can it be sprinkled with cultic waters (להזות במי נדה) and be sanctified by the cleansing water (להתקדש במי דוכי; *Dead Sea Scrolls Electronic Library* trans. alt.).

Although the terminology is not quite as consistent as in Josephus,[6] the basic point is the same: ritual bathing accomplishes nothing unless it is preceded by spiritual cleansing. Similarly, 1QS 5:13–14 emphasizes that no one may "enter the waters" until he has first repented: "He shall not enter the waters (לוא יבוא במים) to touch the purity [= pure food] of the men of holiness, because they will not be purified unless they have repented of their evil (כיא לוא יטהרו כי אם שבו מרעתם); because he is unclean, as are all who transgress [God's] word" [my trans]. In these Qumran passages, as in the Josephus passage about John, we see a common theme. Ritual bathing alone cannot bring about spiritual purity, which can only be accomplished by repentance. When repentance has taken place, however, the subsequent physical bathing symbolizes the spiritual regeneration that has already occurred.[7] It seems unlikely that this overlap is accidental, both because the similarity is so striking,[8] and because, as chapter 2 has shown, John was probably at one time a member of the Qumran community.

· ·

John's Baptism as a Sacrament

But are the Qumran parallels and Josephus's anti-sacramental account of John the definitive word on his baptismal theology? There are several reasons for doubting this. First, Josephus, by his own account, experienced the sectarian life of the Essenes, the parent group of the Qumran sect (*Life* 10–11), and he seems to be reasonably well informed about them; it is possible, then, that he is interpreting John's rite through the distorting lens of his knowledge of Essene lustrations.[9] Second, the Josephus passage seems to be polemical, and often when Josephus becomes polemical about religious matters he is trying to cover things up.[10] In this particular case, his attitude sounds not only like that of 1QS but also like that of enlightened Hellenistic philosophers, who disparaged magical understandings of religious rites common among the populace and instead offered rationalizing interpretations of them.[11] But this sort of rationalizing interpretation frequently reduces the rite itself to an unnecessary feature and thus proves inadequate to the task of explaining what it means to its practitioners.[12]

Josephus's interpretation of John's ministry, indeed, transforms John's baptism into a mere pendant to repentance. But this is in tension with the fact that John was remembered primarily as John *the Baptist,* not as John the Proclaimer of Repentance. It seems inconceivable, moreover, that so many people would have left their homes to make the long journey into the desert to be baptized by John if they had thought that they had *already* been purged by repentance, if they had not believed that his baptism would confer some sort of spiritual blessing. And they probably would not have thought so unless John himself encouraged the belief.[13] Whatever one thinks of the grammar of Mark 1:4, moreover, it has John proclaiming *baptism,* not in the first instance repentance. Repentance, then, is *part* of the baptismal gestalt but not its leading edge.

As for the Qumran evidence, it does not univocally support Josephus, even if we limit ourselves to 1QS. Although 1QS 3:4–9, which describes the community's present practices, describes purification by the Spirit as a necessary *preliminary* to cleansing of the flesh by immersion in water, 1QS 4:20–22, which depicts a future, eschatological event, uses the image of sprinkling with purificatory water to describe God's refinement of both body and soul through the Spirit.[14] "By His truth," the passage reads, "God shall then purify all human deeds (כול מעשי גבר), and refine some of humanity so as to extinguish every perverse spirit from the inward parts of his flesh (מתמכי בשרו), cleansing him from every wicked deed by a holy spirit (לטהרו ברוח קודש). Like purifying waters, He shall sprinkle each with a spirit of truth (ויז עליו רוח אמת כמי נדה), effectual against all the abominations of lying and sullying by an unclean spirit" (*Dead Sea Scrolls Electronic Library* trans. alt.). The sprinkling spoken of in 1QS 4, then, does not *follow* spiritual purification but is *concomitant* with it. Both ideas, then, are present in succeeding columns of 1QS: 1QS 3, which describes life in the penultimate age, is coherent with *Jewish Antiquities* 18.117, but 1QS 4, which describes life in the eschatological era, is coherent with the idea that John's baptism itself conferred forgiveness of sins.

The crucial question, then, is which era John saw himself as belonging to.
....

The Gospels on John's Baptism

This question can best be approached by a critical look at what the Gospels report about John. A critical approach is necessary because it is not only Josephus who transmits questionable information about John; the Gospels do so as well. Exhibit A, in my opinion, is the way in which all four canonical Gospels show John contrasting his baptism in water with a coming baptism in the Holy Spirit (Mark 1:8; cf. John 1:33) or in the Holy Spirit and fire (Matt. 3:11//Luke 3:16 = Q). Some scholars have argued for the historicity of the version with Spirit and fire,[15] while others have preferred the one with Spirit only.[16] Still others, however, and most influentially Martin Dibelius, have contended that neither is to be followed exactly, although Q is closer to being historical. But the original form of the saying, according to Dibelius, did not speak of the Spirit at all, merely contrasting John's *water* baptism with a coming *fire* baptism: "I baptize you with water, but he will baptize you with fire."[17]
....

Jesus as Sole Spirit Bestower

This conclusion arises mainly from the observed tendency of early Christian literature to ascribe to Jesus and the Christians, for theological reasons, sole possession of the Spirit,[18] an attitude epitomized by John 7:39: "For as yet there was no Spirit (οὔπω γὰρ ἦν πνεῦμα), because Jesus had not yet been glorified."[19] Dibelius's basic contention is that the separation of John's water baptism from Jesus's Spirit baptism serves this Christian interest, which is part of a more general tendency to subordinate John to Jesus (see, for example, Matt. 11:11//Luke 7:28; John 1:8a; 3:30).[20] It does so in this particular case by identifying the Spirit with Jesus and the Christians to the detriment of John.

This is a theme in all four Gospels, but especially in Luke's two-volume work, and particularly in his second volume (see, for example, Acts 1:5 and 11:16.). Most important for Dibelius's case is the tale in Acts 19 about Ephesian followers of the Baptist who have not even heard of the Spirit—a position that, as John Meier points out, would, if taken literally, mean "that they had never heard about the 'spirit of holiness' spoken of in the Old Testament and reflected upon further in intertestamental literature and the documents of Qumran."[21] This hardly seems likely; as Ernst Käsemann puts it, "These Ephesian disciples seem to be living in a vacuum."[22] This explains why some ancient Christian scribes altered the text of Acts 19:2 and some modern commentators have paraphrased it in a way that contradicts its grammar.[23]

A more satisfying solution to the conundrum posed by the verse is provided by Dibelius, who argues that the incongruity of the narrative is a sign that, whatever its historical roots,[24] the tale has been shaped by Christian interests, reflecting the way in which "the Holy Spirit" had become "a shibboleth in the controversy of the Christians with the disciples of the Baptist."[25] This can be seen in the way that Paul, in the continuation of the Acts story, ascribes to John's "baptism of repentance" a merely preliminary character, looking forward to the coming of Jesus (19:4)—a point of view that is then confirmed by the fact that the Ephesian disciples, once they have been baptized in the name of Jesus, receive the Spirit.[26] Moreover, there is a revealing overlap between Acts 19:2 ("we have not even heard that there was a Holy Spirit") and John 7:39 ("for as yet there was no Spirit, because Jesus had not yet been glorified"): both reflect the Christian conviction that the Risen Jesus alone imparts the Spirit.[27] But the ignorance of the Baptist's disciples about the Spirit in Acts 19:2 is as tendentious as the ignorance of Jesus's disciples about the resurrection in Mark 9:10.[28] Both serve the theological interests of post-Easter Christians: resurrection and Holy Spirit, the expected gifts of the new age in Jewish apocalyptic thought, are linked in an exclusive and definitive way with the Risen Jesus. The first reason for suspecting that the reference to the Spirit in Mark 1:8 pars. is a Christian interpolation, then, is that it fits so neatly into the Christian interest in putting the Baptist in his place.

To be sure, Luke is not consistent in pursuing this and others of his theological tendencies; here as elsewhere in his two-volume work, he has preserved traditions that are in tension with them.[29] In fact, as Peter Böhlemann points out, Luke himself records instances in which people close to the Baptist are filled with the Spirit, including his mother Elizabeth (Luke 1:41) and his father Zechariah (Luke 1:67), not to mention John himself, who is described in Luke 1:80 as being "strengthened by the Spirit" (ἐκραταιοῦτο πνεύματι) until his manifestation to Israel. In Acts 18:25, moreover—a few verses before the story of spiritually challenged followers of the Baptist—Luke describes Apollos, a man who knows only the baptism of John, as "bubbling with the Spirit" (ζέων τῷ πνεύματι, my trans.). The Luke 1 passages may very well reflect the fact that, as many scholars have argued, this chapter incorporates a source from Baptist circles.[30] It is possible that this is true of Acts 18:25 as well: all reflect traditions preserved in Baptist circles that tied John (contrary to Luke's theological tendency) to the Spirit.[31]

Whereas, then, there is a significant tendency for early Christian theology to portray Jesus as the first and only imparter of the Spirit, the truth probably is that John already saw himself as possessing it and thought that his baptism would impart it to those who came to him with repentant hearts.[32] As shown above, this would be in line with John's apparent determination to model himself after Elijah, since the latter is portrayed in a famous Old Testament passage as a possessor of the Spirit (2 Kgs. 2:9; cf. 1 En. 70:1–2), who also imparts it to his disciple (2:15; cf. Sir 48:12)—and that in a story that involves crossing the Jordan River (2:7–8, 13–14), the site of John's baptismal activity. In the Synoptics, moreover, Jesus himself receives the Spirit during, or immediately after, his baptism in the Jordan at John's hands (Mark 1:10//Matt. 3:16//Luke 3:21–22)—evidence that runs counter to the Christian tendency to dissociate John from the Spirit.[33] Later Christians were aware of this tension; Jerome, for example, asks rhetorically, "What do we mean by saying that John in his baptism could not give the Holy Spirit to others, yet gave him to Christ?"[34]

....

Old Testament and Jewish Parallels

In a little-noticed essay from 1970, Otto Böcher observed this "denial of Spirit" tendency of early Christian sources vis-à-vis John and his baptism and convincingly argued that, contrary to this tendency, John probably saw himself not only as a forerunner but also as himself a transmitter of salvation *(Heilsmittler)*, which included the eschatological gift of the Spirit.[35] Part of Böcher's argument is the strong connection between water imagery and the eschatological Spirit already in important prophetic texts from the Old Testament, which may have influenced John (Isa. 44:3; Ezek. 36:25–27; Joel 2:28–29; Zech. 13:1–2). Particularly significant, in Böcher's opinion, are Ezek. 36:25–27 and Zech. 13:1–2, which speak of the eschatological divine gift as a cleansing bath that bestows God's Spirit and removes "the unclean spirit."[36]

Böcher also notes that this connection continues to be made at Qumran, citing especially the two passages from the Community Rule investigated above. As we have seen, 1QS 3:6–9 connects the present immersion practices of the community with the purifying action of God's Holy Spirit, and 1QS 4:20–23 uses the image of purificatory waters to describe a future cleansing of humanity by that Spirit.[37] The Qumran community thus linked the Holy Spirit both with its present immersions and with a future "sprinkling" by God. While it is theoretically possible that John decoupled his baptism from the Spirit when he struck out on his own, it seems more likely that he retained his home community's connection between immersion and the Spirit. Both his predecessors, the Qumranians, and his successors, the Christians, connected the Spirit with immersion in water.[38] It makes sense that John, the link between the two groups, did so, too,[39] especially since the Spirit was sometimes conceived as a sort of invisible supernatural fluid, and the act of water baptism itself could thus suggest the Spirit.[40]

....

Forgiveness and the Spirit

A further and most important argument against the Gospels' form of the saying about the two baptisms, and in favor of John's association of his own baptism with the Spirit, has to do with the Gospel linkage between John's baptism and forgiveness of sins (Mark 1:4//Luke 3:3)—a linkage that seem intrinsically plausible, given the strong Old Testament connection between water rites and imagery, on the one hand, and the theme of forgiveness of sins, on the other (see, for example, Num. 8:7;[41] Isa. 1:15–18, 4:4; Ps. 51:1–2; Ezek. 36:25–33; Zech. 13:1).[42] This connection continues in Second Temple Jewish texts in general[43] and the Qumran literature in particular (see, for example, 1QS 3:1–9; 4:20–22). In the Old Testament, however, forgiveness of sins is also strongly associated with the action of God's Spirit (for example, Ps. 51:1–2, 10–12; Ezek. 11:18–20, 18:30–31, 36:25–31; cf. Jer. 31:31–34), an association that, again, continues at Qumran (see, for example, 1QS 3:6–7, 4:20–23, 9:3–5; 1QH[a] 17[9]:32–34, frag. 2 1:13; 4Q506 frags. 131–132 11–14). In view of these deep Old Testament linkages and John's own rootedness in Qumran, it may be asked whether he would have proclaimed a baptism that brought forgiveness of sins without associating it with the eschatological action of the Spirit. The answer is probably no.

To be sure, some scholars, such as James Dunn, have attempted to preempt this argument by denying that John thought his baptism imparted forgiveness. Dunn interprets the formula from Mark 1:4, εἰς ἄφεσιν ἁμαρτιῶν ("unto forgiveness of sins"), as a reference to a *future* act of divine forgiveness, not one occurring concurrently with John's baptism, which was preparatory rather than initiatory.[44] For Dunn, "the very idea of a rite which effected forgiveness was wholly foreign to the prophetic genius of the OT"—an assertion that Dunn backs up, not with citations from the Hebrew Bible itself, but with a reference to 1QS 3:3–9. The latter shows, for Dunn, that the Qumran sect "certainly rejected any idea that sprinkled water could be efficacious to cleanse from sins and restricted the cleansing effects of water to the flesh."[45] When he does finally turn to the Old Testament purification rites, Dunn offers a rationalistic interpretation, asserting that they were "symbols of the cleansing which God himself immediately effected apart from this ritual"[46] and "the means God used to encourage the humble and give confidence to the repentant to approach him, by indicating his gracious will to forgive and receive such." But according to Dunn, such purification rites were never intended to cleanse the heart or take away sins, for they could not possibly do so—an assertion that Dunn reinforces not with Old Testament or Jewish texts but with a citation of the New Testament's Epistle to the Hebrews (9:9–14, 10:1–4)! For Dunn, then, John's baptism was not intended to convey forgiveness; rather, "it is the repentance expressed in the baptism which resulted in forgiveness," and that forgiveness was conceived as a future, eschatological act.[47]

Dunn's arguments, however, do not carry conviction, first because John apparently associated his baptismal ministry with the description in Isa. 40:3

of the preparation of a way in the wilderness (see app. 8). The previous verse in Isaiah links this description with the proclamation that Jerusalem's "penalty" (that is, God's punishment for her sinfulness) has already been paid, and the Targum appropriately renders the latter announcement as "her sins have been forgiven her" (Tg. Isa. 40:2)—an announcement of an accomplished forgiveness, not a promise of a future one.[48]

Dunn's case for an anti-sacramental interpretation of John's baptism, moreover, ignores central features of the texts to which he alludes. Numbers 8:6–7, for example, refers straightforwardly to "waters of expiation" (מי חטאת, lit. "waters of sin") as the means for purifying the Levites; the dichotomy Dunn posits between cleansing the flesh from impurity and cleansing the heart from sin is foreign to this sort of priestly text. Similarly, in 1QS 3:4, "he will not be declared innocent by ceremonies of atonement" (לוא יזכה בכפורים) parallels "he will not be purified by waters of cleansing" (לוא יטהר במי נדה); here again, atonement and rituals of cleansing are conjoined rather than separated.[49] To be sure, Dunn is right to claim that, according to 1QS 3:3–9, unrepentant people cannot be purified by immersion, but this does not mean the author of that text believed that immersion had no atoning effect; the point of the passage, rather, is that, in the case of the unrepentant, the waters do not have their normal, expected consequence (cf. 1 Cor. 11:27–30). Nor is this an idiosyncratic Qumran perspective; as Jonathan Klawans points out, the default ancient Jewish view is that expiation of sin is accomplished by sincere repentance *in combination with* rituals of atonement.[50]

Dunn, moreover, does not take into account some relevant evidence from the New Testament itself, which suggests that early Christians were aware of and troubled by the expiatory implication of Mark 1:4. Matthew, for example, in redacting Mark, removes from his account of John's baptism (Matt. 3:1, 11) the phrase εἰς ἄφεσιν ἁμαρτιῶν ("unto forgiveness of sins"), inserting it instead into the cup word in the Last Supper narrative (see Matt. 26:28//Mark 14:24)—presumably because he wants to associate forgiveness with Jesus's death rather than John's baptism.[51] This seems like an attempt to suppress an inconvenient memory, namely that John's baptism *was* meant to expiate the sins of its recipients—a memory that ran the risk of rendering Jesus's death superfluous.[52] Contrary to Dunn, then, John's baptism *was* understood by some of his contemporaries to convey forgiveness; and therefore, in view of the strong tie between forgiveness and the Spirit, it is reasonable to suppose that it was understood to convey the Spirit as well.

This inconvenient linkage between the forgiveness of sins associated with John's baptism and impartation of the Spirit was well known to post–New Testament Christian theologians, and we can see them wrestling with its implications, sometimes in ways that anticipate the struggles of Dunn and other modern commentators. Tertullian, for example (*Baptism* 10.5–6), says that John's baptismal preaching of forgiveness of sins "was an announcement made in view of a future remission" *(in futuram remissionem enuntiatum est);* his baptism did not impart forgiveness, since it had reference only to the human act of repentance, not to the divine act of forgiveness, which came about through Christ.[53] Many of the writers of the Patristic period agrees with Tertullian in emphasizing the purely preparatory character of John's baptism; as one of them puts it, that baptism was merely "a prelude to the gospel of grace,"[54] and some of the Latin Fathers make this point by interpreting *praedicabat* ("he proclaimed") in the Vulgate of Mark 1:4//Luke 3:3 as a prediction of a future forgiveness rather than an announcement of a present one.[55] Bede, similarly, in his commentary on Acts 19:2, says that John's baptism "could not grant the remission of sins, but only teach repentance," though it also "figuratively pointed to Christ's baptism, by which remission of sins would be given."[56] Several centuries later, Thomas Aquinas moved in a similar direction when he denied that John's baptism was a sacrament, asserting that it was only a sacramentalistic rite that looked forward to the true sacrament, Christian baptism (*Summa* 3.38.1).[57]

Of all the Christian reinterpretations of John's baptism, however, none reveals the stakes in that process more clearly than Jerome's discussion of the issue in his *Dialogue Against the Luciferians* 7 (PL 23.162C–163A). The Luciferians were a group of Christian rigorists, followers of the fiercely anti-Arian bishop Lucifer of Cagliari (d. 370 or 371), who insisted on rebaptizing people who had been baptized by Arian bishops. Lucifer compared these baptizands to the disciples of John in Acts 19:1–6, who needed to be rebaptized to receive the Spirit. Jerome responds that the cases are not parallel, since those described in Acts 19 were not yet Christians, whereas the Arians were and had therefore received the Spirit at their (Christian) baptism. To establish this contrast, Jerome expands on Tertullian's point about the provisional nature of John's baptism:

> The baptism of John did not so much consist in the forgiveness of sins
> as in being a baptism of repentance for the remission of sins, that is,
> for a future remission, which was to follow through the sanctification
> of Christ.[58] . . . But if John, as he himself confessed, did not baptize
> with the Spirit [cf. Mark 1:8 pars.], it follows that he did not forgive
> sins either, for no one has their sins remitted without the Holy Spirit.[59]
> Or if you contentiously argue that, because the baptism of John was
> from heaven, therefore sins were forgiven by it, show me what more
> there is for us to get in Christ's baptism.[60] Because it [John's baptism,
> according to the contrary argument] forgives sins, it releases from

Gehenna. Because it releases from Gehenna, it is perfect. But [I say that] no baptism can be called perfect except that which depends on the cross and resurrection of Christ.[61] Thus, although John himself said, "He must increase, but I must decrease" [John 3:20], in your perverse scrupulosity you give more than is due to the baptism of the servant[62] and destroy that of the master to which you leave no more than to the other.[63] (Trans. alt. from Nicene and Post-Nicene Fathers.)

Note the retrospective nature of Jerome's logic: the baptism of John could not have imparted forgiveness of sins, since if it had, it would have been perfect—but only the redemption wrought by Christ's death and resurrection is perfect. To say the contrary is to ascribe to John a status and office equal to that of Christ, and that cannot be, for if John's water baptism had already imparted forgiveness, what more was to be obtained from Christ's baptism in the Spirit? John's baptism, then, did not impart forgiveness of sins, and "unto forgiveness of sins" in Mark 1:4 must therefore be interpreted as a reference, not to that baptism, but to the future redemption wrought by Christ. Jerome here makes clear how heavily invested he is in the idea that Jesus alone, through the Spirit, imparts forgiveness of sins, and that therefore John's water baptism could not have done so. It is probable that the same sort of retrospective logic was used by the early Christians to efface the historical memory that John and his followers believed that his baptism imparted the Spirit.

All of this confirms Böcher's contention that John saw himself, not only as a *preparer* for salvation, but as an *imparter* of salvation, in that his baptism bestowed on its recipients the eschatological gift of the Spirit and with it forgiveness of sins. This understanding is consonant with the portrait of John in Luke 1, a section of Luke that may very well go back to Baptist circles and that speaks of John being *"filled with the Holy Spirit"* from his mother's womb (1:15) and imparting "knowledge of *salvation* to [God's] people *in the forgiveness of their sins*" (Luke 1:77).[64] Indeed, the ending of the Benedictus, from which the latter phrase is taken, presents a strikingly high estimate of John:

> [76]And you, child, will be called the prophet of the Most High;
> for you will go before the Lord to prepare his ways,
> [77]to give knowledge of salvation to his people
> in the forgiveness of their sins,
> [78]through the tender mercy of our God,
> by which the sunrise from on high has visited[65] us
> [79]to give light to those who sit in darkness and in the shadow of death,
> to guide our feet into the way of peace. (Luke 1:76–78, RSV alt.)

Not only will John go before the Lord to prepare his ways and give God's people knowledge of salvation in the forgiveness they experience through his baptism, but in so doing he will manifest the mercy of God, giving light to people who sit in darkness and the shadow of death. John, then, will be not only a *forerunner* (of God and/or the Messiah) but also a *minister* of "the tender mercy of our God." Indeed, it is not too much to say that, if we take the imagery of 1:79 with the seriousness it deserves, it comes close to suggesting what John 1:8 is at pains to deny: *John* will be the light.

....

Sociological Considerations

A final argument against the Gospels' reservation of the Spirit to "the Coming One," and in favor of John's claim to it, is a factor to which I alluded above,[66] and that is the popularity of John's baptism. If we accept the Gospel portrayal of crowds going into the wilderness to receive this baptism (Mark 1:5//Matt. 3:5; Matt. 11:7–10//Luke 7:24–27; cf. Josephus, *Ant.* 18.118), why would they have done so except to receive a spiritual blessing? And reception of the Spirit, of course, ranks as the spiritual blessing par excellence. To be sure, it is not the only spiritual gift, and it is theoretically possible that John promised his baptizands some other religious benefit, such as forgiveness of sins, but held reception of the Spirit in reserve as a future gift of the Coming One. This, indeed, is the picture that Mark seems to present. But it seems intrinsically unlikely. As just shown, forgiveness of sins and reception of the Spirit go hand in hand in the Old Testament and at Qumran, and it therefore seems probable that, if John promised one of these gifts to his baptizands, he promised them both. And that is why multitudes followed John into the desert.

All of this makes it seem probable that John, contrary to the impression conveyed by Mark 1:8b and parallels, associated his own baptismal rite with the Spirit.[67] Early Christians had a strong motive for denying this association—their desire to link the Spirit exclusively with Jesus and his followers. But that is their view, not John's. John would have been going against both the Old Testament and his Qumran background if he had delinked his baptism from the Spirit, and he would have created a theological incongruity by promising forgiveness of sins without also promising the Spirit.

The original form of the saying about baptism in water and the Spirit, therefore, probably was something like this:

JOHN	"THE COMING ONE"
I baptize you	but he will baptize you
in water	in fire
and the Holy Spirit	

It is easy to see how this form could have been revised into the Markan and Q forms to meet the Christian conviction that only Jesus baptizes with the Spirit. Both forms move the Spirit from John to "the Coming One." The Markan form substitutes "in the Holy Spirit" for "in fire," while the Q form *adds* it to "in fire."

But if John did originally contrast his baptism in water and the Spirit with the future baptism of "the Coming One" in fire, then those modern interpreters who have—often with a subtle or not so subtle anti-Jewish bias—contrasted John, the judgmental Jew, with Jesus, the merciful transcender of Judaism, have gotten things exactly wrong.[68] John was, in his own self-understanding, as Otto Böcher puts it, a *Heilsmittler,* a transmitter of salvation.[69] In his eyes, *he* was the preacher of the good news that God's eschatological victory was already manifesting itself in the earthly sphere. And as a sign of that spreading eschatological victory, and as its vanguard, his baptism was conveying the joyful realities of the new age: forgiveness of sins, and the Spirit that made such forgiveness possible.[70] For John, then, *now* is the day of salvation, though the window of opportunity is closing; John urges his hearers to avail themselves of this last opportunity before it is too late. Soon there will be time only for the visitation of fire, brought by the warlike Davidic Messiah.[71]

. . . .

John's Baptism and Ritual Purity

Taylor vs. Klawans

According to the above argument, John thought that his baptism conveyed forgiveness of sins to its recipients through the action of the Spirit. But this conclusion leaves unanswered the question of how John thought his baptism was related to the sort of cleansing from ritual impurity that was usually associated with water rites in ancient Judaism. Joan Taylor and Jonathan Klawans deserve credit for engaging this question, although they reach opposite conclusions: for Taylor, John's baptism was directed at ritual impurity rather than forgiveness of sins; for Klawans, the reverse.[72]

Taylor's point of departure is the fact that, in the Old Testament and Second Temple Jewish texts, most forms of Levitical impurity are cleansed by immersion or sprinkling, sometimes in combination with other rites, and almost all water rites are directed at Levitical impurity—the sort of ritual defilement that, in biblical and Second Temple Jewish texts, is contracted through childbirth or contact with the dead, with leprosy, with semen, with menstrual blood, and with other fluxes.[73] Taylor concludes that "to Jews in general John's call for immersion would have been understandable as a call to become ritually clean."[74] A corollary for her is that John's baptism was *not* directly connected with forgiveness of sins, which for John was dealt with by repentance rather than washing. She envisages a sequential, four-stage process: "(1) one repents and practices righteousness; (2) one's sins are remitted (= one is cleansed inwardly); (3) one immerses; (4) one's immersion is considered acceptable by God, and one becomes outwardly clean." Repentance, then, results in forgiveness of sins, which is followed by immersion, which leads to ritual purity.

This understanding, however, seems problematic, first of all because of the discrepancy between the sequence Taylor envisages and Mark 1:4//Luke 3:3, which speaks not of "a repentance unto forgiveness of sins and then baptism" but of "a baptism of repentance unto forgiveness of sins"; baptism, then, comes before forgiveness of sins, not after it.[75] Moreover, Old Testament and Second Temple Jewish passages such as Num. 8:6–7, Ps. 51:7, Ezek. 36:25–31, and 1QS 3:8–9 (cf. Sib. Or. 4:165–169) do link water rites with forgiveness, and the Ezekiel passage describes a forgiveness that results from sprinkling (and the concomitant action of the Spirit), both of which precede the people's repentance. Taylor's sequencing of Johannine baptism, then, and her limitation of its effect to a state of ritual purity, are questionable. But her suggestion that ritual cleansing was at least involved in John's baptism is worth consideration. It may be that she is wrong in what she denies (that John's baptism was linked with forgiveness of sins) but right in what she affirms (that it was linked with ritual cleansing).

Jonathan Klawans, however, opposes the latter linkage. His main argument is that, in ancient Judaism, ritual defilement was a constantly recurring and unavoidable phenomenon tied to natural activities such as sexual intercourse, menstruation, and contact with the dead. If John's baptism had been conceived as a means of treating this sort of defilement, it would have had to be frequently repeated (as, for example, happens among the Mandeans, who do link their baptismal rites with ritual purity and therefore practice frequent rebaptism).[76] Our most reliable evidence, however, suggests that John's baptism was a once-and-for-all event.[77] Klawans therefore concludes that John's baptism was probably not directed at ritual impurity.

There is a significant hole in this argument, however: most ancient Jews seem to have believed that, in the conditions of the present world, moral transgression was no less inevitable than the contraction of Levitical impurity.[78] Would the idea of a once-and-for-all cleansing from ritual impurity, then, be less utopian than the idea of a once-and-for-all cleansing from sin? The subsequent history of Christian involvement with the issue of post-baptismal sin, beginning with the Epistle to the Hebrews (6:4–8; 10:26–31) and the Shepherd of Hermas (Herm. Vis. 15.3 = III.7.3; Herm. Mand. 31.1–6 = IV.3.1–6), suggests that this remained a pressing concern. The idea of post-baptismal sinlessness, then, is no less removed from everyday reality than the concept of a permanent buffer against ritual impurity; and on the occasions when a robust notion of sinlessness has arisen in the history of religions, it has most often done so in the context of millenarian movements with a vibrant sense of imminent or realized eschatology.[79]

Klawans's objection to the idea of a once-and-for-all ritual cleansing, then, rather than showing that John could not have believed in such a cleansing, instead points to a factor that Klawans underplays: the impact of John's eschatological convictions on his views about both forgiveness of sins and cleansing of ritual impurity—which he, in common with the Qumran community, may have conflated.[80] If the guide cut has already been made for the tremendous eschatological hewing (Matt. 3:10//Luke 3:9),[81] a once-and-for-all cleansing may be all that is required to sanctify the elect, preparing them ritually to become the beneficiaries of God's imminent act of redemptive holy war.[82]

Early Christian Evidence

There is evidence within the New Testament itself that some of the Baptist's contemporaries connected his baptism with ritual purity. John 3:25 records a dispute between the disciples of the Baptist and a Jew over καθαρισμός ("purification"). The most likely interpretation of this puzzling notice is that the dispute concerns the sort of cleansing practice referred to a chapter earlier, in the allusion to large water jugs standing at the wedding in Cana κατὰ τὸν καθαρισμὸν τῶν Ἰουδαίων ("according to the purification rites of the Jews," my trans. of John 2:6). The dispute, then, would seem to entail a comparison between these purificatory Jewish water rites and John's baptism—perhaps a disagreement about whether or not the latter rendered the former superfluous (see app. 11).[83]

This continued to be an issue among Christians for several centuries. We see it prominently on display, for example, in the early-third-century Christian text *Didascalia Apostolorum*,[84] which is only preserved in a (slightly) later Syriac translation, in passages that discuss whether or not sexual intercourse, menstruation, or contact with the dead produce real defilement. The author thinks not and thus is on the opposite side of the fence from the author of the Pseudo-Clementine *Homilies*,[85] but the energy he expends on it shows that it was a real question in his environment.[86] Significantly for our investigation, a major part of his counterargument has to do with baptism, which the Christians took over from John. Does baptism relieve a person from going to the ritual bath (as the author of the *Didascalia* thinks), or does it merely deal with a different sort of defilement than that cleansed by the *miqveh* (as his Jewish Christian opponents apparently believe)? The author repeatedly rails against those who participate in Jewish rituals of cleansing, and insists on the all-sufficiency, for purposes of Levitical purification, of a once-and-for-all baptism:[87]

ܘܥܠ ܡܥܡܘܕܝܬܐ ܬܘܒ ܚܕܐ ܣܦܩܐ ܠܟܘܢ. ܗܝ ܕܓܡܝܪܐܝܬ ܫܒܩܬ ܠܟܘܢ ܚܛܗܝܟܘܢ.
ܠܐ ܓܝܪ ܐܡܪ ܐܫܥܝܐ ܕܣܚܘܬܘܢ ܗܘܝܬܘܢ ܐܠܐ ܕܣܚܘ ܘܐܬܕܟܘ.

And about baptism also, one is sufficient for you, that which has perfectly forgiven you your sins. Indeed, Isaiah did not say "be washing," but "wash and be cleansed." (Cf. Isa. 1:16; *Didascalia* 24 [232.22–233.2/215.9–11)], alt.)

ܡܛܠ ܕܒܝܕ ܡܥܡܘܕܝܬܐ ܡܩܒܠܝܢ ܪܘܚܐ ܩܕܝܫܐ. ܗܘ ܕܥܡ ܐܝܠܝܢ ܕܥܒܕܝܢ ܙܕܝܩܘܬܐ
ܐܝܬܘܗܝ ܟܠܙܒܢ. ܘܠܐ ܦܪܩ ܡܢܗܘܢ. ܡܛܠ ܪܕܝܐ ܕܟܝܢܐ ܘܫܘܬܦܘܬܐ ܕܙܘܘܓܐ. ܐܠܐ
ܟܠܙܒܢ ܐܡܝܢ ܠܘܬ ܐܝܠܝܢ ܕܩܢܝܢ ܠܗ ܘܢܛܪ ܠܗܘܢ.

For through baptism they receive the Holy Spirit who is always with those that work righteousness, and does not depart from them by reason of natural fluxes and the intercourse of marriage, but always perseveres with those who possess her [= the Spirit], and keeps them. (*Didascalia* 26 [255.16–20/238.13–17], alt.)

ܘܐܢ ܬܣܚܝܢ. ܒܗܘ ܡܕܡ ܕܡܣܒܪܐ ܐܢܬܝ. ܕܡܬܕܟܝܐ ܐܢܬܝ. ܬܫܪܝܢ ܡܥܡܘܕܝܬܐ
ܡܫܠܡܢܝܬܐ ܕܐܠܗܐ. ܗܝ ܕܫܒܩܬ ܠܟܝ ܚܛܗܝܟܝ ܓܡܝܪܐܝܬ. ܘܬܫܬܟܚܝܢ ܒܒܝܫܬܐ
ܕܚܛܗܝܟܝ ܩܕܡܝܐ ܘܬܫܬܠܡܝܢ ܠܢܘܪܐ ܕܠܥܠܡ.

And if you shall bathe yourself, through that which you suppose that you [fem.] are purified [that is, if you go to the *mikveh*], you shall abrogate the perfect baptism of God which completely forgave you your sins, and you will be found in the evils of your former sins, and you will be delivered to the eternal fire. (*Didascalia* 26 [259.9–13/241.27–242.1], alt.)

ܘܐܢ ܥܠ ܓܪܡܐ ܬܕܘܫ ܐܘ ܠܒܝܬ ܩܒܘܪܐ ܬܥܘܠ. ܣܢܝܩ ܐܢܬ ܠܡܣܚܐ. ܘܠܐ

ܡܬܕܟܐ ܬܬܕܟܐ. ܘܡܥܡܘܕܝܬܐ ܕܐܠܗܐ ܬܫܪܐ. ܘܡܚܕܬ ܐܢܬ ܣܘܪܚܢܝܟ. ܘܡܫܬܟܚ
ܐܢܬ ܒܚܛܗܝܟ ܩܕܡܝܐ. ܘܠܬܢܝܢ ܢܡܘܣܐ ܡܫܪܪ ܐܢܬ. ܘܕܝܠܬ ܦܠܚܘܬܐ ܕܥܓܠܐ ܡܩܒܠ
ܐܢܬ ܥܠܝܟ.

And if you tread upon a bone, or enter a tomb, you [think that you] are obliged to be bathed, but you will never be cleansed. And so you will abrogate the baptism of God, and renew your offenses and be found in your former sins, and affirm the second legislation, and take upon you the idolatry of the [Golden] Calf. (*Didascalia* 26 [260.5–10/242.18–22], alt.)

ܠܒܪ ܗܘ ܐܢܬܬܐ ܕܟܕ ܗܘܬ ܠܘܬܗ ܕܐܢܬܬܐ ܐ : ܗܘܢ ܕܘܒܪ ܘܐ ܐ ܐ : ܐ

ܘ ܐ ܐ ܗ ܘܐ ܐ ܐ : ܐ ܐ : ܘ ܘ ܘ ܐ ܐ ܐ ܘ ܐ ܐ

ܬܘ ܐ ܘ ܐ ܐ ܘ ܘ.

On this account, a woman when she is in the way of women, and a
man when an issue comes forth from him, and a man and his wife when
they have intercourse and rise up from one another—let them assemble
without restraint, without bathing, for they are clean. (*Didascalia* 26
[262.21–263.2/245.7–11].)

In all these passages, the question under dispute is whether Christian baptism provides a once-and-for-all antidote not only to sin but also to Levitical
uncleanness, or whether it needs to be supplemented by repeated, purificatory water rites that treat the latter. This is precisely the idea that Klawans
deems impossible: that John thought his baptism dealt once and for all with
the problem of Levitical uncleanness. In a way, my interpretation of John is
actually more conservative than Klawans's: the Baptist took an existing Jewish rite, immersion to cleanse from ritual impurity, and *broadened* it to include cleansing from impurity in general (including the impurity of sin). In
Klawans's view, however, the Baptist *transformed* the immersion rite from
one having to do with ritual impurity to one having to do with moral impurity.

Proselyte Baptism?

There is one other factor[88] that comes into consideration in discussing John's
baptism and its relationship to Jewish rites of cleansing: the possibility that
John's most immediate model was what scholars have dubbed Jewish "proselyte baptism." It is certain that, at least by Talmudic times, converts to Judaism
in rabbinic circles were required to undergo not only circumcision (if male)
but also immersion in a ritual bath. The latter rite, which is first unambiguously attested in a baraita (see glossary) in the Babylonian Talmud (b. Yebam.
47b), may imply that Gentiles are intrinsically impure,[89] and Solomon Zeitlin
has argued that the institution of the rite was probably connected with the
emergence of the concept of Gentile impurity.[90] If, therefore, it could be
shown that a rite of proselyte baptism or the idea of Gentile impurity was
established in John's day, that would make it more likely that John's baptism,
which may have been a modification of the Jewish rite, was also directed
at least partly at ritual impurity. This scenario of John modifying the rite of
proselyte baptism would cohere with the message of the Q logion Matt. 3:9//
Luke 3:8, which quotes him as saying that born Jews ("children of Abraham")
have no advantage over Gentiles in escaping the coming divine wrath: *all*

humans, including Jews, are intrinsically impure, and all (not just Gentiles) therefore need to be cleansed by baptism.

Unfortunately, the external evidence for the practice of proselyte baptism and the idea of Gentile impurity in the early first century CE is fragmentary, and as the notes to the following pages show, many contemporary scholars question its relevance.[91] With regard to proselyte baptism, the Stoic philosopher Epictetus (late first–early second century CE) compares a person who cannot make up his mind to adopt the philosophic lifestyle with a would-be Jew who has not yet been "dipped" (βεβαμμένος) and therefore is a "false baptist" (παραβαπτίστης; Discourses 2.9.19–21). There are also reports in the Mishnah (m. Pesaḥ 8:8) and Tosefta (t. Pesaḥ 7:13–14) about Gentiles who immersed in order to consume the Passover offering, which was permissible only to Jews; the Mishnaic account situates its report in the context of a dispute between the early-first-century "houses" of Hillel and Shammai.[92] Shaye Cohen has questioned the relevance of these citations, arguing that they may not refer to proselyte baptism but to immersion to remove some other sort of impurity or to mark a different sort of transition.[93] He acknowledges, however, some doubt about this conclusion.[94] In any case, none of these texts is an unambiguous testimony to an early-first-century rite of proselyte baptism.[95]

As for the impurity of Gentiles, this is unambiguously stated in t. Zabim 2:1[96] and may be implied by earlier texts. Letter of Aristeas 139–142, for example, speaks of the danger of Jews being polluted by association with people from other nations, and Josephus describes the high priest Hyrcanus, prodded by Herod's enemy Malichus, refusing to let aliens enter Jerusalem because it is a holiday and the Jews are in a state of ritual purity (J.W. 1.229; Ant. 14.285). Similarly, in Ant. 12.145–146, Josephus conflates excluding foreigners from the Temple enclosure with keeping unclean animals out of the holy city. In J.W. 2.150, the same author describes the strict Levitical hierarchy of the Essenes: "A senior if but touched by a junior, must take a bath, as after contact with an alien." And, within the New Testament, Peter in Acts 10:28 seems to link Jewish segregation from Gentiles with purity concerns: "You yourselves know how unlawful it is for a Jew to associate with or visit an alien; but God has shown me that I should not call anyone common or unclean" (κοινὸν ἢ ἀκάθαρτον; RSV alt.).

Jonathan Klawans disputes the relevance of these passages, arguing that the Letter of Aristeas is concerned not with the ritual impurity of Gentiles but with their morally impure behavior and that Malichus and Hyrcanus were just deploying purity concerns to keep Herod out of Jerusalem. As for the passages in which foreigners are forbidden access to the Temple, this, Klawans claims, is not because they were considered unclean (the opposite of ritually pure) but because they were considered profane (the opposite of sacred).[97] The Qumran passage about bathing after contact with an alien is dismissed as a Qumran peculiarity, not a general Jewish conception, and the passage from Acts as an exaggeration reflecting the fact that its author was a Gentile and "by no means sympathetic to Jews or Judaism."[98]

These refutations, however, are unconvincing. On the point about Josephus's reference to Essene avoidance of contact with Gentiles, for example, the passage does not actually say that such avoidance was an Essene peculiarity. Rather, it seems to imply that, just as Jews in general avoided the touch of Gentiles, so the Essenes avoided the touch of those Jews lower down on the Essene hierarchy of impurity. The fact is that all the passages under review do associate Gentiles with ritual impurity, no matter what other issues may be involved. On the wider issue of proselyte baptism, a question raised by Robert Webb bears repeating: if Gentile men were initiated into the Jewish community by circumcision, how, if not by proselyte baptism, were women initiated?[99] This question may not have been so pressing in earlier ages, when Judaism was basically the religion of an ethnic group living in Judea, but it became a question once Jews were spread over the Mediterranean world and it became possible for non-Jews to convert.[100] I am not suggesting that proselyte baptism was universally practiced in all Jewish circles open to Gentile converts (there were some that were not),[101] but that, in the pluralistic Jewish environment of early-first-century Palestine, it may have been well enough known to provide part of the conceptual background for John's rite.

....

Summary

This chapter has dealt with the central and distinctive feature of John's ministry, his baptism, and is thus the fulcrum of the study. It has attempted to analyze and compensate for the competitive slant of the Christian sources on this subject, a slant that was analyzed in general terms in chapter 1, as well as for the apologetic and anti-apocalyptic slant of Josephus. This process has led to the conclusion that John saw his baptism not just as a preparatory rite but as a sacrament of salvation. For John, the power of God's new age was already invading the earthly sphere, cleansing definitively from both ritual impurity and sin those who came to his baptism. And this cleansing was necessary, and took place, regardless of the baptizand's place within the Jewish community—or even whether the baptizand was Jewish at all.

Both in his realized eschatology, which this chapter has emphasized, and in his challenge to covenantal nomism, which was discussed in chapter 2, John anticipated Jesus. This raises the question of exactly how far Jesus's debt to John extended, and what the precise relation between the two men was. Those questions will be explored in the following chapter.

CHAPTER FIVE

Jesus

Among those who came to be baptized by John was a young man from Naza-reth named Jesus. His baptism is either described or alluded to in all four canonical Gospels (Mark 1:9–11, Matt. 3:13–17, Luke 3:21–22, John 1:29–34). This is one of the few things we can feel confident about in his biography. As already noted, it is not the sort of thing the church is likely to have made up, since it posed a problem: John's rite was a "baptism of repentance unto forgiveness of sins" (Mark 1:4), but the early church believed that Jesus had no sins to forgive (2 Cor. 5:21; John 8:46; Heb. 4:15, 7:26; 1 Pet. 2:22; 1 John 3:5).[1]

We can already see the Gospel writers dealing in various ways with the problem of what Jesus's baptism may have implied about him and his rela-tionship to John. As noted in chapter 1, Matthew constructs a dialogue, not present in any other Gospel, in which John protests the baptism; it is he who needs to be baptized by Jesus, not the other way around, since the superior baptizes the inferior (Matt. 3:14–15). For a similar reason, Matthew also, as noted in the previous chapter, removes the phrase "unto forgiveness of sins" from his description of the purpose of John's baptism and plugs it into his account of Jesus's Last Supper (Matt. 26:28). Luke deals with the problem in a different way by saying that Jesus joined in the rite "when all the people were being baptized" (Luke 3:31, Revised Standard Version alt.); his baptism, then, was an act of solidarity with his nation, not an expression of his own need for spiritual cleansing. And the author of the Fourth Gospel, although reflecting the tradition about the descent of the Spirit, which occurs in the Synoptics at Jesus's baptism, omits any account of Jesus's baptism. Indeed, the Fourth Evangelist never calls John "the Baptist," though he does mention his baptismal activity (1:31, 33; cf. 3:23). But the whole purpose of this activity is to reveal Jesus to Israel (John 1:29–34), to testify to his divine status and superiority to John himself.

It is not only in the Fourth Gospel, however, that John acknowledges his inferiority to Jesus. All four Gospels and all three main Gospel sources (Mark, Q, and John), have a version of a saying in which John contrasts his baptism in water with the baptism of a "coming one," to whom he is inferior, and whom all the Gospel writers understand to be Jesus (Mark 1:7–8//Matt. 3:11//Luke 3:16//John 1:26–27). Although the previous chapter has examined this passage for the light it sheds on John's understanding of his baptism, the focus now is on the light it may shed on John's relation to Jesus. The Q form of the saying probably ran something like this: "I baptize you with water, but the one who comes after me is stronger than me, the thong of whose sandal I am not fit to loosen; he will baptize you with fire."[2] In Q this saying is followed by another logion (Matt. 3:12//Luke 3:17) that explicates the reference to the coming baptizer-in-fire: "His pitchfork is in his hand, and he will cleanse his threshing floor, and gather the grain into the barn; but the chaff he will burn with unquenchable fire" (my trans.).

John, then, acknowledges his inferiority to a coming figure whom he expects to separate the wheat from the chaff, that is, good from evil human beings, rewarding the former and destroying the latter—attributes of the coming king in Isa. 11:1–9 and of the Messiah, "powerful in the Holy Spirit," who will purify Jerusalem, in the first-century BCE Psalms of Solomon (17:21–46). Another Jewish text, perhaps from the first century CE, speaks of a figure who is alternately called God's Elect One (for example, 1 En. 49:3), his Anointed One or Messiah (48:10; 52:4), and "that Son of Man," whose most consistent function is to be an end-time judge (for example, 45:3, 55:4, 62:3, 5), a role that God's Anointed One performs in a classic biblical messianic text, Isa. 11:3–5.[3] John's sayings in their present form, therefore, definitely seem to refer to the Messiah.[4] And the juxtaposition between these sayings and the baptism of Jesus, which immediately follows in the Synoptics, leaves no doubt that the Gospel writers think John was talking about Jesus playing this messianic role.[5]

....

Doubts

But *was* he talking about Jesus? Doubts arise from a number of factors:

(1) The assertion that John regarded Jesus as the "coming one" whom he prophesied clearly serves a key agenda of the Gospels: to show that Jesus indeed *was* the Messiah. While this in itself does not disprove that John believed in Jesus—apologetic writers sometimes base their arguments on truths—it does alert us to the possibility that the tradition of John's acknowledgment of Jesus may have been created by the needs of later Christian apologetics.

(2) There is nothing in John's words about the "coming one" that relate distinctively to Jesus. What is reflected is rather a standard Jewish expectation about the coming Messiah, who will set the world to rights when

he comes. In the Synoptics, the link with Jesus is provided only by the juxtaposition between John's prophecy and the immediately subsequent account of his baptism of Jesus. Here the Spirit descends on Jesus (thus perhaps "anointing" him) and a heavenly voice acclaims him as God's Son (a synonym for the Messiah in some texts found at John's onetime home at Qumran); thus the baptismal account displays Jesus's messiahship in symbolic form.[6] It is difficult, however, to know what may be historical in this highly mythological account of Jesus's baptism, and the earliest version, that of Mark, has Jesus alone registering the Spirit's descent and the heavenly voice. The later Gospels have all made the baptismal revelations into more public, "objective" events, visible to John as well as to others, but they have done so at least partly for apologetic reasons.[7] Therefore the standard Christian understanding of John as the self-acknowledged forerunner of Jesus, which is explicit already in John 1:6–8, 15, 20, 29–34, and 3:25–31, appears to be a theological rereading of history.

(3) This understanding of John as a witness to Jesus's messiahship is, moreover, challenged by a later passage from Q, Matt. 11:2–6//Luke 7:18–23. Here John, in prison towards the end of his life, hears about the things Jesus has been doing and sends some of his disciples to ask, "Are you the coming one, or are we waiting for someone else?" (my trans.). Jesus, in response, describes his healing miracles in scriptural language, drawn especially from Deutero-Isaiah—a pastiche remarkably similar to what turns up in a Qumran passage about God's Messiah (4Q521). This weighs as a factor in favor of its historicity, especially in view of John's linkage with Qumran.[8]

The implication of the passage would seem to be that Jesus is answering John's question about his being the "Coming One" with an implied "yes," and the very indirectness of the claim is an argument for its historicity. Significantly, the story does not end with John being won over. This is surely a revealing omission and, again, an indication that some sort of historical memory underlies the exchange: if Christians had invented the story out of whole cloth, they probably would have pictured John being convinced.[9]

Carl Kraeling argues against the passage's historicity, suspecting John's question from prison because "the transcendent Coming One whom [John] expected to destroy the wicked in unquenchable fire would scarcely be evoked by the figure of Jesus."[10] But we cannot know that John's expectations for the Messiah were limited to that figure's judgmental side. In Jewish traditions, the judgmental Messiah usually has a compassionate side as well: he will deliver his suffering people while obliterating their enemies. This is already true in Isaiah 11, where the shoot from Jesse's stem not only kills the wicked with the breath of his mouth but also judges the poor with righteousness, that is, has mercy on them. It is also true in the larger context of 4Q521, where a later fragment couples the raising of the dead with a reference to judgment: "those who curse" are destined to die when "the one who revives" raises the dead (4Q521, Fragment 7, lines 5–6).

John, then, could have believed both that the "Coming One" would soon execute fiery judgment and that the sorts of miracles attributed to Jesus might be among "the works of the Anointed One" (Matt. 11:2, my trans.). In any case, for present purposes the issue of the historicity of Matt. 11:2–6//Luke 7:18–23 is not crucial; even if it was made up by the early church, as Kraeling asserts, it would still reflect a common perception that John did not accept Jesus's messiahship.[11] Either way, then, the passage is a powerful testimony against the assumption that John recognized Jesus as the fulfillment of his messianic hopes in the way the Gospels imply.[12]

(4) As for evidence outside the Gospels, the testimony of Josephus also casts doubt on the thesis that John saw the primary purpose of his ministry as preparing the way for Jesus. Indeed, Josephus treats the two men separately, describing John in one passage of the *Jewish Antiquities* (18.116–119) and Jesus in another (18.63–64)—or, if the latter is a Christian interpolation, not at all.[13] He does not link the two figures, and his description of John actually comes at a point in his narrative subsequent to his description of Jesus.[14] This clashes with the presentation in the Gospels, whereby John, the Elijah-like preparatory figure, appears on the scene first and goes to death first, prefiguring Jesus's fate by his proclamation, suffering, and death (cf. Mark 9:11–13).

It is true that Josephus, like the Gospels, uses John for his own purposes, above all, as Steve Mason says, in the service of "his ongoing demonstration that violation of the divine laws brings inevitable punishment."[15] But it seems unlikely that he has therefore glossed over the connection between the two men; he probably did not know about it. Despite this, it is probable that John and Jesus were indeed connected, as the embarrassing memory of Jesus's baptism by John shows. It is also probable that John's death preceded Jesus's, as in the Gospels.[16] But Josephus's evidence at least reveals that some people remembered John without reference to Jesus and thus makes questionable a presentation in which John's main purpose is to prepare Jesus's way.[17] Similarly, a later development of the Baptist legend, the Slavonic Josephus, does not link the two men except in one glancing reference (2.168).[18]

(5) We also need to consider the wide range of evidence mobilized in chapter 3, which shows that followers of the Baptist who did not become part of the Jesus movement are already reflected in the New Testament and continued to be a significant factor, especially in Syria, at least through the fourth century. If John viewed himself merely as a precursor to Jesus, why did so many of his followers not get the message?

We have noted in chapter 1 that the evidence for this competitive Baptist mission is strongest in the Fourth Gospel, which puts the greatest emphasis of all the canonical documents on John's subordination to Jesus. The Fourth Evangelist, as argued earlier, seems to be in touch with, and trying to refute the claims of, a group of followers of the Baptist who exalted him over Jesus. The very strength of this polemic suggests the strength of the claim it is trying to refute, and one possible explanation for the strength of that claim about John's supremacy is that it rests on a truth: Jesus began as a follower of the Baptist.

6) It is particularly interesting that one of the ways the Fourth Evangelist rebuts this point is by having the Baptist himself say, "The one coming after me has gotten priority over me, because he was before me" (John 1:15, my trans.).[19] This formulation, which is echoed in 1:27, advances the Evangelist's case by reinterpreting a potentially damaging fact about the relation between the two men: John appeared before Jesus on the stage of history. For the Fourth Evangelist, however, this does not mean—as he seems to be afraid one might think—that John was the more important figure.[20] The situation was actually the reverse: *Jesus* was first, since he existed "in the beginning," that is, from eternity (cf. 1:1).

Nevertheless, it is striking that the phrase the Baptist uses for Jesus in John 1:15, "the one coming after me" (ὁ ὀπίσω μου ἐρχόμενος), could be taken as a reference to a disciple,[21] and this nuance is even closer to the surface in 1:27. In that context, John appears to be saying to the Pharisees who come to interrogate him, "You do not recognize the one who is standing in your midst, whom you think is just 'the one coming after me,' that is, my disciple. But he is actually my superior, whose sandal-thong I am not fit to loosen." These Johannine texts acknowledge the possibility that people might think that Jesus was just John's follower but label this a misinterpretation: the "one coming after" John was actually his predecessor and therefore his superior. But, in so doing, these texts protest too much, and may inadvertently reveal the opposite of what they are trying to establish: Jesus actually started out within the Baptist movement, as John's follower, "the one coming after him."

....

Jesus the Baptizer

The Fourth Gospel's depiction of Jesus's early baptismal ministry (John 3:22–24; 4:1–2) points in the same direction. These references are curious because the Gospel first matter-of-factly reports that Jesus was baptizing in Aenon-by-Salem (3:23), then says that, in general, Jesus was baptizing and making more disciples than John (4:1), then qualifies this by saying that Jesus himself did not baptize, but only his disciples (4:2). We have no other early reports, either in the New Testament or elsewhere, about Jesus baptizing. Why does only John report this—and why does he do so only to immediately deny it?

On the one hand, we might, with Dibelius, ascribe the motif of Jesus's baptizing to the Fourth Gospel's desire to emphasize his superiority to John. Both Jesus and John have baptismal ministries, but Jesus's is more popular (4:1); he baptizes, and *all* come to him (3:26; cf. the emphasis on Jesus's universal appeal in 12:19, 32).[22] On the other hand, we might, with C. H. Dodd, take the notices about Jesus's baptizing as a historical memory, one that the final redactor of the Gospel is concerned to contradict lest readers think Jesus was just John's imitator.[23]

Dodd seems to have the better argument here; as John Meier points out, the denial of Jesus's baptismal activity in 4:2 "supplies us with perhaps the best New Testament example of how the criterion of embarrassment works." Memories that early Christians seek to suppress are likely to be true.[24] Although the Fourth Evangelist does use the memory of Jesus's baptismal activity to score points about his superiority to John, it is hard to see the record of that activity as a mere setup to the assertions of superiority in 3:26 and 4:1, since the Fourth Evangelist could have made the general point, as the Synoptic authors do, without recourse to a dominical baptismal ministry, and the latter creates more problems than it solves. What the Fourth Evangelist really seems to be doing is damage control: trying to turn an uncomfortable memory to his advantage. In this endeavor he was not entirely successful, as shown by 4:2, which is probably a later gloss.[25]

Jesus, then, probably did have a baptismal ministry, first as John's emissary, then perhaps independently. The Fourth Evangelist has developed this memory into an argument for Jesus's superiority to John: they both baptized, but Jesus baptized more people. The final editor or a later glossator, however, has contradicted this because the original memory reveals too much about Jesus's dependence on John—which may also explain why the Synoptic tradition has mostly suppressed it. The memory may, however, be indirectly reflected in the controversy about Jesus's authority in Mark 11:27–23. Here Jesus answers the question about his authority by a counter-question about the authority of John's *baptism*. This may imply that Jesus's ministry was thought to derive its authority from John's baptismal ministry because Jesus continued it.[26]

A later product of a Johannine community, 1 John 5:6, bolsters this reconstruction. This verse defines Jesus as "the one who came through water and blood, . . . not in the water only but in the water and in the blood."[27] As Martinus C. de Boer has shown,[28] "came through/in water" is probably a reference to Jesus's baptismal ministry, the ministry he performed through the instrumentality of water,[29] just as "came through/in blood" is a reference to the ministry he performed through his redemptive death.[30] This suggests that the memory of Jesus's baptismal ministry—a ministry that began as a continuation of John's baptism—was firmly established in the community of the Epistle writer and considered by some there to be the central aspect of his redemptive work. This is why the epistle's author has to emphasize, "not in the water only."[31] The point of the counterargument in 1 John 5:6 is that it is not the baptismal water, which was already present in John's ministry, that cleanses from sin, but only the blood of Jesus (cf. 1:7). John's baptism—contrary to what John himself seems to have thought—did not wash away sin.[32]

. . . .

John and Jesus: Elijah and Elisha?

John 3:3 and 4:1, then, provide a snapshot of Jesus at an early stage of his ministry, when he was still more or less within the orb of the Baptist's message and influence, though he was starting to move out into his own independent mission. What did they think of each other, and of their relationship, at this point? Perhaps Jesus's opinion of John at this stage is reflected in the Q saying Matt. 11:16–19//Luke 7:31–35: they were beginning to have distinct ministries (Jesus ate and drank in a normal way, whereas John did not), but they were still messengers of divine wisdom in a parallel way.

How about John's opinion of Jesus? As seen above, it is unlikely that he acknowledged his former pupil as the Messiah, if the later question he poses in Matt. 11:3//Luke 7:19 has any claim to historicity (as I have argued it does). But, on the other hand, it also seems unlikely that he thought of Jesus as just another disciple. This is already evident from the fact that John 3:3 and 4:1 present Jesus alone as carrying on John's baptismal ministry in a semi-independent manner during John's lifetime. Perhaps there were others who did so, but we have no evidence for their existence. And if Jesus alone extended John's baptismal outreach into new areas during the latter's lifetime, he probably could not have done so without some sort of acknowledgment from John of his special status among his followers.

Further evidence that John did in some way publicly acknowledge Jesus comes in the important controversy story in Mark 11:27–33. Here Jesus, challenged about the authority for his audacious actions, above all the cleansing of the Temple (Mark 11:15–19),[33] responds with a question of his own about the authority for John's baptism—a counter-question that only makes sense if John's authority and Jesus's were somehow thought to be linked. The indirect nature of this rebuttal, the lack of a strong Christological assertion, and the fact that the argument runs counter to the later tendency to present Jesus as one who abjures human witnesses (cf. John 5:35, 41), all suggest that some sort of historical memory lies behind it.[34] John, then, probably did in some way point towards Jesus.[35] But how did he do so, if not as the Messiah?

A possible answer is suggested by the conclusion in chapter 3 that John thought of himself as the returning Old Testament prophet Elijah. If so and if he saw Jesus as his heir apparent, he may have thought of Jesus as being like Elijah's successor, Elisha. Although there is slight evidence for a concrete expectation in pre-Christian Judaism that Elisha, like Elijah, would return before the end,[36] eschatological conceptions and figures were fluid,[37] and there are certainly Elisha-like features in the New Testament's picture of Jesus.[38] This is especially true of Jesus in his relation to John: he starts out as a follower of the established prophet, but eventually succeeds and trumps him, both in terms of possession of the Spirit and in terms of his interrelated ability to work miracles.[39] Similarly, according to the biblical account, Elisha asked for, and received, a double portion of Elijah's spirit when the latter was taken up into heaven (2 Kgs. 2:9, 15); several later interpreters take this as a reference to his superior miracle-working power.[40]

These pictures of John and Jesus, of course, are taken from later Christian narratives, so we cannot automatically assume that John and his followers would have applied the Elijah/Elisha typology to his relationship with Jesus. But it still seems likely that the New Testament's picture of Jesus as an Elisha-like figure did not come out of nowhere, and given the close relation between John and Jesus, their association in ministry, and the probability that John saw himself as Elijah, it makes sense that he would have seen his heir apparent as Elisha—and Jesus, at least initially, may have concurred. If so, they may have agreed that Jesus had a more powerful spiritual endowment than John but would not have posited the absolute dichotomy the New Testament does with regard to possession of the Spirit.

It may even be that the terms the Baptist uses in the messianic prophecy in Mark 1:7//Matt. 3:11//Luke 3:16//John 1:27, "the one coming after me" (ὁ ὀπίσω μου ἐρχόμενος) and "the one stronger than me" (ὁ ἰσχυρότερός μου), originally identified Jesus as an Elisha-like figure.[41] "The one coming after me" is an ambiguous phrase: it could mean "the one who will succeed me," and this is the way the Gospels take it here. It could also mean, however, "the one who follows me as my disciple or petitioner"—and this is actually the more frequent implication of ὀπίσω in the Gospels.[42] There is a similar ambiguity about the phrase used in 1 Kings 19:16 to speak about Elisha in relation to Elijah, נביא תחתיך, which can connote either subservience or succession. The term literally means "a prophet under you" and may most immediately designate Elisha as Elijah's servant and disciple, who is subservient to him. This interpretation accords with the immediate Old Testament context: a few verses later, we read that Elisha "went after Elijah, and served him" (19:21, my trans.).[43] It also accords with 2 Kings 3:11, in which King Jehoram of Israel describes Elisha as a prophet "who used to pour water on the hands of Elijah" (NIV). The implication of servanthood in the phrase "a prophet under you," therefore, is strong. But "a prophet in your place" is also a possible nuance of the phrase, and this is the way the phrase is translated in the Septuagint (εἰς προφήτην ἀντὶ σοῦ) and the Peshitta (ܢܒܝܐ ܚܠܦܝܟ).[44] This translation also fits the larger context, which describes Elijah's discouragement and God's decision to replace him with Elisha (1 Kgs. 19:4–18).[45]

If, then, John the Baptist, who saw himself as Elijah, thought of Jesus as an Elisha figure, that may originally have meant that he saw him as his chief assistant—a prophet "under him," who followed him as a disciple. Later on, however, as Jesus manifested special abilities, and even outstripped John in certain regards (baptismal ministry, reputation for miracles), John came to regard him, perhaps, as "the one stronger than me," an Elisha figure in the sense of the prophet who would succeed him—a being who still operated on more or less the same level as John but did a better job of it because he possessed a double rather than a single portion of the Spirit. And still later, he may have begun to wonder if Jesus was actually a being of a different order—not just Elisha, but the Messiah.

....

Competition

John may have accepted Jesus's transition from assistant to successor with good grace. But it seems more likely that a rivalry developed between the two men. And if they modeled their relationship in some way on the biblical duo of Elijah and Elisha, they may have found the germs of such a rivalry in the biblical model itself. Ancient exegetes, for example, seem to have wondered why Elisha was not content to ask for the same spiritual endowment as Elijah, instead requesting a double portion of it (2 Kgs. 2:9). The Greek translators of Sir. 48:12 omit the Hebrew text's reference to Elisha having double the miracle-working power of Elijah, perhaps "because this bicolon seems to make Elisha a greater person than Elijah."[46] Rabbinic interpreters show a similar sensitivity: in b. Sanh. 105b, for example, R. Jose b. Ḥoni cites Elijah's acquiescence to Elisha's request for a double portion of his spirit as an illustration of the rule that a man is jealous of everyone except his son and his disciple. This seems to imply that a lesser man than Elijah would have been upset at Elisha's desire for supremacy.

There is a suggestion of a similar competition—at least from the side of Jesus—in the important Q saying Matt. 11:7–11//Luke 7:24–28. Here Jesus, on the one hand, acclaims John as "a prophet, and more than a prophet" and interprets his ministry through an allusion to Mal. 3:1 (which probably means endorsing the view that John is Elijah).[47] On the other hand, he concludes with this marvelously mixed message: "ἀμὴν λέγω ὑμῖν, οὐκ ἐγήγερται ἐν γεννητοῖς γυναικῶν μείζων Ἰωάννου τοῦ βαπτιστοῦ· ὁ δὲ μικρότερος ἐν τῇ βασιλείᾳ τῶν οὐρανῶν μείζων αὐτοῦ ἐστιν" ("Amen I say to you, among those born of women no one has arisen who is greater than John the Baptist—but the least person in the dominion of God is greater than him" [Matt. 11:11// Luke 7:28, my trans.]).[48]

The first half of the verse asserts that John is the greatest person of all time. But the second half immediately undermines this hyperbolic praise, proclaiming John's inferiority to even the least person in the dominion of God—that is, the least of Jesus's own disciples.[49] How can John be the greatest person who ever lived and yet inferior to the least important citizen of the kingdom?

One way of solving this problem is to say, with Dibelius, that the tension between the two halves of the verse is so intense that both could not have come from the same mouth. For Dibelius, the assertion in the first half, "no one is greater," is not so much qualified as contradicted by the assertion in the second half. The first half, then, reflects the historical Jesus's veneration for John, whereas the second half reflects not Jesus but the later church, which was competitive with the Baptist movement.[50]

Other scholars, who have not wanted to accept such redactional surgery, have argued that the contrast here is eschatological: although John was the greatest citizen of the old era, a new age is about to dawn, and in that era, as Davies and Allison put it, "the least in the kingdom will be greater than the greatest is now."[51] Eschatology certainly seems to be present in the Q context, since Matt. 11:12–13//Luke 16:16 goes on to oppose "the days of John the Baptist," which is the end of the era of "the Law and the prophets," with the era of the dominion of God. But the problem with Davies and Allison's formulation is that Matt. 11:11//Luke 7:28, like the continuation of the passage, seems to imply that the dominion of God is present, not future. The least in the kingdom *is* greater than John; it is not said that that person *will be* greater than John.[52] The kingdom, then, is already present, and John, who is still alive at this point in the narrative, does not belong to it. Similarly, Matt. 11:12// Luke 16:16 seems to separate John's era from the era of the dominion of God, which is presently being proclaimed by Jesus. If this is true, then Jesus placed

John, whom he interpreted as his forerunner, on the "old age" side of the eschatological ledger.

That is an estimate with which John would not have agreed, if the argument in the previous chapter was correct: John saw his baptism as *presently* conveying the eschatological gift of forgiveness, and probably the associated eschatological gift of the Spirit as well. For John, the new age was already dawning, and baptism at his hands was the way to get into it. Jesus seems to have agreed with this analysis and prescription early in his ministry, as shown by his participation in the Baptist movement, even to the point of becoming a baptizer himself.

Later, apparently, he changed his mind. And if we reject Dibelius's redactional surgery and maintain the integrity of Matt. 11:11//Luke 7:28, we will be forced to admit that Jesus emerged from that transformation expressing a somewhat ambivalent attitude to John. He still revered him as "a prophet, and more than a prophet" (Matt. 11:9//Luke 7:26) and the greatest human who had existed up to his own time. But he also felt the need to put him in his place, perhaps after John had already passed from the scene. And that place was, according to Jesus, in the old era (contrary to John's own self-estimate), outside of the new aeon of which Jesus was, in his own eyes, the proclaimer and agent.[53] He thus expressed towards John what Harold Bloom has termed "the anxiety of influence": the need on the one hand to acknowledge the importance of the "parent-poet," but on the other hand to supersede, downgrade, or creatively misread him.[54]

....

History-of-Religions Comparisons

This phenomenon of a successor figure acknowledging and even lauding his predecessor, yet on a deep level competing with him or his memory, has precedents in the history of other prophetic and messianic movements. Often, the successor claims merely to be carrying on the work of the predecessor, usually after the latter has passed from the scene,[55] and this can lead to what Max Weber termed "routinization of the charisma."[56] But such routinization does not always occur. Denis MacEoin, for example, calls early Shiʿism "a clear and useful example of extended hereditary charismatic leadership" and claims that "a tendency to avoid premature routinization of the charisma . . . is . . . a marked feature of Bābi and Bahaʾi history."[57] Margrit Eichler, similarly, says that in studying the Münster Anabaptists of the early sixteenth century "we are dealing with the relatively rare case in which one charismatic leader is immediately succeeded by another."[58]

Such successions can be accompanied by competition. The relation between Elijah Muhammad, the founder of the Nation of Islam, and his erstwhile lieutenant, Malcolm X, is a case in point. Malcolm eventually left the

Nation, partly because of political and religious differences that developed between him and Muhammad, partly because of disillusionment caused by his discovery of Muhammad's extramarital affairs, and partly because of Muhammad's jealousy, which sprang from the intense media attention to Malcolm. As one of Malcolm's loyal followers later put it: "I felt that eventually [he] would have to leave the Nation of Islam. . . . He was developing too fast."[59] Perhaps something similar was felt within the Baptist movement when Jesus began attracting more disciples and baptizing more adherents than John (cf. John 4:1). Nor did the ill will of Elijah Muhammad and his followers end with Malcolm's departure from his group: Malcolm died in a hail of bullets from the guns of Nation of Islam members, and Elijah Muhammad was probably at least indirectly responsible for the assassination.

I am not suggesting that John the Baptist felt a similar level of animosity for Jesus; indeed, if we accept the substantial historicity of John's question to Jesus from prison, he acknowledged and respected Jesus and was even willing, late in life, to entertain the possibility that he might be the Messiah. From the side of Jesus, as we have seen, the picture seems more complicated, a combination of acknowledgment and undercutting, betraying among other things, perhaps, the "anxiety of influence."

....

The Bābī/Bahā'ī Parallel

Something similar seems to have occurred in the history of the interrelated Bābī and Bahā'ī movements in the nineteenth century,[60] which provide some fascinating parallels to the interrelated Baptist and Jesus movements of the first.[61] Bahā'ism grew out of the millenarian Bābī movement of the 1840s, whose leader, Sayyid 'Ali Muhammad, began in 1844 to call himself the Bāb (= Gate), an epithet that originally connoted the Gate to the Hidden Imam, the eschatological redeemer figure expected by Twelver Shi'a Muslims (the majority of Shi'ites).[62] Then, in 1848, the Bāb began hinting that he was not merely the Gate to the Hidden Imam but the Hidden Imam himself, as well as the *Qa'im* = "the One Who Rises," which he glossed as "he who prevails over all people, whose rising is the resurrection."[63] This title was based on the Shi'ite belief that from time to time God sends a major "manifestation" to the earth, starting with Adam and continuing in the great prophets Abraham, Moses, Jesus, and Muhammad.[64] The Bāb came to think that he was the greatest of these manifestations so far, thus explicitly contradicting the Qur'ān, according to which Muhammad was the last and greatest of the prophets. In the movement that the Bāb inspired, these claims were combined with an apocalyptic militancy that the Iranian authorities found deeply unsettling. The Bāb was imprisoned in 1848 and executed in 1850 after armed revolts by his followers broke out in several Persian cities. This Bābī militancy continued after the Bāb's death, climaxing in an 1852 attempt on the Shah's life by three of the Bāb's followers.[65]

Meanwhile, a succession struggle broke out amongst the Bābīs, despite the fact that the Bāb had actually designated a successor, Subh-i-Azal.[66] This figure, however, lacked the personal force of the Bāb (Denis MacEion speaks of his "premature routinization" of the charisma),[67] and he sought seclusion rather than the limelight. But the Bāb had unwittingly introduced a further destabilizing factor into the succession struggle by prophesying the advent of another redemptive figure, "The-One-Whom-God-Will-Make-Manifest," who would be even greater than himself. In his mind this expectation was a hope for the distant future, since he expected his own dispensation to last as long as the previous dispensations of Adam, Abraham, Moses, Jesus, and Muhammad. "The-One-Whom-God-Will-Make-Manifest" would come between 1511 and 2001 years later;[68] the expectation of his advent, therefore, was distinct from the question of the Bāb's immediate successor.

After the Bāb was martyred in 1850, however, these two expectations began to coalesce, as various of the Bāb's disciples (but not Subh-i-Azal) presented themselves as "The-One-Whom-God-Will-Make-Manifest."[69] The most successful of these claimants was Subh-i-Azal's half-brother, Mirza Husayn 'Ali, who became known as Bahā' Allāh ("The Glory of God"). Bahā' Allāh, who had been a prominent adherent of the Bāb during the latter's lifetime but had not met him personally, was imprisoned after the Bābī attempt on the Shah's life, and during this period, according to his own testimony, he experienced a vision in which a heavenly maiden—"the embodiment of the remembrance of the name of my Lord"—greeted him as "the Best-Beloved of the worlds . . . the Mystery of God and His Treasure. . . . He Whose Presence is the ardent desire of the denizens of the Realm of eternity."[70] This revelation eventually led to a thorough reinterpretation of the Bāb's holy writing, the Bayān, which was now taken to demonstrate that the Bāb had, in fact, anticipated the imminent appearance of "The-One-Whom-God-Will-Make-Manifest," that is, Bahā' Allāh himself.[71] Exiled to Baghdad after his imprisonment, Bahā' Allāh publicly declared himself to be "The-One-Whom-God-Will-Make-Manifest" in 1863.[72] Not surprisingly, Subh-i-Azal rejected his half-brother's claims, but his lack of charisma caused him to lose most of his influence among Bābīs. Meanwhile, the movement led by Bahā' Allāh dropped the Bābī emphasis on literal holy war, instead proclaiming that non-violent proselytizing was the true *jihād*.[73]

Most interestingly, the increased reverence for Bahā' Allāh led to a corresponding denigration of the Bāb. While still acknowledging the Bāb's prophetic authority, Bahā' Allāh and his followers demoted him vis-à-vis Bahā' Allāh; no longer was he the Major Manifestation of God for the age, but merely the precursor to Bahā' Allāh, who was the *real* Major Manifestation. The Bāb's chief function, then, was not to be a revealer himself but to prepare the way for Bahā' Allāh, "The-One-Whom God-Will-Make-Manifest." Bahā' Allāh himself frequently referred to the Bāb as "my forerunner," and in Bahā'ī literature, already from an early date, his relation to Bahā' Allāh is explicitly compared to John the Baptist's relation to Jesus.[74] In any case, he is definitely subordinated to Bahā' Allāh, reduced to being a witness to the latter. Consider the following quotations from Bahā'ī writers, which illustrate this demotion:

> The Bāb had made it unequivocally clear that the primary purpose of His Mission was to herald the advent of "Him Whom God shall manifest." The worth of every man and everything, including His own book, the *Bayán*, . . . he made dependent upon approval by the Manifestation of God Who was to come after Him. . . . The entirety of . . . the *Bayán* is one continuous, unbroken paean of praise and adoration, submission to and glorifying of "Him Whom God shall make manifest."[75]

> In the same book [the *Bayán*] and at the same time that the Báb finally uses his full authority to establish the laws of his religious dispensation, he states that his system is to be short-lived and sharply focused. It is to prepare the way for the imminent advent of another, greater revelation. . . . The entire purpose of his system and his cause was to prepare his followers for the recognition and acceptance of a further, greater Manifestation of God soon to come, clarifying thereby the true meaning of the title "Bab."[76]

Here, as in Christian traditions about John the Baptist, we see not only the relegation of the Bāb to the status of forerunner but also the notion that his dispensation is a penultimate one (cf. Matt. 11:12–13//Luke 16:16). And we can well imagine the Bāb, as described by these Bahā'ī authors, employing or having applied to him the sort of language that the Fourth Evangelist uses about and puts into the mouth of the Baptist: "He was not the light, but came to bear witness to the light" (1:8); "for this I came . . . , that he might be manifested" (1:31); "he must increase, but I must decrease" (3:30).[77] Here, as in the case of the John/Jesus relationship, we see (a) a founder figure who believed himself to have a salvific role, yet also alluded to the coming of a figure greater than himself, and (b) a successor figure who both acknowledged his predecessor and relegated him to a preparatory status, implicitly denying to him and his epoch the independent redemptive function he claimed for himself and his epoch. In the latter way, the Bāhā'ī attitude towards the Bāb reproduces Islam's relegation of Jesus to a merely preparatory role, pointing ahead to Muhammad as "the seal of the prophets." In Qur'ān 61:6, for example, Jesus announces the coming of Muhammad after him, "whose name is more highly praised."[78]

This tendency to subordinate the Bāb to Bahā' Allāh frustrated the great British Orientalist, Edward Granville Browne, who was fascinated by the Bāb and traveled all over Persia in 1887–88 seeking information about him. He found to his chagrin, however, that Bahā'īs usually tried to change the subject to Bahā' Allāh.[79] As Browne puts it in his firsthand account, *A Year Amongst the Persians:*

> Rejoiced as I was at the unexpected facilities which appeared to be opening out to me [of finding Bahā'īs who would talk to him, despite the threat of persecution], there was one thing which somewhat distressed me. It was the Báb whom I had learned to regard as a hero, whose works I desired to obtain and peruse, yet of him no account appeared to be taken. I questioned my [Bahā'ī] friend about this, and learned . . . that much had taken place amongst the Bábís since those events of which Gobineau's vivid and sympathetic record [of the Bāb and his movement] had so strangely moved me.[80] That record was written while Mírzá Yaḥyá, *Ṣubḥ-i-Ezel* . . . was undisputed vicegerent of the Báb, and before the great schism occurred which convulsed the Bábí community. Now, I found, the Báb's writings were but little read even amongst his followers, for Behá had arisen as "He whom God shall manifest" (the promised deliverer foretold by the Báb), and it was with his commands, his writings, and his precepts that the Bábí messengers went forth from Acre to the faithful in Persia.[81]

One can easily imagine an admirer of John the Baptist saying something similar in the middle or end of the first century CE:

> Happy as I was to finally encounter members of the movement started by John, there was one thing which somewhat distressed me. It was John whom I had learned to regard as a hero, whose wisdom I desired to hear; yet of him no account appeared to be taken amongst most of those who claimed to revere him. Now, I found, the genuine teachings of the Baptist were but little remembered even amongst his followers, for Jesus had arisen as "the Coming One" (the promised deliverer foretold by the Baptist), and it was with his commands, his parables, and his precepts that the baptizing messengers went forth from Jerusalem to the faithful in Palestine and the Diaspora.

Yet the absorption of the Baptist movement by the Jesus movement in the first century, like that of the Bābī movement by the Bahā'ī movement in the nineteenth, was incomplete. Browne still found in his travels in Persia some reminders of the earlier, more heterogeneous situation. While most Bābīs had come to recognize Bāhā᾽ Allāh as the complete fulfillment of the hopes the Bāb had generated, Browne encountered some who rejected or remained agnostic about those claims, thinking that the arrival of "The-One-Whom-God-Will-Make-Manifest" was, or might be, a hope for the future. Browne describes, for example, an encounter in 1888 with a young Bābī who refused to identify either with the Bāhā᾽īs or the Bāhā᾽-skeptics. "When asked by the Behá'ís," he writes, "to recognize Behá as the one foretold by the Báb, he would only reply, 'His Highness the Point of Utterance [= the Bāb] is sufficient for me'; yet he did not categorically deny the claims of Behá like the Ezelís."[82]

This is the sort of viewpoint that the predominantly Christian nature of our sources about John the Baptist mostly prevents us from seeing,[83] but that probably existed in the first century and beyond. For those Christian sources, as for Bāhā᾽ī sources about the Bāb, the situation is all or nothing: one either accepts that John's main goal was to point to Jesus, or one has entirely missed the purpose of his ministry. But in the beginning the situation was probably much more mixed: there were Baptists who became part of the Jesus movement, Baptists who resisted the claims made for Jesus, and Baptists who were unsure whether those claims were true or not. And it is this sort of mixed-up situation that helps explain the sometimes contradictory attitude of the New Testament and later Christian sources towards the Baptist. A play is made for followers of the Baptist who are unsure about Jesus, but it is also emphasized that the Baptist was secondary to Jesus.[84] And this mixed message probably goes back to Jesus himself.

. . . .

Conclusion: John and Jesus

The main concern here, however, is not with Jesus but with John. How, overall, did he regard his erstwhile disciple? This question comes up more than once in the Gospel tradition (see Matt. 11:2–3//Luke 7:18–19; John 3:26), and when it does, John does not disparage Jesus. This seems plausible; if he *had* done so, it seems unlikely that Christian memory would have retained him in the role of witness to Jesus, even appealing to his positive attitude in an indirect way in a passage that has a strong claim to historicity (Mark 11:27–33).[85] If John had been as qualified in his praise of Jesus as Jesus later was about him ("the least person in the dominion of God is greater than he"), he probably would not have become an established element in the Christian history of salvation.

But this does not mean that John was the full-throated advocate of Jesus's messiahship that Christian sources picture him being. Early on in their association, he probably realized that the young man from Nazareth was not an ordinary disciple; indeed, I have argued elsewhere that, even before becoming part of the Baptist movement, Jesus had already gained a reputation for healings and other extraordinary powers.[86] With a generosity of spirit not always characteristic of the founders of religious movements, John decided not to treat Jesus as a rival but to give him free rein and acknowledge his gifts, putting him on a par with himself and appointing him as his emissary to places removed from his own sphere of activity. He may even have acknowledged that Jesus's powers transcended his own, as Elisha's transcended those of Elijah—though not that they were of a completely different nature, any more than Elisha's ministry differed substantially from Elijah's. And he probably saw Jesus's activities, as well as his own, as signs that the age of redemption had indeed broken into the world with his own baptismal ministry and that all that remained was for the Messiah to come and finish the job.

But what did John expect the Messiah to do, and how did he expect the redemptive process to be completed? These questions are interrelated with the one explored in the next and final chapter, where the reasons for John's execution by Herod Antipas are examined.

CHAPTER SIX

Herod Antipas

The Gospels and Josephus on the Death of John

John, like Jesus, was executed by one of the supreme authorities in Palestine—in John's case, Herod Antipas. Josephus (*Ant.* 18.116–119) and the Synoptic Gospels (Mark 6:17–29//Matt. 14:3–12, Luke 9:9) independently attest that Antipas put John to death,[1] though the motivation for the act varies in Mark, Matthew, and Josephus.[2] In Mark, Antipas is sympathetic and even reverential towards John, and tries to keep him alive. He only executes him because of the scheming of his wife, Herodias, who bears a grudge against John because John has denounced her marriage to Antipas as incestuous.[3] She uses the occasion of Antipas's birthday, her daughter's erotic dance, and Antipas's rash promise to give the daughter anything she wants to manipulate him into the execution.[4]

The picture Josephus paints is quite different: Antipas himself feels alarmed by John's popularity with the crowds and determines to have him killed before things get out of hand and a revolt ensues.[5] As Ernst Lohmeyer points out, Josephus implies that Antipas's fears were not unfounded, since according to him John called on the Jewish people to unite together[6] by joining in his baptismal movement (χρωμένοις βαπτισμῷ συνιέναι). Josephus, then, presents John as a teacher of virtue but also something of an activist or even a revolutionary,[7] who is rightly feared by Herod.[8] Mark, on the other hand, presents him as a moral rigorist who objects to Herod's marriage but is protected by Herod himself.

Matthew splits the difference between Mark and Josephus in an interesting way. He retains the basic Markan story (the occasion for John's execution is Herodias's hatred for him and Salome's dance at Antipas's birthday party) but gives it a different motivation, one consistent with Josephus: Antipas *wants* to kill John and is only restrained from doing so by his fear of the people's displeasure (Matt. 14:5).[9] Both Josephus and Matthew, then, mention John's popularity with the crowds, the first as the reason for Antipas's desire to do away with him, the second as the reason he stays his hand. Both may be right: for a time Antipas held back, not wanting to anger the populace, but when he saw that they were so enamored of John that the situation was growing dangerous, he decided to kill him (*Ant.* 18.118). Matthew and Josephus, then, supports each other on the politically explosive nature of John's popularity.

The situation, as noted, is different in Mark's Gospel, where Antipas is well intentioned toward John but confused, and tries but fails to keep him alive in the face of his wife's animosity. This is quite similar to the failed attempt of another weak leader in Mark, Pontius Pilate, to keep alive another Jewish prisoner—Jesus. In both cases, we may suspect that the portrayal of the ruler's sympathy is largely an apologetic device to demonstrate the spiritual power of the martyr and the perfidy of those who manipulate the ruler into putting him to death. With Pilate and Jesus, as with Antipas and John, Josephus paints a darker picture that seems intrinsically more credible.[10] And Mark's narrative of John's death also contains lurid, soap-opera-like features and biblical echoes (for example, "up to half my kingdom" [my trans.] in 6:23; cf. Esth. 5:3) that make it more questionable historically than Josephus's sober and prosaic account.[11]

. . . .

Revolution and Self-Critique

Josephus is probably right that Antipas had good cause to fear the revolutionary tendencies of the movement the Baptist spawned.[12] This conclusion, however, raises a question about my analysis in chapter 2. There I argued, on the basis of the Q saying about raising up Abrahamic children out of stones (Matt. 3:7b-10//Luke 3:7-9) and Josephus's reference to John's appeal to "others" (*Ant.* 18.118), that John challenged the notion of the eternal election of Israel. Indeed, this Q saying implies that some Gentiles have a better claim to membership in God's kingdom than some Jews.[13] Is that consistent with my present assertion that Antipas viewed John as a revolutionary leader who might unite the Jews of his realm against him? Is there not a tension between Josephus's term συνιέναι ("unite themselves") and the internal division implied by Matt. 3:7b-10//Luke 3:7-9? Does not the latter suggest that John believed that some of his fellow Jews had placed themselves outside the bounds of God's covenant with Abraham? And, if John believed that, would Antipas have feared him as a firebrand who might unite Jews and Gentiles against him?

The answer to all these questions is, I believe, yes. The leaders of rigorist, millenarian religious movements often castigate their countrymen for apostasy from God's will, warning that they will be cut off from their favored status unless they repent, and this can make them unpopular with their contemporaries, especially religious and secular elites. But that does not necessarily make these judgmental prophets politically irrelevant; on the contrary, their denunciations often have a broad appeal to sectors of society, especially the disenfranchised, who see their leaders as corrupt—a contrast that is echoed in the Gospel references to John's embrace by "tax collectors and sinners" even while he is rejected by religious elites (Matt. 21:31–32; Luke 7:29–30).

Norman Cohn's classic study of medieval millenarian movements, *The Pursuit of the Millennium,* offers several examples of this sort of combination. For example, the early twelfth-century prophet, Tanchelm of Antwerp,

> like so many other wandering preachers, . . . started by condemning unworthy clerics . . . and then broadened his attack to cover the Church as a whole. He taught not merely that sacraments were invalid if administered by unworthy hands but also that, things being as they were, holy orders had lost all meaning, sacraments were no better than pollutions, and churches no better than brothels. This propaganda proved so effective that people stopped partaking of the Eucharist and going to church. And, in general, as the Chapter [of Utrecht] ruefully remarked [in a letter to the Archbishop of Cologne], things came to such a pass that the more one despised the Church the holier one was held to be. . . .
>
> According to the Chapter of Utrecht, Tanchelm formed his followers into a blindly devoted community that regarded itself as the only true church, and he reigned over them like a messianic king. . . .
>
> The canons in the Chapter of Utrecht freely admitted their helplessness. Tanchelm, they insisted, had long been a danger to the church of Utrecht; if he were to be released and allowed to resume his work they would not be able to resist him and the diocese would be lost to the Church without hope of recovery. And even after his death (he is believed to have been killed by a priest, around 1115) Tanchelm long continued to dominate the town of Antwerp. A congregation of canons specially established for the purpose was unable to counteract his influence but on the contrary succumbed to it.[14]

Here we have a prophet who regards himself and his adherents as the only true church, who denounces the rest of the church as apostate, and who acts like a messianic king. The authorities are rightly upset by his wide influence, and one of them kills him, but (like John the Baptist and Jesus) he continues to sway people even after his death.

Similarly, the renegade monk Jacob, known as "the Master of Hungary," the leader of the so-called *Pastoureaux* ("shepherds"), preached, surrounded by an armed guard,

> attacking the Mendicants as hypocrites and vagabonds, the Cisterians as lovers of land and property, the Premonstratensians as proud and gluttonous, the canons regular as half-secular fast-breakers; and his

attacks on the Roman Curia knew no bounds. His followers were taught to regard the sacraments with contempt and to see in their own gatherings the sole embodiment of the truth. . . . The murder of a priest was regarded as particularly praiseworthy; according to Jacob it could be atoned for by a drink of wine. It is not surprising that the clergy watched the spread of this movement with horror.[15]

Nor is it surprising that the movement was eventually suppressed by violence and Jacob himself cut to pieces.

The most interesting medieval parallel to the incendiary potential of a mass penitential movement such as the Baptist's, however, is the flagellants of the thirteenth and fourteenth centuries. Religiously motivated flagellants first appeared in Italy in the mid-thirteenth century, catalyzed by famine, a serious outbreak of plague, and the incessant warfare between the Guelphs and the Ghibellines:

> Yet all these afflictions were felt to be but a prelude to a final and over-whelming catastrophe. A chronicler remarked that during the flagellant processions people behaved as though they feared that as a punishment for their sins God was about to destroy them all by earthquake and by fire from on high. It was in a world which seemed poised on the brink of the abyss that these penitents cried out, as they beat themselves and threw themselves upon their faces: "Holy Virgin take pity on us! Beg Jesus Christ to spare us!" and: "Mercy, mercy! Peace, peace!"—calling ceaselessly, we are told, until the fields and mountains seemed to echo with their prayers and musical instruments fell silent and love-songs died away.[16]

It was not in Italy but in Germany, however, that the movement really took root and assumed more militant features. Here, too, it was explicitly apocalyptic, warning of the judgment hanging over humanity unless it changed its ways; indeed, the heavenly letter that inspired the movement declared that God had first decided to kill all living things on earth but had been moved by the intercession of the Virgin to grant humankind one last chance to repent. Such warnings, with their threat of punishment if ignored, were given sharper emphasis by the Black Death of 1348–49, which according to modern estimates killed a third of the population of western Europe.

The movement that emerged out of this maelstrom was sharply anticleri-cal; indeed, if a priest (or a woman) entered the circle of flagellants, the whole action became invalid and had to be recommenced. This anticlericalism mir-rored that of the populace as a whole; clerics themselves, in fact, were often the sharpest critics of their fellows. The flagellant leaders—who had to be laymen—usurped priestly prerogatives, imposing penances and granting absolution, both during public flagellations and in private—a usurpation that shocked both ecclesiastical and secular authorities. As the movement gathered steam in the wake of the Black Death, it became more radical in other ways as well. Leadership passed into the hands of dissident or apostate priests, and there were masses of new recruits from the margins of society, including vagabonds, bankrupts, outlaws, and other criminals. Religious elites became a special target:

> As the flagellant movement turned into a messianic mass movement its behaviour came to resemble that of its forerunners, the People's Crusades. The German flagellants in particular ended as uncompromising enemies of the Church who not only condemned the clergy but utterly repudiated the clergy's claim to supernatural authority. They denied that the sacrament of the Eucharist had any meaning; and when the host was elevated they refused to show it reverence. They made a practice of interrupting church services, saying that their own ceremonies and hymns alone had value. They set themselves above pope and clergy, on the grounds that whereas ecclesiastics could point only to the Bible and to the tradition as the sources of their authority, they themselves had been taught directly by the Holy Spirit which had sent them out across the world. The flagellants absolutely refused to hear criticism from any cleric; on the contrary . . . they declared that any priest who contradicted them should be dragged from the pulpit and burnt at the stake. . . . At times flagellants would urge the populace on to stone the clergy. Anyone, including any member of their own fraternity, who tried to moderate their fury against the Church did so at his peril. The Pope complained that whenever they had the chance these penitents appropriated ecclesiastical property for their own fraternity; and a French chronicler said that the flagellant movement aimed at utterly destroying the church, taking over its wealth and killing all the clergy. There is no reason to think that either was exaggerating.[17]

While there is nothing in available sources about John the Baptist to suggest that he himself was similarly inclined to violence, these passages illustrate the potential for violence of a mass penitential movement convulsed by millenarian hope and fear. Moreover, the denunciation of the corruption of the church, which is sick from head to toe; the flouting of its sacraments; and the denial of its ultimacy in the name of one's own perfectionist group—all this negates the traditional view of the church as the ark of salvation and comes close to John's denunciation of elites who rely on descent from Abraham to shield them from "the wrath to come" (cf. Matt. 21:32//Luke 7:29–30, in which elites reject John the Baptist, but tax collectors and sinners embrace him).

....

The Jewish Identity of Herod Antipas

In light of all this, Josephus's portrayal of John as a potential revolutionary whose danger is rightly sensed by Antipas seems more plausible than Mark's portrayal of him as a holy man whom the monarch indulgently protects. But it would be a mistake to dismiss the Markan story altogether. While some differences between the two accounts cannot be reconciled,[18] they show intriguing commonalities. Both, for example, link John's death with Antipas's scandalous marriage to Herodias, though in different ways.[19] The basic stories, moreover, are compatible with each other, if we accept that Matthew and Josephus are right that Antipas wanted to get rid of John. In a colonial system in which imperial authorities exercise their dominion through local client rulers, an attack on the religious validity of the client ruler's marriage comes close to open sedition,[20] since such rulers depend not only on imperial force but also on the support of a native populace strongly influenced by religion. On this issue, the Herodians were always on the defensive because of their Idumean background, their usurpation of the Hasmonean dynasty, and their alliance with Rome.[21]

Herod Antipas was not indifferent to his reputation among his Jewish subjects, and that included his religious reputation. Indeed, he probably would not have lasted as tetrarch for forty-three years (4 BCE–39 CE) if he had systematically outraged public opinion in this regard. On the contrary, he did defend Jewish interests, and he seems to have been careful not to flout the Torah publicly. He appears to have made a habit of attending the pilgrimage festivals in Jerusalem (cf. Luke 23:7; Josephus, *Ant.* 18.122), and he probably led the delegation of "the four sons of the king [Herod the Great]" who successfully appealed to Tiberius against Pontius Pilate's decision to introduce golden shields into the holy city, an offense against Jewish sensibilities (see Philo, *Embassy* 299–305).[22] This may have been the cause of the hostility between Antipas and Pilate mentioned in Luke 23:12, if that is a historical recollection,[23] though Pilate's murder of some of Antipas's Galilean subjects who were engaged in a religious rite (Luke 13:1) may also have played a role. In any event, as Mary Smallwood notes, the existence of a party of "Herodians" among early first-century Jews (cf. Mark 3:6; 12:13//Matt. 22:16) may be a testimony to Antipas's relative popularity."[24]

Another indication of Antipas's sensitivity to Jewish religious concerns is the fact that his coinage avoids pictorial representations, which were considered by many Jews to be a violation of the Second Commandment— despite the fact that his own palace at Tiberias was full of animal images (see

Josephus, *Life* 65). Morten Jensen argues that, while Antipas personally did not object to images, he avoided them on his coinage out of respect for his countrymen's scruples. Similarly, though he tried to curry favor with the emperor Caligula by striking a coin dedicated to him in 38/39 CE ("Antipas the Tetrarch to Gaius Caesar Germanicus"), this act of homage was far less questionable from a Jewish point of view than that of his nephew Agrippa I, who struck a coin in the same year featuring an *image* of Caligula.[25] Jensen argues that Antipas was the Jewish ruler in the Hasmonean and Herodian periods who adhered most closely to the aniconic tradition in his coinage.[26] This is ironic, since Josephus judges him harshly for perceived infractions of Jewish law and morality but presents Agrippa as a model of Jewish piety (*Ant.* 19.293–296, 331). It has also been argued by Monika Bernett, drawing on earlier work by Manfred Lämmer, that the stadium in Tiberias, which she thinks Antipas built, was of a peculiarly "kosher" variety: "There were no sacrifices, no holy processions with cult images, and probably no iconic representations of the honored imperial persons."[27] As Jensen points out, however, this is essentially an argument from silence, and we cannot be sure that the stadium was constructed in Tiberias's time.[28] At least in his coinage, though, Antipas seems to have successfully negotiated the challenge of recognizing the claims of the Romans without violating Jewish sensibilities.

This apparent caution contrasts with the portrayal of Antipas in Josephus, who, as Jensen points out, tends to depict him, like his father, Herod the Great, as impious—in Antipas's case, because of his founding of Tiberias on a gravesite (*Ant.* 18.38), his murder of John the Baptist (*Ant.* 18.116–119), and the undue influence of his wife, Herodias (*Ant.* 18.255).[29] As Jensen notes, however, Josephus's negative descriptions of Antipas often have a way of deconstructing themselves. His murder of John the Baptist, for example, though brutal, is presented as effective in preventing the revolution that John was about to inspire (*Ant.* 18.118). And although he blames Antipas for founding Tiberias on the site of tombs, "knowing that this settlement was contrary to the law and tradition of the Jews,"[30] the larger context of the passage softens the condemnation by presenting Antipas as a benefactor to many of the settlers, whom he liberated from slavery and gave gifts of houses and land.

Moreover, the legal basis for Josephus's statement about the unlawfulness of building on a gravesite is unclear. The Torah does not actually condemn building on abandoned graves; it only provides rites for purifying those who have become ritually defiled by touching dead bodies (Num. 19:11–22). Josephus's wording in *Ant.* 18.38 ("our law declares that such settlers are unclean for seven days") seems to generalize this uncleanness to anyone who lives in such a place, but it also seems to imply that, after the initial period of uncleanness, impurity is no longer a problem. Lee Levine has pointed out other problems with Josephus's statements about the uncleanness of the Tiberians: "True, Numbers 19:11–16 does speak of the impurity incurred by contact with the dead. However, later Jewish tradition applied these rules to the priestly class exclusively. . . . How a potentially large urban population might be affected is unclear. Furthermore, if indeed the graves had been obliterated, then the obstacles to settlement should have been minimal. Later rabbinic law, for examples, notes a series of possible rectifications which would have made such land usable" [citing t. 'Ohal. 17–18].[31] Levine theorizes that Josephus's own bad relations with the Tiberians during the Jewish Revolt may be part of the reason he slurs them. And Jensen points out that Josephus himself did not always act as if residence in Tiberias were unlawful, since he did in fact visit the city several times (see, for example, *Life* 91–93, 155–157, 164, 188).

It is true that some rabbinic stories speak of R. Simeon b. Yoḥai, a second-century rabbi, cleansing Tiberias of its impurity (Gen. Rab. 79:6–7; b. Šabb. 33b-34a), and Levine believes that these stories probably have a historical basis and reflect priestly uneasiness about living in the city[32]—uneasiness that Josephus, a priest himself, may have shared. But such uneasiness was probably not widespread; as Levine points out, a number of prominent rabbis lived in the city in the late first and early second centuries. It is doubtful, therefore, that many people shared Josephus's belief that Antipas's founding of Tiberias was a stain on his character.

Herod Antipas, then, showed sensitivity to his reputation as a Jewish leader, and this was undoubtedly at least in part because he recognized what a powerful influence Judaism exercised within his realm. Consequently any serious attack on his religious legitimacy, including the legitimacy of his marriage, would have posed a threat to his power—and may have been intended as such. This would have been especially the case if John, Nathan-like (cf. 2 Sam. 12), denounced Antipas for the marriage, as Mark 6:18//Matt. 14:4 implies, perhaps even doing so in public.[33]
. . . .

Sedition and Attack on Royal Marriages

This principle that an attack on a ruler's marriage is often a veiled threat to his sovereignty can be illustrated by various instances ancient and modern. In the early fifth century the Bishop of Constantinople, John Chrysostom, denounced Eudoxia, the wife of the emperor Arcadius, as a "Jezebel" for supporting a churchman who had intrigued against him. In retaliation, she had Chrysostom deposed as bishop. He, however, was popular in the city, and riots broke out, followed by an earthquake, at which point the superstitious Eudoxia recalled Chrysostom. After this there was a period of amity, but later Chrysostom became enraged by the pagan nature of the ceremonies conducted to inaugurate an image of Eudoxia, and he preached a sermon beginning with the words, "Herodias is raging again. Again she is dancing. Again she demands the head of John on a charger." This time, the royal couple decided they had had enough, and Arcadius deposed and exiled Chrysostom. "On the night of his departure a fire broke out that destroyed not only Saint Sophia but the Senate House next door also. Chrysostom and his friends were accused of arson."[34] Some of Chrysostom's adherents were tortured, but since the inquisition was inconclusive they were eventually released. Chrysostom himself carried on an active correspondence with his supporters but died of exhaustion three years later.[35] Whether or not the charges against him and his adherents were true, the incident shows how religious opposition to a ruler's wife can be linked with popular unrest and charges of sedition.

Similarly, in the Carolingian period, scandalous marriages by two kings, Louis the Pious (!) and Lothar II, stirred up political opposition and popular resentment. As Stuart Airlie emphasizes, the seriousness of these challenges reflected the public and sacral nature of Carolingian royalty: "The royal household was conceived as a model for good order in the kingdom at large, in accordance with divine commandments. Harmony in the royal household was necessary for harmony to exist in the realm as a whole; the realm, in turn, was seen, in this scheme of patrimonial rule, as the royal household writ large."[36] This meant that, if disorder was present within the royal house-hold, the kingdom itself was threatened and drastic action called for; and it is possible that remnants of a similar ideology were present in Herodian Palestine as an inheritance from the Hasmonean monarchy. In any event, the Carolingian theology of royal marriage is reflected in a negative way in the case of Louis the Pious, since the rebels against his rule in the 830s focused their complaints on the allegedly adulterous behavior of his queen, Judith. As Airlie puts it, these accusations about the king's marriage "were a way of cod-ing an attack on Louis' government."[37]

The second Carolingian instance, that of Lothar II, was more compli-cated. It began when Lothar tried to divorce his queen Theutberga, whom he had wed in 855 for political reasons, and to marry his old flame, Waldrada. To pave the way for this change, he accused Theutberga in 857 of commit-ting incest—sodomite incest at that—with his brother Hubert, then aborting the fetus that was conceived. This sensational case became an international cause célèbre and stirred up all levels of society, with Hincmar, archbishop of Reims, playing the John the Baptist role by denouncing the king's charges against his wife as spurious and therefore his divorce and remarriage as sin-ful. Pope Nicholas I also got into the act, berating Lothar in 863 for letting the needs of his body control him. As Airlie paraphrases Nicholas, "A king who could not rule his body was unworthy to rule his kingdom"[38]—a moral that would also apply to Antipas as pictured in Mark 6:14–29.[39] In 865 the political pressure generated by these protests forced Lothar to take Theutberga back and repudiate Waldrada.

To Lothar's opponents, the denouement of the affair confirmed that he had rendered himself unfit for royal rule by his unseemly marital actions. His authority was considerably weakened by the scandal, and when in 869 he died of a fever contracted on a trip to Italy to curry favor with Nicholas's successor as Pope, Hincmar and others saw his death "as the angry judgment of a God whose patience had been abused once too often . . . not only a manifestation of divine wrath against the divorce-raddled Lothar but against all his kingdom."[40] Once again, then, a questionable divorce and remarriage was seen not just as a private affair but as fateful for the kingdom as a whole, and those who denounced it presented themselves as the guardians of the kingdom against divine judgment. It is easy to see how such a theology could contribute to political turmoil and even revolt.

Indeed, revolt *was* the result of a similar case later in the Middle Ages. This involved King John of England, who in 1199 had his marriage to his first wife annulled and in 1200 wed Isabella of Angoulême in France, who was the heiress of a splendid fortune in gold and lands.[41] Isabella, however, was already betrothed, and perhaps legally married, to a French noble, Hugh IX de Lusignan. Nicholas Vincent argues that the reason Hugh had not yet consummated his marriage with Isabella was that she was underage; in carrying her off, therefore, John committed two sacrileges, marrying a minor and taking a bride who was legally bound to another man.[42] This led the Lusignans, who were soon joined by other barons and King Philip II of France, into rebelling against John. The net result was that John lost his major territories in France, which not only delivered a blow to his prestige but also put a major strain on his finances. The measures he took to alleviate the strain only made matters worse by increasing the financial burden on the people, many of whom blamed the chain of events on John's "Jezebel," Isabella, who was also accused of adultery and incest.[43] As W. G. van Emden points out, these events repeated in history themes found earlier in two fictional twelfth-century "epics of revolt," *Girart de Vienne* and *Girart de Roussillon*. Here Charlemagne's susceptibility to women and consequent misalliances bring disastrous wars on his kingdom.[44]

A case similar to that of King John occurred in thirteenth-century Aragon, where Alvaro, the Count of Urgel, married Costanza, the daughter of Pedro de Moncada and niece of James I of Aragon. When the dowry James had promised Alvaro failed to materialize, Alvaro repudiated Costanza and married Cecilia, the sister of Count Roger of Foix; later, however, he returned to Costanza, then abandoned her again for Cecilia, in each case arguing for the legality of the marriage to which he was presently committed. This turned on three questions, summarized by James Brundage: "first, whether Alvaro and Costanza were of marriageable age (i.e., fourteen and twelve respectively) at the time of their wedding; second, whether the marriage was consummated then or later; and third, whether both parties freely consented to the marriage."[45] As with several of the other cases mentioned above, things ended badly for the much-married count: King James invaded the county of Urgel, and Alvaro was forced to take refuge with Cecilia's family at Foix, where, in Brundage's words, "he fell ill and in March 1268 died at the age of twenty-eight, having spent exactly one-half of his life in litigation about his marriages."[46] According to Brundage, the prime mover in the whole affair was actually King James, whose "aim was to bring the county of Urgel more closely under the control of the Aragonese crown." For this purpose he married off his niece to Alvaro, but when Alvaro balked at James's stinginess and left Costanza for Cecilia, James used the marital issue as a pretext for military intervention in and occupation of Urgel, thus accomplishing his primary purpose of control in a more direct way.[47]

For present-day readers, however, the most famous instance of a disputed royal marriage linked with political unrest is that of Henry VIII in the sixteenth century. The lawfulness of Henry's marriage to Anne Boleyn was not just a religious issue but also a political one, and he treated protests against the marriage as sedition.[48] After his death, these protests were transferred to the fruit of his union with Boleyn, his daughter Elizabeth; many Catholics viewed her birth and hence her claim to the throne as illegitimate, and some tried to depose her in favor of Mary, Queen of Scots, in the unsuccessful Northern Rebellion of 1569.[49] Here again, political revolt was linked with protest against an illegitimate royal marriage.

The relevance for the study of Antipas and John the Baptist of this survey of "illegitimate" marriages by rulers can be summarized in three points:

(1) In a state in which religion is central, the legality of a ruler's marriage is not a private affair but perceived by broad swaths of society to involve the spiritual and social welfare of the nation. Forces opposed to the ruler, therefore, can use the marriage's perceived illegality as a way of attacking the government.

(2) These resistant forces may be both internal and external to the state, and the latter is especially common when the ruler has entered into an alliance with a foreign power through marriage.

(3) In some cases the attack on the ruler's marriage can help precipitate a revolt.

All these points have correspondences in the story of Antipas and John the Baptist. Since most of Antipas's subjects were Jews, he had to be careful not to commit overt violations of Jewish law—and, as noted, he generally was careful not to do so. He probably did not think that his marriage to Herodias constituted such a violation, as the relevant scriptures, Lev. 18:16 and 20:21, do not make clear whether the ban on marrying one's brother's wife includes the case of a *half*-brother's wife.[50] Therefore John's attack on the legality of Antipas's marriage was a potentially seditious act. Moreover, it was not only the good opinion of local Jews that was important to Antipas, but also that of non-Jews, both within his realm and in neighboring areas, especially the Nabatean kingdom.[51] Many of these Gentiles were probably offended by Antipas's repudiation of his former wife. John's denunciation of Antipas's marital status, therefore, may have resonated not only with his Jewish subjects but also with his non-Jewish subjects and neighbors.[52] It may not be accidental, then, that Josephus reports that Antipas took action against John when the latter's sermons stirred up both the Jewish crowds and "others" (τῶν ἄλλων συστρεφομένων, *Ant.* 18.118). Carl Kraeling suggests that Herod's divorce in 27 CE of a Nabatean princess, the daughter of King Aretas IV, in order to marry Herodias, created volatility among his Jewish and non-Jewish subjects, and that John's denunciation of this marriage threatened to ignite this political dynamite. As Kraeling puts it: "In view of the explosive situation created by the flight of the Nabataean princess [to her father Aretas in Petra when she heard of Antipas's plan to divorce her],[53] the sudden appearance of a man in the Jordan Valley and in Peraea publicly denouncing Antipas and saying, 'It is not lawful for thee to have thy brother's wife' was not only embarrassing, it was politically explosive. It meant aligning the pious Jewish inhabitants of Peraea with those of Arabic stock against their sovereign and thus fomenting sedition and encouraging insurrection."[54]

Though Herod seems to have succeeded in the short term in damping down revolutionary manifestations by executing John, the grievances stirred up by his divorce and remarriage—now compounded by his execution of John—probably continued to fester, stoking alienation among both Jews and non-Jews in the population. This alienation may have contributed to Herod's sound military defeat by Aretas in 36 CE. Josephus presents this war as catalyzed both by the insult to Aretas's daughter and by a border dispute between Herod and Aretas (*Ant.* 18.113–114), though he also mentions a popular theological interpretation: "But to some of the Jews it seemed that Herod's army had been destroyed by God, and justly so, as a punishment for what he had done to John, who was called the Baptist" (*Ant.* 18.116).[55] Thus Josephus portrays John as being deeply implicated in the Herodian political situation and rightly feared by Herod Antipas, and although he does not mention John's denunciation of Antipas's divorce and remarriage in this regard, it probably aggravated the problem. This is especially true because the divorce and remarriage had something in it to offend both Palestinian Jews and Nabatean Gentiles—two groups that, Josephus hints, were both attracted to John's ministry, a tacit alliance that Antipas feared (*Ant.* 18.118).

....

John the Baptist and "The Violent"

There is one other intriguing bit of evidence that fits with this picture of John as a firebrand. This is a Q logion that some have interpreted as a criticism of John's militant tendencies. Matthew's version runs as follows:

> ἀπὸ δὲ τῶν ἡμερῶν Ἰωάννου τοῦ βαπτιστοῦ ἕως ἄρτι ἡ βασιλεία τῶν οὐρανῶν βιάζεται καὶ βιασταὶ ἁρπάζουσιν αὐτήν. πάντες γὰρ οἱ προφῆται καὶ ὁ νόμος ἕως Ἰωάννου ἐπροφήτευσαν·

> From the days of John the Baptist until now the dominion of heaven has been subjected to violence (or: has acted violently), and violent people take it by force. For all the prophets and the Law prophesied until John. (Matt. 11:12–13, my trans.)

Luke's version is more condensed:

> Ὁ νόμος καὶ οἱ προφῆται μέχρι Ἰωάννου· ἀπὸ τότε ἡ βασιλεία τοῦ θεοῦ εὐαγγελίζεται καὶ πᾶς εἰς αὐτὴν βιάζεται.

> The Law and the prophets were until John; since then the good news of the dominion of God has been preached, and everyone acts violently to get into it. (Luke 16:16, my trans.)

The reconstructions of and interpretations of the underlying Q form are numerous. The main exegetical questions are whether the dominion of heaven suffers violence or itself acts violently, whether this violence is literal or metaphorical, and on which side of the dividing line between "the Law and prophets," on the one hand, and the dominion of God, on the other, John stands. Luke seems to evaluate the violence positively and to make it into a metaphor for pressing forcefully into the spiritual realm of God. But in Matthew the violence seems to be literal and to be evaluated negatively—and most scholars think that Matthew's version is more likely to approximate the original sense of the logion.[56] Here, as in text criticism, the principle is that the more difficult reading is likely original.

The saying, then, seems to associate John with violent people who, since his appearance on the scene, have been trying to establish the dominion of God by force. Ulrich Luz may be right to think of "overzealous followers of the Baptist and of Jesus" with militant tendencies, like those described in John 6:15, who try to force (ἁρπάζειν) Jesus to become king—the very verb used for "forcing" the dominion of God in Matt. 11:12.[57] In our saying,

Jesus criticizes such followers, not John himself directly, but he still associates John with this violent apocalyptic tendency.[58] And such an association is more likely in view of John's background in the Qumran community, which was discussed in chapter 2; the community's War Scroll, which was probably written close to or in John's lifetime,[59] is an extended fantasy about an apocalyptic war by Jewish holy warriors against the Kittim (= Romans) and their Jewish allies. And Herod Antipas belonged to the latter group.

....

Challenges to the Thesis of John's Militancy

David Flusser has challenged this thesis of Johannine militancy by arguing that both the Qumran community and the Baptist, who was influenced by that community, were politically passive with regard to the Romans. Regarding the Qumran community, Flusser claims that "the apparent rejection of radical principles was one of the key elements of the Essene *Weltanschauung*," citing the Essenes' "conditional pacifism"—that is, the idea that one had to be a pacifist *now*, hiding one's hate for the Romans and their allies (see 1QS 9:21–23; Josephus, *J.W.* 2.140). When the end-time came, however, God would unleash his fury and destroy these enemies, and the time of clandestine hatred would be over.[60] Earlier in his book, however, Flusser acknowledges that the Essenes were not always so pacifistic, as the War Scroll shows; they only became so, in his view, when their hope for a quick end failed to materialize.[61] The proof texts for this change in attitude are 1QpHab 7:7–8; 1QH^a 6:4, 15–16; 1QS 9:21–25; 10:17–19; 11:1–2. But this scenario, in which the War Scroll was earlier than the Habbukuk Pesher, the Hodayot, and the Community Rule, does not conform to the consensus of today's scholarship, which makes the War Scroll later than all the other texts cited.[62]

The other key piece of evidence is Luke 3:10–14, in which John instructs the crowds to share their food and garments with the poor, tax collectors not to overcharge, and soldiers not to extort money. Flusser says that this passage shows that "in practical terms, [John] recognized the status of the tax collectors working on behalf of Rome."[63] And, indeed, this summary of John's sociological teaching does not sound very revolutionary. Although John enjoins full-hearted charity and fair dealing, he does not forbid either tax collectors or soldiers to practice their profession, both of which were essential to the smooth functioning of the state. By contrast, the later *Apostolic Tradition* of Pseudo-Hippolytus (16:17) forbids more intrinsic aspects of the soldier's profession, such as taking the military oath and participating in executions.[64] For this reason, however, and because the timeless ethical instruction of the section contrasts with the apocalyptic tension that prevails in the traditions about John in the previous verses (Luke 3:3–9), it is questionable whether Luke 3:10–14 really goes back to the Baptist.[65]

....

Summary

What, then, can we say about John's execution by Herod Antipas? First, that it definitely happened, and probably before Jesus's public ministry was far advanced (cf. Mark 6:14). Second, that Antipas had good reasons for wanting the Baptist out of the way. Not only was he the leader of a religious renewal movement with a large popular following (Mark 1:5 pars.; Josephus, *Ant.* 18.118)—always a threat to a despot—but that movement was explicitly apocalyptic, looking forward to the imminent overthrow of the structures of this world (cf. Matt. 3:10//Luke 3:9, Matt. 3:11–12//Luke 3:1–17). It may, moreover, have united Jews with Gentiles—a dangerous mix for Antipas, especially given the powerful Nabatean kingdom on his eastern border, whose king and populace he had offended by his cavalier divorce of the king's daughter and marriage to Herodias. When John denounced this marriage, therefore, he may have intended to ignite a metaphorical firestorm that would soon be confirmed and completed by a literal firestorm from heaven instituted by God's baptizer-in-fire, the Messiah.

The consequences were predictable: John was arrested and executed. Josephus's account gives us a realistic political motivation for this execution: Antipas was afraid of John's effect on the people. The Synoptic Gospels offer a more lurid scenario, with their vindictive mother, dancing daughter, scripture-echoing king, and head on a platter, and it is doubtful whether they should be followed 100 percent; the story is too good (or too bad) to be true. But the basic point that John denounced Antipas's divorce and remarriage and that this had something to do with his death seems plausible and dovetails nicely with Josephus's Realpolitik analysis.

Conclusion

This study has attempted to grasp the historical figure of John the Baptist by exploring his relationship with several different contexts: the Qumran community, which shaped his thinking and practice; the biblical image of the returning Elijah, with which he came to identify; Jesus of Nazareth, who began as his disciple; and Herod Antipas, who put him to death. It has also explored John's baptismal practice, which was distinctive but partly derived from his experience at Qumran and reinterpreted by both Josephus and the Christian tradition in line with the theology of each. These explorations have permitted different aspects of John to come into focus, and they add up to a coherent picture. Like the Qumranians, and indeed like his disciple Jesus, John was an apocalyptic thinker, expecting an imminent end to the world. Like the Qumranians, he believed that this consummation would overthrow the ruling authorities of his day; therefore it is no surprise that the ruler most directly connected with him, Herod Antipas, put him to death. His apocalypticism also comports with his belief in himself as Elijah, whose return from the dead becomes the harbinger of the new age in Malachi and later Jewish traditions. But, since the line between expectation of an imminent end and belief that the end has begun often thins to the vanishing point,[1] he also seems to have believed that, through his baptismal rite, the new age, with its concomitant gifts of the Spirit and forgiveness of sins, was already sacramentally present.

This last conclusion points up one of the tensions between the results of this historical study about John on the one hand and Christian faith as it has normatively expressed itself on the other. As noted in chapter 4, Christians have usually associated forgiveness of sins, the advent of the Spirit, and the beginning of the new age with Jesus's death and resurrection, not John's baptism. It is symptomatic, as we have seen, that Matthew displaces the phrase "unto the forgiveness of sins" from the account of John's baptism (Mark 1:4) to the description of the atoning effect of Jesus's death (Matt. 26:28). Similarly, the Q saying Matt. 11:12–13//Luke 16:16 seems to place John in the old age ("the Law and the prophets"), before the eschatological divide, rather than in the new age ("the dominion of God")—where he probably thought he belonged.

Nor are these the only tensions with traditional Christian faith that our study has turned up. Christians picture John foretelling the advent of a "Stronger One," the Messiah, whose sandal latch he is unworthy to loosen, and then realizing that Jesus is this Stronger One when he sees the Spirit descend on him at his baptism.[2] This study, on the other hand, has posited that, while John did baptize Jesus and did look forward to the coming of the Messiah, he did not at that time consider Jesus the Messiah. Only towards the end of his life did he begin to consider it a possibility, but still an open question.

All of this is to say that the Christian tradition, in its natural emphasis on the centrality of Jesus, has emptied John's ministry of independent significance. For Christians the baptismal rite taken over from John *does* impart forgiveness through the Spirit—but only because it incorporates its recipients into Jesus's death and resurrection (see, for example, Rom. 6:3–4; Col. 2:12–13). John's own baptism, which preceded those salvific events, was merely their precursor, a shadow of the good things to come, to apply the words of the Epistle to the Hebrews (10:1; cf. 8:5, Col. 2:17). Historically, however, something of the reverse was true. Jesus began his career by shadowing John, first undergoing baptism at his hands—a fact that itself had to be explained by the later church[3]—and then participating in John's baptismal ministry in a way that implied dependence on him and embarrassed subsequent Christians (see John 3:22, 26, 4:1–2). It is only natural, then, that Jesus should have felt the need, when he finally struck out on his own, both to acknowledge his former mentor (the greatest of those born of women) and to relativize him (less than the least in the dominion of God: Matt. 11:11//Luke 7:28). Following Jesus, the Christian tradition has diminished John further. The epitome comes in what are perhaps the last words John speaks in the Fourth Gospel: "He must increase, but I must decrease" (John 3:30). That is exactly what the Christian tradition has done to John: diminished him to magnify Jesus.

This has happened because Christianity naturally focuses on Jesus, interpreting everything from its conviction of his messiahship and his crucial eschatological significance. Since John was remembered as proclaiming the imminent arrival of the Messiah, it was reasoned, he must have been talking about Jesus, and indeed the whole purpose of his own ministry must have been to prepare for him. And since, for Christians, only Jesus's ministry, death, and resurrection inaugurated the new age, imparting the Spirit and forgiveness of sins, John's baptism could not have done so.

As noted, however, this probably does not correspond to John's own self-understanding. In John's view, his baptism was an eschatological sacrament—not only because it *anticipated* the eschaton but because it already *imparted,* through the Spirit, the forgiveness that was intrinsic to God's new age. In his own self-understanding, John did not belong on the side of "the Law and the prophets"; he was already the first citizen in the dominion of God. The coming Davidic Messiah would purge the world of the wicked, but John himself had already performed a more important purgation by proclaiming and becoming the human instrument for a "baptism of repentance unto forgiveness of sins." Christian supersessionism (see glossary), which permeates both the early Christian sources and much Christian scholarship about John, is partially responsible for obscuring the evidence for John's sense of his own salvific importance and restricting him to anticipation. John himself, by contrast, intensifying a tendency already present at Qumran, probably had a partially realized eschatology or, in Joachim Jeremias's formulation (vis-à-vis Jesus), an eschatology in the process of being realized.[4] Despite frequent claims to the contrary, then, "realized eschatology" was not the invention of Jesus;[5] some Jewish apocalypticists already shared in it.[6] And John the Baptist was a bridge figure here between these Jewish apocalypticists, on the one hand, and Jesus and early Christianity, on the other.

This study, then, has called attention to the inaccuracy of sweeping contrasts between the eschatology of John and that of Jesus, such as this classic one from Jeremias: "John the Baptist remains within the framework of *expectation;* Jesus claims to bring *fulfilment.* John still belongs in the realm of the *law,* with Jesus, the *gospel* begins. . . . Here is the gulf which separates the two men, despite all the affinities between them."[7] James Dunn draws the same sort of contrast, but more expansively:

> It is important to recognize that John's ministry was essentially preparatory. John himself did not bring in the End. It was the Coming One who would do that. With John the messianic Kingdom has drawn near but it has not yet come. The note of the unfulfilled "not yet" predominates. John is only the messenger who makes ready the way, the herald who goes before arousing attention and calling for adequate preparation. His baptism is thus preparatory also. It does *not* mark the beginning of the eschatological event; it does *not* initiate into the new age; it is the answer to John's call for preparedness: by receiving the Preparer's baptism the penitent prepares himself to receive the Coming One's baptism.[8]

Jeremias and Dunn present a thinly scholasticized version of the traditional Christian conception of John, which is found already in the New Testament. One of the chief aims of this study has been to challenge the adequacy of this reconstruction of the thought of the historical Baptist.

....

A Slanted History

It would seem, then, that the early Christians distorted history when they made John's ministry exclusively anticipatory and focused on Jesus. The following points, however, balance this judgment.

First, the Christian tradition itself, from the New Testament onward, is not univocal about John. The main line of that tradition presents him as significant only in relation to "the Stronger One," Jesus, in whose messiahship he believed from the start. But the early Christian tradition also contains Matt. 11:2–6//Luke 7:18–23, in which John, towards the end of his life, seems to be considering for the first time the *possibility* that Jesus might be the Messiah. Sending messengers (from prison, in Matthew) to Jesus, he asks whether or not Jesus is "the Coming One." Jesus responds with an implicit affirmation and a somewhat threatening warning, apparently directed to his former teacher as well as to others: "Blessed is the one who takes no offense at me" (my trans.). The passage does not record John's positive response to this affirmation; we must assume there was none.

As at many other points, therefore, the tradition here contains a contradiction; and it was observation of such contradictions, and an unwillingness to ignore or explain them away, that helped give rise to modern historical criticism of the Bible.[9] Among other merits, that criticism has revealed a more human John the Baptist as well as a more human Jesus of Nazareth—a Jesus who, for example, can threaten his former teacher and subsequently undermine him even as he heaps praises on his head (Matt. 11:11//Luke 7:28). If this revelation poses a problem for Christian dogmatics, it may turn out to be a creative challenge, one that helps us see something about the human side of the Chalcedonian formulation "true God and true man."

Second, the challenge posed by the apparent distortion of John's role in the main line of Christian tradition is in some ways analogous to that posed by the phenomenon of Christian interpretation of the Old Testament, beginning with the New Testament. If John, from the Christian point of view, erred in not recognizing Jesus as the Messiah whose advent he prophesied, the Old Testament writers, from the Christian point of view, erred in thinking that their prophecies of eschatological advent referred to their own time, rather than to one centuries later. A less polemical way of saying this is to assert that the New Testament's hermeneutic, like the hermeneutic of other Second Temple Jews (and indeed like the hermeneutic of the later writers of the Old Testament itself), is a creative rereading of Old Testament traditions in the light of later concerns and circumstances.[10] The comparison between the creative reinterpretation of John's mission and the creative interpretation of the Old Testament is especially apt because, as we have just seen, some

Christian theology, beginning with the Q saying Matt. 11:12–13//Luke 16:16, puts John on the Old Testament side of the eschatological ledger. The charge that Christians misinterpret John's ministry, then, is analogous to the charge that they twist the Old Testament scriptures when they interpret the Old Testament as a series of prophecies about Jesus.[11] Over the past twenty centuries, non-Christians have often vociferously expressed this charge.[12]

A mature Christian response to this challenge is the assertion that later events can reveal new meanings in old writings, meanings perhaps hidden from the authors themselves.[13] This sort of hermeneutical theory is neither a modern nor a Christian invention. In the Habakkuk Pesher from Qumran, for example, the author says that God disclosed his *words* to the biblical prophets but their *meaning* centuries later to the Teacher of Righteousness. The latter revealed, among many other things, that the last days would extend beyond what the prophets themselves expected (that is, until the Teacher's own time), "for God's revelations are truly mysterious" (1QpHab 7:1–8). Here the author clearly implies that the prophets misunderstood their own words, at least as far as timing is concerned.[14] Eighteen hundred years later, the mystical poet William Blake developed a similar hermeneutical theory, claiming, for example, that he understood John Milton's poetry better than Milton himself.[15] The true poet, for Blake, is one who is inspired to say things that transcend his own understanding or conscious will.[16] Later, in the twentieth century, Harold Bloom spoke of one "strong poet" interpreting another as an act that "always proceeds by a *misreading* of the prior poet, an act of creative correction that is actually and necessarily a misinterpretation"[17]—a misinterpretation from a technical point of view but, in the successor's mind, a creative correction that conveys the true meaning of the predecessor's words.[18] As Dennis Feeney said in a BBC radio discussion of Roman satire, "Poets always create their own predecessors."[19]

So, the Christian apologist might say, John the Baptist did not know that he was pointing to Jesus as Messiah—but he was. And he did not know that the forgiveness he proclaimed would be achieved through Jesus's death and resurrection, to which the church related the baptismal practice it took over from him. But it was.

What is the value of pointing up the discrepancy between what John himself thought he was doing and what Jesus and the later Christian tradition thought? A similar question is raised by research into the historical Jesus: is not the *real* Jesus the one who has been transmitted by Christian tradition rather than a reconstructed historical figure who may be a figment of the scholar's imagination?[20] If one is not primarily motivated by a desire to debunk traditional views, what is the value of this sort of historical inquiry? Does it not just raise unnecessary questions about what the Gospels proclaim?

One recalls the crucial paragraph from Julius Wellhausen's 1882 letter of resignation from his position as professor of theology at the University of Greifswald: "I became a theologian because the scientific treatment of the Bible interested me; only gradually did I come to understand that a professor of theology also has the practical task of preparing the students for service in the Protestant Church, and that I am not adequate to this practical task, but that instead despite all caution on my own part I make my hearers unfit for their office. Since then my theological professorship has been weighing heavily on my conscience."[21] Should historical work on John the Baptist also weigh heavily on the conscience of a scholar who claims to be Christian? By writing a book like this one, has he helped make theological students unfit for their ministry (assuming that any of them read it)? After all, John's witness to Jesus, like the Old Testament's witness to him, is an important article of faith for most Christians. Is it worth challenging?

I think it is, first, because the truth is the truth, and Christians ultimately have nothing to fear from it: "For we cannot do anything against the truth, but only for the truth" (2 Cor. 13:8). The observations upon which a book such as this is based arise largely out of the biblical texts themselves. The Gospels, with their different views of the details and sometimes the meaning of Jesus's life and death, stand side by side in the canon of scripture, and the discrepancies between them became an invitation to analyze them historically as well as wrestle with them hermeneutically, once critical tools such as Gospel Synopses and modern methods of historiography had developed. And trying to make sense of these discrepancies hermeneutically can be a constructive theological process, and indeed it is demanded by the fact that we are citizens both of the Enlightenment and of what Karl Barth calls "the strange new world within the Bible."[22] What Daniel Boyarin says about the Babylonian Talmud also applies to the Gospels, the New Testament, and the Bible as a whole: they enshrine disagreement and thus invite conversation and debate, and this conversation can be seen as part of the continuing process of revelation.[23] On the other hand, if we try to deny or tone down these discrepancies, others will point them out, and our avoidance strategy may end up discrediting both ourselves and the gospel.

As we have seen, the early Christian view of John the Baptist developed over time. While all four of the Gospel writers suggest that John pointed to Jesus, in Mark, the earliest Gospel, he does so indirectly, through the editorial juxtaposition between John's prophecy of the coming of a "Stronger One" (1:7–8) and Mark's description of Jesus's baptism, which is accompanied by the descent of the Spirit (1:9–11). The Baptist himself does not witness that descent, and elsewhere in Mark we get only a hint that John in some way acknowledged Jesus and not necessarily as the Messiah (11:27–33). Matthew and

Luke both make the baptism story more explicit, implying that John saw the Spirit descending on Jesus, and Luke has John acknowledge Jesus while still in his mother's womb (Luke 1:44). And the Fourth and latest canonical Gospel makes John's witness to Jesus and subordination of his own ministry the most explicit of all. Just as Christology developed through continued reflection on the events of Jesus's life, as illuminated by scripture and subsequent events,[24] so did the Christian view of John develop, though in the opposite direction: John decreased so that Jesus might increase.

This is a theologically as well as a historically significant observation: memory and the meaning of tradition are transfigured by later events, which may reveal dimensions of the faith that were unclear to earlier generations. For thousands of years, for example, people thought that the Bible justified slavery, or at least tolerated it. Exegetically, they may have been right. But when a new movement of the Spirit occurred, the Bible began to be interpreted differently—and, we would say, more rightly.[25] Something similar may be happening in our own time with regard to the Bible's strictures about gay and lesbian people. "The letter killeth, but the Spirit giveth life" (2 Cor. 3:6 KJV); sticking by traditional answers may sometimes strangle the Spirit. At the same time, however, there is a limit to the malleability of tradition: Christians remembered that John had baptized Jesus and that Jesus had once had a derivative baptismal ministry, even though those memories embarrassed them.[26]

The discovery that John the Baptist had a more exalted view of himself and his ministry than Christian tradition has normally accorded him is itself hermeneutically suggestive. It reminds us that revelation always exists within the confusion of human uncertainty and error, "where cross the crowded ways of life," and that there are no unmistakable markers of its presence. We may be mistaken about where and how God is acting, even if we fancy ourselves among the prophets—even if, in fact, we *are* prophets. God's word always enters into the arena of humanity, that is, into an arena of error. But if we follow faithfully on the path set before us, we may find that our life has attained a different meaning and become part of a grander plan than we had imagined.

These conclusions about John the Baptist also have implications for the historical Jesus and *his* hermeneutical significance. If the thesis of this book is right and John believed that his baptism inducted people into the new age, at least some of the elements of realized eschatology in Jesus's own teaching may have derived from John. After all, in the Gospel stories themselves Jesus receives the Spirit, the power of the new age, when he experiences baptism at John's hands. This does not imply that there was nothing new about Jesus's eschatology, only that he derived some of his key insights from the Baptist.

This study, then, can be seen as an appendix to Luke 2:52, which Origen (*Comm. Matt.* 13.26) already cites as an argument for Jesus's humanity: "And Jesus increased in wisdom and in stature, and in favor with God and human beings" (Luke 2:52, RSV alt.).[27] Jesus, in other words, learned from others—perhaps above all, from John the Baptist. If he subsequently felt the need to deemphasize as well as affirm this connection, that also was part of his humanity.

But this book is not centrally about Jesus, and its implications for Christology are not its main point. The point of the book is John the Baptist, and I hope to have restored to him some of the dignity he deserves not only as the proclaimer of Jesus, not only as his predecessor in the way of suffering and death, but also in his combination of realized and futuristic eschatology, his openness to Gentiles, and his sharp modification of covenantal nomism. If he, like Jesus, ended up being executed by the ruling authorities, that is another sign that the two of them preached a similarly explosive message.

When was John born, when did he die, and when did he begin his public ministry?

We know the least about the year of John's birth. The only information we possess is from Luke's Gospel, which has John, like Jesus, being born around the time of Quirinius's census, which occurred in 6 CE (Luke 1:57; cf. 2:1–2). However, since Luke himself seems confused about the date of the census,[1] and since his whole presentation of John's birth is controlled by his desire to link him with Jesus,[2] we cannot rely on this datum. It is generally true, however, that John was a contemporary of Jesus, perhaps a slightly older one, since Jesus started out as a member of John's movement. And since Jesus's birth is usually dated around 6 BCE.[3] we might guess that John was born a little earlier, perhaps around 10 or 15 BCE.

As for when he began his public ministry, Luke again is our main source. In his Gospel he tells us that "the word of the Lord" came to John in the fifteenth year of the reign of Tiberius Caesar (Luke 3:1–3). There is some doubt about exactly what Luke means by this. As Joseph Fitzmyer observes, however, most commentators interpret it by invoking the Julian calendar and reckoning Tiberius's regnal years either from the death of his predecessor Augustus or from the vote of the Roman senate to acknowledge him as emperor. This makes the fifteenth year of Tiberius August or September 28–29 CE.[4] Again, we may wonder how good Luke's information is, but a date in the late twenties CE for the start of John's ministry seems plausible.

The year of John's execution is more complicated. The most consistent assertion in the Gospels is that John's death preceded Jesus's. In fact, the usual New Testament claim is that John's ministry and arrest preceded the beginning of Jesus's ministry, and the general impression given is that he was dead by the time Jesus's ministry was well underway (Mark 1:14//Matt. 4:12; Mark 6:17–29//Matt. 14:3–12; Mark 9:9–13//Matt. 17:9–13; Mark 11:27–33//Matt. 21:23–27//Luke 20:1–8; Acts 1:22, 10:37–38, 13:24–25). Even the Fourth Evangelist, who presents John and Jesus as carrying out concurrent ministries for a time (John 3:22–4:1), has the beginning of John's ministry precede the beginning of Jesus's ministry (John 1:19–42), and we do not hear from John again after his prophetic utterance, "He must increase, but I must decrease," in 3:30. By chapter 5, the Johannine Jesus is speaking of John as a figure of the past (John 5:31–35; cf. 10:40–41). If we follow this general New Testament schema of "John first, Jesus second" and accept the usual consensus that Jesus died between 30 and 33 CE,[5] John's death must have occurred in the late twenties or early thirties.

But there is a problem in reconciling this estimate with the information gleaned from Josephus. The latter links John's death with Herod Antipas's defeat by the Nabatean king Aretas IV, saying that many people saw that defeat as a divine judgment for Antipas's execution of John (*Ant.* 18.116). Josephus says that a major cause of the war was Aretas's anger over the way in which Antipas had repudiated his wife, Aretas's daughter, to marry his niece Herodias (*Ant.* 18.109–115). This is a point of rough chronological overlap with Mark and Matthew, since, in these Gospels, Antipas executes John after John denounces this same marriage.

When did the marriage of Antipas to Herodias, which both Josephus and the Gospels link with John's death, occur? Josephus describes it right after relating the death of Herod of Trachonitis, an event that he dates to the twentieth or twenty-second year of Tiberius's reign, that is, 34 or 36 CE.[6] And he introduces the account of the marriage with the words "in the meantime" (ἐν τούτῳ), seemingly linking it temporally with Herod of Trachonitis's death. He follows the account of the marriage and of Aretas's military response to it with a description of how the Roman general Vitellius attempted to punish Aretas for attacking Antipas. Vitellius's punitive expedition was called off when Tiberius, who had ordered it, died in March of 37 CE. We thus arrive at the following chronology from Josephus:

(1)   Herod of Trachonitis dies in the twentieth or twenty-second year of Tiberias's rule = 34 or 36 CE (*Ant.* 18.106–108).
(2)   "In the meantime" (ἐν τούτῳ), Antipas repudidates Aretas's daughter and marries Herodias (*Ant.* 18.109–110).
(3)   Aretas, incensed by the news from his daughter, goes to war with Antipas and destroys his army (*Ant.* 118.111–114).
       [Sometime before this, Antipas had executed John the Baptist, and some people interpreted his defeat by Aretas as a divine judgment for this killing (*Ant.* 18.116–119)].
(4)   Tiberius, angered by Aretas's war against Antipas, orders Vitellius to punish him militarily (*Ant.* 118.115).
(5)   Vitellius musters his forces for war against Aretas, but before he can go into battle Tiberius dies on March 15, 37 CE, and Vitellius calls the campaign off.

Kirsopp Lake sums up the situation in this way:

It is clear from these statements of Josephus that he regards the marriage of Herod and Herodias, and the war between Aretas and Herod, as closely connected events belonging to the same period as the death of Herod of Trachonitis, which he dates in the twentieth or twenty-second year of Tiberius. As he relates these events after mentioning the death of Herod of Trachonitis, it is *prima facie* probable that he regards them as slightly later; but too much must not be made of this argument, as Josephus often turns back and relates incidents in one part of the country after he has completed the narrative of events of a later date which had taken place in another district. More important for fixing the chronology is what follows. Vitellius endeavoured to carry out the command of the emperor and to punish Aretas. . . . But before the expedition could get further than Jerusalem news reached him that Tiberius was dead, and all the preparations were postponed until the will of the new emperor could be ascertained. Now, Tiberius died in March 37 A.D. It is thus practically certain that the war in which Herod was defeated took place in the year 36 A.D., and the suggestion is certainly very strong that the marriage of Herod and Herodias which occasioned this war had not taken place more than a year or two before the outbreak of hostilities; so that the year 35 A.D. is the most probable for the marriage of Herod and Herodias, although a few months earlier is not entirely inconceivable.[7]

If we accept this line of reasoning, John must have died sometime around 35 CE—a date later than the usually accepted one for Jesus's death. And if that is right, two conclusions are possible:

(1) Either we may preserve the New Testament order of "John first, then Jesus," but move the death of Jesus into the late thirties CE, or
(2) We may preserve the usual dating of Jesus's death in the early thirties, but revise the New Testament placement of John's death before Jesus's.

Lake favors the first solution. If Herod and Herodias were married in 35 and John was executed in the same year, Jesus probably died at Passover time in the following year, 36. This is the last possible date for his crucifixion, since Pontius Pilate's prefecture ended in 36, and, if there is one secure datum in New Testament chronology, it is that Jesus died "under Pontius Pilate."[8] Among other weaknesses, though, this theory has Jesus dying on a Saturday (if his death is dated at 14 Nisan) or a Sunday (if it is dated at 15 Nisan), whereas the universal testimony of the Gospels is that he died on a Friday.[9] For this and other reasons, Lake's theory has not gained much traction among scholars.[10]

The second position, which makes John's death later than Jesus's, has recently been argued by Johannes Tromp, who thinks Jesus died in 30 CE, and that John died five years later. The New Testament's "John first, Jesus second" order, for him, is a theological imposition: the historical chronology has been reversed in order to relegate John to the status of forerunner.[11] In support of this thesis, Tromp points out that Josephus does not even connect John with Jesus and that he describes Jesus at an earlier point in his narrative (*Ant.* 18.63–64) than he does John (*Ant.* 18.116–119).[12]

Tromp's thesis, however, seems unlikely, above all because both Jesus's baptism by John and his following him in time were problems for the early church and thus unlikely to have been invented. The baptism was a problem because it seemed to imply John's superiority to Jesus as well as Jesus's sinfulness.[13] And John's precedence in time was a problem because of the established principle that, in matters of immediate historical succession, the earlier is better.[14] Why, then, would the church have invented a Jesus who followed John in time and came to be baptized by him for the forgiveness of his sins?

If we do not accept either the hypothesis that Jesus preceded John in time or the hypothesis that Jesus died in the late thirties, how should we deal with the chronological problems highlighted by Lake? The key, it seems to me, is to follow up on the hint Lake himself provides when he says that Josephus often completes his account of events in one part of Palestine and then moves to another part and begins with events that occurred at an earlier date elsewhere. In other words, Josephus (like the Gospel writers and like ancient historians in general) often arranges his material thematically or geographically rather than in strict chronological order.[15] As E. P. Sanders puts it: "It is best to think that the story of Antipas, Herodias and the execution of John is a 'flashback', out of its historical sequence. The story of John's execution, in fact, is quite obviously a flashback: Josephus refers to it after the event that it is said to have caused. In this entire section . . . Josephus arranged the material topically; this explains why the stories about Herodias, Aretas' invasion and the execution of John come so close together."[16]

So the ἐν τούτῳ ("in the meantime") in *Ant.* 118.109, which correlates the death of Herod of Trachonitis in 34/36 CE with Antipas's repudiation of Aretas's daughter, cannot be pressed; it just indicates a general connection, perhaps within the same decade. Neither can we be certain that the insult to Aretas's daughter led to an immediate war against Antipas; he might have nursed the grudge for years before finding an opportunity for revenge.[17] And we certainly cannot conclude that Antipas's murder of the Baptist must have occurred shortly before the disastrous war that was popularly believed to be a punishment for that murder.[18] After all, if Christians could think that the destruction of the Temple in 70 CE was a punishment for the execution of Jesus in the thirties, it does not seem implausible that Palestinian Jews known to Josephus could think that Antipas's defeat around 36 CE was a punishment for his execution of John several years earlier.

The correlation Josephus makes between John's death and Herod's defeat by Aretas, therefore, is not strong enough evidence to overturn the persistent and somewhat embarrassing New Testament tradition that John preceded and baptized Jesus. Assuming that John died a year or two before Jesus did and that Jesus died in either 30 or 33, John's death probably occurred at the end of the twenties or the beginning of the thirties.

Is Josephus's Account of John the Baptist a Christian Interpolation?

Recently, Rivka Nir has revived the old theory that the account of John the Baptist in Josephus, *Antiquities* 18.116–119 is a Christian interpolation.[1] After reviewing some of the older arguments against Josephan authorship of the *Antiquities* passage, Nir develops her own original attack. Before looking at this new argument, it will be helpful to review the former ones she mentions and the reasons most scholars accept the authenticity of *Ant.* 18.116–119 (unlike the situation with regard to the passage about Jesus in *Ant.* 18.63–64, about which there continues to be substantial debate).[2]

Although the passage about John is first cited by Origen in the mid-third century in his refutation of a pagan critic of Christianity (*Against Celsus* 1.47), it fails to conform to the basic Christian attitude about the Baptist. It does, however, correspond to typical Josephan emphases.[3] The John of the *Jewish Antiquities* passage is a "good man," a preacher of piety toward God and justice towards humanity, a version of the double commandment that, as Steve Mason points out, "is Josephus' usual way of describing Jewish ethical responsibility."[4] It would also appeal to Josephus's Hellenistic readers, since it turns the Baptist into something like a typical philosopher, which is exactly what Josephus does to the Pharisees, Sadducees, Essenes, and even Zealots.[5] The omissions in the *Jewish Antiquities* portrayal of John also fit into a regular Josephan pattern, since Josephus's Baptist lacks eschatological trappings and makes no prophecy of a coming Messiah, corresponding to Josephus's tendency to suppress eschatology and messianism.[6] This deeschatologized version of the Baptist is far from the picture of him in the Gospels and hard to credit to a Christian author. Even more startling, neither this passage nor the one about Jesus, if that is genuine, links the two figures—an absence that is even harder to attribute to a Christian.[7]

Why, then, did some scholars question Josephus's authorship of *Ant.* 18.116–119—to such an extent that the great nineteenth-century Jewish historian Heinrich Graetz pronounced it a "shameless forgery"?[8] *Jewish Antiquities* 18.116–119, it was claimed, was disruptive in its context, which concerned Herod Antipas's defeat by Aretas IV, and the narrative flowed better if it was removed. The passage, moreover, was too sympathetic to John to be written by a "fierce opponent of anyone seeking to challenge the legitimate government or promote change or rebellion." The vocabulary of baptism employed in the passage (βαπτιστής, βαπτισμός, βάπτισις) was taken as another sign that it was Christian in inception, since it departed from Josephus's usual vocabulary for Jewish immersions (λούεσθαι, ἀπολούεσθαι).[9]

These arguments, however, are either weak or point towards different conclusions. The disruptiveness of the passage in its context is not unusual in Josephus's narrative, which is full of such digressions (see, for example, the long excurses on Jewish sects in *J.W.* 2.119–166 and *Ant.* 18.11–25).[10] Neither is it unusual for Josephus to show sympathy towards Jewish prophets and others whose adherence to God caused them to oppose arbitrary rule,[11] including that of the Herodians,[12] even if they were executed or threatened with execution.[13] The picture of Herod fearing that John might start a revolution does not make John one of the violent revolutionaries Josephus despised; it places him among the righteous men whom unjust rulers feared.[14] And the different vocabulary used by Josephus for John's lustrations may reflect John's own vocabulary, which differed from the norm among his Jewish contemporaries, including his former colleagues at Qumran—perhaps partly to signal his distinctiveness.[15]

Nir's new argument against Josephan composition of *Ant.* 18.116–119 centers on the theology of Josephus's description of John's baptism rather than its vocabulary. Josephus asserts that John's baptism was not meant to wash away sins but to attest that the soul had already been cleansed by righteousness; internal, spiritual cleansing thus preceded rather than followed physical baptism. Nir points out the similarity between this and the Jewish-Christian Pseudo-Clementine literature (*Hom.* 11.28, which is part of the reconstructed *Kerygmata Petrou* source). Her conclusion is that the *Jewish Antiquities* passage must be an interpolation influenced by similar, Jewish-Christian circles, since this idea "did not exist amid mainstream Jewish circles of the Second Temple period." John's demand for inner purity as a precondition for baptism, rather, was "a step in a completely new direction."[16]

Nir, however, acknowledges that a very similar idea is found at Qumran (see above, chap. 2, on 1QS 3:4–9 and 5:13–14 [p. 31]). The paradox is resolved by the realization that in her view Qumran was not a part of "mainstream Judaism." The latter, in her view, consisted of various "component groups and movements, with the Pharisees at the fore, [which] shared fundamental principles, beliefs and ideas which, despite differences, formed the common ground marking the boundary between Judaism and what lay outside it." This "mainstream Judaism," in Nir's view, is attested by the Apocrypha, Philo, Josephus, and the early layers of the Talmudic literature. It is *not* attested by the Pseudepigrapha or the Qumran literature—not to mention the traditions about John the Baptist and the early Christians.

This is an old-fashioned approach, reminiscent of George Foot Moore's construct of "normative Judaism," a term that most scholars today find misleading.[17] Scholars in recent years have, rather, recognized that, in Second Temple times and well into the early centuries of the Common Era, there was no such thing as "normative" or "mainstream" Judaism, but rather a variety of Judaisms all claiming normativity and competing with and anathematizing each other. Nir recognizes that her approach is itself somewhat out of the mainstream, "going against today's ascendant view."[18] But the major fallacy in her argument is that it scarcely matters, for the present discussion, how "mainstream" Qumran was. It *was* a form of Judaism, mainstream or not, and, as shown in chapter 2, a form that probably influenced John. There is no need to posit a Christian source for Josephus's assertion that repentance must precede baptism when we have such a good parallel from a Jewish group that we know influenced John as well as, probably, Josephus.[19] And it is plausible that certain Jewish-Christian groups continued aspects of John's baptismal theology that were already foreshadowed at Qumran—thus producing the consonance with the Pseudo-Clementines that is the fulcrum of Nir's argument.

APPENDIX 3   *Database by Source of Information about*
John the Baptist in the Canonical Gospels
and Josephus

I.   The Synoptic Gospels speak about the Baptist in approximately twenty-five
     passages. A plurality of these come from either Mark or Q and are shared by
     at least two of the Synoptics.

     A. Passages from Mark

     1. Editorial linkage of John with Exod. 23:20 + Mal. 3:1 (Mark 1:2; cf. I.B.4
         and I.C.1 below)
     2. Editorial linkage of John with Isa. 40:3 (Mark 1:3//Matt. 3:3//Luke 3:4–6)
     3. Description of John's rite as "a baptism of repentance for the forgive-
         ness of sins" (Mark 1:4//Luke 3:3)
     4. Description of John's garb and diet (Mark 1:6//Matt. 3:4)
     5. Description of Jerusalemites and Judahites coming to be baptized by
         John (Mark 1:5//Matt. 3:5)
     6. John's prophecy of "the Stronger One," who will baptize in the Spirit
         (Mark 1:7–8; cf. I.B.2, I.C.2, and II.E below)
     7. Jesus's baptism by John, including the descent of the Spirit on Jesus
         (Mark 1:9–11//Matt. 3:13–17//Luke 3:21–22)
     8. John's disciples fast (Mark 2:18; + and pray, Luke 5:33)
     9. Herod's opinion that Jesus is John returned from the dead (Mark
         6:14–16//Matt. 14:1–2//Luke 9:7–9)
     10. Herod's execution of John (Mark 6:17–29//Matt. 14:3–12)
     11. Jesus's reference to John as Elijah, who goes before him in the way of
         suffering and death (Mark 9:11–13//Matt. 17:10–13)
     12. Jesus's response to the challenge to his authority, in which he asks
         whether the baptism of John was from "heaven" or "human beings"
         (Mark 11:27–33//Matt. 21:23–27//Luke 20:1–8)

     B. Passages from Q

     1. John's warning about the coming judgment (Matt. 3:7–10//Luke 3:7–9)
     2. John's testimony to "the Coming One" who will baptize in Spirit and
         fire, clear the threshing floor, gather the wheat into the barn, and burn
         the chaff (Matt. 3:11–14//Luke 3:15–18; cf. I.A.6 above and I.C.2 and II.E
         below)

3. Jesus's testimony to John as "a prophet and more than a prophet" (Matt. 11:7–9//Luke 7:24–26)

4. Jesus's testimony to John's fulfillment of Exod. 23:20 + Mal. 3:1 (Matt. 11:10//Luke 7:27; cf. I.a.1 above and I.C.1 below)

5. Jesus's testimony to John as the greatest of those born of women, but less than the least in the dominion of God (Matt. 11:11//Luke 7:28; cf. II.K below)

6. Jesus's placement of John within the history of salvation (Matt. 11:12–13//Luke 16:16)

7. Jesus's parable of the children in the marketplace (Matt. 11:16–19//Luke 7:31–35)

8. John's question to Jesus about whether or not he is "the Coming One" (Matt. 11:2–6//Luke 7:18–23)

9. Contrast between acceptance of John by tax collectors [and prostitutes in Matt; and the whole nation in Luke] and his rejection by religious leaders [Pharisees and scribes in Matthew] (Matt. 21:32//Luke 7:29–30)

C. Mark/Q overlaps

1. Linkage of John with Exod. 23:20/Mal. 3:1 (Mark 1:3; Matt. 11:10//Luke 7:27)

2. John's prophecy of "the Coming One," who baptizes in the Spirit (Mark 1:7–8//Matt. 3:11–12//Luke 3:15–16; cf. II.E below)

D. Special Matthean passages about the Baptist

1. John's reluctance to baptize Jesus (Matt. 3:14–15; an insertion in I.A.7)

2. Jesus's testimony to the Baptist as Elijah returned from the dead (Matt. 11:14, an addendum to I.A.11 above)

E. Special Lukan pericopes about the Baptist

1. From Luke 1, probably reflecting a source (see app. 4)

   a) Description of John's parents, Zechariah and Elizabeth (Luke 1:5–7)

   b) The archangel Gabriel's announcement to Zechariah that Elizabeth will have a child in her old age (Luke 1:8–20)

   c) Zechariah struck with muteness, and the couple returns home (Luke 1:21–23)

   d) Elizabeth's pregnancy (1:24–25)

   e) Mary's visit to Elizabeth, at which Elizabeth's baby leaps in her womb (Luke 1:39–45)

   f) The birth of Elizabeth's baby (Luke 1:57–58)

   g) Circumcision and naming of the baby, accompanied by cure of Zechariah's muteness (Luke 1:59–66)

   h) Zechariah's praise of God for the birth of John (Luke 1:67–75)

   i) Zechariah's prophecy about John's future role (1:76–79)

   j) John's boyhood in the Judean wilderness (Luke 1:80)

2. Outside of Luke 1
   a) John's ethical advice (Luke 3:10–14)
   b) Herod's imprisonment of John (Luke 3:19–20; cf. I.A.10)
   c) John teaches his disciples to pray (Luke 11:1)

II. The Gospel of John speaks about the Baptist in approximately ten passages, some of which have partial parallels in the Synoptics, others of which are in tension with or even contradict the Synoptics.

   A. Author's assertion that John was not the Light, but came to bear witness to the Light (John 1:6–8)
   B. John's testimony that he is neither the Christ nor Elijah nor the prophet, but only the fulfillment of Isaiah 40:3 (John 1:19–23; cf. I.A.2 above)
   C. John's prophecy of the Coming One (John 1:25–28; cf. I.C.2 above)
   D. John's acclamation of Jesus as "the Lamb of God" (John 1:29–31)
   E. John's flashback to the descent of the Spirit on Jesus (John 1:32–34; cf. I.A.7 above)
   F. John's reiterated identification of Jesus as "the Lamb of God" (John 1:35–36)
   G. The defection of two of John's disciples to Jesus (John 1:35–40)
   H. The simultaneous baptismal ministries of John and Jesus (John 3:23–24)
   I. John's response to a question about Jesus's baptismal ministry, emphasizing Jesus's superiority to him (John 3:25–30)
   K. John's (or the author's) identification of Jesus as the one who comes "from above" and "the Son," in contrast to the one who comes "from below" (John 3:31–36)
   L. Jesus's departure for Galilee, occasioned by the Pharisees having heard that he has been making and baptizing more disciples than John (John 4:1–3)

III. Josephus has one passage about John, *Antiquities* 18.116–119. Since it may not be accessible to all readers of this book, I give it below, both in Greek and in my own translation.

116) Τισὶ δὲ τῶν Ἰουδαίων ἐδόκει ὀλωλέναι τὸν Ἡρώδου στρατὸν ὑπὸ τοῦ θεοῦ καὶ μάλα δικαίως τινυμένου κατὰ ποινὴν Ἰωάννου τοῦ ἐπικαλουμένου βαπτιστοῦ. 117) κτείνει γὰρ δὴ τοῦτον Ἡρώδης ἀγαθὸν ἄνδρα καὶ τοῖς Ἰουδαίοις κελεύοντα ἀρετὴν ἐπασκοῦσιν καὶ τὰ πρὸς ἀλλήλους δικαιοσύνῃ καὶ πρὸς τὸν θεὸν εὐσεβείᾳ χρωμένοις βαπτισμῷ συνιέναι. οὕτω γὰρ δὴ καὶ τὴν βάπτισιν ἀποδεκτὴν αὐτῷ φανεῖσθαι μὴ ἐπί τινων ἁμαρτάδων παραιτήσει χρωμένων, ἀλλ᾽ ἐφ᾽ ἁγνείᾳ τοῦ σώματος, ἅτε δὴ καὶ τῆς ψυχῆς δικαιοσύνῃ προεκκεκαθαρμένης. 118) καὶ τῶν ἄλλων συστρεφομένων, καὶ γὰρ ἤρθησαν ἐπὶ πλεῖστον τῇ ἀκροάσει τῶν λόγων, δείσας Ἡρώδης τὸ ἐπὶ τοσόνδε πιθανὸν αὐτοῦ τοῖς ἀνθρώποις μὴ ἐπὶ ἀποστάσει τινὶ φέροι, πάντα γὰρ ἐῴκεσαν συμβουλῇ τῇ ἐκείνου πράξοντες, πολὺ κρεῖττον ἡγεῖται πρὶν

τι νεώτερον ἐξ αὐτοῦ γενέσθαι προλαβὼν ἀνελεῖν τοῦ μεταβολῆς γενομένης μὴ εἰς πράγματα ἐμπεσὼν μετανοεῖν. 119) καὶ ὁ μὲν ὑποψίᾳ τῇ Ἡρώδου δέσμιος εἰς τὸν Μαχαιροῦντα πεμφθεὶς τὸ προειρημένον φρούριον ταύτῃ κτίννυται. τοῖς δὲ Ἰουδαίοις δόξαν ἐπὶ τιμωρίᾳ τῇ ἐκείνου τὸν ὄλεθρον ἐπὶ τῷ στρατεύματι γενέσθαι τοῦ θεοῦ κακῶσαι Ἡρώδην θέλοντος.

116) But to some of the Jews it seemed that Herod's army had been destroyed by God, and justly so, as a punishment for what he had done to John, who was called the Baptist. 117) For Herod had killed this John, although he was a good man, and had exhorted the Jews to exercise virtue by practicing righteousness towards each other and piety towards God, and thus to be joined together by baptism. For in his eyes baptism was unacceptable as a way of gaining remission of sins, but [acceptable] as a way of obtaining cleanliness of the body, inasmuch as the soul had already in fact been purified by righteousness. 118) And when others began to gather around him, for they were aroused to the highest extent by hearing his words, Herod, fearing that such persuasive power over people might lead to a revolt—for they seemed ready to do anything on his advice—he thought it was much better to execute him preemptively before something else could happen through his influence, rather than fall into difficulties and repent [of his leniency] when an insurrection arose. 119) And John, having been sent bound to Machaerus, the prison previously referred to, because of Herod's suspicion about him, was put to death in that place. But the opinion of the Jews was that the destruction visited on the army was a retribution for John by God, who wished to do evil to Herod.

From this passage we learn about:

A. Some Jews' opinion that Aretas's destruction of Herod's army was a divine punishment for Herod's his execution of John
B. John's moral goodness
C. John's exhortation to the Jews to do justice towards each other and to revere God
D. The nature of his baptism
    1. Not for forgiveness of sins
    2. Only a cleansing of the body, when the soul had already been purified by righteousness
E. The great popular reaction to John, both by Jews and "others"
F. Herod's execution of John in Machaerus, motivated by his fear that John might start a revolt

According to Luke 1, John's father Zechariah and his mother Elizabeth were both from a priestly background (1:5), and John's coming birth was revealed in the Jerusalem Temple, where Zechariah was serving (1:8–23). This information, however, is not corroborated elsewhere in the New Testament, and in view of the legendary nature of much of the material in both the Lukan and the Matthean birth narratives, the saturation of both with Old Testament themes, and their almost total lack of agreement, many scholars dismiss them as sources of historical information about either John or Jesus. There are, to be sure, several details shared by Matthew and Luke (for example, the role of the Holy Spirit in Jesus's conception, the virginity of Mary, the heavenly imposition of his name), suggesting preexistent traditions[1]—but John's priestly descent is not among them. In fact, Matthew's birth story completely ignores John.

However, it seems unlikely that the narrative about John is a Lukan invention, since it ascribes such critical importance to John and only connects him with Jesus in the Visitation scene (Luke 1:39–56) and the verses leading up to it (1:36–37). The Visitation may have been created by Luke precisely to link two independent birth narratives, the first of which came from Baptist circles, the second from Christian ones,[2] or else to link the preexistent story of John's nativity with the story of Jesus's nativity, which Luke created on the pattern of the Baptist nativity story.[3] In the scenes that center on John, no mention is made of Jesus; John himself, rather, is called "great before the Lord" and prophesied to be "filled with the Holy Spirit, even from his mother's womb" (1:15)—a departure from the usual Christian view that the Spirit is a gift imparted through Jesus (see chap. 4). True, John is assigned a preparatory function, consonant with his identification with Elijah (1:17), and in 1:76 it is said that he will go before the Lord to prepare his ways—an allusion to Isa. 40:3, which seems to have been central to John's self-understanding (see app. 8). But it is never made clear who this "Lord" is—God? the Messiah?—either here or in 1:16–17.

Factors such as these have caused even hard-nosed critics such as Bultmann[4] and Dibelius[5] to posit that Luke's Baptist narrative goes back to a Baptist source,[6] and Brown, who is skeptical about the existence of such a source, is willing to accept that the narrative may reflect an accurate tradition about John's priestly background. This is partly because the knowledge shown of priestly terms of service, the incense offering, and the cult in 1:8–10 goes beyond what could be derived from the Old Testament and contrasts with Luke's "confused picture of presentation and purification in 2:22–24."[7]

There is circumstantial evidence that backs up Luke's claim that John was from a priestly background. First of all, as I show in chapter 2, a good case can be made that John was at one time a member of the Dead Sea community, which was priestly in origin and led by priests, and which most scholars think was part of the group called "Essenes" by Philo and Josephus. Josephus describes the Essenes adopting other people's children (τοὺς δ' ἀλλοτρίους παῖδας ἐκλαμβάνοντες, *J.W.* 2.120), and if there is any truth to the Lukan assertion that John's parents, who were of priestly lineage, were elderly when he was born (Luke 1:17–18), it would make sense that, at a young age, he might have been orphaned and adopted by Essenes. This reconstruction dovetails with Luke's notice that, as a child (παιδίον), John was "in desert places" (ἐν ταῖς ἐρήμοις) until the day of his manifestation to Israel" (Luke 1:80, RSV alt.), and it unties a knot in the Lukan narrative: "How could this little child, the only son of aged parents, grow up in the wilderness?"[8]

Another factor in favor of John's priestly identity is the priestly associations of his baptism. In the Old Testament and Second Temple Jewish literature, as Jonathan Lawrence puts it, there are "quite a few references to washing practices that appl[y] specifically to priests, centered around their service in the Temple,"[9] and it appears to have been a priest's prerogative to pronounce forgiveness of sins, sometimes after the penitent had confessed them (see, for example, Lev. 4:20, 26, 31, 35; 5:5, 10, 13, 16, 18).[10] John's baptism, of course, was also a water rite, and according to Mark, it was a "baptism of repentance unto forgiveness of sins" (1:4), in which people confessed their sins while they were being baptized (1:5). It thus corresponds in some ways to priestly practice.

Finally, there is John's association of himself with Elijah (see chap. 3). Although Elijah is not described as a priest in the Old Testament, he does perform priestly functions, building an altar and offerings sacrifices (1 Kgs. 18:30–39) and anointing a king (1 Kgs. 19:15–16; cf. 1 Sam. 10:1; 16:13).[11] Partly because of these passages, the Targumim, Jewish midrashim, and many Church Fathers refer to Elijah as a priest or imply that he was one,[12] often equating him with the zealous priest Phinehas, who in the time of the wilderness wanderings killed an Israelite man and the Midianite woman he had espoused (Num. 25:6–8). The earliest instance of this equation of Elijah with Phinehas is in LAB 48:1, which may date to the first century CE.[13] If the equation of Elijah with Phinehas was already existent in the first century, Phinehas's strong objection to an illicit union is an interesting and perhaps significant parallel to John's repudiation of Herod Antipas's marriage to Herodias (Mark 6:17–18; see chap. 6). John's action may have reflected his sense of himself as Elijah = Phinehas returned from the dead.

All in all, then, there seems to be a good chance that the prophet John, like the prophet Jeremiah (Jer. 1:1), was from a priestly background.

The "Others" in Josephus, Antiquities *18.118*

In *Jewish Antiquities* 18.117, Josephus describes John the Baptist's exhortation to his fellow Jews: to practice virtue, cultivate piety towards their neighbors and God, and gather together in his baptismal rite. Then, in paragraph 118, Josephus notes that when "others" also began to respond to John, Herod Antipas became alarmed and decided to do away with him (for the text in Greek and English, see app. 3). But who were these "others"?

Since the Jews have been explicitly mentioned as John's target audience in paragraph 117, the "others" of paragraph 118 should probably be understood as non-Jews. John Meier points out that this interpretation has the advantage of paralleling what Josephus says (in Meier's view mistakenly) about Jesus in the famous *Testimonium Flavianum* of *Ant.* 18.63–64 (assuming, as Meier does, that the latter is authentic): "He won over many Jews *and many of the Greeks*" (emphasis added).[1] But Meier and several other interpreters find this interpretation of "others" hard to accept. Meier writes that "there is no support for such an idea in the Four Gospels,"[2] and he and other scholars instead suggest that the "others" are a different group of Jews from those referred to in paragraph 117. For example, the editor of the Loeb Classical Library volume containing the passage, Louis Feldman, conjectures that the reference may be to unjust people.[3] Meier himself, similarly, takes the "others" as Jews who have *not* done what John exhorts Jews to do in paragraph 117: cleanse their souls of unrighteousness before coming to be baptized. In a slight variation, Roland Schütz takes the "others" as Jews outside the circle of the Baptist.[4] All these interpretations, however, seem to go against the grammar of *Ant.* 18.117–118,[5] which contrasts John's original addressees, the Jews, with "others" who later began flocking to him.[6]

Meier counters with a revisionist reading of the syntax of *Ant.* 18.117a. He takes the circumstantial participles ἐπασκοῦσιν and χρωμένοις as conditional and translates the sentence, "For Herod in fact killed him, although he was a good man and bade the Jews—if [or provided that] they were cultivating virtue and practicing justice toward one another and piety toward God—to join in baptism." Thus John was not addressing all Jews but only those who were assiduous about virtue, justice, and piety; the "others" who later streamed to him were less worthy Jews.[7] This conditional reading comports with what follows in the second half of 18.117, which emphasizes that John's baptism did not cleanse from sin unless the soul had already been cleansed by righteousness.

But nothing in the previous context suggests that the participles are to be read conditionally, and therefore the natural tendency would be for the reader who has not yet read 117b to take 117a as a summary of John's message to all his fellow Jews, analogously with the picture presented in Mark 1:4–5, 7–8. If Josephus had intended the conditional meaning, he probably would have found a clearer way to express it, such as using attributive participles.[8] Moreover, if Meier's interpretation were correct, Josephus would be saying that John, after preaching to worthy Jews, began preaching to unworthy ones, and this is why Herod became alarmed and killed him—an action that, in the context, seems not only rational, but justified. But this would not fit with the general tenor of the passage, which is to blame Herod for executing John.

Another interpretation of τῶν ἄλλων in *Ant.* 18.118 has been offered by Michael Winger: "Originally, John was alone; then he accumulated followers; 'others' just means people other than John himself."[9] This, however, seems unlikely, since "the Jews" have been mentioned twice previously in the paragraph as the object of John's exhortations. It seems most likely that they are also indirectly indicated by the immediately following coordinate participle συστρεφομένων ("gathering themselves together"): first the Jews gathered together around John, then they began to be joined by "the others," that is, Gentiles, and *that* is when Herod decided things had gotten out of hand.[10]

The equation of "the others" with Gentiles makes perfect sense, given the location of John's ministry. As Robert Webb points out, John "could have had contact with Gentiles who traveled the trade routes coming from the East, as well as with Gentiles living in the region of the Trans-Jordan."[11] Later, Webb mentions the Nabateans specifically,[12] a group John may already have encountered at Qumran (see the section "The Qumran Attitude toward Gentiles" in chap. 2). Contrary to Meier, moreover, it is not exactly true that there is no hint in the Four Gospels that John appealed to an audience wider than Jews. Samuel Tobias Lachs, for example, refers to Matt. 3:5 ("all the region about the Jordan") in support of the opinion that John's audience may have included non-Jews.[13]

The hypothesis that the ἄλλων of *Ant.* 118.118 may be Gentiles is strengthened when one looks at Josephus's other instances of ἄλλοι. He frequently uses the term to contrast Jews with Gentiles.[14] It is especially striking to see how concentrated the term is in the short *Against Apion,* a polemical work designed to defend the Jews against charges brought against them by Gentiles. All in all, then, ἄλλων in *Ant.* 18.118 seems to hint that the Baptist's proclamation was beginning to extend into the non-Jewish world when he was executed by Herod Antipas.[15]

Acts 19:1–7 seems to describe Paul preaching in Ephesus to followers of John the Baptist who are ignorant of Jesus. Knut Backhaus, however, offers a different interpretation of Acts 19:1–7.[1] For him the Ephesians to whom Paul preached were not adherents of the Baptist but Christians, since elsewhere Luke uses the terms "disciples" (μαθηταί, 19:1) and "believers" (πιστεύσαντες, 19:2) only of followers of Jesus. They were, however, in Backhaus's view, strangely isolated Christians, or "semi-Christians"—people who earlier had had some contact with the historical Jesus and his followers, as well as with the associated Baptist circle, but who lost touch with the Jesus movement sometime between their baptism by John and the Easter/Pentecost events. Consequently, they were ignorant of the kerygma about Jesus's resurrection, knowing him as a teacher rather than the exalted Lord (cf. 19:5: "On hearing this, they were baptized into the name of *the Lord* Jesus").

This reading, however, presumes a scarcely credible isolation of the Ephesian "disciples" from the rest of the burgeoning Christian movement.[2] If they, moreover, knew about the historical Jesus but not about his resurrection, it is curious that Paul fails to mention the latter in his kerygmatic proclamation in 19:4. Contrary to Backhaus, the impression left by 19:4–5 is that these Ephesian "disciples" are not yet believers in Jesus (as can be seen from the implicit exhortation to believe in him in 19:4). Indeed, they seem never to have heard of Jesus.[3]

Backhaus asserts that the point of 19:4 is not to introduce Jesus to the Ephesian "disciples" but to connect him with John's proclamation of the "Coming One." The pitch is: "You know something about John and you know something about Jesus, but you don't know that John pointed to Jesus as the one in whom people should believe." This interpretation, however, is unconvincing. The logic of Acts 19:4, rather, seems to be that Paul is informing the Ephesians of three facts:

(1) John's baptism, which they have experienced, is not self-referential but only a baptism of repentance preparing people for something else.
(2) That "something else" is a person in whom John wanted his baptizands to believe.
(3) The name of that person is Jesus.

The words τοῦτ᾽ ἔστιν εἰς τὸν Ἰησοῦν ("that is, into Jesus"), in this context, imply the unveiling of a previously unknown name; it is upon hearing this name, and into it, that the Ephesians are immediately baptized.[4] If Luke calls these baptizands "believers" and "disciples," terminology that he elsewhere reserves for Christians, this is because he has refashioned the image of the Ephesian adherents to fit his own Christian theology, in which followers of the Baptist *of course* believe in Jesus too.[5] Although this superimposition introduces a narrative inconsistency into Acts, that is a small price for Luke to pay for being able to assert that followers of John are naturally followers of Jesus as well—and that, if any are not, they will quickly become so on hearing the good news.

APPENDIX 7   *The "Day-Baptists"*

··························

Patristic Evidence

The Pseudo-Clementine *Homilies,* in a generally disparaging passage that probably formed part of the basic writing underlying this document and therefore goes back to the end of the second or beginning of the third century CE, describes John as a "Day-Baptist" (ἡμεροβαπτιστής; *Hom.* 2.23).[1] The first attestation of this term is in Hegisippus's listing of Jewish sects in the latter part of the second century CE (Eusebius, *Ecclesiastical History* 2.22.7): "Now there were various opinions among the circumcision, among the children of Israel, against the tribe of Judah and the Messiah, as follows: Essenes, Galileans, Day-Baptists, Masbothei, Samaritans, Sadducees, and Pharisees" (trans. alt. from Loeb Classical Library).

As Kurt Rudolph points out, this first reference to "Day-Baptists" unfortunately tells us nothing about the group except its name, and in general the passage appears garbled (was there really a Jewish sect called "the Galileans"?). Moreover, "Day-Baptists" seems to be the same thing as "Masbothei," since the latter is probably derived from the Aramaic *maṣbūʿtā* (= "dipping, baptism"), which became a technical term among the Mandeans for their most important form of ablution, a repeated ritual immersion in running water.[2] Hegisippus's list overlaps significantly with a similar enumeration in Justin, *Dialogue* 80.4, where the corresponding sect is referred to simply as "Baptists" (Βαπτιστῶν). The fourth-century Apostolic Constitutions (6.6.5) adds that the Day-Baptists "every day, unless they wash, do not eat—no, and unless they cleanse their beds and tables, or platters and cups and seats, do not make use of any of them" (Ante-Nicene Fathers trans. alt.). This phrasing, however, seems to be derived from the mocking description in Mark 7:3–4 of the practices of "the Pharisees, and all the Jews," and it is questionable whether we can glean historical information from it.

We are on slightly firmer ground with the fourth-century church father Epiphanius, who devotes a chapter of his *Panarion,* a sometimes fanciful refutation of heresies, to a description of the Day-Baptists (*Anacephalaeosis* 1.17). Here we learn that this group has the same ideas as the scribes and Pharisees, but they insist on being baptized every day of the year, since they "alleged that there is no life for a man unless he is baptized daily with water, and washed and purified from every fault."[3]

....

Tosefta Yadayim 2:20

Still, we might be inclined to dismiss these reports from the Church Fathers about "Day-Baptists" as a malign Christian fantasy about overly scrupulous Jews if there were not similar descriptions in rabbinic literature of a group known as the "Dawn Immersers" (טובלי שחרין).[4] The overlap with the Patristic expression "Day-Baptists" is especially strong because the Greek word ἡμέρα can mean "dawn" as well as "day."[5] The earliest of these rabbinic references is in Tosefta Yadayim 2:20b, a passage that reads as follows in the text from the Vienna manuscript (Library Vienna, Hebr. 20, early fourteenth century).[6]

אומרין טובלי שחרין: קובלנו עליכם פרושין שאתם מזכירין את השם בשחרית בלא טבילה.
אומ׳ פרושין: קובלנו עליכם טובלי שחרין שאתם מזכירין את השם מן הגוף שיש בו טומאה.

(a) The Dawn Immersers say: We complain about you, O Pharisees, because you make mention of the Name [of God] at dawn without having immersed.

(b) The Pharisees say: We complain about you, O Dawn Immersers, because you make mention of the Name from a body that has impurity in it. (My trans.)

Here, as happens in 2:20a and elsewhere in Tannaitic literature,[7] there is a complaint against the Pharisees that is answered by the Pharisees—often with a complaint against the complainers. But the passage seems somewhat at variance with what Epiphanius says about the Day-Baptists, since here it is the Pharisees—not the Dawn Immersers—who complain about the impurity of the other party.

The *editio princeps* of the Tosefta, however (Venice, 1521–522), which is based on a manuscript now lost, gives a shorter text, which is closer to Epiphanius's report: אומרין ר׳ טיבלני שחרית: קובלני עליכם פרושין שאתם מזכירי׳ את השם מן הגוף שיש בו טומאה ("The Dawn Immersers say: We complain about you, O Pharisees, because you make mention of the Name from a body that has impurity in it"). This could be a corruption of Vienna text created by parablepsis (see glossary), since the phrase שאתם מזכירין את השם ("because you make mention of the Name") occurs in both halves of the Vienna text:

a) The Dawn Immersers say
b) We complain about you, O Pharisees,
c) **because you make mention of the Name**
d) at dawn without having immersed.

a') The Pharisees say:
b') We complain about you, O Dawn Immersers,
c') **because you make mention of the Name**
d') from a body that has impurity in it.

The eye of the scribe could have skipped from c to c', leaving out d, a', and b', and thus creating the *editio princeps* text.[8]

It is also possible, however, that the shorter *editio princeps* text is the earlier form. It is inherently logical that people such as the "Dawn Immersers," who bathed daily, would complain about the ritual impurity of the Pharisees, who had not immersed themselves.[9] This would make the original Toseftan text close to the report from Epiphanius, who says that the Day-Baptists are baptized daily to be purified from faults and attain eternal life. A rabbinic scribe, however, might have taken umbrage at this accusation and might have made a "correction," swapping the Pharisees and the "Dawn Immersers," so that now it was the former who complained about the uncleanness of the latter, as in the second half of the Vienna text. Once that had happened, however, he would have had to ascribe some other complaint to the Dawn Immersers, so he created the text in the first half of the Vienna text.

Even if the Vienna text is original, however, we still see the Dawn Immersers implying (though not lodging openly) the complaint that the Pharisees have by their impurity sullied the divine name, since they have not immersed before reciting it.[10] This text, then, is still close to what Epiphanius says about the Day-Baptists— though not as close as the *editio princeps* text.

....

Was John a "Day-Baptist"?

Thus both Christian and Jewish sources present a picture of a group of Jewish rigorists who immerse themselves daily[11] to be cleansed from ritual impurity and sin. But what to make of the report in the Pseudo-Clementines that John himself was such a daily immerser? Is it historical?

Unlikely. About the only corroborating evidence is that the Mandeans, who revere John, practice frequent immersions, the most important of which they call "baptism" (*maṣbūʿtā*) and practice weekly.[12] But the Mandean connection with John is tenuous,[13] and all of the other sources about John imply that his baptism was a once-and-for-all event (see the section "John's Baptism and Ritual Purity" in chap. 4). The Pseudo-Clementine report, moreover, comes in a context that is hostile to John. It is true that the basic writing underlying the Pseudo-Clementines, of which the report about John is a part, is not unremittingly hostile to post-baptismal washings, and indeed argues that women after menstruation and both sexes after copulation need to wash themselves (βαπτίσεσθαι) or be washed (βαπτισθείσῃ; *Hom.* 11.30, 33).[14] But *daily* immersion is apparently regarded as excessive, much as it is by the Pharisees in t. Yad. 2:20. The Pseudo-Clementine description of John as a Day-Baptist, then, is likely a slander designed to associate him with excessive bathing.

The Gospel of Mark begins with a series of Old Testament allusions, followed by a short account of John the Baptist's ministry in the Jordan Valley:

> 1¹ The beginning of the good news of Jesus Christ, as it has been written in Isaiah the prophet: ²"Look, I am sending my messenger before your face [cf. Exod. 23:20], who will set your way in order [cf. Mal. 3:1].³ The voice of someone shouting in the wilderness: 'Prepare the way of the Lord; make his paths straight!'" [Isa. 40:3]
>
> ⁴John appeared, baptizing in the wilderness and proclaiming a baptism of repentance unto forgiveness of sins . . . (my trans.)

Here the Isaian reference to a "voice . . . shouting in the wilderness" to prepare the Lord's way is merged with the Exodus prophecy that God will send a messenger before the Israelites to lead them through the desert and the Malachi prophecy that he will send them a messenger to prepare his way. Later in Malachi this messenger is identified as Elijah (Mal. 3:23 MT/4:5 ET). This conflated citation itself "prepares the way" for the Markan portrayal of the Baptist's preparatory, Elijah-like mission (1:7–8; 9:11–13).[1]

Matthew and Luke give the merged citation from Exodus and Malachi in another context, the Q narrative of Jesus's declaration about the Baptist's identity: John is a prophet, and more than a prophet, for he is the one to whom God was referring when he spoke of the messenger who would prepare his way (Matt. 11:10// Luke 7:27). Here it is Jesus rather than the Evangelist who links John with Exod. 23:20 and Mal. 3:1. Perhaps partly as a consequence of this shift and perhaps also because they realizes the inaccuracy of Mark's ascription of the entire passage to Isaiah, Matthew and Luke retain only the Isaianic part of Mark's opening quotation (Matt. 3:3//Luke 3:4).

If the Exodus and Malachi texts were already combined and referred to John the Baptist in Q on the basis of the shared phrase "Behold, I am sending a messenger,"[2] Mark may have gotten the combination from a source and added a reference to Isaiah 40:3, partly on the basis of the shared motif of clearing a path for God.[3] Mark 1:2–3, then, would be a complex conflation of Old Testament texts that developed through the Jewish exegetical principle of *gezerah shavah* (analogy; see glossary). This conflation inaugurates Mark's Gospel with an impressive

Old Testament testimony suggesting that the Baptist was both the voice in the wilderness described by Isaiah and the returning Elijah pictured by Malachi, and that his preparatory and guiding mission was foreshadowed by the "Angel of the Presence" of the exodus era.

The Markan opening thus reflects early Christian convictions about the biblical lineaments of John the Baptist. But do these convictions correspond to John's own understanding of himself? In chapter 3 we take up the Elijan side of this question; here we attempt to assess whether or not John thought of himself as the Isaian wilderness voice. Did the Baptist interpret his own ministry through Isa. 40:3?

This would be a simple question to answer if we could be sure that we could trust the Fourth Gospel, since there the Baptist, while denying that he is either the Messiah, Elijah, or "the prophet," affirms that he *is* "the voice of someone shouting in the wilderness, 'Make straight the way of the Lord'" (John 1:23 RSV alt.). Unfortunately, we cannot always trust the historicity of the Fourth Gospel, although C. H. Dodd, Raymond E. Brown, and others have done much to rehabilitate its status.[4] Nevertheless, the Gospel's theological tendencies must be taken into account, and in this particular case, as Dodd admits, it is possible to see the Evangelist's placement of Isa. 40:3 into the Baptist's mouth as a reflection of his own concern to portray John as the witness par excellence (cf. John 1:7). In support of this possibility, Dodd compares the way in which the same Evangelist, in contrast to the other Gospel writers, locates the descent of the dove within "the testimony of John" (John 1:32–34; contrast Mark 1:10//Matt. 3:16//Luke 3:22).[5] Moreover, the movement in the Fourth Gospel toward explicit self-identification by the Baptist corresponds to the parallel movement to self-identification by Jesus, as seen especially in the famous "I am" statements (John 6:35; 8:12; 10:9, 11; 11:25; 14:6; 15:5)

These Johannine tendencies, however, cannot predetermine our answer to the question of whether or not the Baptist saw himself as the Isaian voice shouting in the wilderness. Even if the tradition that came down to him had shown the Baptist using the words of Isa. 40:3 with reference to himself, Mark may have wanted to transform this into a testimony *about* him from the scriptures and to frontload this biblical testimony onto his Gospel; and Matthew and Luke merely follow Mark in this regard. After all, Mark may well have done something similar with the Exodus/Malachi conflation, which came down to him as a testimony by Jesus (cf. again Matt. 11:10//Luke 7:27 = Q). Mark deliberately constructs his Gospel to begin with an impressive citation of the word of God; the crucial affirmation for him is not that "the beginning of the good news" has taken place as described by a recent human being, even John the Baptist or Jesus, but that it has occurred "as it had been written" hundreds of years previously in the book of "Isaiah the prophet" (Mark 1:1–2).[6]

Moreover, John 1:23 is somewhat in tension with its Johannine context and therefore likely to reflect a pre-Gospel tradition. Two verses earlier, in 1:21, the Evangelist has John *deny* that he is Elijah or "the [eschatological] prophet." Here in 1:23, however, John identifies himself as the Isaian "voice of one shouting in the wilderness" to make the Lord's ways straight. This certainly sounds like the self-description of a prophet, and straightening the Lord's way is close to preparing it, which is what the eschatological Elijah does in Mal. 3:1, 23.[7] John 1:23 may be a deliberate revision of an earlier tradition in which the Baptist affirmed that he was both the voice shouting in the wilderness and the preparer of the way of the Lord—that is, Elijah—especially since the latter was associated with the Judean wilderness referred to in Isa. 40:3.[8]

That the Isaianic self-testimony in John 1:23 reflects the consciousness of the historical Baptist is also supported by the Qumran parallels noted in the section "Similarities" in chapter 2, especially 1QS 8:12–14 and 9:18–20. These passage link Isa. 40:3 with the Dead Sea Sect's location in the Judean wilderness and its mission of observing the true Torah of God in preparation for the eschaton. As Dodd puts it, "If the men of Qumran believed themselves to have been called (or adopted) to fill the role of the Voice in the Wilderness, so may John the Baptist have believed himself called."[9] This is especially likely since, as I show in the same section of chapter 2, Isa. 40:3 was a favorite passage of the sectarians and was little used elsewhere in Second Temple Judaism. Moreover, an allusion to Isa. 40:3 occurs in the Benedictus (Luke 1:76), which seems not to show Christian influence and probably goes back to Baptist circles.[10] Another occurs, in a rather incidental way, in the account in Acts 18:24–28 of Apollos, who "knows only the baptism of John" and is instructed in "the way of the Lord." This passage also may reflect a Baptist source.[11]

An objection has been voiced to Dodd's reasoning: the Qumran usages of Isa. 40:3 and the Hebrew text of Isaiah on which those usages are based do not actually speak of a voice shouting in the wilderness. Rather, for the author of 1QS 8–9, as probably for the Deutero-Isaian original, "in the wilderness" modifies the imperative to prepare the Lord's way:

> A voice cries:
> > in the wilderness
> > > prepare
> > > > the way of the LORD,
> > > make straight
> > in the desert
> > > a highway for our God. (Isa. 40:3 MT)

As the parallelism indicates, "in the wilderness" in the Isaian original designates the place where the Lord's way is prepared rather than the location of the shouting voice. Correspondingly, neither 1QS 8:12–14 nor 1QS 9:18–20 mentions the shouting voice; both concentrate instead on preparing the way in the wilderness, which is what the sectarians saw themselves doing by their study of the Law at Qumran. The Gospel usages, on the other hand, reflect the Septuagint, which makes "in the wilderness" go with the calling voice by dropping the parallel phrase "in the desert":

> A voice of one shouting in the wilderness:
> Prepare the way of the Lord;
> Make straight the paths of our God. . . .

In accordance with this altered text, the Gospels, in their use of Isa. 40:3, stress the calling activity of an individual, whom they identify with John; the Qumran texts, on the other hand, stress the scholarly activity of a community, which they identify with themselves.[12] These differences make it likely that the Gospels' use of the Isaian text reflects Greek-speaking Christianity rather than the historical Baptist. So runs the argument.[13]

This argument, however, is not cogent, first because it exaggerates the contrast between the collective interpretation of Isa. 40:3 at Qumran and the individual interpretation in the New Testament. In fact, two passages in the Qumran literature, one from the Aramaic Levi Document and the other from the Community Rule, use Isa. 40:3 in reference to an individual. The first presents a striking parallel to the Gospel usage of Isa. 40:3, since the person who alludes to the Isaian text, the patriarch Levi, is involved in a rite of immersion: "I washed myself entirely in living water and made all my ways straight" (πάσας τὰς ὁδούς μου ἐποίησα εὐθείας). The Isaian text is also alluded to in 1QS 4:2–3, where the job of the Prince of Light is to "enlighten a person's heart, and to straighten before him all the ways of true righteousness (וליישר לפניו כל דרכי צדק אמת), and to cause his heart to fear the laws of God" (*Dead Sea Scrolls Electronic Library* trans. alt.). In both instances, Isa. 40:3 is referred to the activity of an individual (in the one case Levi, in the other the ideal sectarian). Both Qumran writers have thus taken a favorite biblical text—one that the Community Rule author elsewhere uses in a collective way—and here applied it to the work of an individual. This fits with what we know about ancient Jewish exegesis in general: exegetes were usually not concerned with preserving original contexts, often preferring creative misreadings, and they frequently reinterpreted biblical collective figures as individuals (for example, the Suffering Servant from Isaiah and the "one like a son of man" from Daniel).[14]

Another blow to skepticism about the Baptist's use of Isa. 40:3 emerges from the ambiguity of that verse in the Hebrew. Although Isa. 40:3 MT is most smoothly read as speaking of the preparation of a way in the wilderness, the text *can* actually be read as a reference to a voice shouting in the wilderness.[15] In fact, the (infrequent) rabbinic citations of the verse, which use the MT, usually cite just its first six words, (קול קורא במדבר פנו דרך ה'), which lack the parallelism of the full verse and are most easily read as a reference to the location of the voice: "A voice crying in the wilderness, 'Prepare the way of the Lord!'"[16] Strikingly, this is almost exactly the form in which the verse is rendered in the Gospel of John—the same Gospel that has the Baptist proclaiming the verse, rather than the Evangelist.[17]

The Baptist's usage of Isa. 40:3 to refer to himself as "the voice crying in the wilderness," then, could be a creative "misreading" of a biblical text whose importance he first registered as a member of the Qumran community but later reactualized to fit his changed circumstances—just as his Qumran predecessors had reactualized it to refer to theirs. John learned a process of biblical interpretation from his time in the sect; it would make sense that he extended it in other ways after he left it.[18] The Gospel writers may have conformed this reactualization to the LXX, the form of scripture used in their churches, but they did not thereby distort John's meaning.

John the Baptist in the Slavonic Version of Josephus's Jewish War

The translations that follow are from *Josephus' Jewish War and Its Slavonic Version: A Synoptic Comparison of the English Translation by H. St. Thackeray with the Critical Edition by N. A. Meščerskij of the Slavonic Version in the Vilna Manuscript Translated into English by H. Leeming and L. Osinkina*, ed. H. Leeming and K. Leeming, Arbeiten zur Geschichte des antiken Judentums und des Urchristentums 46 (Leiden, the Netherlands: Brill, 2003). Meščerskij follows the Vilna manuscript, but variant readings from the Volokolam manuscript are given in braces—that is, { }. The words in square brackets—[ ]—have been added by the English translators for stylistic reasons.

In Meščerskij's opinion, the Slavonic Josephus is a periphrastic translation of Josephus's Greek original. It shows the influence of the Slavonic translation of the chronicle of George Hamartolus, which was made in the tenth or eleventh century (72–73). Meščerskij convincingly refutes the argument of Alexander Berendts and Robert Eisler that it contains Aramaisms that suggest the translation was made from a putative Aramaic original of Josephus's *War* (41–42).[1]

....

2.110

And at that time a certain man was going about Judaea, [dressed] in strange garments. He donned {Vol: stuck} the hair of cattle on the parts of his body which were not covered with his own hair. And he was wild of visage. And he came to the Jews and called them to freedom, saying, "God has sent me to show you the lawful way, by which you will be rid of [your] many rulers. But there will be no mortal ruling {Vol + over you}, only the Most High, who has sent me." And when they heard this, the people were joyful. And all Judaea and the environs of Jerusalem were following him. And he did nothing else for them, except to immerse them in Jordan's stream, and to dismiss them, bidding them refrain from their wicked deeds, and a king would be given to them, saving them and humbling all the unsubmissive, while he himself would be humbled by no one. Some mocked his voices {Vol: words}, others believed them. And when he was brought before Archelaus and the experts of the Law were assembled, they asked him who he was and where he had been up until then. In answer he said, "I am a man. Where {Vol: As} the divine spirit leads me, I feed on the roots of reeds and the shoots of trees." When those [men] threatened him with torture if he did not cease those words and deeds, he said, "It is you who should cease from your foul deeds and adhere to the Lord, your God." And arising in fury, Simon, an Essene by origin [and] a scribe, said, "We read the divine scriptures every day,[2] and you who have [just] now come in {Vol: come out} like a beast from the woods dare to teach us and to lead people astray with your impious words." And he rushed forward to tear his body apart. But he, reproaching them, said, "I am not revealing to you the mystery which is [here] among you, because you have not wished it. Therefore, there will come {Vol: has come} [down] on you an unutterable calamity, because of you {Vol + and all the people}." Thus he spoke and left for the other side of the Jordan. And as no one dared to prevent him, he was doing just what he had done before.

. . . .

2.168

{Vol: And in those days} Philip, while being in his own domain, saw [in] a dream an eagle tear out both his eyes. And he called together all his wise men. And when others were resolving the dream otherwise, the man we have already described as walking about in animal hair and cleansing people in the streams of Jordan, came to Philip suddenly, unsummoned, and said, "Hear the word of the Lord. The dream you have seen: the eagle is your rapacity, for that bird is violent and rapacious. Such also is that sin; it will {Vol: And that sin will} pluck out your eyes which are your domain and your wife {Vol: "your wife" is erased}.

And when he had spoken thus, Philip passed away by evening and his domain was given to Agrippa. And his wife Herodias was taken by Herod, his brother. Because of her all those who were learned in the Law detested him but did not dare accuse him to his face. Only that man they called wild {Vol and other mss. + but we call John, Baptizer of the Lord}, came to him in fury and said, "Since you, lawless one, have taken your brother's wife, just as your brother died a merciless death, so you too will be cut down {corrected by a later hand to: reaped} by heaven's sickle. For divine providence will not remain silent but will be the death of you through grievous afflictions in other lands, for you are not raising seed for your brother but satisfying your carnal lust and committing adultery, since there are four children of his own."

Hearing this, Herod was enraged and ordered him to be beaten and thrown out. He, however, did not cease but wherever he encountered Herod, {spoke thus [and] accused him; Vol: there accused him} until {he put him in a dungeon; Vol: he was exasperated and gave orders to behead him}. {Vol - And} his character was strange and his way of life not that of a human being, for he existed just like a fleshless spirit. His mouth knew not bread nor did he even taste the unleavened bread at Passover, saying that it was in remembrance of God, who had delivered the people from servitude, but it had been given to eat for escape, [since] the journey was urgent. Wine and fermented liquor he would not allow to come near himself. And he detested {Vol: the eating of} all animal [meat]. And he denounced all injustice. And for his needs there were tree shoots {Vol: and locusts and wild honey}.

APPENDIX 10   *Apocalyptic Belief and Perfectionism*

In chapter 4, I argue that John thought his baptism provided a once-and-for-all cleansing from both ritual impurity and sin, and I link this belief with John's sense of an erupting apocalypse. Such a linkage is not unusual in the history of religions: a robust sense of sinlessness often goes along with a vibrant sense of imminent or realized eschatology.

In his study of the genesis of the idea of perfectionism in 1 John, for example, John Bogart maintains that "a genuine, full-blown perfectionism" appeared in Judaism only in the apocalyptic literature of the Maccabean period and later (citing 1 Enoch, Jubilees, and the Testaments of the Twelve Patriarchs).[1] Elsewhere Bogart generalizes: "A perfectionist self-understanding can occur in history when two *sine-qua-non* elements co-exist in the same community at the same time: ethical dualism and imminent eschatological hope."[2] Although I am leery about calling imminent eschatological hope a sine qua non for perfectionism or a belief in sinlessness,[3] the two often go together. In the Christian sphere, one can cite the second-century Montanists,[4] the medieval Free Spirit movement,[5] and the nineteenth-century Campbellites, Shakers, and Oneida Community.[6] Also relevant is Albert Schweitzer's famous treatment of the "interim ethic" of Jesus.[7]

A similar connection is visible in some Jewish messianic circles. Most influential in this regard has been Gershom Scholem's study of the idea of the holiness of sin in the Frankist offshoot of the Sabbatai Zevi messianic movement in the seventeenth century. Scholem argues that, in the history of religions, this idea is almost invariably coupled with the notion that

> the elect are fundamentally different from the crowd and not to be judged by its standards. Standing under a new spiritual law and representing as it were a new kind of reality, they are beyond good and evil. It is well known to what dangerous consequences Christian sects in ancient and modern times have been led by the idea that the truly new-born is incapable of committing a sin, and that therefore everything he does must be regarded under a higher aspect. Similar ideas made their appearance very soon in the wake of Sabbatianism especially in Salonica. The inner reality of redemption, which has already been inaugurated in the hidden world, was held to dictate a higher law of conduct to those who experience it.[8]

But a connection with antinomianism is not inevitable; the Chabad messianic movement, for example, has remained generally within the parameters of Orthodox practice at the same time that it sees the divine energy as transforming earthly limitations.[9] In practice, however, here, as in other Hasidic movements, sinlessness is predicated only of the Rebbe, not his followers.[10]

A connection between belief in sinlessness and eschatological expectation is also visible outside of the Judeo-Christian sphere. There are numerous examples in Bryan Wilson's study of modern cargo cults and other millenarian movements.[11] The Aum Shinrikyô movement that was responsible for the sarin gas attacks in Tokyo is a horrifying contemporary example; interestingly, purity language is prominent in the group's literature.[12]

John 3:23–30 begins with an account of John baptizing in Aenon near Salem, "where there was much water" (3:23). This site cannot now be identified; all that can be said for sure is that the Fourth Evangelist conceives it to be somewhere west of the Jordan (see 3:26 and cf. 1:28).[1] As the story progresses, John's baptismal activity at Aenon (and also perhaps the baptismal activity of Jesus in Judaea, referred to in 3:22) sets off a dispute between "a Jew" and John's disciples concerning καθαρισμός (= "purification" [3:25]).

It would be nice to know the exact nature of this dispute.[2] Knut Backhaus rightly labels it one of the most enigmatic passages in Johannine literature.[3] Raymond Brown delineates the main alternatives: "Are we to think [the controversy] was about the relative value of the baptisms of John the Baptist and Jesus? Or, since the word 'purification' reminds us of the water 'prescribed for Jewish purifications' in ii 6, are we perhaps to think of a dispute about the relative value of John the Baptist's baptism and of standard Jewish purificatory washings? Was this Jew posing questions about John the Baptist's baptism like those by the Pharisees in i 25? Or was there a general controversy about the value of all the types of purification by water (like the various baptisms of the Pharisees; Essene lustrations)?"[4] Of these four possibilities, the first two are supported by the strongest contextual clues.

On the one hand, the οὖν ("therefore") in 3:25 seems to associate the dispute with what has immediately preceded in 3:22–24, which is an account of the simultaneous baptismal ministries of John and Jesus. The latter could be seen as raising the question of the relative value of those two baptisms—which, if either of them, has the power to "cleanse" people, presumably from their sins? The continuation of the passage, in which John acknowledges his inferiority to Jesus (3:26–30), might then point toward the intended answer: Jesus's baptism, not John's, imparts purification, a message that agrees with the many New Testament passages, including Johannine ones, that link Jesus or the new Christian reality with cleansing from sin.[5] There is, however, a problem with this interpretation: it is not clear how a statement about the relative effectiveness of John's baptism and Jesus's is a logical response to a purity dispute between John's disciples and *"a Jew."* If a Jew disputes with John's disciples about καθαρισμός, that would seem to suggest a discrepancy between the Baptist's understanding of the term and the Jewish understanding of it, not the Christian one.

This suggests, in turn, that the καθαρισμός at the center of the dispute is a "Jewish" form of cleansing, and if so the prime candidate is purification from Levitical uncleanness, the sort of ritual defilement that, in biblical and Second Temple Jewish texts, is contracted through childbirth or contact with the dead, with leprosy, with semen, with menstrual blood, or with other fluxes.[6] A plurality of the Septuagint's usages of καθαρισμός refer to this sort of ritual cleansing,[7] and this meaning makes sense in the Johannine context. There is a strong correlation in biblical and Second Temple Jewish texts between water rites and cleansing from Levitical impurity,[8] and this association helps explain the οὖν in John 3:25: the baptisms practiced by John and Jesus are reminiscent of Jewish rites of ritual purification, so the question naturally rises whether they are meant to deal with the same sort of impurity. And the removal of Levitical uncleanness is precisely what is in view in the only other Johannine usage of καθαρισμός, the reference in 2:6 to the six large water jugs that are present at the Cana wedding κατὰ τὸν καθαρισμὸν τῶν Ἰουδαίων ("according to the purification process of the Jews," my trans.). Both passages involve purification, water rites, and Jews.

But what more precisely was the dispute about? Among Jews themselves, there were frequent disagreements about what sorts of substances caused Levitical defilement and how these defilements should be cleansed, disagreements that usually arose because of the vagueness or contradictory evidence of the Pentateuchal laws. Such disputes are visible, for example, throughout the Qumran Halakhic Letter (4QMMT)[9] and in rabbinic accounts of the arguments between the Schools of Hillel and Shammai (for example, m. ʿEd. 4:6),[10] between the Pharisees and the Sadducees (for example, m. Par. 3:7; m. Yad. 4:6–7),[11] and between specific rabbis and the rest of the sages (for example, m. ʿEd. 3:7–9).[12]

The dispute alluded to in John 3:25 may well be of a similar nature. Indeed, as shown in chapter 4, it was, in early Christianity in general, a controversial subject whether the Levitical laws of cleanness still applied or whether they had been abrogated along with the rest of the Torah (cf. Rom. 10:3). This question arose partly because the Levitical purity laws themselves treat processes associated with the powers of life and death and thus subject, in various religions, to taboos. For Christians, therefore, the question naturally arose whether such laws were just a matter of Jewish custom, and hence safe to ignore, or whether they were built into the very structure of the universe, and therefore perilous to ignore. This question continued to be debated for several centuries in the church.[13]

. . . .

Kathar Words in the Septuagint Divided by Category

καθαρίζειν

Ritual:[14] Exod. 29:36–37; 30:10; Lev. 8;15; 9:15 (A): 12:7–8, 13: 7, 13, 17, 23, 28, 34, 35, 37, 59; 14:2, 4, 7–8, 11, 14, 17, 18, 19, 20, 23, 25, 28, 29, 31, 48, 57; 15:13, 28 (2x); 16:19, 20, 30 (2x), 22:4; Num. 6:9; 8:15; 12:15; 31:23–24; 1 Kgdms. 20:26; 4 Kgdms. 5:10, 12,

13, 14; 2 Chron. 29:15; 2 Esd. 6:20; Neh. 12:30 (2x); 13:9; Jud. 16:18; Job 1:5; Isa. 66:17; Ezek. 39:12, 14, 16; 43:26; 44:26; Dan. 8:14; 1 Macc. 4:36, 41, 43

"Moral": Exod. 20:7; 34:7; Num. 14:18; 30:6, 9, 13; Deut. 5:11; 19:13; Josh. 22:17; Pss. 18:13–14; 38:8 (‫א‬); 50:4, 9; Sir. 23:10; 38:10; Mal. 3:3; Isa. 53:10; Jer. 32:29; 40:8; Ezek. 24:13; 36:25, 33; Dan. 11:35; 4 Macc. 1:11; 17:21—24x

Idolatry: Gen. 35:2; 2 Chron. 34:3, 5, 8; Hos. 8:5; Jer. 13:27; Ezek. 27:23; 1 Macc. 13:47, 50; 2 Macc. 2:18; 10:3, 7; 14:36—13x

Ambiguous, neutral: Ps. 11:7; Prov. 25:4; Sir 31:4; 38:30; Isa. 57:14

καθαριότης

"Moral": 2 Kgdms. 22:21, 25; Pss. 17:21, 25
Ambiguous, neutral: Exod. 24:10; Wis. 7:24 (‫א‬); Sir. 43:1

καθαριοῦν

Ambiguous, neutral: Lam. 4:7

καθάρσις

Ritual: Lev. 12:4, 6

καθαρισμός

Ritual: Exod. 29:36; Lev. 14:32; 15:13; 1 Chron. 23:28; Neh. 12:45; Job 7:21; 4 Macc. 7:6

Moral: Num. 14:18; Job 7:21; Ps. 88:45; Prov. 14:9: Sir 51:20; Dan. 12:6
Idolatry: 2 Macc. 1:18; 2:16, 19; 10:5
Ambiguous, neutral: Exod. 30:10; 2 Macc. 1:36

καθαρός

Ritual: Gen. 7:2 (2x), 3 (2x), 8 (2x), 8:20 (2x); Lev. 4:12; 6:11; 7:9; 10:10; 11:32, 36, 37, 47; 13:6, 13, 17, 34, 37, 39 (2x), 40, 41, 58; 14:4, 7, 8, 9, 49, 53; 15:8, 12, 13; 17:15; 20:25 (2x); 22:7; Num. 5:17; 8:7; 9:13; 18:11, 13; 19:3, 9 (2x), 12 (2x), 18, 19; Deut. 12:15, 22; 14:11, 20; 15:22; 23:11; 1 Kgdms. 20:26; 2 Chron. 13:11; 2 Esd. 6:20; Jud. 10:5; 12:9; Mal. 1:11; Isa. 65:5; Ezek. 22:26; 44:23

Moral: Gen. 20:5–6; 24:8; 44:10; Num. 5:28; Tob. 3:14; Job 4:7, 17; 8:6; 9:30; 11:4, 13; 14:4; 15:15; 16:17; 17:9; 21:16 (A); 22:25, 30; 25:5; 33:3, 9, 26; Pss. 23:4; 50:12; Prov. 12:27; 20:9; Wis. 7:23; 14:24; Hab. 1:13; Isa. 1:16, 25; 14:20; Sus. 46; 2 Macc. 7:40 (v.l.)

Idolatry: Ezek. 36:25

Ambiguous, neutral: Exod. 25:10, 16, 27, 28, 30, 35, 37, 38; 27:20; 28:8 (v.l.), 13, 14, 22, 32; 30:3–4, 35; 31:8, 36:22, 37; 38:2, 9, 25; 39:16; Lev. 22:2, 4, 6, 7; 2 Chron. 3:4, 5, 8; 4:16, 20, 21; 9:15; 2 Esd. 2:69; Tob. 8:15; 13:16; Job 11:15; 28:19; Prov. 8:10; 14:4; 25:4; Eccl. 9:2; Wis. 15:7; Zech. 3:5 (2x); Isa. 35:8; 47:11; Jer. 4:11; Dan. 2:32 Th (AB²); 7:9

καθαρότης

Ambiguous, neutral: Exod. 24:10 (A); Wis. 7:24

καθάρσιος

Moral: 4 Macc. 6:29

κάθαρσις

Ritual: Lev. 12:4, 6
Moral: Jer. 32:29
Ambiguous, neutral: Ezek. 15:4

κάθαρτος

Ritual: Lev. 14:41 (A)

καθαρῶς

Moral: 2 Macc. 7:40

LIST OF ABBREVIATIONS

AB Anchor Bible

BZNW Beihefte zur Zeitschrift für die neutestamentliche Wissenschaft

JBL *Journal of Biblical Literature*

NTS *New Testament Studies*

WUNT Wissenschaftliche Untersuchungen zum Neuen Testament

NOTES

Introduction

1. See Raymond E. Brown, *The Gospel According to John*, AB 29 and 29A (Garden City, N.Y.: Doubleday, 1966–70), 1:159–60, who argues that the speaker switches to Jesus in John 3:31.

2. Knut Backhaus, "Echoes from the Wilderness: The Historical John the Baptist," in *Handbook for the Study of the Historical Jesus*, vol. 1, *How to Study the Historical Jesus*, ed. Tom Holmén and Stanley E. Porter (Leiden, the Netherlands: Brill, 2011), 1753, punctuation slightly altered. A photograph of the famous Isenheim altar of Matthias Grünewald is on the cover of the present study.

3. For the chronology of John and Jesus, see app. 1.

4. For the theory that *Ant.* 18.116–119 is a later interpolation into Josephus's writing, see app. 2.

5. John Reumann, "The Quest for the Historical John the Baptist," in *Understanding the Sacred Text: Essays in Honor of Morton S. Enslin on the Hebrew Bible and Christian Beginnings*, ed. John Reumann (Valley Forge, Pa.: Judson Press, 1972), 187.

6. For further analogies with Islam, see the section "The Islamic Analogy" in chap. 1.

7. Wilhelm Baldensperger, *Der Prolog des vierten Evangeliums: sein polemisch-apologetischer Zweck* (Freiburg, Germany: J. C. B. Mohr [Paul Siebeck], 1898); Martin Dibelius, *Die urchristliche Überlieferung von Johannes dem Täufer*, Forschungen zur Religion und Literatur des Alten und Neuen Testaments 15 (Göttingen, Germany: Vandenhoeck & Ruprecht, 1911). For a good summary but poor critique, see C. W. Rishell, "Baldensperger's Theory of the Origin of the Fourth Gospel," *JBL* 20 (1901): 38–49. Baldensperger's hypothesis attained almost canonical status when it was adopted by Rudolf Bultmann in his classic commentary on the Gospel of John; see Rudolf Bultmann, *The Gospel of John: A Commentary* (1941; Eng. trans., Philadelphia: Westminster, 1971), under "Baptist and the Baptist sect."

8. For Dibelius, this tendency is already apparent in the secondary 11:11b//Luke 7:28b. I disagree with Dibelius on the incompatibility of Matt. 11:11a//Luke 7:28a with Matt. 11:11b//Luke 7:28b; the mixed attitude may reflect the sort of ambivalence often encountered in a successor figure's attitude towards a founder. See the section on "History-of-Religions Comparisons" in chapter 5.

9. Backhaus, "Echoes from the Wilderness," 1755. Backhaus labels this "the criterion of counter-tendency," but in n. 32 he paraphrases it as "the criterion of dissimilarity and embarrassment." On the problems that John's baptism of Jesus caused for Christians, see chap. 5.

10. See Chris Keith and Anthony Le Donne, eds., *Jesus, Criteria, and the Demise of Authenticity* (London: T&T Clark, 2012).

11. This is denied by Robert L. Webb, "Jesus' Baptism: Its Historicity, and Implications," *Bulletin for Biblical Research* 10 (2000): 291–92, apparently for apologetic reasons.

12. I do not follow a recent trend to distinguish "embarrassment" from "dissimilarity"; see, for example, John P. Meier, *A Marginal Jew: Rethinking the Historical Jesus,* Anchor Bible Reference Library, 5 vols. (New Haven: Yale University Press, 1991–2016), 1:171. "Embarrassment" is actually a subset of "dissimilarity," especially when the latter is understood, as it should be, as "single dissimilarity" (from the teachings of the church) rather than "double dissimilarity" (from the teachings of both first-century Judaism and the church); cf. Tom Holmén, "Doubts About Double Dissimilarity: Restructuring the Main Criterion of Jesus-of-History Research," in *Authenticating the Words of Jesus,* ed. Bruce Chilton and Craig A. Evans, New Testament Studies and Tools 28.1 (Leiden, the Netherlands: Brill, 1999), 75.

13. On Jesus's apocalypticism, see E. P. Sanders, *Jesus and Judaism* (Philadelphia: Fortress, 1985); Dale C. Allison, *Jesus of Nazareth: Millenarian Prophet* [Minneapolis: Fortress, 1998]. For the continuity argument, see Dale C. Allison, "A Plea for Thoroughgoing Eschatology," *JBL* 113 (1994): 654–55; Dale C. Allison, *Constructing Jesus: Memory, Imagination, and History* (Grand Rapids, Mich.: Baker Academic Press, 2010), 54–55. Allison, however, makes the case about the linkage with Jesus the other way around: since Jesus's predecessor and teacher, John the Baptist, was an apocalypticist, and since his followers, the early Christians, were apocalypticists, so probably was he.

14. I have borrowed the phrasing from Allison, "Plea for Thoroughgoing Eschatology," 652.

15. There is one saying about the Baptist in the second-century Gospel of Thomas, logion 46: "Jesus says, 'From Adam to John the Baptist, among those born of a woman there is no one who surpasses John the Baptist, so that his (i.e. John's) eyes need not be downcast. But I have (also) said, Whoever among you becomes little will know the kingdom and will surpass John'" (trans., with punctuation slightly altered, from Uwe-Karsten Plisch, *The Gospel of Thomas: Original Text with Commentary* [Freiburg, Germany: Deutsche Bibelgesellschaft, 2008], 121–22.) As Plisch argues, this seems to be a secondary version of Matt. 11:11//Luke 7:28, though it preserves the essential intention of its source, especially in the second sentence.

16. Albert Schweitzer, *The Quest of the Historical Jesus: First Complete Edition* (1913; English trans., Minneapolis: Fortress, 2001), 198, makes the decision between John and the Synoptics the second of the three "great alternatives" whose gradual recognition marks the progress of life-of-Jesus research in the nineteenth century; the others are "either purely historical or purely supernatural" and "either eschatological or non-eschatological." On the priority of the Synoptics in life-of-Jesus research, see also E. P. Sanders, *The Historical Figure of Jesus* (London: Penguin Press, 1993), 57; Gerd Theissen and Antoinette Merz, *The Historical Jesus: A Comprehensive Guide* (London: SCM, 1998), 25.

17. I accept the consensus of scholarship that Mark and the hypothetical Q document were the earliest Gospel sources, which were subsequently used independently by Matthew and Luke; for a summary of recent research, see Christopher M. Tuckett, "The Current State of the Synoptic Problem," in *New Studies in the Synoptic Problem: Oxford Conference, April 2008; Essays in Honour of Christopher M. Tuckett,* ed. Paul Foster et al., Bibliotheca Ephemeridum Theologicarum Lovaniensium 239 (Leuven, Belgium: Peeters, 2011), 9–50. For a challenge to the consensus, see Mark Goodacre, *The Case Against Q: Studies in Markan Priority and the Synoptic Problem* (Harrisburg, Pa.: Trinity Press

International, 2002); for a rebuttal, see John S. Kloppenborg, "On Dispensing with Q? Goodacre on the Relation of Luke to Matthew," *NTS* 49 (2003): 210–36.

18. On John's "realized eschatology," see Rudolf Bultmann, *Theology of the New Testament*, 2 vols. in 1 (New York: Scribner's, 1951–55), 2:75–92; Brown, *Gospel According to John*, 1:cxv–cxxi; Jörg Frey, *Die johanneische Eschatologie*, WUNT 96, 3 vols. (Tübingen, Germany: J. C. B. Mohr [Paul Siebeck], 1997–2000).

19. On the expectation that Elijah would precede the Messiah, see chap. 3, n. 1 (p. 187–88).

20. See C. H. H. Scobie, *John the Baptist* (London: SCM, 1964), 129. In the view of John A. T. Robinson, "Elijah, John and Jesus: An Essay in Detection," *NTS* 4 (1958): 263–81, the idea was an invention of Jesus himself.

21. John 1:21 is an exception and will be weighed carefully in chap. 3.

22. Cf. Meier, *Marginal Jew*, 2:19–233, who divides his book-length treatment of the Baptist into two sections, "John Without Jesus" and "Jesus With and Without John."

....

CHAPTER ONE   The Competition Hypothesis

1. Baldensperger, *Prolog des vierten Evangeliums.*

2. Knut Backhaus, *Die "Jüngerkreise" des Täufers Johannes: eine Studie zu den religionsgeschichtlichen Ursprüngen des Christentums*, Paderborner Theologische Studien 19 (Paderborn, Germany: Ferdinand Schöningh, 1991), 365–66, 370.

3. Ernst Bammel, review of *Die 'Jüngerkreise' des Täufers Johannes*, by Klaus Backhaus, *Journal of Theological Studies* 43 (1992): 583–84.

4. On John 1:6–8 as an editorial insertion into a preexistent Logos Hymn, see Brown, *Gospel According to John*, 1:21–23, 27–28.

5. Baldensperger, *Prolog des vierten Evangeliums*, 59, calls particular attention to the repeated emphasis in John 1:20: "And he confessed, and he did not deny, and he confessed: 'I am not the Christ'" (my trans.). Oscar Cullmann, "Ὁ ὀπίσω μου ἐρχόμενος," in *The Early Church: Studies in Early Christian History and Theology* (1947; Eng. trans., Philadelphia: Westminster, 1956), 178, referring to this passage, speaks of the Fourth Evangelist's "emphatic insistence which can only be explained as aimed at an assertion to the contrary." Although ὁμολογεῖν = "to confess" in the New Testament often has the nuance "to declare publicly" and can lack the note of admission of an uncomfortable truth, its three Johannine usages (1:20, 9:22, 12:42) all seem to strike this note (see also Heb. 11:13 and BDAG 708 [3]).

6. See especially Cullmann, "Ὁ ὀπίσω μου ἐρχόμενος"; cf. Joseph Thomas, *Le mouvement baptiste en Palestine et Syrie (150 av. J.-C.-300 ap. J.-C.)*, Universitas Catholica Lovaniensis, Dissertationes ad gradum magistri in Facultate Theologica vel in Facultate Iuris Canonici Consequendum Conscriptae 2.58 (Gembloux, Belgium: J. Duculot, 1935), 125n1. Cullmann points to the way in which the Pseudo-Clementines reverse this principle, for example in *Hom.* 2.16: "For whereas from [God] the greater things come first, and the inferior second, we find the opposite in human beings—the first worse, and the second superior" (Ante-Nicene Fathers trans. alt.). The author goes on in *Hom.* 2.17 to cite the relation between John the Baptist and Jesus as an illustration of the latter principle. But this makes all the more striking his acknowledgment in 2.16 that the default order is: superior first, inferior second. On this principle, see also Stephanie von Dobbeler, *Das Gericht und das Erbarmen Gottes: Die Botschaft Johannes des Täufers und ihre Rezeption bei den Johannesjüngern im Rahmen der Theologiegeschichte des Frühjudentums*, Bonner Biblische Beiträge 70 (Frankfurt: Athenäum, 1988), 229, who cites Odes Sol. 28:17–18 (= Charlesworth 28:18–19). Satan uses similar logic in Life of Adam

and Eve 14:3. See also Moses's superiority to Joshua and Peter's preeminence amongst the disciples of Jesus.

7. Walter Wink, *John the Baptist in the Gospel Tradition,* Society for New Testament Studies Monograph Series 7 (Cambridge: Cambridge University Press, 1968), 98.

8. See Cullmann, "Ὁ ὀπίσω μου ἐρχόμενος," 180–82.

9. On Acts 18:24–28; 19:1–7 as evidence for competition between early Christians and followers of John the Baptist, see already Baldensperger, *Prolog des vierten Evangeliums,* 93–99. See also the influential 1952 essay by Ernst Käsemann, "The Disciples of John the Baptist in Ephesus," English translation in *Essays on New Testament Themes* New Testament Library (Philadelphia: Fortress Press, 1964), 142–43.

10. Although Acts 18–19 describes events that took place much earlier in the century, around the fifties (see C. K. Barrett, *A Critical and Exegetical Commentary on the Acts of the Apostles,* International Critical Commentary, 2 vols. [Edinburgh: T&T Clark, 1994–98], 2:lvi), the peculiar emphasis that Luke gives to these stories, even at the risk of anachronism and illogic (see Käsemann, "Disciples of John the Baptist"), suggests that the Baptist movement was still a factor to be reckoned with when he wrote Acts.

11. On Knut Backhaus's different interpretation of Acts 19:1–7, see app. 6.

12. See Peter Böhlemann, *Jesus und der Täufer. Schlüssel zur Theologie und Ethik des Lukas,* Society for New Testament Studies Monograph Series 99 (Cambridge: Cambridge University Press, 1997), passim.

13. Morton Smith, "The Account of Simon Magus in Acts 8," in *Harry Austryn Wolfson Jubilee Volume: On the Occasion of His Seventy-Fifth Birthday; English Section* (Jerusalem: American Academy for Jewish Research, 1965), 2:737–38, notes that in Acts 8:9–24 Simon Magus is similarly inferior to Philip, who baptizes him.

14. Συγγενίς ("relative") here is sometimes translated as "cousin" (see, for example, the KJV), but as Joseph A. Fitzmyer, *The Gospel According to Luke,* AB 28 and 28A (New York: Doubleday, 1981–85), 1:352, notes, Luke does not use the usual word for "cousin," which is otherwise attested in the New Testament (ἀνέψιος; see Col. 4:10): "The phrase implies the kinship of John and Jesus as well, which must be considered in the light of John 1:33, where John the Baptist says that he did not know Jesus. The traditions here are obviously mixed." Given Luke's interest in emphasizing the salvation-historical continuity between John and Jesus, it is probable that Luke's picture of a family relation between the two is unhistorical.

15. For other parallels between John and Jesus in the Gospel tradition, see Allison, *Constructing Jesus,* 82–83.

16. On the locales of Matthew, Luke, and John, see Burnett Hillman Streeter, *The Four Gospels: A Study of Origins* (London: Macmillan, 1924), 500–23, 531–39; Raymond E. Brown, *An Introduction to New Testament Christology* (New York: Paulist Press, 1994), 212–16, 269–71, 375.

17. Backhaus, *Die "Jüngerkreise" des Täufers Johannes,* 112; cf. 340–41.

18. Manuel Vogel, "Jesusgemeinden und Täufergruppen zwischen Abgrenzung und Wertschätzung—eine Skizze," in *Juden und Christen unter römischer Herrschaft. Selbstwahrnehmung und Fremdwahrnehmung in den ersten beiden Jahrhunderten n. Chr.,* ed. Niclas Förster and Jacobus Cornelis de Vos (Göttingen, Saxony: Vandenhoeck & Ruprecht, 2015), 77.

19. For recent discussion of the date of the Pseudo-Clementine *Recognitions* and *Homilies* and their sources, see Georg Strecker, *Das Judenchristentum in den Pseudoklementinen,* Texte und Untersuchungen 70 (Berlin: Akademie-Verlag, 1981), passim;

F. Stanley Jones, *An Ancient Jewish Christian Source on the History of Christianity: Pseudo-Clementine Recognitions 1.27–71*, Texts and Translations 37 (Atlanta: Scholars Press, 1995), 166; Annette Yoshiko Reed, "'Jewish Christianity' After the 'Parting of the Ways': Approaches to Historiography and Self-Definition in the Pseudo-Clementines," in *The Ways That Never Parted: Jews and Christians in Late Antiquity and the Early Middle Ages*, ed. Adam H. Becker and Annette Yoshiko Reed, Texte und Studien zum antiken Judentum 95 (Tübingen, Germany: Mohr Siebeck, 2003), 197; Jürgen Wehnert, "Taufvorstellungen in den Pseudoklementinen," in *Ablution, Initiation, and Baptism*, ed. David Hellholm et al., BZNW 176 (Berlin: De Gruyter, 2011), 2:1073–77.

20. Strecker, *Judenchristentum in den Pseudoklementinen*, 221–54, identifies the source, the Ascents of James, with *Rec.* 1.33–71 and locates it at Pella in the second half of the second century CE; similarly Robert E. Van Voorst, *The Ascents of James: History and Theology of a Jewish-Christian Community*, Society of Biblical Literature Dissertation Series 112 (Atlanta: Scholars Press, 1989), 180. Jones, *Ancient Jewish Christian Source*, 157–68, identifies it with *Rec.* 1.27–71 and thinks it was written under the name of Matthew by a Jewish-Christian author around the year 200, "quite possibly in Judaea or Jerusalem."

21. *Sed et ex discipulis Iohannis, qui videbantur esse magni, segregarunt se a populo et magistrum suum velut Christum praedicarunt;* translation mine. The Syriac version runs, in Jones's translation, "Now the pure disciples of John (ܐܠܡܝ̈ܕܐ, ܕܝܢ ܕܕܟܝܐ) separated themselves greatly from the people (ܣܓܝ ܦܪܫܘ ܠܗܘܢ ܡܢ ܥܡܐ) and spoke to their teacher as if he was concealed [or: said that their teacher was, as it were, concealed]." In the view of Thomas, *Le mouvement baptiste*, 121n2, this version may reflect the Jewish idea of the hidden Messiah. The phrase "the pure disciples of John" may be ironic, equivalent to "those who thought of themselves as pure," analogous to "those who are well" and "the righteous" in Mark 2:17. It also suggests a connection between John and the theme of ritual purity; see the section "John's Baptism and Ritual Purity" in chap. 4.

22. The fourth-century Syrian churchman Ephrem seems to have referred to this same tradition in a prayer appended to his commentary on Tatian's harmony of the Gospels. The Syriac original is not extant, only an Armenian translation. A Latin translation of the latter is given in Georg Moesinger, ed., *Evangelii Concordantis Expositio facta a Sancto Ephraemo Doctore Syro* (Venice: Libraria PP. Mechitaristarum in Monasterio S. Lazari, 1876), 288; and this is displayed synoptically with the *Recognitions* passage in Thomas, *Le mouvement baptiste*, 117. See also n. 52 below.

23. Thomas, *Le mouvement baptiste*, 122.

24. The classic example of this theology is 1 John 2:18–19, on which see below; other New Testament examples include Jude 3–4 and Acts 20:29–30. For later examples see Walter Bauer, *Orthodoxy and Heresy in Earliest Christianity* (1934; Eng. trans., Philadelphia: Fortress, 1971), 38, 82–84, 90, who cites as the prototype Ephrem, *Hymns Against Heretics* 24.20: "For years the apostles preached, and others after them, and still there were no weeds [= heretics]"—the weeds first appearing with Simon Magus (not Marcion, as Bauer mistakenly claims), who according to Ephrem withdrew from the orthodox church (*Orthodoxy and Heresy*, 38–39; cf. Edmund Beck, ed., *Des heiligen Ephraem des Syrers Hymnen contra haereses*, Corpus scriptorum christianorum orientalium 169–70/Scriptores Syri 76–77 [Leuven, Belgium: Imprimerie Orientaliste L. Durbecq, 1957], 169.96–97//170.90). See also Alain Le Boulluec, *La notion d'hérésie dans la littérature grecque, IIe-IIIe siècles* (Paris: Etudes Augustiniennes, 1985), subject index under "nouveauté (de l'hérésie)." Page 99 includes an explicit reference to "the axiom that error

is an innovation"; among the passages cited (p. 179) is Irenaeus, *Against Heresies* 3.4.2, which contrasts "the inventions of the heretics" with "the ancient tradition of the apostles."

25. Bauer, *Orthodoxy and Heresy,* 28–29.

26. Ibid., 92. I have altered the translation from "setting the pace" to "setting the tone"; cf. Walter Bauer, *Rechtgläubigkeit und Ketzerei im ältesten Christentum* (1934; repr., Beiträge zur historischen Theologie 10; Tübingen, Germany: Mohr, 1964), 96 ("tonangebend").

27. ܪܐܬ̈ܝܟ ܐܪ̈ܗ ܝܟܝܐܬ̈ܣܟ ܐܟ ܣ ܟ ܐܬ̈ܣ ; trans. Jones, emphasis added. Rufinus's Latin, similarly, has, "These began to separate themselves from the assembly of the people as more righteous than the others and to deny the resurrection of the dead [Jones trans., alt.]" (*hique ut ceteris iustiores segregare se coepere a populi coetu et mortuorum resurrectionem negare).*

28. Jon D. Levenson, *Resurrection and the Restoration of Israel: The Ultimate Victory of the God of Life* (New Haven, Conn.: Yale University Press, 2006), emphasizes the roots of the idea of resurrection in the pre-exilic period, but even he recognizes that the doctrine received its first explicit articulation in the Hasmonean era; cf. Benjamin D. Sommer, review of *Resurrection and the Restoration of Israel,* by Jon D. Levenson, *Journal of Religion* 90 (2010): 555. Cf. George W. E. Nickelsburg, *Resurrection, Immortality, and Eternal Life in Intertestamental Judaism,* Harvard Theological Studies 26 (Cambridge, Mass.: Harvard University Press, 1972), 180: "The evidence indicates that in the intertestamental period there was no single Jewish orthodoxy on the time, mode, and place of resurrection, immortality, and eternal life." On the traditionalism of the Sadducees, see Jacob Z. Lauterbach's 1913 essay "The Sadducees and Pharisees," reprinted in *Rabbinic Essays* (Cincinnati: Hebrew Union College Press, 1951), 27–39.

29. *et ecce unus ex discipulis Iohannis adfirmabat, Christum Iohannem fuisse, et non Iesum; in tantum, inquit, ut et ipse Iesus omnibus hominibus et prophetis maiorem esse pronuntiaverit Iohannem.* Translations from Jones, *Ancient Jewish Christian Source.*

30. On this saying and its significance for the question of the relation between Jesus and John, see chap. 5.

31. On the term "Day-Baptist," see app. 7.

32. Although in one sense all humans are "born of women," the *Homilies* uses the phrase in a spiritual sense, to designate those who follow the false, female kind of prophecy; see *Hom.* 2.15 and Hans-Joachim Schoeps, *Theologie und Geschichte des Judenchristentums* (Tübingen, Germany: J. C. B. Mohr [Paul Siebeck] 1949), 163.

33. On this principle, a reversal of the usual assumption that the better comes first, see n. 6 above. Mandean texts reverse the valence here: John is the true prophet whereas Jesus is a false one; see Edmondo Lupieri, *The Mandaeans: The Last Gnostics,* Italian Texts and Studies on Religion and Society (Grand Rapids, Mich.: Eerdmans, 2002), 162–65, 224–53. On the Mandeans, see the section "The Mandean Literature" below.

34. Thomas, *Le mouvement baptiste,* 129, calls the Baptist of *Hom.* 2.23–24//*Rec.* 2.8 "Jean l'hérésiarche par excellence, père de toutes les hérésies."

35. Oscar Cullmann, *Le problème littéraire et historique du roman pseudo-clémentin: Étude sur le rapport entre le Gnosticisme et le Judéo-Christianisme,* Etudes d'Histoire et de Philosophie religieuses 23 (Paris: Librairie Félix Alcan, 1930), 240; cf. Backhaus, *Die "Jüngerkreise" des Täufers Johannes,* 291.

36. Wehnert, "Taufvorstellungen in den Pseudoklementinen," 2:1108, finds a

softening of John's image in later strata of the Pseudo-Clementines, but his argument is not compelling, being mostly based on silences such as the absence of John from the syzgies in *Rec.* 3.61. Wehnert also does not reckon enough with the inclusion of the earlier strata in the later versions of the work.

37. Backhaus, *Die "Jüngerkreise" des Täufers Johannes*, 275–98.

38. C. H. Dodd, *Historical Tradition in the Fourth Gospel* (Cambridge: Cambridge University Press, 1963), 298n1.

39. Backhaus, *Die "Jüngerkreise" des Täufers Johannes*, 283.

40. Ibid., 285–86.

41. Ibid., 286.

42. Ibid., 289. Backhaus finds it inconceivable that a Baptist community would appeal to a saying of Jesus, but as Thomas, *Le mouvement baptiste*, 131n2, already pointed out, non-Christian sects such as the Elchasites, the Simonians, and other Gnostic groups seem to have taken account of Christianity and to have incorporated Gospel texts into their own systems.

43. Backhaus, *Die "Jüngerkreise" des Täufers Johannes*, 290–92.

44. Ibid., 295.

45. Ibid., 290.

46. Ibid., 294.

47. See Thomas, *Le mouvement baptiste*, 130–31.

48. See for example Backhaus, *Die "Jüngerkreise" des Täufers Johannes*, 292–93, 295, 297.

49. Thomas, *Le mouvement baptiste*, 125; cf. Schoeps, *Theologie und Geschichte*, 165, 401–2; Cullmann, "Ὁ ὀπίσω μου ἐρχόμενος," 179. The sole possible exception is the pair of Simon Magus and Peter, which may reflect reaction against a form of Gnosticism linked with Simon. The Pseudo-Clementines themselves link Simon with the Samaritan Gnostic Dositheus (*Rec.* 2.8–11; *Hom.* 2.24), but it is hard to know whether or not there was actually a connection between the two, or between the historical Simon and later Simonian Gnosticism; see Wayne A. Meeks, "Simon Magus in Recent Research," *Religious Studies Review* 3 (1977): 142. Moreover, for the Pseudo-Clementines themselves, Simon himself is a derivative figure, a disciple of John the Baptist (*Hom.* 2.23; *Rec.* 2.8). Smith, "Account of Simon Magus," mounts an argument for the accuracy of this tradition.

50. Cf. Thomas, *Le mouvement baptiste*, 130.

51. Backhaus, *Die "Jungerkreise" des Täufers Johannes*, 295, 298.

52. In his commentary on the Diatessaron, Ephrem says the following, which seems to combine elements of *Rec.* 1.54.8 and 1.60.1: "And the disciples of John exult about John and say that he is greater than Christ, because he himself [Christ] bore witness to it, saying, 'There is no one among those born of woman who is greater than John.'" The original Syriac of this passage is not available; the above is my translation of a modern Latin rendering of an Armenian version (from Moesinger, *Evangelii Concordantis Expositio*, 287–88); cf. Thomas, *Le mouvement baptiste*, 116–18.

53. Thomas, *Le mouvement baptiste*, 130–33; cf. 123, where he says that the violent passage *Hom.* 2.23–24//*Rec.* 2.8, which makes John into a heresiarch, was probably part of the basic writing underlying the Pseudo-Clementines, which was composed around 230 CE; it was perhaps retained in the *Homilies* two centuries later because anti-Baptist polemic had again become necessary. Backhaus, *Die "Jüngerkreise" des Täufers Johannes*, 297–98, seems to cite Thomas with approval on this point, but it is hard to see how he could do so without undermining his own position. Cf. Strecker, *Judenchristentum in*

den Pseudoklementinen, 46, 243, 267, who agrees with Thomas in placing *Hom.* 2.23–24 in the basic writing, but dates this source between 220 and 300 CE. Wehnert, "Taufvorstellungen in den Pseudoklementinen," 2:1074, 1103–5, locates the passage in the Peter-Simon novella, which he dates to the end of the second or the beginning of the third century CE.

54. See Thomas, *Le mouvement baptiste,* 130.

55. On ancient polemic, see Luke Timothy Johnson, "The New Testament's Anti-Jewish Slander and the Conventions of Ancient Polemic," *JBL* (1989): 419–44.

56. See Pierluigi Piovanelli, "The *Toledot Yeshu* and Christian Apocryphal Literature: The Formative Years," in *Toledot Yeshu ("The Life Story of Jesus") Revisited: A Princeton Conference,* ed. Peter Schäfer, Michael Meerson, and Yaacov Deutch (Tübingen, Germany: Mohr Siebeck, 2011), 99, who concludes that "the earliest *Toledot Yeshu* stories were the *oral* product of Jewish communities that were living, probably in Syria-Palestine, in close contact and connection with a group, or multiple groups, of Jewish Christians." Piovanelli thinks these stories were already collected in book form by the end of the fourth or the beginning of the fifth century CE and that fourth-to-sixth-century "orthodox" Christian apocrypha such as Acts of Pilate, the Lament of Mary, and the Book of the Cock were a response to them; cf. Thomas, *Le mouvement baptiste,* 131n1, who compares the vitriolic rhetoric in *Hom.* 2.23–24//*Rec.* 2.8 to that in *Toledot Yeshu.*

57. Cf. John Barclay, "Apologetics in the Jewish Diaspora," in *Jews in the Hellenistic and Roman Cities,* ed. John R. Bartlett (London: Routledge, 2002), 134–35.

58. See Majella Franzmann, "Mandaeism," in *Religion Past and Present* (1998; repr., Leiden, the Netherlands: Brill, 2010), 8:21; Jorunn Jacobsen Buckley and Ezio Abrile, "Mandaean Religion," in *Encyclopedia of Religion,* ed. Lindsey Jones (Detroit: Macmillan Reference USA, 2005), 8:5634. Edmondo Lupieri, *Giovanni Battista fra storia e leggenda,* Biblioteca di Cultura Religiosa (Brescia, Italy: Paideia, 1988), 198, notes a consensus of recent studies that locate the origin of the Mandean movement in the Jordan Valley prior to the third century CE.

59. See Kurt Rudolph, *Die Mandäer,* Forschungen zur Religion und Literatur des Alten und Neuen Testaments 74, N.F. 56 (Göttingen, Germany: Vandenhoeck & Ruprecht, 1960), 1:62–66; Lupieri, *Mandaeans,* 13–14.

60. E. S. Drower, *The Mandaeans of Iraq and Iran: Their Cults, Customs, Magic, Legends, and Folklore* (Leiden, the Netherlands: Brill, 1962), 100–123 (quote at p. 100); cf. Lupieri, *Mandaeans,* 15–19.

61. For representative texts, see Lupieri, *Mandaeans,* 224–39; for a more extensive sampling and analysis, see Lupieri, *Giovanni Battista fra storia e leggenda,* 195–395.

62. For representative texts, see Lupieri, *Mandaeans,* 240–53. The other false prophets, with whom Jesus is frequently grouped, are Abraham, Moses, and Muhammad.

63. *Book of John* 30. Mandaic text and German translation in Mark Lidzbarski, *Das Johannesbuch der Mandäer* (Berlin: A. Töpelmann, 1915), 103–8; English translation in Lupieri, *Mandaeans,* 232–33; description and analysis in Lupieri, *Giovanni Battista fra storia e leggenda,* 227–30.

64. Rudolph, *Mandäer,* 1:76; on Mandean water rites, see further Lupieri, *Mandaeans,* 15–22.

65. See, however, the Pseudo-Clementine *Hom.* 2.23, which describes John as a "Day-Baptist"; on this passage, see further the discussion of the Pseudo-Clementine literature above and app. 7 on "The Day-Baptists."

66. Lupieri, *Mandaeans,* 165, says that the figure of John as the Mandaean predecessor

to Jesus was "present in Mandaeanism right from the beginning" but that his importance grew over time. Rudolph, *Mandäer,* 1:70, says that full Mandean narratives about John (rather than incidental references) leave the impression of being late.

67. Rudolph, *Mandäer,* 1:70, claims that John never appears in liturgical texts, but Lupieri, *Mandaeans,* 238, notes that his name has entered into perhaps the most common and best-known Mandean prayers, the *Abahatan Qadmaya* and the *Asut Malkiya,* though he is by no means central to these prayers. Lupieri, *Giovanni Battista fra storia e leggenda,* 279, quantifies this: in the Mandean liturgical texts so far published in the West, there are seven references to the Baptist, five of which are from *Abahatan Qadmaya.* For a partial translation of this prayer, see Lupieri, *Mandaeans,* 238–39. On the *Asut Malkiya,* see Lupieri, *Giovanni Battista fra storia e leggenda,* 282–83.

68. Lupieri, *Mandaeans,* 238, concludes that "his figure has not penetrated to the deepest level of the myths that characterize Mandaean religion." Cf. p. 165, where Lupieri writes, "Despite occasional exaltation, it remains something of an adventitious or secondary character." See also Rudolph, *Mandäer,* 1:73: "Johannes ist für die mandäische Religion überhaupt nicht konstitutiv." For Mandean stories about Adam and his sons, see Lupieri, *Mandaeans,* 45–51.

69. Rudolph, *Mandäer,* 1:70.

70. Lupieri, *Mandaeans,* 162–63.

71. See Hans Lietzmann, "Ein Beitrag zur Mandäerfrage," in *Kleine Schriften I: Studien zur spätantiken Religionsgeschichte,* Texte und Untersuchungen 67 (1930; rpt. Berlin: Akademie-Verlag, 1958), 124–31; Rudolph, *Mandäer,* 1:67–68.

72. See Lietzmann, "Beitrag zur Mandäerfrage," 139. Christian influence seems more likely to me than the speculative derivation of Mandean Sunday observance from an extension of the Jewish Sabbath; on this theory, see Rudolph, *Mandäer,* 2:322–31.

73. See Rudolf Bultmann, "Der religionsgeschichtliche Hintergrund des Prologs zum Johannes-Evangelium," in *Eucharistērion: Studien zur Religion und Literatur des Alten und Neuen Testaments; Hermann Gunkel zum 60. Geburtstage, dem 23. Mai 1922 dargebracht von seinen Schülern und Freunden,* 2 Teil, *Zur Religion und Literatur des Neuen Testaments,* Forschungen zur Religion und Literatur des Alten und Neuen Testaments 36.2//N.F. 19.2 (Göttingen, Germany: Vandenhoeck & Ruprecht, 1923), 1–26; Rudolf Bultmann, "Die Bedeutung der neuerschlossenen mandäischen und manichäischen Quellen für das Verständnis des Johannesevangeliums," *Zeitschrift für die neutestamentliche Wissenschaft und die Kunde der älteren Kirche* 24 (1925): 100–146; Bultmann, *Gospel of John,* 17–18. In Bultmann's view, the Fourth Gospel's prologue was originally a hymn to the Baptist rather than to Jesus. The Gospel's author turned it into a pro-Jesus, anti-Baptist hymn through the prose insertions in 1:6–8, 15. As Rudolph, *Mandäer,* 1:80, points out, however, the Mandeans, in contrast to the polemic behind John 1:6–8, do not revere John as Messiah or Savior.

74. Against Lietzmann, "Beitrag zur Mandäerfrage," 139; Alfred Loisy, *Le Mandéisme et les origines chrétiennes* (Paris: Émile Nourry, 1934), 27.

75. Rudolph, *Mandäer,* 1:70.

76. On the contacts with the Protoevangelium of James, see Rudolph, *Mandäer,* 1:71; Lupieri, *Giovanni Battista fra storia e leggenda,* 462 ("Indice dei luoghi," under "Prot. Iac.").

77. Rudolph, *Mandäer,* 1:70–71.

78. For a strong argument that Protoevangelium of James was composed in Syria in the late second or early third century, see Lily C. Vuong, *Gender and Purity in the Protevangelium of James* WUNT 2.358 (Tübingen, Germany: Mohr Siebeck, 2013), 193–239.

79. See Rudolph, *Mandäer*, 1:72, 75.

80. Lupieri, *Giovanni Battista fra storia e leggenda*, 198–200, 392.

81. The question is comparable to that about the knowledge of the historical Jesus in the Pauline churches, an issue that continues to spark lively debate; for a survey of recent contributions, see Yongbom Lee, *Paul, Scribe of Old and New: Intertextual Insights for the Jesus-Paul Debate*, Library of New Testament Studies 512 (London: Bloomsbury–T&T Clark, 2015), 7–21.

82. On the Christianization of Syria, see Hans Drijvers, "Syrian Christianity and Judaism," in *Jews Among Pagans and Christians in the Roman Empire*, ed. Judith Lieu, John North, and Tessa Rajak (London: Routledge, 1994), 124–46; Bas ter Haar Romeny, "Hypotheses on the Development of Judaism and Christianity in Syria in the Period After 70 C.E.," in *Matthew and the Didache: Two Documents from the Same Jewish-Christian Milieu?*, ed. Huub van de Sandt (Assen, the Netherlands: Van Gorcum; Minneapolis: Fortress, 2005), 13–33; Frank Trombley, "Overview: The Geographical Spread of Christianity," in *The Cambridge History of Christianity*, vol. 1, *Origins to Constantine*, ed. M. Mitchell and F. Young (Cambridge: Cambridge University Press, 2006), 302–13; Manuel Sotomayor, "Los grandes centros de la expansión del cristianismo," in *Historia del cristianismo: I. El mundo antiguo*, ed. Manuel Sotomayor and José Fernández Ubiña (Madrid: Universidad de Granada, 2006), 196–207.

83. See Steven Kaplan, *The Beta Israel (Falasha) in Ethiopia: From Earliest Times to the Twentieth Century* (New York: New York University Press, 1992), 53–78; Seth D. Kunin, *Juggling Identities: Identity and Authenticity Among the Crypto-Jews* (New York: Columbia University Press, 2009), 146–91.

84. Vogel, "Jesusgemeinden und Täufergruppen," 77–82, here 78, citing Johannes Tromp, "John the Baptist According to Flavius Josephus, and His Incorporation in the Christian Tradition," in *Empsychoi Logoi—Religious Innovations in Antiquity: Studies in Honour of Pieter Willem Van der Horst*, ed. Alberdkina Houtman, Albert de Jong, and Magda Misset-van de Weg (Leiden, the Netherlands: Brill, 2008), 146.

85. The distinction corresponds to that between the Pseudo-Clementine *Recognitions* passages and those from the *Homilies*. In the former, John is not a false Messiah, and it is only his followers who claim that he is superior to Jesus; in the latter, he claims to be the Messiah but is actually the latter's evil counterpart.

86. See Walter Bauer, *Das Johannesevangelium*, Handbuch zum Neuen Testament 6 (Tübingen, Germany: J. C. B. Mohr [Paul Siebeck], 1925), 60–61; C. K. Barrett, *The Gospel According to St John: An Introduction with Commentary and Notes on the Greek Text* (London: S.P.C.K., 1962), 187; Wink, *John the Baptist*, 169.

87. Wink, *John the Baptist*, 94n4.

88. Bauer, *Johannesevangelium*, 15, unconvincingly asserts that the Fourth Evangelist means his readers to contrast the "burning and shining lamp" of John invidiously with the "true light' of Jesus (cf. 1:8–9). There is a tension between 1:8–9 and 5:35, but it is not to be resolved in this way.

89. Michael Theobald, *Das Evangelium nach Johannes, Kapitel 1–12*, Regensburger Neues Testament (Regensburg, Germany: Friedrich Pustet, 2009), 292; cf. Vogel, "Jesusgemeinden und Täufergruppen," 81n32. It seems tendentious, however, to interpret the "other laborers" who have prepared the way for the ministry of Jesus's disciples in Samaria in 4:36–38 as followers of the Baptist and to speak on the basis of these verses of a synergy between the Baptist movement and the early Christian mission from the perspective of the Fourth Evangelist (Vogel, "Jesusgemeinden und Täufergruppen," 81; cf.

John A. T. Robinson, "The 'Others' of John 4.38: A Test of Exegetical Method," in *Twelve New Testament Studies*, Studies in Biblical Theology [1959; repr., Naperville IL: Alec R. Allenson, 1962], 61–66; Backhaus, *Die "Jüngerkreise" des Täufers Johannes*, 363–64). We have even less evidence that followers of the Baptist paved the way for the Christian mission in Samaria than that John the Baptist himself did (cf. Brown, *Gospel According to John*, 1:183–84). On the other hand, also to be rejected is the attempt of Cullmann, "Ὁ ὀπίσω μου ἐρχόμενος," 181, to identify the "thieves and robbers" of John 10:8 with the Baptist sect. In neither case are there any contextual clues suggesting an identification with followers of the Baptist. It is more likely that the "other laborers" of 4:36–38 were earlier Christian missionaries in Samaria, who preceded the Johannine community's outreach there; see Acts 8:1, 4, 14, and Oscar Cullmann, "Samaria and the Origins of the Christian Mission," in *The Early Church: Studies in Early Christian History and Theology*, ed. A. J. B. Higgins (1953–54; Eng. trans., Philadelphia: Westminster, 1956), 190.

90. Wink, *John the Baptist*, 102–5.

91. Ibid., 102.

92. Ibid., 104–5.

93. See Jacob Neusner, "'Judaism' After Moore: A Programmatic Statement," *Journal of Jewish Studies* 31 (1980): 141–56; John M. G. Barclay, *Jews in the Mediterranean Diaspora from Alexander to Trajan (323 BCE–117 CE)* (Edinburgh: T&T Clark, 1996), 83–88.

94. Philipp Vielhauer, "Das Benedictus des Zacharias (Luk 1,68–79)," in *Aufsätze zum Neuen Testament*, Theologische Bücherei: Neudrucke und Berichte aus dem 20. Jahrhundert 31 (1952; repr. Munich : Chr. Kaiser Verlag, 1965), 45.

95. Here Vogel, "Jesusgemeinden und Täufergruppen," 82n37, cites Carol Newsom, "Constructing 'We, You, and the Others' Through Non-Polemical Discourse," in *Defining Identities: We, You, and the Other in the Dead Sea Scrolls*, Proceedings of the Fifth Meeting of the IOQS in Groningen, ed. Florentino García Martínez and Mladen Popović (Leiden, the Netherlands: Brill, 2008), 21, who writes about the Qumran sect: "We need to pay as much attention to the non-polemical discourses of the community as we do to the explicitly polemical language of 'we' and 'they.'" Newsom, however, is talking about passages in the Hodayot and the Community Rule (for example, 1QH^a 5:19–22; 9:21–23; IQS 10:1–11:22) that emphasize the nothingness and corruption of the speaker's human condition, not the speaker in comparison to outsiders. Vogel's citation of her would be more appropriate if she had been discussing, say, the irenic attitude of 4QMMT, on which see Elisha Qimron and John Strugnell, *Qumran Cave 4. V: Miqṣat Maʿaśe Ha-Torah*, Discoveries in the Judaean Desert 10 (Oxford: Clarendon Press, 1994), 109–21.

96. Rudolf Bultmann, *History of the Synoptic Tradition* (1921; Eng. trans., New York: Harper & Row, 1963), 164.

97. David Marshall, "Christianity in the Qurʾān," in *Islamic Interpretations of Christianity*, ed. Lloyd Ridgeon (New York: St. Martin's Press, 2001), 22–23. The translation of the Qurʾān passage here is by Marshall but based on Arthur J. Arberry, *The Koran Interpreted* (New York: Macmillan, 1955).

98. See Gerd Lüdemann, *Early Christianity According to the Traditions in Acts: A Commentary* (London: SCM, 1989), 124–33, 166–77. See already the classic account of the discrepancies between Acts 15 and Galatians 2 in Ferdinand Christian Baur, *Paul the Apostle of Jesus Christ: His Life, Works, His Epistles and Teaching* (1875–76; repr., Peabody Mass.: Hendrickson Publishers, 2003), 109–51.

99. Cf. Philip Alexander on the "loud silence" of the rabbis about early Jewish

Christianity: Philip S. Alexander, "Jewish Believers in Early Rabbinic Literature (2d to 5th Centuries)," in *Jewish Believers in Jesus: The Early Centuries*, ed. Oskar Skarsaune and Reidar Hvalvik (Peabody, Mass.: Hendrickson Publishers, 2007), 660–61; Philip S. Alexander, "'In the Beginning': Rabbinic and Patristic Exegesis of Genesis 1:1," in *The Exegetical Encounter Between Jews and Christians in Late Antiquity*, ed. Emmanouela Grypeou and Helen Spurling, Jewish and Christian Perspective Series 18 (Leiden, the Netherlands: Brill, 2009), 4–5.

100. See David M. Levy, "The Hostile Act," *Psychological Review* 48 (1941): 356–61.

· ·

CHAPTER TWO   Qumran

1. See the section "Competition" in chapter 5.

2. A wadi is a streambed or riverbed that remains dry except in the rainy season.

3. For the story of the discovery of the Scrolls, see Weston W. Fields, *The Dead Sea Scrolls: A Full History*, vol. 1, *1947–1960* (Leiden, the Netherlands: Brill, 2009).

4. For an exploration of the sources and the debate about the connection between Qumran and the Essenes, see Martin Goodman and Geza Vermes, *The Essenes According to the Classical Sources*, Oxford Centre Textbooks 1 (Sheffield, U.K.: JSOT Press, 1989); Jodi Magness, *The Archaeology of Qumran and the Dead Sea Scrolls*, Studies in the Dead Sea Scrolls and Related Literature (Grand Rapids, Mich.: Eerdmans, 2002), 39–43. The main ancient sources on the Essenes are Philo, *Good Person* 75–91, *Contempl. Life* 1–2 and *Hypothetica* 11.1–18; Josephus, *J.W.* 2.119–161 and *Ant.* 18.18-22; Pliny, *Natural History* 5.73.

5. Karl Heinrich Georg Venturini, *Natürliche Geschichte des grossen Propheten von Nazareth* (Copenhagen: Bethlehem, 1806), 1:295–320. What principally intrigued Venturini and many subsequent biographers of Jesus was the Essenes' reputation as a secret society of holy men; he also noted such commonalities as asceticism, fame for prophetic powers and interpretation of the Bible, and belief in resurrection. Even before Venturini, at the end of the eighteenth century, Karl Friedrich Bahrdt had linked Jesus with the Essenes; see Schweitzer, *Quest of the Historical Jesus*, 38–39. On Luke's unhistorical presentation of Jesus and John as "cousins," see chap. 1, n. 14 (p. 164).

6. On the presence of the Essenes by the Dead Sea, see Pliny, *Natural History* 5.73. On their water rites, see Josephus, *Jewish War* 2.129, 138. On their asceticism, see in general the sources listed in n. 4.

7. Heinrich Graetz, *History of the Jews*, vol. 2 (1863; Eng. trans., Philadelphia: Jewish Publication Society, 1893), 145–46.

8. David Friedrich Strauss, *A New Life of Jesus* (London: Williams and Norgate, 1865), 252–54. Strauss thought Jesus was influenced by Essenism but that he transcended his Essene background, whereas John did not; ibid., 257.

9. J. B. Lightfoot, *St. Paul's Epistle to the Galatians: With Introductions, Notes and Dissertations* (1875; repr., Lynn, Mass.: Henrickson, 1981), 399–407. In the judgment of Alfred Edersheim, *The Life and Times of Jesus the Messiah* (1883; repr., Grand Rapids, Mich.: Eerdmans, 1971), 1:325, Lightfoot "conclusively disposed of" the hypothesis that there was any connection between Essenism on the one hand and John, his baptism, and the teaching of Christianity on the other.

10. Christian D. Ginsburg, *The Essenes: Their History and Doctrines; The Kabbalah: Its Doctrines, Development, and Literature* (1864; repr., London: Routledge & Kegan Paul, 1955), 24.

11. See Schweitzer, *Quest of the Historical Jesus*, 39, 43–45, 150–51, 290.

12. See for example Adolf Schlatter, *Johannes der Täufer* (1880; repr., Basel, Switzerland: Verlag Friedrich Reinhardt AG., 1956), 132, who claims that Essene dogma and praxis were foreign to John.

13. Dibelius, *Die urchristliche Überlieferung*, 137n1, mentions Essene baths, along with priestly ablutions and Jewish proselyte baptism, as possible backgrounds to John's baptism. He also mentions (p. 133) possible foreign influences on John, such as those that shaped the Essene community. See also Ernst Lohmeyer, *Das Urchristentum*, vol. 1, *Johannes der Täufer* (Göttingen, Germany: Vandenhoeck & Ruprecht, 1932), 33, 47, 123, 145.

14. Recent and influential naysayers include Josef Ernst, *Johannes der Täufer: Interpretation–Geschichte–Wirkungsgeschichte*, BZNW 53 (Berlin: De Gruyter, 1989), 329–30; Jonathan Klawans, *Impurity and Sin in Ancient Judaism* (New York: Oxford University Press, 2000), 138–43; Joan E. Taylor, *The Immerser: John the Baptist Within Second Temple Judaism* (Grand Rapids, Mich.: Eerdmans, 1997), 16–29.

15. See Magness, *Archaeology of Qumran*, 158; Eric M. Meyers, "Khirbet Qumran and Its Environs," in *The Oxford Handbook of the Dead Sea Scrolls*, ed. Timothy H. Lim and John J. Collins, Oxford Handbooks in Religion and Theology (Oxford: Oxford University Press, 2010), 34. According to the latter, the Qumran *miqva'ot* are the largest in the country, occupy 17 percent of the site's total area, and represent the highest density of immersion pools for any site in the country. For a chart of the distribution of *mikveh* remains in Israel/Palestine, see Jonathan David Lawrence, *Washing in Water: Trajectories of Ritual Bathing in the Hebrew Bible and Second Temple Literature*, Academia Biblica 23 (Atlanta: Society of Biblical Literature, 2006), 251–68.

16. See Dieter Sänger, "'Ist er heraufgestiegen, gilt er in jeder Hinsicht als ein Israelit' (bYev 47b). Das Proselytentauchbad im frühen Judentum," in *Ablution, Initiation, and Baptism*, ed. David Hellholm et al., BZNW 176 (Berlin: De Gruyter, 2011), 1:301.

17. Taylor, *Immerser*, 22–23, downplays the similarity between John's baptism and the Qumran immersions by noting that *miqva'ot* are ubiquitous at first-century Jewish archaeological sites and that the Mishnah records disputes between Sadducees and Pharisees in which purity issues are fundamental. On the first point, see n. 15 above. The second assertion misses the point that, both for the Baptist and for Qumran, the cleansing is *eschatological* in orientation and involves not just ritual purity but also remission of sins. On the latter point, see the section "John's Baptism and Ritual Purity" in chap. 4.

18. I argue in chap. 4, however, that John associated the Spirit not with the baptism of the "Coming One" but with his own baptism; the reference to the Spirit in Mark 1:7–8//Matt. 3:11–12//Luke 3:16–17, therefore, is not an original part of the logion. The original form of this logion probably was something like, "I baptize you with water and the Spirit, he will baptize you with fire."

19. "I will sprinkle clean water upon you, and you shall be clean from all your uncleannesses, and from all your idols I will cleanse you. A new heart I will give you, and a new spirit I will put within you; and I will take out of your flesh the heart of stone and give you a heart of flesh. And I will put my spirit within you, and cause you to walk in my statutes and be careful to observe my ordinances." For references to this text at Qumran, see 1QH[a] 21:10, 13 ; ALD 3:13; and esp. 1QS 3:9, 4:21–22. On the latter texts see Robert L. Webb, *John the Baptizer and Prophet: A Socio-Historical Study*, Journal for the Study of the New Testament: Supplement Series 62 (Sheffield, U.K.: JSOT Press, 1991), 144–45, 157. For the importance of Ezek. 36:25–27 in the thought of the Baptist, see Webb, *John the Baptizer*, 207, 274n35, 292.

20. On the common eschatological orientation of the water rites of John and Qumran, see Joachim Gnilka, "Die essenischen Tauchbäder und die Johannestaufe," *Revue de Quman* 3 (1961): 205; Herbert Braun, *Qumran und das Neue Testament*, 2 vols. (Tübingen, Germany: J. C. B. Mohr [Paul Siebeck], 1966), 2:3–4; Ernst, *Johannes der Täufer* (1989), 325–26. But Everett Ferguson, *Baptism in the Early Church: History, Theology, and Liturgy in the First Five Centuries* (Grand Rapids, Mich.: Eerdmans, 2009), 87, denies this, saying that while there was a strong eschatological orientation at Qumran, it was not connected with its washings. He undermines this assertion immediately, however, by acknowledging in n. 22 that 1QS 4:19–22 "does use 'purifying waters' as an image for eschatological cleansing." This is not the only parallel between this eschatological passage and the description of the community's lustrations one column earlier in 1QS 3:4–12. Both speak of God's holy spirit, the spirit of truth, as the active agent in cleansing, and both describe it as designed to root out the iniquity or the unclean spirit that is opposed to it. Thus the ceremonial washings practiced in the community were one of the many factors of community life that anticipated the life of the new age; that is why the community could be referred to in 1QS 3:12 as "the *eternal Yahad*" (unity). On other elements of "realized eschatology" at Qumran, see Heinz-Wolfgang Kuhn, *Enderwartung und gegenwärtiges Heil: Untersuchungen zu den Gemeindeliedern von Qumran mit einem Anhang über Eschatologie und Gegenwart in der Verkündigung Jesu*, Studien zur Umwelt des Neuen Testaments 4 (Göttingen, Germany: Vandenhoeck & Ruprecht, 1966); David Edward Aune, *The Cultic Setting of Realized Eschatology in Early Christianity*, Novum Testamentum Supplements 28 (Leiden, the Netherlands: Brill, 1972), 29–44; E. P. Sanders, *Paul and Palestinian Judaism: A Comparison of Patterns of Religion* (Philadelphia: Fortress, 1977), 280–81.

21. See the archaeological evidence for *miqva'ot* cited in the first bullet point, as well as the survey of texts in Webb, *John the Baptizer*, 95–162.

22. Sibylline Oracles 4:162–170 does exhort its audience to escape from the coming fiery judgment by repenting and being baptized, but this is a post–70 CE text; it must be dated to 80 CE or later because of the references to Nero's supposed flight to Parthia in the year of his death, 68 CE (4:119), to the destruction of Jerusalem in 70 CE (4:116–118), and to the eruption of Vesuvius in 79 CE (4:130–134); see John J. Collins in *Old Testament Pseudepigrapha*, ed. James H. Charlesworth, 2 vols. (Garden City, N.Y.: Doubleday, 1983), 1:382. Earlier scholars such as Thomas, *Le mouvement baptiste*, 50–52, and Aurelio Peretti, "Echi di dottrine esseniche negli Oracoli Sibillini giudaici," *La parola del passato* 17 (1962): 247–95, argue that the Jewish Sibyllines themselves reflect Essene thought and practice, but the overlaps are too general to warrant such a conclusion; see Valentin Nikiprowetzky, "Réflexions sur quelques problèmes du quatrième et du cinquième livre des Oracles Sibyllins," *Hebrew Union College Annual* 43 (1972): 29–76.

23. Antje Labahn, "Aus dem Wasser kommt das Leben: Waschungen und Reinigungsriten in früjüdischen Texten," in *Ablution, Initiation, and Baptism*, ed. David Hellholm et al., BZNW 176 (Berlin: De Gruyter, 2011), 1:157n2.

24. Ibid., 1:157–219. Labahn also finds this association in T. Levi 9, but I do not regard the Testaments of the Twelve Patriarchs as a witness for pre-Christian Judaism; see Joel Marcus, "The *Testaments of the Twelve Patriarchs* and the *Didascalia Apostolorum*: A Common Jewish-Christian Milieu?" *Journal of Theological Studies* 61 (2010): 596–626. For the Jubilees fragments at Qumran, see James C. VanderKam, "Jubilees, Book of," in *Encyclopedia of the Dead Sea Scrolls*, ed. Lawrence H. Schiffman and James C. VanderKam (Oxford University Press, 2000), 1:434–38.

25. See Gen. 19:24; Lev. 10:2; Num. 11:1, 16:35; Deut. 32:22; 2 Sam. 22:9; 2 Kgs. 1:10; Isa. 33:14; 66:24; Ezek. 22:21; Mal. 3:2–3, 19; Pss. 18:8, 50:3, 97:3; 1 En. 102:1; cf. Michael Edward Stone, *Fourth Ezra: A Commentary on the Book of Fourth Ezra,* Hermeneia (Minneapolis: Fortress, 1990), 387.

26. Steve Mason, "Fire, Water and Spirit: John the Baptist and the Tyranny of Canon," *Studies in Religion* 21 (1992): 171.

27. It is partly foreshadowed in Isa. 30:27–28, which speaks of the arrival of "the name of the Lord," which is hypostasized and comes "burning with his anger, and in thick rising smoke," having a tongue "like a devouring fire" and hot breath "*like an overflowing stream that reaches up to the neck.*" More important, Dan 7:10 describes a river of fire issuing forth from God's throne, and the next verse speaks of the destruction by fire of the fourth beast (a symbol for the climactic anti-God kingdom).

28. From the later first century CE, the motif of the destructive stream of fire is found in the Jewish apocalyptic work 4 Ezra (13:10–11); also possibly from the first century, but very hard to date, is 2 En. 10:2. For even later Jewish instances of the idea of the river of fire (rabbinic traditions, Hekhalot literature, and so on), see Carl-Martin Edsman, *Le baptême du feu,* Acta seminarii neotestamentici upsaliensis 9 (Leipzig, Germany: Alfred Lorentz; Uppsala, Sweden: A.-B. Lundequistska Bokhandeln, 1940), 19–31. Early Christian attestations include Sib. Or. 3:54, 84–85. See also the "lake of fire" in Rev. 19:20, 20:10, 14–15, 21:8.

29. See W. H. Brownlee, "John the Baptist in the New Light of Ancient Scrolls," in *The Scrolls and the New Testament,* ed. Krister Stendahl (London: SCM, 1957), 42; David Flusser, "The Baptism of John and the Dead Sea Sect [Hebrew]," in *Essays on the Dead Sea Scrolls in Memory of E. L. Sukenik* (Tel Aviv: Hekhal Ha-Sefer, 1961), 226. Before the discovery of the Qumran scrolls, it was suggested that the origin of the Baptist's imagery of a judgmental, destructive stream of eschatological fire was in Zoroastrianism; see, for example, Carl H. Kraeling, *John the Baptist* (New York: Scribner's, 1951), 117; cf. *Bundahishn* 30:19–21, cited in John J. Collins, *Daniel: A Commentary on the Book of Daniel,* Hermeneia (Minneapolis: Fortress Press, 1993), 302n225. Zoroastrian influence and Qumran influence are not mutually exclusive, since the Qumran literature itself seems to have been influenced by Zoroastrianism; see Shaul Shaked, "Qumran and Iran: Further Considerations," *Israel Oriental Studies* 2 (1972): 433–46.

30. On the possible localizations of Aenon, see Brown, *Gospel According to John,* 1:151. But despite the linkage of the Baptist with the east bank of the Jordan in John 1:28, 3:26, and 10:40, I do not think that one can locate him exclusively on the East Bank and use that as the key for understanding his ministry, as does Hartmut Stegemann, *The Library of Qumran: On the Essenes, Qumran, John the Baptist, and Jesus* (Grand Rapids, Mich.: Eerdmans; Leiden, the Netherlands: Brill, 1998), 212–13. Other plausible sites for Aenon are on the West Bank (see Brown, *Gospel According to John,* 1:151; Jerry A. Pattengale, "Aenon," in *Anchor Bible Dictionary* [New York: Doubleday, 1992], 1:87), and the Fourth Gospel itself seems to locate the town west of the Jordan. In 3:26, which also takes place in Aenon, John's disciples refer to his witness to Jesus when the two were together "beyond the Jordan," and the only passage that fits this description is 1:19–34, which took place in "Bethany beyond the Jordan" (1:28). Since Bethany is apparently an East Bank town (for the various theories about its location, see Brown, *Gospel According to John,* 1:144–45), Aenon must be a West Bank town. Stegemann's other evidence for an East Bank Baptist is John's execution by Herod Antipas at his stronghold of Machaerus in the mountains east of the Dead Sea in Perea, according to Josephus (*Ant.*

18.119). But here, too, there is a division in the sources, since Mark 5:21 identifies "the leading men of Galilee" as present at the banquet at which John is executed. (Antipas was tetrarch of both Perea and Galilee.) Mark 1:5, moreover, locates John's baptismal activity on the west bank of the Jordan, and Matt. 3:1 specifies the realm of his preaching as "the wilderness of Judea," which would seem to rule out the East Bank. With such conflicting testimony, dogmatism about John's preference for a particular side of the Jordan seems out of place; both included Jewish areas and he may have operated on both. Also overly confident about where John was baptizing (and that it was not near Qumran) is Taylor, *Immerser,* 42–48. Better is Webb, *John the Baptizer,* 363, who draws on the work of McCown and Funk to demonstrate that "'the wilderness' and 'the region around the Jordan' [Matt. 3:5] refer to the southern portion of the Jordan valley extending as far north as Wadi Far'ah [about on the same latitude as Shechem, and a few miles east of it] and including both the western and eastern slopes [of the valley]."

31. See app. 8 on the Baptist's use of Isa. 40:3. As Brownlee, "John the Baptist," 34–35, notes, both in the case of John and of the Qumran sect, Isa. 40:3 was interpreted with reference to the Judean Desert, rather than the Sinaitic one, partly "because Isa. 40:3 employed a word for wilderness *(arabah)* which was the proper designation of the deep depression in which are found the Jordan River and the Dead Sea."

32. וליישר לפניו כל דרכי צדק אמת. Michael A. Knibb, *The Qumran Community,* Cambridge Commentaries on Writings of the Jewish and Christian World, 200 BC to AD 200, vol. 2 (Cambridge: Cambridge University Press, 1987), 99, says that this is "perhaps an allusion to Isa. 40:3 (quoted in 8:14), but 'before him' refers here to man, not God," and he compares Psalm 5:9. P. Wernberg-Møller, *The Manual of Discipline,* Studies on the Texts of the Desert of Judah 1 (Grand Rapids, Mich.: Eerdmans, 1957), 73, says that the Qumran passage echoes not only these two Old Testament texts but also Isa. 45:13 (which, like 1QS 4:2–3, reapplies the phrasing of Isa. 40:3 to the ways of humanity). He also compares Pss. Sol. 10:3, ὀρθώσει γὰρ ὁδοὺς δικαίων ("for he will straighten the ways of the righteous"). If Wernberg-Møller were right, the author of 1QS 4:2 might just be employing stereotyped biblical verbiage, not a specific allusion to Isa. 40:3, but the fact that the same author specifically cites Isa. 40:3 twice a little later in his work tells against this.

33. καὶ ὅλος ἐλουσάμην ἐν ὕδατι ζῶντι· καὶ πάσας τὰς ὁδούς μου ἐποίησα εὐθείας. The passage is part of a lacuna of four lines in the Aramaic document, but a Greek translation of those lines is interpolated into an eleventh-century manuscript of the Testaments of the Twelve Patriarchs found at Mt. Athos (Monastery of Koutloumous, Cod. 39 [cat. no. 3108]), and this seems to be a reliable translation; see Jonas C. Greenfield, Michael E. Stone, and Esther Eshel, *The Aramaic Levi Document: Edition, Translation, Commentary,* Studia in Veteris Testamenti pseudepigraphica 19 (Leiden, the Netherlands: Brill, 2004), 5, 58; Henryk Drawnel, *An Aramaic Wisdom Text from Qumran: A New Interpretation of the Levi Document,* Journal for the Study of Judaism: Supplement Series 86 (Leiden, the Netherlands: Brill, 2004), 14–55. The case for these words being part of the original Qumran text is strengthened by the similarity to the language of 1QS 4:2, cited above; both texts offer an ethicizing and individualizing interpretation of Isa. 40:3.

34. Although Drawnel, *Aramaic Wisdom Text,* 210, notices the link between ALD 2:5 and Isa. 40:3, he does not remark on the similarity between that text and the Gospel usages of Isa. 40:3 with reference to the ministry of John the Baptist.

35. Armin Lange and Matthias Weigold, *Biblical Quotations and Allusions in Second Temple Jewish Literature,* Journal of Ancient Judaism: Supplement Series 5 (Göttingen, Germany: Vandenhoeck & Ruprecht, 2011), 133, record only allusions from the Qumran literature (including the Aramaic Levi Document). Bradley H. McLean, *Citations and Allusions to Jewish Scripture in Early Christian and Jewish Writings Through 180 C.E.* (Lewiston, N.Y.: Edwin Mellen Press, 1992), 90, also lists Pss. Sol. 8:17 and Sib. Or. 1:336, but the latter is a Christian text reflecting New Testament usages of the Isaian verse. In contrast to my argument here, Ian McDonald plays down the relevance of the fact that both the Qumranians and John the Baptist associated themselves with Isa. 40:3, claiming that "this text represents a well known *crux interpretum,* and it seems likely that John read the text in a different way" (J. Ian H. McDonald, "What Did You Go Out to See? John the Baptist, the Scrolls, and Late Second Temple Judaism," in *The Dead Sea Scrolls in Their Historical Context,* ed. Timothy H. Lim [Edinburgh: T&T Clark, 2000], 57). To back up these claims, McDonald cites Taylor, *Immerser,* 25–29, but the only Second Temple Jewish texts Taylor cites on these pages, apart from the LXX, are from Qumran, so "well known *crux interpretum*" is a considerable exaggeration. As for the differences between John's interpretations and those of Qumran, see the section "The Differences and Their Significance" below.

36. For the rabbis, see Sanders, *Paul and Palestinian Judaism,* 157–80.

37. On the Philo text, see E. P. Sanders, *Judaism: Practice and Belief 63 BCE–66 CE* (London: SCM; Philadelphia: Trinity Press International, 1992), 230; and Taylor, *Immerser,* 86–87. Sanders also points to Let. Aris. 305–306, in which the custom of "all the Jews" to wash their hands in the sea while praying is evidence that they have done no evil.

38. "On your lives (I swear), it is not the corpse that defiles and it is not the water that purifies, but the ordinance of the Holy One, Blessed be He" (my trans.); חייכם לא המת מטמא ולא המים מטהרים אלא גזירתו של הקב"ה; cited by Ferguson, *Baptism in the Early Church,* 63n18); cf. also Num. Rab. 19:8.

39. See Rivka Nir, "Josephus' Account of John the Baptist: A Christian Interpolation?" *Journal for the Study of the Historical Jesus* 10 (2012): 56; cf. Hannah K. Harrington, *The Purity Texts,* Companion to the Qumran Scrolls (London: T&T Clark, 2004), 22–23, who mentions the parallel between the Qumran texts, the Philo text, and the tradition about John the Baptist. Earlier scholars who notice the parallel between the Qumran texts and the Josephus passage include Brownlee, "John the Baptist," 39–41, and Flusser, "Baptism of John," 214.

40. Ferguson, *Baptism in the Early Church,* 84n7, translates χρωμένοις βαπτισμῷ συνιέναι as "to participate in baptism" but notes that the phrase literally means "to come together in baptism." He comments, "The verb may mean to form an identifiable group, and baptism in the dative case may mean "by means of baptism." But he asserts (without saying why) that it is more likely that it means "to come together for baptism." On this question, see chap. 6, n. 7 (p. 214).

41. Revised Standard Version: "They hatch adders' eggs," but in the MT צפעוני is singular. The LXX changes the singular adder to a plural (ἀσπίδωνι), and this plural reading is preserved in 1QIsaᵃ LXX (see Martin Abegg, Peter Flint, and Eugene Ulrich, *The Dead Sea Scrolls Bible: The Oldest Known Bible* [San Francisco, Calif.: HarperSan Francisco, 1999], 368).

42. My trans. Both צִפְעוֹנִי and אֶפְעֶה and their LXX translations ἀσπίς and βασιλίσκος are terms for poisonous snakes; see the respective entries in David Clines, ed., *The*

Dictionary of Classical Hebrew (8 vols.; Sheffield: Sheffield Academic Press, 1993–2011) and T. Muraoka, *A Greek-English Lexicon of the Septuagint* (Louvain/Walpole, MA: Peeters, 2009). The Q saying Matt 3:7//Luke 3:7 uses a different Greek word, ἔχιδνα, which does not appear in the LXX, although Aquila employs it as a rendering for אֶפְעֶה.

43. This has been verified by a check of McLean, *Citations and Allusions,* Lange and Weigold, *Biblical Quotations,* and Aaron Hyman, *Torah Haketubah Vehamessurah* (Tel Aviv: Dvir, 1979).

44. Otto Betz, "Was John the Baptist an Essene?" *Bible Review* 6, no. 6 (December 1990): 24. Besides denoting a venomous snake, אֶפְעֶה can also mean "nothing, worthlessness" (see Clines, *Dictionary of Classical Hebrew,* 1.359–60). Carol Newsom, taking up a suggestion of C. G. Frechette, utilizes both senses, translating אפעה as "venomous vanity" (see Hartmut Stegemann, Eileen Schuller, and Carol Newsom, *1QHodayot^a: With Incorporation of 1QHodayot^b and 4QHodayot^{a-f}* [Discoveries in the Judaean Desert 40; Oxford/New York: Clarendon Press/Oxford University Press, 2009], 156).

45. It is, however, mentioned by David Flusser in Flusser, "Baptism of John," 210 n. 6.

46. In 19:22–24, however, the vipers/snakes themselves are Gentiles; cf. CD 8:9–13, in which the תנינים are "the kings of the Gentiles," mention is made of their poison, and they are linked with the enemies of the Sect. See also 1QH^a 13(5):26–28, mentioned by Brownlee, "John the Baptist," 37, which uses two other terms for snakes, תנינים and פתנים, for the enemies of the sect.

47. On John's possible priestly background, see app. 4.

48. Gnilka, "Tauchbäder," 205–6.

49. On Matt. 12:34 and 23:33 as redactional M material, see Ulrich Luz, *Matthew: A Commentary* Hermeneia, 3 vols. (Minneapolis: Fortress Press, 1989–2005), 2:202, 3:131.

50. Charles Darwin, *The Annotated Origin: A Facsimile of the First Edition of* On the Origin of Species (1859; repr. Cambridge, Mass.: Belknap Press of Harvard University Press, 2009), 425–26 (chap. 13). The alternative is to say that the similarities result from convergent evolution, but this becomes less likely the more similarities there are; see Keith A. Crandall, "Convergent and Parallel Evolution," in *Encyclopedia of Evolution,* ed. Mark Pagel (Oxford: Oxford University Press, 2002), 1:201–5.

51. See the classic treatment of this subject in Darwin's *Origin of Species,* chaps. 11 and 12.

52. For these differences, see Flusser, "Baptism of John," 211; Taylor, *Immerser,* 15–48; Klawans, *Impurity and Sin,* 141–42; and Ferguson, *Baptism in the Early Church,* 87.

53. This and the once-and-for-all nature of John's baptism (see next point) are key aspects of the rite that were taken over by the Christians.

54. There is no indication they were administered by another, such as the leader of the sect, whose duties are carefully spelled out in passages such as CD 9:18–22, 13:6–22, 14:8–13, 15:7–15; 1QS 3:13–15, 6:11–12, 19–20, 9:12–26; 1QSb 5:20; 4Q266 fr. 11:14–16; 4Q271 fr. 3:12–15. In default of such evidence, it seems safe to assume that Qumran immersions proceeded in the way other Jewish immersions did.

55. Meier, *Marginal Jew,* 2:51, and Klawans, *Impurity and Sin,* 209n24, have pointed out that this is never explicitly said by either the Gospels or Josephus. But it is a reasonable inference, since those who received John's baptism returned to their daily lives and thus separated themselves from the baptizer. As Klawans puts it, since John's baptism had to be administered by John, it "could not be repeated at will but only when one who wished to repeat it could track John down," which seems impractical and unlikely.

56. This is never explicitly said, but it follows from the fact that they immersed before dining. Josephus (*J.W.* 2.129) says that the Essenes bathe before entering the refectory "as though into a holy precinct," and this corresponds to the fact that some of the largest Qumran *miqva'ot* are located by the entrances to the communal dining rooms; see Magness, *Archaeology of Qumran,* 153.

57. In the section "Challenges to the Thesis of John's Militancy" in chapter 6, I question the historicity of Luke 3:10–14. But it probably is based on the accurate memory that John did not demand that people leave their professions as a condition for joining in his baptism.

58. Qumran, however, was probably part of a larger Essene movement, which included adherents who did not segregate themselves but lived side by side with nonsectarians. See CD 7:6–9, 12:19–23, which speak of those who live in "camps," "the assembly of the towns of Israel," and "the assembly of the camps," and who, unlike strict sectarians, marry; cf. Josephus (*J.W.* 2.160–161), who speaks of "another order of Essenes," who, unlike other Essenes, marry. Cf. Goodman and Vermes, *Essenes According to the Classical Sources,* 12–13; James C. VanderKam, *The Dead Sea Scrolls Today* (Grand Rapids, Mich.: Eerdmans; London: SPCK), 57, 90–91.

59. For other similarities and differences between the use of Isa. 40:3 at Qumran and in other Jewish traditions, on the one hand, and its usage with reference to John the Baptist in the Gospels, on the other, see app. 8.

60. Klawans, *Impurity and Sin,* 41, who is quoted here, inaccurately calls John a "wandering loner"; see the references to his disciples in Mark 2:18 pars., Mark 6:29 pars., Matt. 11:2//Luke 7:18, Luke 11:1, and John 1:35–37. In Matt. 11:2//Luke 7:18 and John 1:35–37, at least, it is clear that these disciples are actually with John.

61. See Roy A. Rappaport, *Ritual and Religion in the Making of Humanity,* Cambridge Studies in Social and Cultural Anthropology (Cambridge: Cambridge University Press, 1999), passim, including the italicized words on pages 6–7: "Structural transformations in some subsystems [make] it possible to maintain more basic aspects of the system unchanged."

62. See Daniel Boyarin, *Border Lines: The Partition of Judaeo-Christianity,* Divinations (Philadelphia: University of Pennsylvania Press, 2004), 1–33.

63. Taylor, *Immerser,* 28, who also enunciates a stringent attitude toward the burden of proof: "Only if the interpretation is *precisely the same* can we suppose that the two may have been linked" (p. 25, emphasis added). This line of reasoning would imply, for example, that ancient Christianity and ancient Judaism were completely unrelated.

64. Cf. Jean Steinmann, *Saint John the Baptist and the Desert Tradition* (New York: Harper, 1958), 60: "It is certain that John was not simply an Essene; he appeared rather as a dissenter from the Essene community."

65. Or, we may suggest, a different way of reading that reference; see app. 8.

66. Brownlee, "John the Baptist," 35–36.

67. On the importance of this question, see James H. Charlesworth, "John the Baptizer and Qumran Barriers in the Light of the *Rule of the Community,*" in *The Provo International Conference on the Dead Sea Scrolls: Technological Innovations, New Texts, and Reformulated Issues,* ed. Donald W. Parry and Eugene Ulrich, Studies on the Texts of the Desert of Judah 30 (Leiden, the Netherlands: Brill, 1999), 360.

68. On the historicity of this passage, see the section "Revising the Jewish/Gentile Antinomy" in this chapter.

69. Cf. Charlesworth, "John the Baptizer," 369, who speculates that John's progress in the sect may have been hindered by the *Maskil.* On the role of the *Maskil* at Qumran, see Shane A. Berg, "An Elite Group Within the *Yaḥad:* Revisiting 1QS 8–9," in *Qumran Studies: New Approaches, New Questions,* ed. Michael Thomas Davis and Brent A. Strawn (Grand Rapids, Mich.: Eerdmans, 2007), 174–76.

70. Against Alex P. Jassen, *Mediating the Divine: Prophecy and Revelation in the Dead Sea Scrolls and Second Temple Judaism,* Studies on the Texts of the Desert of Judah, 68 (Leiden, the Netherlands: Brill, 2007), 188–94, who makes too sharp a distinction between the eschatological prophet "who teaches righteousness at the end of days" (CD 6:11) and "the Interpreter of the Law" (דורש התורה). The latter is described in one passage as a figure of the past, perhaps identical with the Teacher of Righteousness (CD 6:7), and in two others as an eschatological figure complementary to the royal Messiah (CD 7:18; 4QFlor. 1:11–12). This suggests a continuity of office, which in turn implies that the priestly leader of the sect was ascribed a potentially eschatological role—if only the eschaton would come and confirm it! For a similar dynamic, in which potential messianism easily shades over into actual messianism, see the recent history of Chabad messianism; cf. Joel Marcus, "Modern and Ancient Jewish Apocalypticism," *Journal of Religion* 76 (1996): 18–20; Joel Marcus, "The Once and Future Messiah in Early Christianity and Chabad," *New Testament Studies* 47, no. 3 (2001): 383–86; Samuel C. Heilman and Menachem M. Friedman, *The Rebbe: The Life and Afterlife of Menachem Mendel Schneerson* (Princeton, N.J.: Princeton University Press, 2010), passim. The Lubavitcher Rebbe, Menachem Mendel Schneerson, transitioned seamlessly from being identified as "the prophet of this generation" to being identified as a potential Messiah to being identified as the real Messiah.

71. Such schisms are common in sects begun by charismatic leaders; see the sections "History-of-Religions Comparisons" and "The Bābi/Bahā'ī Parallel" in chap. 5.

72. Cf. Charlesworth, "John the Baptizer," 358–66. Charlesworth asserts that this difference means that John came to dissent from the rigid determinism of the sect, in which all outsiders were children of darkness and had no possibility of repentance. John does, however, use the "brood of vipers" terminology, which is implicitly deterministic (those so designated come from a bad seed), though this denunciation is immediately followed by a call to repent (Matt. 3:7–8//Luke 3:7–8). But there is a similar murkiness in CD 19:15–17, where the "Boundary-Movers," who later are linked with viperous snakes (19:22–24), "entered the covenant of repentance but did not turn away from the path of the traitors" (באו בברית תשובה ולא סרו מדרך בוגדים, my trans.). Moreover, the Qumran sect seems to have retained hope for the conversion of the nonsectarian portion of Israel; see the discussion below and cf. Sanders, *Paul and Palestinian Judaism,* 244–57, esp. 247: "The community believed that eschatological Israel would be formed by the conversion of the rest of Israel to the way of the sect."

73. See Magen Broshi, "Qumran: Archaeology," in Schiffman and VanderKam, *Encyclopedia of the Dead Sea Scrolls,* 738.

74. See Jürgen Zangenberg, "Opening up Our View: Khirbet Qumran in a Regional Perspective," in *Religion and Society in Roman Palestine: Old Questions, New Approaches,* ed. Douglas R. Edwards (New York: Routledge, 2004), 175, who lists the numerous harbors on the Dead Sea and concludes, "Clearly, a complex network of local and regional transportation emerges that connects all inhabited areas around the Dead Sea with each other *and* the whole region with the Judean hill country to the west and Peraea and the Decapolis to the east. The entire region, not only Qumran, formed a compartmentalized,

but closely connected *local network* of pockets of habitation that relied upon specialized agriculture and easy connections provided by the Dead Sea" (emphasis in original). Zangenberg also notes that while "no anchorage has been found at Qumran or En Feshka [a nearby and perhaps associated settlement] yet, . . . both sites could be reached from [the harbor at] Rujm el-Bahr in less than two hours."

75. Meyers, "Khirbet Qumran and Its Environs," 27. Jericho is twenty-eight kilometers from Qumran on the ancient north-south path through the Buqei'a region; see Shimon Gibson and Joan E. Taylor, "Roads and Passes Round Qumran," *Palestine Exploration Quarterly* 140 (2008): 225–27.

76. See Catherine M. Murphy, *Wealth in the Dead Sea Scrolls and in the Qumran Community*, Studies on the Texts of the Desert of Judah 40 (Leiden, the Netherlands: Brill, 2002), 359: a connection of Qumran with Nabatea is suggested by "the grave architecture and orientation, so similar to the cemetery on the Nabatean coast of the Dead Sea, by the presence of a Nabatean name on a storage jar (רומא, Gr7Q 6), and by the presence of a few Nabatean coins." See also Zangenberg, "Opening up Our View," 177: "Trade across the Dead Sea is attested by the presence of 'cream ware,' documenting that Nabatean trade interest extended across the Dead Sea and found customers there"; for more detail on this type of pottery, see Jodi Magness, "The Community at Qumran in Light of Its Pottery," in *Methods of Investigation of the Dead Sea Scrolls and the Khirbet Qumran Site: Present Realities and Future Prospects*, ed. Michael O Wise et al., Annals of the New York Academy of Sciences 722 (New York: New York Academy of Sciences, 1994), 45.

Philip C. Hammond, *The Nabateans—Their History, Culture and Archaeology*, Studies in Mediterranean Archaeology 37 (Gothenburg, Sweden: P. Åströms Förlag, 1973), 120, lists a Nabatean inscription at Khirbet Qumran but gives no details. There is a fragmentary letter in Nabatean script, apparently of a legal nature, among the Cave 4 fragments (4QLetter nab = 4Q343); see Hannah M. Cotton and Ada Yardeni, *Aramaic, Hebrew and Greek Documentary Texts from Naḥal Ḥever and Other Sites: With an Appendix Containing Alleged Qumran Texts (the Seiyâl Collection II)*, Discoveries in the Judaean Desert 27 (Oxford: Clarendon Press, 1997), 286–88. I would like to thank Ben Gordon for helping to clarify my thinking on the regional setting of Qumran.

77. Cf. Joseph M. Baumgarten, "Gentiles," in Schiffman and VanderKam, *Encyclopedia of the Dead Sea Scrolls*, 305.

78. See, for example, the restrictive attitude of Ezra-Nehemiah, Jubilees, and Pseudo-Philo, as described by Christine E. Hayes, *Gentile Impurities and Jewish Identities: Intermarriage and Conversion from the Bible to the Talmud* (New York: Oxford University Press, 2002); Terence L. Donaldson, *Judaism and the Gentiles: Jewish Patterns of Universalism (to 135 CE)* (Waco, Tex.: Baylor University Press, 2007); Matthew Thiessen, *Contesting Conversion: Genealogy, Circumcision, and Identity in Ancient Judaism and Christianity* (New York: Oxford University Press, 2011).

79. See Joseph M. Baumgarten, "Proselytes," in Schiffman and VanderKam, *Encyclopedia of the Dead Sea Scrolls*, 2:700–701; Donaldson, *Judaism and the Gentiles*, 203–15.

80. Joseph M. Baumgarten, "The Exclusion of *Netinim* and Proselytes in 4Q Florilegium," in *Studies in Qumran Law*, Studies in Judaism in Late Antiquity 24 (Leiden, the Netherlands: Brill, 1977), 75, somewhat misleadingly says that this passage "lists *ger nilwah*, 'the proselyte who joins,' in the enumeration of the classes of the congregation," by which Baumgarten seemingly means the Qumran community. But though 4QpNah 2:5 does use the phrase "from the midst of their congregation" (מקרב עדתם), the

"congregation" here seems to be Palestinian Jewish society as a whole, not the Qumran community, as is clear from the threat to the followers of the "Seekers of Smooth Things" in 2:4–6 and the reference to "kings" and "princes" at the beginning of 2:9.

81. Cf. Shaye J. D. Cohen, *The Beginnings of Jewishness: Boundaries, Varieties, Uncertainties* (Berkeley: University of California Press, 1999), 162n75: "It is possible that *gēr* in the Qumran texts means not 'proselyte' but 'resident alien.'" The latter is the way the word is translated in *The Dead Sea Scrolls Electronic Library.* Wise, Abegg Jr., and Cook, *The Dead Sea Scrolls: A New Translation* (San Francisco: HarperSanFrancisco, 2005), 219, similarly, render גר here with "foreigner."

Donaldson, *Judaism and the Gentiles,* 207 argues against such renderings, asserting that the language of joining or attachment (נלוה) suggests conversion and citing Esth. 9:27, where the same verb is used in a context that speaks of adhesion to Judaism. But nothing in the immediate context of 4QpNah 2:9 suggests that converts are in view, and the reference to "nations" (גוים) in line 7 may suggest the contrary; the *niphal* of לוה, moreover, can denote a political alliance, without religious connotation (see, for example, Ps. 83:9; Dan. 11:34), although the religious connotation is more common in the Old Testament and at Qumran (Isa. 14:1, 56:3, 6; Zech. 2:15; CD 4:3; 1QS 5:6; cf. Clines, *Dictionary of Classical Hebrew,* 4:523). On the evolution of the meaning of *ger* from the Bible, where it denotes a resident alien, to rabbinic literature, where it denotes a convert, see Cohen, *Beginnings of Jewishness,* 120–22, 161–62.

82. As Donaldson, *Judaism and the Gentiles,* 208, points out, this courtyard "displaces the court of the Gentiles, which has no counterpart in the *Temple Scroll.*" According to Josephus, *Ag. Ap.* 2.103–104, the outer, fourth courtyard of the Second Temple was open to all, foreigners included, "women during their impurity" alone being excepted; the third courtyard was accessible to all Jews, "and, when uncontaminated by any defilement, their wives."

83. Donaldson, *Judaism and the Gentiles,* 208, argues that the *gerim* here are proselytes because of (1) their commensurality with Israelite women and (2) 11QT[a] 44:7–8, which seems to refer to people in the same area of the Temple as "children of Israel." The reference to 11QT[a] 44:7–8 appears to be a mistake resulting from transposition of Roman numerals (XLIV vs. XLVI); the intended reference is to 11QT[a] 46:7–8.

84. Unless women were mentioned in the lacuna at the beginning of line 4, but this seems unlikely. On the common restorations, see George J. Brooke, *4Q Florilegium in the Context of Early Jewish Exegetical Method,* Journal for the Study of the Old Testament: Supplement Series 2 (Sheffield, U.K.: JSOT Press, 1985), 100–101.

85. "This (is) the house which these will not enter: a [for]ever, nor an Ammonite, a Moabite, a bastard, a foreigner (בן נכר), or a *ger* forever, for [God's] holy ones (are) there" (*Dead Sea Scrolls Electronic Library* trans. alt.). But I do not think that Sanders, *Paul and Palestinian Judaism,* 243, is correct in his assertion that 1QS 6:13–14 ("if anyone *from Israel* volunteers [וכולה מתנדב מישראל] for enrollment in the party of the *Yahad*") limits membership in the sect to those who are natural-born Jews; the text merely describes the two-year novitiate for those aspirants (surely the majority) who were Jewish. There may have been a different and perhaps even lengthier procedure for the proselytes.

86. Donaldson, *Judaism and the Gentiles,* 210–15, argues against translating *ger* here as "resident alien" because (a) the term always means "proselyte" elsewhere in the Qumran scrolls and (b) the term does not appear in Deut. 23:2–3 and Ezek. 44:9 (which

excludes כל־בן־נכר, "every alien," from God's sanctuary), from which the Florilegium lines are derived; if the Qumran authors have deliberately added it to the biblical list, this "seems to indicate that they were not simply replicating biblical categories in an antiquarian sort of way but were using the term with the sense it had acquired subsequently." But, as for (a), Donaldson himself acknowledges (p. 205) that *ger* in CD 6:21 may simply mean "resident alien," and this is especially likely in view of the word's association there with widows, orphans, and the poor, with whom resident aliens are frequently linked in the Pentateuch through their shared state of economic dependence. We have already seen, moreover, that there is an argument for interpreting *ger* in 4QpNah 2:9 as "resident alien." Despite Donaldson's awareness of the danger of "homogenizing" Qumran texts, therefore, that may be what he is doing. As for (b), the mere fact that the *gerim* have been tipped into the biblical allusions indicates nothing in particular about the word's meaning here; the author may have wished to emphasize that neither the foreign alien (בן נכר) nor the resident alien (גר) will have access to the eschatological Temple, though the convert to Judaism, presumably, will. This seems to me at least as likely as Donaldson's way of reconciling the Florilegium text with CD 14:3–6 and 11QTᵃ 40:5–6, which is to say that the Florilegium does not exclude the *ger* from membership in eschatological Israel, only from access to the eschatological Temple because of purity concerns. And the "resident alien" translation would seem to be supported by the parallel in Pss. Sol. 17:28: καὶ πάροικος καὶ ἀλλογενὴς οὐ παροικήσει αὐτοῖς ἔτι ("the alien and the foreigner will no longer live near them"), where the first word, πάροικος, is the LXX rendering for גר in eleven Old Testament passages and the second is the translation of בן־נכר in Ezek. 44:9. On this passage and its similarity to 4QFlor 1:3–4, see Baumgarten, "Exclusion of *Netinim*," 84–85.

87. In view of CD 14:6, I do not see how Donaldson, *Judaism and the Gentiles*, 215, can say that "there were proselytes within the Qumran worldview but not within the Qumran community." Sanders, *Paul and Palestinian Judaism*, 243n11, rightly asserts that "different Essene groups may have followed different practices" with regard to proselytes, but I do not agree with his further assertion that "admitting proselytes was probably not in any case a live issue."

88. On the location of John's ministry, see above, n. 30 (pp. 175–76).

89. On this interpretation of "the others" in *Ant.* 18.118, see app. 5.

90. See Luke 4:26–28 in which, contrary to Amy-Jill Levine, Jesus gives offense to a hometown crowd precisely because he refers pointedly to the conversion of two Gentiles (Amy-Jill Levine and Marc Zvi Brettler, eds., *The Jewish Annotated New Testament: New Revised Standard Version Bible Translation* [Oxford; New York: Oxford University Press, 2011], 107). Some later rabbinic traditions overcome this problem by constructing an Israelite genealogy for the widow of Zarapheth and her son (y. Sukkah 5:1 [55a]; Gen. Rab. 98:11; Pirqe R. El. 33), and another possibly portrays Naaman converting to Judaism (Mek. Amalek 3 [Lauterbach 2.176]; cf. *JE* s.v. "Naaman"), though Bernard J. Bamberger, *Proselytism in the Talmudic Period* (1939; repr., New York: KTAV Publishing House, 1968), 205, does not think conversion is implied by the *Mekilta* passage. Traditions in the Babylonian Talmud, however (Git. 57b; *Sanh.* 96b), portray Naaman as a גר תושב, which in this case means a semi-convert to Judaism (see Bamberger, *Proselytism in the Talmudic Period*, 137).

91. We may also note Luke 3:14, which portrays John responding helpfully to a question about how to live from soldiers (στρατευόμενοι), whom Luke may have thought of as Roman soldiers and hence Gentiles (see François Bovon, *Luke*, Hermeneia, 3 vols.

[Minneapolis: Fortress, 2002–12], 1:124n44), although most of the commentators take them as Jewish mercenaries of Antipas. Fitzmyer, *Gospel According to Luke,* 1:470, for example, says, "These were not Roman soldiers, since there were no legions stationed in Palestine in this time, nor auxiliaries from other provinces. They should be understood as Jewish men enlisted in the service of Herod Antipas." C. F. Evans, *Saint Luke,* New Testament Commentaries (London: SCM; Philadelphia: Trinity Press International, 1990), 241, adds the good point that "Luke would hardly introduce Gentiles so indirectly." I. Howard Marshall, *The Gospel of Luke: A Commentary on the Greek Text,* New International Greek Testament Commentary (Exeter, U.K.: Paternoster; Grand Rapids, Mich.: Eerdmans, 1978), 143, however, points out that the forces of Antipas stationed in Perea may have included non-Jews, as his father's army had (see Josephus, *Ant.* 17.198–199). In any case, I doubt the historicity of the saying attributed to the Baptist in Luke 3:12–14; see chap. 6, section on "Challenges to the Thesis of John's Militancy."

92. The other differences are relatively minor. Matt. 3:8a has the singular καρπὸν ἄξιον whereas Luke 3:8a has the plural καρποὺς ἀξίους ("fruits worthy"). Matt. 3:9a has μὴ δόξητε λέγειν ("do not *think* to say"), whereas Luke 3:8b has μὴ ἄρξησθε λέγειν ("do not *begin* to say"). Luke 3:9a has the seemingly superfluous καί, which is absent in Matt. 3:10: ἤδη δὲ καὶ ἡ ἀξίνη.

93. See Paul Hoffmann, *Studien zur Theologie der Logienquelle,* Neutestamentliche Abhandlungen 8 (Münster [Westphalia], Germany: Aschendorff, 1975), 17, who points out that Matthew, in 16:1, 11–12, expands a Markan reference to the Pharisees (Mark 8:11) to a reference to the Pharisees and Sadducees. In Matt. 16:6, similarly, he changes a Markan reference to "the leaven of the Pharisees and the leaven of Herod" (Mark 8:15) to "the leaven of the Pharisees and Sadducees."

94. As in James M. Robinson, Paul Hoffmann, and John S. Kloppenborg, eds., *The Critical Edition of Q: Synopsis Including the Gospels of Matthew and Luke, Mark and Thomas with English, German, and French Translations of Q and Thomas,* Hermeneia (Minneapolis: Fortress; Leuven, Belgium: Peeters, 2000), 8.

95. Bultmann, *History of the Synoptic Tradition,* 117; Carl R. Kazmierski, "The Stones of Abraham: John the Baptist and the End of Torah (Matt. 3,7–10 par. Luke 3,7–9)," *Biblica* 68 (1987): 29. The common themes include the threat of imminent judgment for rejecting God's prophets (Mark 12:1–12; Matt. 18:34–35//Luke 11:49–51; Matt. 23:37–39// Luke 13:34–35; cf. 1 Thess. 2:16), the call to repentance (Matt. 11:20–24//Luke 10:35–15), and the relativizing of physical descent from Abraham (Rom. 9:6–7; cf. Matt. 8:11–12// Luke 13:28–30). There is an especially close connection between Matt. 3:7//Luke 3:7 and the saying attributed to Jesus in Matt. 23:33: "You serpents, you brood of vipers, how shall you escape from the judgment of Gehenna?" (my trans.); the Baptist's "brood of vipers" language might therefore be seen as a retrojection. As Meier, *Marginal Jew,* 2:71n40, points out, however, "it is more probable that Matthew, in his great desire to make John and Jesus parallel figures, has taken Baptist material and placed it on the lips of Jesus."

96. See Meier, *Marginal Jew,* 1:32.

97. See, for example, Hoffmann, *Studien zur Theologie,* 26. In his view, the combination might go back to the editor of Q.

98. This connection was already recognized by premodern commentators on Matt. 3:10; see, for example, Chrysostom, *Homilies on Matthew* 11.4; Cornelius à Lapide, *S. Matthew's Gospel—Chaps. I. to IX.,* vol. 1 of *The Great Commentary* (London: John Hodges, 1893), 1:117. Among modern interpreters, some note the possibility that the tree in Matt.

3:10//Luke 3:9 is meant to symbolize Israel; see, for example Ernst, *Johannes der Täufer* (1989), 302–3; Meier, *Marginal Jew*, 2:30; W. D. Davies and Dale C. Allison, *A Critical and Exegetical Commentary on the Gospel According to Saint Matthew*, International Critical Commentary, 3 vols. (Edinburgh: T&T Clark, 1988–97), 1:308–10. But no commentator known to me has made a connection specifically between the tree symbol in Old Testament/Jewish literature, on the one hand, and Abraham and his descendants, on the other. Ernst comes the closest, mentioning that occasionally in the Old Testament a tree symbolizes Israel (Isa. 61:3; Jer. 11:16; Ezek. 15:6 [Jerusalem]) or a people (Amos 2:9 [the Amorites]); the message, then, might be that Israel should use its last chance.

99. See Shozo Fujita, "The Metaphor of Plant in Jewish Literature of the Intertestamental Period," *Journal for the Study of Judaism in the Persian, Hellenistic, and Roman Periods* 7 (1976): 44. The same insight is marvelously expressed in a poem by Emily Dickinson:

Bloom – is Result – to meet a Flower
And casually glance
Would scarcely cause one to suspect
The minor Circumstance

Assisting in the Bright Affair
So intricately done
Then offered as a Butterfly
To the Meridian –

To pack the Bud – oppose the Worm –
Obtain its right of Dew –
Adjust the Heat – elude the Wind –
Escape the prowling Bee

Great Nature not to disappoint
Awaiting Her that Day –
To be a Flower, is profound
Responsibility –
(R. W. Franklin, ed., *The Poems of Emily Dickinson: Reading Edition* [Cambridge
Mass.: The Belknap Press of Harvard University Press, 1999], no. 1038.)

100. Patrick A. Tiller, "The 'Eternal Planting' in the Dead Sea Scrolls," *Dead Sea Discoveries* 4 (1997): 315.

101. See Joel Marcus, "The Intertextual Polemic of the Markan Vineyard Parable," in *Tolerance and Intolerance in Early Judaism and Christianity*, ed. Graham N. Stanton and Guy G. Stroumsa (Cambridge: Cambridge University Press, 1998), 215.

102. Cf. Davies and Allison, *Matthew*, 2:533.

103. See Dale C. Allison, *The Intertextual Jesus: Scripture in Q* (Valley Forge, Pa.: Trinity Press International, 2000), 101–4, who contrasts "The rejected conviction (Isa. 51:1–2)" with "John the Baptist's declaration (Q 3:8)":

In the past God raised up	In the future God can raise up
from the rock that is Abraham	from "these stones" on the ground
children to Abraham	children to Abraham
Israel benefits from its ancestor's merit	Israel does not benefit from its ancestor's merit.

104. On the date of Psalms of Solomon, see R. B. Wright in Charlesworth, *Old Testament Pseudepigrapha*, 2:641, who dates it to the first century BCE.

105. On the date of Pseudo-Philo, see app. 4, "Was John from a Priestly Background?," n. 13 (p. 225).

106. Translations from Pseudo-Philo by Daniel J. Harrington in Charlesworth, *Old Testament Pseudepigrapha*, vol. 2.

107. See Sanders, *Paul and Palestinian Judaism*, passim. Howard Jacobson, *A Commentary on Pseudo-Philo's* Liber Antiquitatum Biblicarum *with Latin Text and English Translation*, Arbeiten zur Geschichte des antiken Judentums und des Urchristentums 31 (Leiden, the Netherlands: Brill, 1996), 1:597, compares LAB 18:10 to the later medieval Jewish midrash, *Yalqut Shimoni* (1, sect. 771): "Further, the Midrash asserts that the plant that is Israel could no more be uprooted than could the heavens and earth, just the point LAB makes here (though LAB's rhetoric is even more emphatic)." On the unconditionality of God's commitment to Israel in Pseudo-Philo, see also John M. G. Barclay, *Paul and the Gift* (Grand Rapids, Mich.: Eerdmans, 2015), 266–79.

108. See Joseph M. Baumgarten, "4Q500 and the Ancient Conception of the Lord's Vineyard," *Journal of Jewish Studies* 40 (1989): 1–6.

109. See Bilhah Nitzan, "302. 4QpapAdmonitory Parable," in *Qumran Cave 4.XV: Sapiential Texts, Part I*, Discoveries in the Judaean Desert 20 (Oxford: Clarendon Press, 1997), 136, 138, 140–41. Cf. Rom. 11:16–24, which also uses a tree parable as a symbol for God's eternal commitment to Israel.

110. The fragments of Jubilees at Qumran are only parts of the first two chapters, but the fragments of 1 Enoch include substantial portions of 1 En. 93, among them the references to the plant in 93:2 and 93:10; see 4QEn^g (Q212) 1 iii 19–20; 1 iv 12–13; cf. J. T. Milik, *The Books of Enoch* (Oxford: Clarendon Press, 1976), 263–69.

111. Translation of O. S. Wintermute from Charlesworth, *Old Testament Pseudepigrapha*, vol. 2; I use this translation rather than the one in the critical edition by James VanderKam because Wintermute's is usually more literal.

112. On the textual and translational problem here, see George W. E. Nickelsburg, *1 Enoch 1*, Hermeneia (Minneapolis: Fortress, 2001), 435; Loren T. Stuckenbruck, *1 Enoch 91–108*, Commentaries on Early Jewish Literature (Berlin: Walter de Gruyter, 2007), 65–66, 76. Either "truth" or "righteousness"/"uprightness" is a possible translation for Aramaic קושטא; see Ludwig Koehler and Walter Baumgartner, *The Hebrew and Aramaic Lexicon of the Old Testament: Study Edition* (Leiden, the Netherlands: Brill, 2001), 2:1974. Unless otherwise noted, translations from 1 Enoch in this chapter are from the Nickelsburg volume.

113. Stuckenbruck, *1 Enoch 91–108*, 101.

114. Nickelsburg, *1 Enoch 1*, 444–45, who goes on to say: "Abraham is himself chosen as the plant, from which comes 'the eternal plant of righteousness.'" Nickelsburg compares this to Jub. 1:16; 16:26; 21:24; and 36:6, where "the plant is historical Israel, explicitly connected with Abraham; it is characterized by righteousness and will thus endure forever."

Stuckenbruck asserts that "plant of righteousness" in 1 En. 93:10 "denotes a group, a 'true Israel' selected from amongst Abraham's offspring, that provides a continuous link between biblical and eschatological time" (Stuckenbruck, *1 Enoch 91–108*, 102). It would be more accurate to say that this group is the new growth that emerges from the devastated plant, but the plant itself is the Abrahamic legacy; cf. Tiller, "'Eternal Planting' in the Dead Sea Scrolls," 320: "It is important to note that the elect are said to be *from* the eternal plant of truth. Presumably, then, the elect are not coterminous with the plant. . . . The elect, which represents the group behind the Apocalypse of Weeks, is only part of the whole plant, which, consequently, must represent either all Israel or possibly an antecedent group of righteous Israel."

115. Amputation of branches is not explicit in 1 En. 93 but would seem to be implied by the reference to the "chosen *root*" (rather than "chosen *plant*," as previously and subsequently) in 93:8.

116. In 1 En. 93, by contrast, the offspring of "the chosen root" are dispersed, but this dispersal turns out to be temporary.

117. Dale C. Allison, "Jesus and the Covenant: A Response to E.P. Sanders," *Journal for the Study of the New Testament* 29 (1987): 158–61; Jon D. Levenson, *Inheriting Abraham: The Legacy of the Patriarch in Judaism, Christianity, and Islam* (Princeton, N.J.: Princeton University Press, 2012), 150. Levenson, however, goes too far, and contradicts one of his own points (for example, p. 157), when he sums up John's message as, "The election of Abraham is irrelevant." As Allison points out, rather, for John, Abraham's election is not irrelevant; it is just a question, as in Gal. 3, of who the true progeny of Abraham are, and whether or not birth into the Jewish community is enough to make one his child.

118. On the Parable of the Vineyard as a warning to Israel as a whole, see Marcus, "Intertextual Polemic of the Markan Vineyard Parable." Matt. 15:13 in its present context is aimed at the Pharisees, but this may be a Matthean narrowing of a saying also originally addressed to Israel as a whole; see T. W. Manson, *The Sayings of Jesus as Recorded in the Gospels According to St. Matthew and St. Luke with Introduction and Commentary* (1937; repr., London: SCM, 1957), 199–200. In Luke 13:6–9 the planter of the fig tree threatens to cut it down because it is fruitless, but the gardener pleads for a year's respite before doing so to see if he can make the tree fruitful. It is possible that Jesus viewed himself as the gardener and his own ministry as a time of respite, the last chance for Israel; see Joachim Jeremias, *The Parables of Jesus*, 2nd rev. ed. (New York: Scribner's, 1972), 170.

119. An alternate hypothesis is that Matt. 3:9–10//Luke 3:8–9 is a Christian invention, ascribing to John the church's rejection of covenantal nomism. This seems unlikely, however, in view of Matt. 11:16–19//Luke 7:31–35, a passage that is probably authentic because it places the Baptist on a par with Jesus as a rejected emissary of Wisdom (and thus goes against the church's tendency to subordinate John to Jesus). The passage suggests that John like Jesus experienced rejection from a significant part of "this generation" and that this fact was well enough known to ground Jesus's prophetic denunciation of his contemporaries. If so, however, a similar denunciation of contemporaries by John would not be unexpected.

....

CHAPTER THREE   The Elijah Role

1. The expectation that the returning Elijah would precede the Messiah is not explicit in the Old Testament or pre-Christian Jewish traditions, but in 1QS 9:11 and 4QTestimonia the eschatological prophet is mentioned before the royal and priestly Messiahs, and this may reflect the belief that he would precede them (cf. Jassen, *Mediating the Divine*, 161–65). In Mark 9:11–13, moreover, the belief that Elijah would precede the Messiah is attributed to Jesus's opponents, the Jewish scribes. This attribution is unlikely to have been invented by the Christians. The passage sounds more like an effort to deal with a real challenge on the part of skeptical Jews: if Jesus was the Messiah,

where was the Elijah, who was supposed to precede him? See Dale C. Allison, "'Elijah Must Come First,'" *JBL* 103 (1984): 256–58; Joel Marcus, *The Way of the Lord: Christological Exegesis of the Old Testament in the Gospel of Mark* (Louisville, Ky.: Westminster–John Knox; Edinburgh: T&T Clark, 1992), 110; Clare K. Rothschild, *Baptist Traditions and Q*, WUNT 190 (Tübingen, Germany: Mohr Siebeck, 2005), 61.

A similar question arose in the case of the seventeenth-century Jewish messianic pretender, Shabbetai Zevi: since the idea had become entrenched that the Davidic Messiah would be preceded not only by Elijah but also by the dying Messiah-son-of-Joseph, "several attempts were made to find the individual who had preceded [Zevi], the messiah of the lineage of Joseph who had fought and died and prepared the way for him, but a convincing candidate was never found. For not a few followers, the absence of a preliminary messiah cast the status of Shabbetai Zvi as the messiah of the lineage of David into such doubt that they abandoned their support of him" (Harris Lenowitz, *The Jewish Messiahs: From the Galilee to Crown Heights* [New York: Oxford University Press, 1998], 150).

2. On this interpretation of Mark 9:11–13, see Joel Marcus, "Mark 9,11–13: As It Has Been Written," *Zeitschrift für die neutestamentliche Wissenschaft und die Kunde der älteren Kirche* 80 (1989): 42–63.

3. The allusion to Mal. 3:1 is editorial in Mark 1:3 and Luke 3:4, though Matthew ascribes it to John himself in Matt. 3:2.

4. On these connections between the Elijah image and the Synoptic image of John, see Brown, *Gospel According to John*, 1:47; Josef Ernst, *Johannes der Täufer, der Lehrer Jesu?*, Biblische Bücher 2 (Freiburg: Herder, 1994), 102.

5. Meier, *Marginal Jew*, 2:28.

6. Cf. John 1:25–27, which is the Fourth Gospel's version of John's prophecy of "the one coming after me," to which the evangelist appends a scene in which the Baptist identifies Jesus as his successor, the Lamb of God and Son of God (1:29–34).

7. On the debate about the identity of the "Stronger One," see Joel Marcus, *Mark: A New Translation with Introduction and Commentary*, Anchor Yale Bible 27 and 27A (New Haven, Conn.: Yale University Press, 2000–2009), 1:151–52. Some (for example, Ernst Lohmeyer, *Das Evangelium des Markus*, [1937; repr., Kritisch-exegetischer Kommentar über das Neue Testament (Meyer-Kommentar), 1:2; Göttingen, Germany: Vandenhoeck & Ruprecht, 1951], 18n1) have thought the reference is to God, since strength in ascribed to God in passages such as Isa. 40:10, Eccl 6:10, and Rev. 18:8, and the judgment attributed to the "Stronger One" is similar to that attributed to God in numerous Old Testament passages. The Achilles heel of this theory, so to speak, is the reference to the sandal of the Coming One. The passage seems to refer to a human figure, more or less on a par with John, but whose superiority he recognizes. The Messiah is the "strongest" candidate, especially given his association with strength and even violence in passages such as Ps. 2:9, Isa. 11:4, Pss. Sol. 17:37, and 1 En. 49:3, and given that a Jewish identification of "the Stronger One" as the Messiah explains why Christians came to identify Jesus, whom they believed to be the Messiah, with "the Stronger One."

8. Cf. Meier, *Marginal Jew*, 2:28. Mark 1:7–8//Matt. 3:11–12//Luke 3:16–17 is a Mark/Q overlap passage, which is an argument for its relative antiquity. For the Isenheim altar of Matthias Grünewald, see the introduction, n. 2 (p. 161).

9. See, for example, Schlatter, *Johannes der Täufer*, 43–47; Robinson, "Elijah, John

and Jesus," 263–81; Raymond E. Brown, "Three Quotations from John the Baptist in the Gospel of John," *CBQ* 22 (1960): 297; Brown, *Gospel According to John*, 2:147–49.

10. Cf. Meier, *Marginal Jew*, 2:32: "*Whether or not* John presented himself as the returning Elijah [emphasis added], the eschatology of [Matt] 3:7–10, without Christianity or its Christ, fits in perfectly with the independent Baptist, who felt no need to define himself by his relation to Jesus of Nazareth." Meier is less qualified on page 40: "Most of John's message would leave one with the impression that he sees himself, Elijah-like, as the direct forerunner of God." Josef Ernst supports an Elijan self-consciousness for John the Baptist in his 1989 work, *Johannes der Täufer* (see p. 297), but is more equivocal in his 1994 volume, *Johannes der Täufer, der Lehrer Jesu?* (see pp. 102–3).

11. Cf. Luke 4:24–26, 7:11–17, with 1 Kgs. 17:1–18:1 (healing of widow's son and drought); Luke 9:51–55, 12:49, with 1 Kgs. 18:38; 2 Kgs. 1:10, 12; 2:11 (calling down fire from heaven); and Luke 12:54–56 with 1 Kgs. 18:44 (cloud rising in the west). See the handy chart of "Elijan echoes in Luke" in Jaroslav Rindoš, *He of Whom It Is Written: John the Baptist and Elijah in Luke*, Österreichische biblische Studien 38 (Frankfurt: P. Lang, 2010), 14–15.

12. On John 1:21b as a reference to the eschatological Prophet-like-Moses, see Brown, *Gospel According to John*, 1:49–50.

13. Brown, *Gospel According to John*, 1:47, citing Georg Molin, "Elijahu: Der Prophet und sein Weiterleben in den Hoffnungen des Judentums und der Christenheit," *Judaica* 8 (1953): 80, claims that Jewish sources combined Isa. 40:3 with Mal. 4:5 and reinterpreted it to refer to Elijah. But I do not see that claim in Molin, nor have I been able to find ancient Jewish sources supporting it.

14. See, for example, Morton Enslin, "Once Again: John the Baptist," *Religion in Life* 27 (1958): 557–66, esp. 563, who thinks that John and Jesus probably never met and that the whole idea of John as a forerunner is a Christian invention. According to one of Enslin's students (Reumann, "Quest for the Historical John the Baptist," 183–84), Enslin went so far as to suggest orally that John, if questioned about Jesus, may have replied, "Jesus who?" For a more recent iteration of the theory that John and Jesus had completely separate ministries, see the view of Johannes Tromp, which is discussed in app. 1.

15. For these arguments, see Schlatter, *Johannes der Täufer*, 43–47; Brown, *Gospel According to John*, 47–49; Ernst, *Johannes der Täufer, der Lehrer Jesu?*, 103.

16. On the Fourth Gospel, see Wink, *John the Baptist*, 89: "For [the Fourth Evangelist] the idea of a forerunner is anathema; notice how carefully he has already applied the antidote to it in 1:1, 15. John is not the forerunner, for the Logos is already πρῶτος (1:15, 30) and can have no forerunner." On Luke's overall retention and even heightening of the Elijah-John association, see Rindoš, *He of Whom*, 193–230.

17. Cf. Taylor, *Immerser*, 283.

18. Scholars affirming a biblical typology in a historical figure's self-consciousness sometimes find themselves in a "damned if you do, damned if you don't" situation. If they detect too few parallels, that becomes evidence that the historical figure did not model himself on the biblical prototype; if they detect too many, that becomes evidence that later followers invented the correspondence.

19. Dale C. Allison, *The New Moses: A Matthean Typology* (Edinburgh: T&T Clark, 1993), 94–95. To cite an example that Allison does not, Bar Kochba is "nowhere . . . said to be of the house of David; he might even have been from a priestly family and thus

outside royal messianic lineage altogether" (Lenowitz, *Jewish Messiahs*, 50–51). Jesus also may have been of non-Davidic lineage, despite frequent claims to the contrary in early Christian tradition (see, however, Mark 12:25–27 and John 7:42). Yet both of these men were acclaimed as, and may indeed have believed themselves to be, the (Davidic) Messiah.

20. Bar Kochba did not call himself Messiah but *nasi'* ("prince, presiding official"), a more equivocal term (see Lenowitz, *Jewish Messiahs*, 51). According to the travel journal of Yakov Sapir, Shukr Kuḥayl, a late-nineteenth-century Yemeni messianic pretender, would sometimes say that he was the Messiah and sometimes that he was merely Elijah's messenger.

Another contemporary source, Moshe Ḥanoch of Aden, writes, "The people of Yemen believe that he is the messiah but he says he is not and merely obeys Elijah and seeks to awaken the people to Redemption." Despite such denials, however, Kuḥayl apparently believed in his own messiahship, and Sapir views his denials as a stratagem: "Kuḥayl was wise not to call himself messiah, . . . but any[one] who possesses an eye that sees and a heart that understands will conclude from his words that he thinks he is a prophet sent from God and the redeemer, the messiah of the lineage of David" (Lenowitz, *Jewish Messiahs*, 236).

21. As Lenowitz, *Jewish Messiahs*, points out, in the Rebbe's case this reluctance to proclaim his messiahship openly may have been partly based on reticence or self-doubt (221–22), a frequent occurrence in the histories of would-be Messiahs; cf. Lenowitz's descriptions of the diffidence of Hayim Vital (1542/43–1620; ibid., 127, 139, 144–45) and Suleiman Jamal (fl. 1667; ibid., 234). As Lenowitz points out, such reticence is usually justified: "The messiah knows of the history of other messiahs and of the texts about them, oral or written. He has good reason to be ambivalent about taking on the task; he knows he can't do it and will probably die in the attempt" (ibid., 274–75). On the Lubavitcher Rebbe's reticence and self-doubt, see also Heilman and Friedman, *Rebbe*, 215, 230–31.

22. See Marcus, "Once and Future Messiah," 392–94; Elliott R. Wolfson, *Open Secret: Postmessianic Messianism and the Mystical Revision of Menaḥem Mendel Schneerson* (New York: Columbia University Press, 2009), passim; Heilman and Friedman, *Rebbe*. Similarly, Shukr Kuḥayl "rectified errors in the texts of the Bible and the Zohar, unscrambling Isa. 45:1, where the messiah's name appears as *koresh*, asserting its 'proper' reading, *shukr*" (Lenowitz, *Jewish Messiahs*, 235–36).

23. See Rappaport, *Ritual and Religion*, 32; Mark Chaves, *Congregations in America* (Cambridge, Mass.: Harvard University Press, 2004), 156.

24. See the discussion of "Criteria for Historicity" in the introduction.

25. Philipp Vielhauer, "Tracht und Speise Johannes der Täufers," in *Aufsätze zum Neuen Testament*, Theologische Bücherei: Neudrucke und Berichte aus dem 20. Jahrhundert 31 (Munich: Chr. Kaiser Verlag, 1965), 53, claims that the parallelism with respect to parts (b) and (c) works only for the LXX version of the 2 Kings passage, not for the MT version, and that therefore John's garb was not meant to invoke that of Elijah. Vielhauer thinks that the Hebrew word used for Elijah's leather garment, אֵזוֹר, means a loincloth, but that if Mark had wanted to indicate a loincloth, he would have written διάζωμα or περίζωμα rather than ζωνή. It is far from clear, however, that אֵזוֹר always indicates a loincloth (see below), and the word, as Vielhauer himself recognizes, is translated with Mark's word ζωνή not only in 2 Kgs. 1:8 but also in Isa. 5:27 and Job

12:18. The other Greek terms never occur in the New Testament, whereas ζωνή occurs not only in the passages about the Baptist's garb but also in Acts 21:11 (in reference to Paul's belt) and in Rev. 1:13; 15:6 (in reference to the golden girdles or sashes worn around the chests of heavenly beings); it is, therefore, the term of choice for an encircling garment.

26. On John's asceticism and the comparison with the Nazirites and Bannus, see Taylor, *Immerser*, index under "Asceticism," "Bannus," and "Nazirite vow." Other ascetic aspects of the Baptist in the Gospel tradition include the descriptions of his fasting (Mark 2:18), abstention from wine (Matt. 11:16–19//Luke 7:31–35; Luke 1:1; cf. Num. 6:3–4), and coarse clothing (Matt. 11:8//Luke 7:25).

27. See Eve-Marie Becker, "'Kamelhaare . . . und wilder Honig,'" in *Die bleibende Gegenwart des Evangeliums. Festschrift für Otto Merk zum 70. Geburtstag* (ed. Roland Gebauer and Martin Meiser; Marburg, Germany: N. G. Elwert, 2003), 13–28.

28. Vielhauer, "Tracht und Speise," 49, though opposing this interpretation of אִישׁ בַּעַל שֵׂעָר as a reference to Elijah's dress, calls it "very common."

29. John Gray, *I & II Kings* (1964; repr., Old Testament Library; London: SCM, 1977), 464; Carol L. Meyers and Eric M. Meyers, *Zechariah 9–14: A New Translation with Introduction and Commentary*, AB 25C (New York: Doubleday, 1993), 379.

30. Douglas E. Edwards, "Dress and Ornamentation," in *Anchor Bible Dictionary* (New York: Doubleday, 1992), 233. Cf. Clines, *Dictionary of Classical Hebrew*, 1:169, which defines אֵזוֹר as "girdle, short waist-cloth of linen or leather."

31. Ernst, *Johannes der Täufer* (1989), 284–85, mentions Zech. 13:4 and the references to Elijah's cloak in 1–2 Kings, along with the influence of the New Testament tradition about the Baptist's clothing, as the basis for "die heute geläufige Übersetzung," according to which 2 Kgs. 1:8 speaks of a hairy garment. Ernst himself opposes this interpretation.

32. Zech. 9–14 is probably to be dated to the first half of the fifth century BCE; see Meyers and Meyers, *Zechariah 9–14*, 27. Elijah is linked with King Ahab of the northern kingdom of Israel, who reigned in the early ninth century BCE. According to Simon J. De Vries, *Prophet Against Prophet: The Role of the Micaiah Narrative (I Kings 22) in the Development of Early Prophetic Tradition* (Grand Rapids, Mich.: Eerdmans, 1978), index under "Elijah cycle," the stories about Elijah and his successor Elisha were probably circulating already during their lifetimes, and were gathered into legendary cycles shortly thereafter, in the reign of Jehu (late ninth century BCE).

In the view of Thomas C. Römer, *The So-Called Deuteronomistic History: A Sociological, Historical and Literary Introduction* (London: T&T Clark, 2005), 153–54, however, most of the Elijah-Elisha stories, including those in 2 Kgs. 1, are post-Deuteronomistic additions appended to the books of Kings in the Persian period (539–331 BCE).

33. See, for example, Prov. 1:17; Eccl. 10:11, 20; Isa. 41:15; Dan. 8:6, 20; cf. Mordechai Cogan and Hayim Tadmor, *II Kings: A New Translation with Introduction and Commentary*, AB 11 (New York: Doubleday, 1988), 26; T. R. Hobbs, *2 Kings*, Word Biblical Commentary 13 (Waco, Tex.: Word Books, 1985), 10.

34. Muraoka, *A Greek-English Lexicon of the Septuagint*, 140, defines δασύς as "thickly, densely covered distinct objects." In the present case, in Gen. 25:25, and in Gen. 27:11, 23, the "distinct objects" are hairs. In Lev. 23:40, Deut. 12:2, Isa. 57:5, Ezek. 6:13 Alexandrinus, Neh. 8:15, and Sir. 14:18, the objects are leaves, and in Hab. 3:3 they are trees.

35. See Arnold Bogumil Ehrlich, *Randglossen zur hebräischen Bibel* (1914; repr., Hildesheim: G. Olms, 1968), 7:278–79; Hobbs, *2 Kings,* 10; Cogan and Tadmor, *II Kings,* 26.

36. Susan Niditch, *My Brother Esau Is a Hairy Man: Hair and Identity in Ancient Israel* (New York: Oxford University Press, 2008).

37. Translation from James B. Pritchard, ed., *Ancient Near Eastern Texts Relating to the Old Testament,* 3rd ed. (Princeton, N.J.: Princeton University Press, 1969), 74.

38. On the Slavonic Josephus, see app. 9.

39. Cf. the description of Esau in Jub. 19:13–14 as "a fierce man, and rustic and hairy," who grew up to be a hunter (trans. O. S. Wintermute in Charlesworth, *Old Testament Pseudepigrapha,* 2:92).

40. 2 Samuel 18:9 mentions Absalom's head rather than his hair being caught in an oak tree; but Josephus (*Ant.* 7.239) interprets this as a reference to his hair, and the interpretation is likely, given the emphasis on Absalom's hair a few chapters earlier; cf. m. Soṭah 1:8: "Absalom gloried in his hair—therefore he was hanged by his hair." This is probably not just "a moralizing exposition," as A. A. Anderson, *2 Samuel,* Word Biblical Commentary 11 (Dallas: Word Books, 1989), 225, asserts, since "head" in the Hebrew Bible frequently stands in for hair by synecdoche (see glossary). See, for example, "do not dishevel your head" (my trans.) in Lev. 10:6 (cf. 21:10; Num. 5:18), "the seven braids of my head" in Judg. 16:13, "no razor shall touch his head" in 1 Sam. 1:11, and "my head is wet with dew" in Cant. 5:2 (cf. 7:5), as well as texts in which kings, priests, or others have their heads anointed (for example, Exod. 29:7; Lev. 21:10; Pss. 23:5, 141:5) or which speak of shaving or shearing the head (Num. 6:9, 18; Job 1:20, etc.; see esp. Isa. 7:20, which links shaving the head with shaving "the hair of the legs," that is, pubic hair). In the New Testament, Jesus warns in Matt. 5:36 against swearing by one's head, "for you cannot make one hair white or black," Luke speaks in Acts 18:18; 21:24 of shearing or shaving the head, and Paul in 1 Cor. 11:4–15 denounces women whose heads are uncovered, since a woman's long hair is her glory. Cf. Clines, *Dictionary of Classical Hebrew,* 7:366, and thanks to Craig Hill for several of these examples.

41. In the case of Esau, whose other name is Edom (אֱדוֹם), this primal quality is suggested not only by his abundant hair but also by his red color, which associates him with the earth (אֲדָמָה); see Gen. 25:25–30 and Niditch, *My Brother Esau,* 114.

42. John is linked with the biblical image of Samson not only by his long hair but also by his diet, which includes wild honey (cf. Judg. 14:8–9).

43. Martin Buber, *The Prophetic Faith* (New York: Macmillan, 1949), 76–77, portrays Elijah both as long haired and as wearing a hairy garment; although I disagree about the latter, Buber's description still captures the spirit of the biblical depiction: "He passes through the midst of the city culture with all its degeneration as the zealous and inflexible nomad, long-haired, wrapped in a hairy garment, with a leather girdle, reminiscent of the Babylonian hero Enkidu of the Gilgamesh epic, except that Enkidu is enticed by the temple whore, whereas Elijah never has any contact with Baal seductions."

44. Pesiqta Rabbati 26:1–2: "You brought it about that curly-haired Elijah rose up to act in their behalf, and they derided him, saying: 'Look how he curls his curls!' And they derided him and called him 'Curly.' And you brought it about that Elisha rose up to act in their behalf, and they said to him: 'Get up, Baldy! Get up, Baldy!'" [cf. 2 Kgs. 2:23; trans. mine]. Note the similarity to the Q saying Matt. 11:18–19//Luke 7:33–34: both the Elijah figure and his successor are mocked, but for opposite reasons.

45. On the theory that Jesus himself invented the identification of John with Elijah, see the introduction, n. 20 (p. 163).

46. It is theoretically possible that the account of John's hair garment and of his diet is historical, reflecting the Baptist's prophetic and ascetic mindset, whereas the leather girdle is ahistorical and was added to create an Elijan typology. But in this case, we face the same dilemma: why weren't the creators of the typology consistent, remaking John into a totally Elijah-like figure? It makes more sense to posit that the basic memory in Mark 1:6 is historical.

47. In contrast, Becker, "'Kamelhaare . . . und wilder Honig,'" 15, quotes Josef Ernst to the effect that "the designation 'camel's hair' has 'no correspondence' in the Old Testament text. Therefore an Elijah typology cannot be established either factually or terminologically on the basis of the prophetic garment." It is precisely the "therefore" ("daher") at the beginning of the second sentence that needs to be challenged.

48. Cf. Becker, "'Kamelhaare . . . und wilder Honig,'" 17–18.

49. The body of the newborn Esau is covered with hair so thick that he seems to be wearing a fur garment. For the way in which the hairiness of Esau in Gen. 25:25 captured the imagination of later exegetes, see James L. Kugel, *Traditions of the Bible: A Guide to the Bible as It Was at the Start of the Common Era* (Cambridge, Mass.: Harvard University Press, 1998), 354n2.

50. See the sections "The Gospels and Josephus on John's Baptism" and "Jesus as Sole Spirit Bestower" in chapter 4.

51. Meier, *Marginal Jew,* 2:26.

52. See, for example, t. 'Ed. 3:4 and b. Qidd. 72b, and cf. Louis Ginzberg, *The Legends of the Jews,* 7 vols. (Philadelphia: Jewish Publication Society, 1909–38), 6:324n35; Joseph Klausner, *The Messianic Idea in Israel: From Its Beginning to the Completion of the Mishnah* (New York: Macmillan, 1955), 454–55; Jassen, *Mediating the Divine,* 141n22.

53. On the historicity of the Synoptic portrayal of the role played by Antipas's marriage in the execution of the Baptist, see chap. 6.

54. On the date of 1 Maccabees, see David A. deSilva, *Introducing the Apocrypha* (Grand Rapids, Mich.: Baker Academic, 2002), 248: it was written sometime between the death of John Hyrcanus in 104 BCE (see 16:23–24) and the Roman intervention in the dispute between Hyrcanus II and Aristobulus II in 63 BCE.

55. See Wolf Wirgin, "Simon Maccabaeus and the *Prophetes Pistos,*" *Palestine Exploration Quarterly* 103 (1971): 35–41. Wirgin, however, thinks that this analysis applies only to 1 Macc. 4:46, not to 14:41, since the "trustworthy prophet" in the latter will not decide halakhic disputes but will make political decisions. This, however, is a false dichotomy; in a theocracy such as ancient Israel, political decisions necessarily involve halakhic disputes; indeed, in the present instance the dispute is precisely about the merging of political and clerical leadership (see Jassen, *Mediating the Divine,* 153). Jewish thinkers understood, on the basis of Old Testament passages such as 2 Sam. 7 and 1 Chr. 17, that the king of Israel was to be from line of David. Simon Maccabeus was not from that line, yet he assumed the royal role. Hence the dispute was a halakhic one. See the criticism of the Hasmoneans in Pss. Sol. 17:6, "instead of their excellence (= high priesthood) they put on kingship," on which see Daniel R. Schwartz, "On Pharisaic Opposition to the Hasmonean Monarchy," in *Studies in the Jewish Background of Christianity,* WUNT 60 (1983; repr., Tübingen: J. C. B. Mohr [Paul Siebeck], 1992), 46.

56. See Julio Trebolle Barrera, "Elijah," in Schiffman and VanderKam, *Encyclopedia of the Dead Sea Scrolls,* 1:246. Louis Ginzberg, *An Unknown Jewish Sect,* (1922; Eng. trans., Moreshet Series 1; New York: Jewish Theological Seminary, 1976), 209–22, who thinks that the Damascus Document's term "Teacher of Righteousness" is a reference to Elijah,

says that the latter "will ultimately, at the End of the Days, decide all doubts and controversies, but until then prime authority is vested in the Founder of the Sect" (222). The founder of the sect, then, was a "Teacher of Righteousness" only in a secondary sense; the real "Teacher of Righteousness" will be the awaited Elijah.

57. The Hebrew of Hos. 10:12b is וְעֵת לִדְרוֹשׁ אֶת־יְהוָה עַד־יָבוֹא וְיֹרֶה צֶדֶק לָכֶם, which the RSV translates: "For it is time to seek the Lord, that he may come and rain righteousness upon you." However, since ירה, which literally means "to throw," can also have the nuance "to teach" (as in the word "Torah" itself), the clause can also be translated, "It is time to seek the Lord, until he comes and teaches righteousness to you."

58. Ginzberg, *Unknown Jewish Sect,* 211–12, points out that, in b. Bek. 24a, the Palestinian R. Yoḥanan (fl. 250 CE) declares that a question of law must remain undecided עד יָבוֹא וְיוֹרה צדק, "until he comes and teaches truth," an echo of Hos. 10:12. Ginzberg concludes that Rashi is correct to see this as a reference to the return of Elijah, pointing to eighteen Talmudic passages in which "Elijah appears as one who, in his capacity of precursor of the Messiah, will settle all doubts on matters ritual and juridical " (b. Ber. 35b; b. Pesaḥ 13a; b. Šabb. 108a; etc.).

59. Brenda J. Shaver, "The Prophet Elijah in the Literature of the Second Temple Period: The Growth of a Tradition" (Ph.D. diss., University of Chicago, 2001), 192.

60. Andrew E. Hill, *Malachi: A New Translation with Introduction and Commentary,* AB 25D (New York: Doubleday, 1998), 366 mentions only that the sentences are transposed in certain LXX mss. (for example, A, B, and Q), but the Göttingen LXX, the New English Translation of the Septuagint, and the volume on Malachi in La Bible d'Alexandrie all print the transposed verses as the original Septuagint text. Cf. Laurence Vianès, ed., *Malachie,* La Bible d'Alexandrie 23.12 (Paris: Les Éditions du Cerf, 2011), 164: "Les trois derniers versets de *Malachie* . . . se présentent dans la LXX dans un ordre différent du TM."

Hill theorizes that the transposition is designed to prevent the canonical book from ending with a curse. But this motivation does not contradict the theory that an additional reason was that Elijah was understood as an eschatological "covenant enforcer" (see next note).

61. Cf. David L. Petersen, *Late Israelite Prophecy: Studies in Deutero-Prophetic Literature and in Chronicles,* Society of Biblical Literature Monograph Series (Missoula, Mont.: Scholars Press, 1977), 43, who terms the Elijah figure in Mal. 3:1, 4:5a (= 3:23a MT) a "covenant enforcer." For other Mosaic features of Elijah, see Allison, *New Moses,* 39–46.

62. Against Vianès, *Malachie,* 167.

63. כי כבשרמה תהיה טהרתמה

64. Yigael Yadin, *The Temple Scroll* (Jerusalem: Israel Exploration Society, 1977–83), 1:310.

65. Becker, "'Kamelhaare . . . und wilder Honig,'" 17–18 uses the Temple Scroll text as evidence that John's coat was not made from a camel's *hide,* but only woven from camel's *hair:* "If John had worn a camel's hide, he would have violate the Jewish purity regulations." There are two problems with this statement: (1) It makes an unjustified equation between sectarian Qumran purity regulations and "*the* Jewish purity regulations" ("die jüdischen Reinheitsvorschriften"). (2) It assumes that the Qumranians would have approved of garments woven from camel hair. But the principle כי כבשרמה תהיה טהרתמה would apply here as well. It is much more likely that John wore a cloak of camel's hide than an expensive garment woven from camel's hair.

66. Against Edmondo Lupieri, "Johannes der Täufer," in *Religion in Geschichte und Gegenwart* (Tübingen: Mohr Siebeck, 1998), 4:515.

67. On the passages about locusts in this paragraph, see James A. Kelhoffer, *The Diet of John the Baptist: "Locusts and Wild Honey" in Synoptic and Patristic Interpretation*, WUNT 176 (Tübingen, Germany: Mohr Siebeck, 2005), 40–56, though I put a different spin on the evidence than Kelhoffer does. As Kelhoffer notes (pp. 5–6, 99n65), Mark's grammar (ἦν . . . ἐσθίων) can be interpreted as suggesting that John's diet *included* locusts and wild honey, not that these were his sole sustenance; Matthew's, however (ἡ δὲ τροφὴ ἦν αὐτοῦ), narrows the implication. In any case, both evangelists agree that these were the foods of John worth noting, and so we must ask why.

68. Kelhoffer, *Diet of John the Baptist*, 54–55.

69. See Jacob Milgrom, *Leviticus: A New Translation with Introduction and Commentary*, AB 3, 3 vols. (New York: Doubleday, 1991–2001), 1:189–90; Kelhoffer, *Diet of John the Baptist*, 80–99.

70. היוצא מן הטמא טמא (m. Bek. 1:2; t. Bek. [Zuckermandel] 1:6, 9; b. Bek. 5b, 7ab). Note the similarity in thought though not in vocabulary to the Qumran principle כי כבשרמה תהיה טהרתמה.

71. See Milgrom, *Leviticus*, 1:189, citing Pliny, *Natural History* 31.14(48), and mentioning that in rabbinic Hebrew הדביש, a verbal form derived from the word for honey, means "turn sour or corrupt" (for example, b. B. Meṣ 38a).

72. See Charlesworth, "John the Baptizer," 367–68.

73. See m. Ned. 6:9: "He who takes a vow . . . not to have honey (הנותר . . . מן הדבש) is permitted to have date honey" (מותר בדבש תמרים). The default assumption, which this mishnah argues against, is that abstention from honey includes abstention from tree honey as well as bee honey.

74. Although Josephus's passage about the Baptist (*Ant.* 18.116–119) does not mention this rebuke as part of the reason that Antipas decided to kill him, it is consonant with Josephus's notice that Herod wanted to do away with him (cf. Matt. 14:5) and goes against the grain of the Markan story, in which he is sympathetic. A prophetic denunciation of a ruler's marriage as contravening Jewish law would, in a first-century theocracy, be a powerful incentive to do away with the prophet; see chap. 6.

75. This half-brother was also named Herod, though Mark calls him Philip, which probably reflects Mark's confusion with Herodias's son-in-law Philip, a mistake that is remedied in Luke 3:19 and D and Latin manuscripts of Matt. 14:3.

76. Steve Mason, *Flavius Josephus on the Pharisees: A Composition-Critical Study*, Studia Post-Biblica 39 (Leiden, the Netherlands: Brill, 1991), 351–53 disputes that this passage says that Josephus became a Pharisee; according to him, it only implies that Josephus, when he entered public life, began to follow Pharisaic rules, since they were the most influential sect (cf. *J.W.* 2.162; *Ant.* 13.288–298, 401, 18.15). This reading, however, seems forced; see Seth Schwartz, review of *Flavius Josephus on the Pharisees: A Composition-Critical Study*, by Steve Mason, *AJS Review* 19 (1994): 87, who calls Mason's interpretation "surely wrong; given the context, Josephus is obviously expressing pride in his fellow-traveling, not confessing his ignominious submission to a bunch of thugs, as Mason argues." Lester L. Grabbe, "The Pharisees: A Response to Steve Mason," in *Judaism in Late Antiquity*, ed. Alan J. Avery-Peck and Jacob Neusner, Handbook of Oriental Studies, Section One: The Near and Middle East, vol. 53 (Leiden, the Netherlands: Brill, 2000), 3:46, says, "I have never known anyone to concede more than necessary to one's opponents. That one's enemies are so strong that they force you to do what you do not want to do may be true, and you may admit it in private, but you are not likely to say that publicly. Yet we supposedly have Josephus saying, . . . 'I don't like the Pharisees. In

fact, I hate their guts. But of course when I decided to go into public life, I followed the Pharisees because they controlled it. I didn't want to but I had to.' It sounds almost like a Monty Python sketch."

77. Ingrid Johanne Moen, "Marriage and Divorce in the Herodian Family: A Case Study of Diversity in Late Second Temple Judaism" (Ph.D. diss., Duke University, 2009), 245.

78. Ibid., 240–45. It is also possible that part of John's problem with Antipas's marriage to Herodias was that she was not only his half-brother's wife but also his niece, though this is not mentioned in the Gospels. Niece marriage was viewed favorably by the rabbis and probably by the Pharisees before them (see, for example, t. Qidd. 1:4; b. Yebam. 62b-63a; Gen. Rab. 17:3; cf. Michael L. Satlow, *Jewish Marriage in Antiquity* [Princeton, N.J.: Princeton University Press, 2001], 157, 330n182), but unfavorably by the Qumran sect (4Q251 12 vii; 11QT^a 66:15–17; CD 5:8–11), who thought it the equivalent of nephew-marriage, which is forbidden in the Torah (Lev. 18:12–13; see William Loader, *Sexuality and the Jesus Tradition* [Grand Rapids, Mich.: Eerdmans, 2005], 110–11). If this is part of John's problem with Antipas's marriage, it again reflects a sectarian position.

79. The alternative is to think that Antipas granted John a private interview, which seems less likely; on the question, see chap. 6, n. 33 (p.216).

80. On the historicity of John's denunciation of Antipas's marriage, see chap. 6.

. . . .

CHAPTER FOUR Baptism

1. The Josephus passage would be even more problematic if it were a Christian interpolation, as claimed by Nir, "Josephus' Account of John the Baptist." I do not think, however, that Nir's case is strong; see app. 2.

2. Translation mine: I use the archaic word "unto" because it preserves the ambiguity of the Greek εἰς ("into/leading to/for the purpose of").

3. Herbert Weir Smyth, *Greek Grammar* (1920; repr., Cambridge, Mass.: Harvard University Press, 1956), §§1289–91. On the elasticity of the genitive, see C. F. D. Moule, *An Idiom Book of New Testament Greek,* 2nd ed. (Cambridge: Cambridge University Press, 1959), 37; Daniel B. Wallace, *Greek Grammar Beyond the Basics: An Exegetical Syntax of the New Testament* (Grand Rapids, Mich.: Zondervan, 1996), 74. Cf. Dibelius, *Die urchristliche Überlieferung,* 136: "And when one interrogates the texts about the relationship between repentance and baptism, one receives no clear information."

4. For the full text of Josephus's passage about John, see app. 3.

5. See Schlatter, *Johannes der Täufer,* 59–65, who thinks that Josephus deliberately contradicts the Gospels on this point, refashioning the Baptist in his own Jewish image. The rest of this chapter demonstrates substantial agreement with Schlatter's point that Josephus inverted John's understanding of his own rite, as reflected in Mark 1:4; see also Meier, *Marginal Jew,* 2:97n179. It is striking, however, how easily Schlatter moves from this valid point to sweeping generalizations about Judaism. For Schlatter, Josephus misconstrues and replaces everything that was good about John, thus showing how incapable not only he but also Judaism in general was of understanding him. Fittingly, according to Schlatter, Josephus's attempt to reclaim John for Judaism failed, and it was only in the church that he continued to be honored. On Schlatter's anti-Judaism, see Anders Gerdmar, *Roots of Theological Anti-Semitism: German Biblical Interpretation and the Jews, from Herder and Semler to Kittel and Bultmann,* Studies in Jewish History and Culture 20 (Leiden, the Netherlands: Brill, 2009), 253–326.

6. In the Josephus passage, physical baptism cleanses the body and thus symbolizes the precedent cleansing of the soul by righteousness. In 1QS 3, the author first says that the flesh is made clean only by humbling of the soul but then speaks of it being purged by the cleansing flow of the cultic waters after the person has repented. The point seems to be that only the water ritual *in combination with* a preceding repentance leads to purity of flesh and soul; cf. the quotation from Jonathan Klawans below in n. 13.

7. Cf. Sänger, "Ist er heraufgestiegen," 1:301, who cites 1QS 3:4–12, 4:21, 5:13–14, to support the conclusion that at Qumran "cleansing from sins is the presupposition for taking part in the ritual bath and not the effective consequence of its accomplishment."

8. Cf. the quotation from Nir, "Josephus' Account of John the Baptist," 56, already cited in chap. 2: "Nowhere in Judaism before Qumran, neither in biblical times nor in the Second Temple period, was the notion that one could be made clean in body only if one was pure in heart ever connected to the rite of immersion."

9. On the credibility of Josephus's report about experiencing Essene life, see app. 2, n. 19 (p. 224).

10. Cf. Tucker S. Ferda, "John the Baptist, Isaiah 40, and the Ingathering of the Exiles," *Journal for the Study of the Historical Jesus* 10 (2012): 170: "It is difficult to see why Josephus would belabor the point if the baptism was a simple Jewish immersion ritual." On Josephus's frequently tendentious polemics, see Martin Hengel, *The Zealots: Investigations Into the Jewish Freedom Movement in the Period from Herod I Until 70 A.D.* (1961; Eng. trans., Edinburgh: T&T Clark, 1989), 15–16, 237–44; Barclay, *Jews in the Mediterranean Diaspora*, 352–53, 358; Mason, "Fire, Water and Spirit," 179; John M. G. Barclay, *Against Apion*, Flavius Josephus, Translation and Commentary 10 (Leiden, the Netherlands: Brill, 2007), xxx–xxxvi, li–liii. Examples include the suppression of the Zealots' messianic expectation and reinterpretation of it in terms of Vespasian (*J.W.* 6.312–313) and the negative reinterpretation of the name "Zealots" in *J.W.* 4.160–161. See also Ernst, *Johannes der Täufer* (1989), 254, who cites Klausner for the point that Josephus transforms the Baptist into a philosopher who wants to spread righteousness and piety—just as he did with religious-political sects such as the Pharisees, Sadducees, Essenes, and even the Zealots/Sicarii (*J.W.* 2.119–166; *Ant.* 18.11–25); cf. Joseph Klausner, *Jesus of Nazareth: His Life, Times, and Teaching* (1925; repr., New York: Macmillan, 1929), 241.

11. On the criticism of traditional understandings of religious rites in Hellenistic philosophy, see Frederick C. Grant, *Hellenistic Religions: The Age of Syncretism*, Library of Liberal Arts (New York: Liberal Arts Press, 1953), 71–104. On the philosophical, rationalizing, Hellenizing nature of Josephus's interpretation of John's baptism, see Schlatter, *Johannes der Täufer*, 59; Dibelius, *Die urchristliche Überlieferung*, 125–26; Ernst, *Johannes der Täufer* (1989), 257; Webb, *John the Baptizer*, 195; Mason, "Fire, Water and Spirit," 178–79; Meier, *Marginal Jew*, 2:61.

12. Cf. von Dobbeler, *Das Gericht und das Erbarmen Gottes*, 173–74.

13. See Klawans, *Impurity and Sin*, 139, who thinks that Josephus is "overemphasizing the prerequisite of repentance over the power of the ritual itself to effect atonement." He grants that John probably would not have baptized a person whom he did not feel to be repentant, but also thinks that "one cannot deny that there was [in John's mind] some power to the ritual itself. . . . Indeed, almost all Jews would have agreed that atonement was effected by sincere repentance *and* rituals of atonement of one sort

or another. If John rejected this consensus and believed that personal repentance alone was effective, then his baptism would not have been necessary."

14. It is often difficult to tell, in Qumran citations, whether the רוח spoken of is the human spirit or the divine one, and sometimes there may be a deliberate ambiguity. Arthur Everett Sekki, *The Meaning of Ruah at Qumran*, Society of Biblical Literature Dissertation Series 110 (Atlanta: Scholars Press, 1989), 225 interprets רוח עצת אמת ("the Spirit of the council/counsel of truth") in 1QS 3:6 as "man's spirit" but רוח קדושה ("the Spirit of holiness") in 3:7 as "God's Spirit."

15. For example, James D. G. Dunn, *Baptism in the Holy Spirit* (London: SCM, 1970), 8–14.

16. See, for example, Rudolf Laufen, *Die Doppelüberlieferungen der Logienquelle und des Markusevangeliums*, Bonner biblische Beiträge 54 (Bonn, Germany: Peter Hanstein Verlag, 1980), 93–108.

17. Dibelius, *Die urchristliche Überlieferung*, 56–58. For scholars who concur with this reconstruction of the saying, see Dunn, *Baptism in the Holy Spirit*, 8n1. Dibelius was partially anticipated by Charles Augustus Briggs, *The Messiah of the Gospels* (New York: Scribner's, 1894), 67n4, though his reasoning was different from Dibelius's. More recently, Mason, "Fire, Water and Spirit," 170, arrived at the same conclusion.

18. Cf. Mason, "Fire, Water and Spirit," 173, who cites 2 Cor. 5:5, Gal. 3:2–5, Rom. 9:9–17 [*sic*; probably Rom. 8:9–18 is meant], Acts 2:16–18, 38, and 1 Cor. 12:13 to make the point that "the first-generation Church considered the holy spirit to be its unique possession" and therefore to exclude the reference to the Spirit from the original form of Matt. 3:11//Luke 3:16. I disagree, however, for reasons that I make clear below, with Mason's conclusion that John's baptism was unconnected with the Spirit.

Besides the sort of history-of-religions considerations adduced here, structural arguments for Dibelius's reconstruction of the saying are sometimes mustered; see, for example, Paul Hoffmann, *Studien zur Theologie*, 25, who claims that, when we eliminate the reference to the Spirit, we obtain a saying "whose succinctness speaks for it being old tradition." Such arguments, however, are inconclusive; for doubts about succinctness as a criterion for antiquity, see E. P. Sanders, *The Tendencies of the Synoptic Tradition*, Society for New Testament Studies Monograph Series 9 (Cambridge: Cambridge University Press, 1969); James R. Royse, *Scribal Habits in Early Greek New Testament Papyri*, New Testament Tools, Studies and Documents 36 (Leiden, the Netherlands: Brill, 2008), 705–36. It is true, however, that the reference to fire but not the reference to Spirit is picked up in Matt. 3:12//Luke 3:17.

19. Cf. also John 16:7, which is cited by Tertullian (*Baptism* 10.4) to make the point of Jesus's superiority to John: "Also our Lord himself said that the Spirit would not come down until he himself should first ascend to the Father" (trans. from Ernest Evans, *Tertullian's Homily on Baptism* [London: S.P.C.K., 1964])).

20. For post–New Testament examples, see Ernst, *Johannes der Täufer* (1989), 244–46, citing, among others, Tertullian, *Baptism* 10; Origen, *Commentary on Romans* 5.8.5–6; *Homilies on Luke* 4.4–5; Epiphanius, *Panarion* 30.13.7–8; Pseudo-Chrysostom, *Homilies on Matthew* 4 [PL 56.658]). The passage from Origen's homilies on Luke illustrates, in a particularly clever way, the tendency of Christians to relativize biblical praises of John. In 4.4, Origen acknowledges that John was filled with the Spirit from his mother's womb [cf. Luke 1:15]—but adds that the Spirit was not the principle of his nature, as it was with Jesus. In 4.5, Origen adds, "John converts *many* [cf. Luke 1:16]; the Lord converts not many but *all*" (trans. Lienhard, emphasis added).

21. Meier, *Marginal Jew,* 2:82n95. John Calvin already raised the same question in his commentary on Acts 19:2; he answered it by appealing to the idea of metonymy (the Ephesians were speaking about the gifts of the Spirit, not the Spirit itself).

22. Käsemann, "Disciples of John the Baptist," 138.

23. For examples of both, see Scott Shauf, *Theology as History, History as Theology: Paul in Ephesus in Acts 19,* BZNW 133 (Berlin: De Gruyter, 2005), 108. Already p[38, 41], as well as D* sy[hmg] sa, change the ἔστιν in 19:2 to λαμβάνουσίν τινες, so that the Ephesian "disciples" end up saying, "We have not even heard that *some have received* the Holy Spirit" rather than "that *there is* a Holy Spirit." Similarly, Theodor Innitzer, *Johannes der Täufer nach der heiligen Schrift und der Tradition* (Vienna: Verlag von Mayer, 1908), 211, first translates the statement literally ("Nein, wir haben nicht gehört, ob es einen heiligen Geist gibt"), then says, "or, better," and gives a paraphrase that totally changes the meaning ("oder besser: ob einige den heiligen Geist empfangen"). This wittingly or unwittingly follows the variant reading just mentioned.

24. Käsemann, "Disciples of John the Baptist," 141 calls the story "an overpainting by Luke of the tradition he had to hand."

25. Dibelius, *Die urchristliche Überlieferung,* 43.

26. Cf. Innitzer, *Johannes der Täufer,* 211.

27. As noted by Shauf, *Theology as History,* 150.

28. On Mark 9:10, see Marcus, *Mark,* 2:643, 647–48.

29. See, for example, Acts 2:36, 3:20–21, 5:31, 10:38, and 13:33, on which see Martin Dibelius, *From Tradition to Gospel* (1933; Eng. trans., Cambridge: James Clarke, 1971), 17–18; Reginald H. Fuller, *The Foundations of New Testament Christology* (New York: Scribner's, 1965), 20, 158–59; Barrett, *Acts,* 1:151–52, 202–7, 524; Brown, *Introduction to New Testament Christology,* 113. Also to be included here are Luke 3:22, if the Western reading is original, as maintained by Bart D. Ehrman, *The Orthodox Corruption of Scripture: The Effect of Early Christological Controversies on the Text of the New Testament* (New York: Oxford University Press, 1993), 62–67; and Luke 22:43–44, if this is part of the original text, as maintained by Raymond E. Brown, *The Death of the Messiah: From Gethsemane to the Grave; A Commentary on the Passion Narratives in the Four Gospels,* Anchor Bible Reference Library (New York: Doubleday, 1994), 1:180–86. As Ehrman shows (*Orthodox Corruption of Scripture,* 62–69, 156), several of these anomalous Lukan traditions were subsequently "corrected" by Orthodox scribes.

30. On this theory, see app. 4, "Was John from a Priestly Background?"

31. Cf. Böhlemann, *Jesus und der Täufer,* 69–70.

32. See Schweitzer, *Quest of the Historical Jesus,* 340: "It is a mistake to regard baptism with water as a 'symbolic act' in the modern sense, and make the Baptist decry his own wares by saying, 'I baptize only with water, but the other can baptize with the Holy Spirit.'"

33. I am grateful to Mark Goodacre for reminding me of this passage and pointing out its relevance to my thesis; cf. Otto Böcher, "Wasser und Geist," in *Verborum Veritas: Festschrift für Gustav Stählin zum 70. Geburtstag,* ed. Otto Böcher and Klaus Haacker (Wuppertal, Germany: Theologischer Verlag Rolf Brockhaus, 1970), 203.

It is noticeable that the Fourth Gospel, which most clearly enunciates the principle that the Spirit only came into existence with Jesus's resurrection (7:39, 16:7), prescinds from directly narrating Jesus's baptismal reception of the Spirit, though its author obviously knows the tradition (see John 1:33).

34. *Quid est hoc, quod Joannes in baptismate suo aliis Spiritum sanctum dare non potuit, qui Christo dedit* (*Dialogue with the Luciferians* 7 [PL 23.161C]).

35. Böcher, "Wasser und Geist," 197–203. Most recent works on the Baptist have ignored Böcher's essay; there is no mention of it in the book-length treatment by Meier, *Marginal Jew*, 2:19–233, nor in various other works—Webb, *John the Baptizer;* Michael Tilly, *Johannes der Täufer und die Biographie der Propheten: die synoptische Täuferüber-lieferung und das jüdische Prophetenbild zur Zeit des Täufers,* Beiträge zur Wissenschaft vom Alten und Neuen Testament, 7th Series 17 [137] (Stuttgart: Verlag W. Kohlhammer, 1994); Taylor, *Immerser;* Rothschild, *Baptist Traditions and Q*—though several mention another article by Böcher about John's diet (Otto Böcher, "Ass Johannes der Täufer kein Brot [Luk. vii. 33]?," *NTS* [1971–72]: 90–92).

An exception is Ernst, *Johannes der Täufer* (1989), whose two mentions of the article (18n59, 98n63) are dismissive. Von Dobbeler, *Das Gericht und das Erbarmen Gottes,* 173, does mention Böcher's article, though not in this connection, but she echoes its thought: "John, the dispenser of baptism, comes close to having a soteriological function, inasmuch as in his preaching and baptism he is the mediator of divine salvation." Rather than Böcher, von Dobbeler here draws on Hartwig Thyen, "Βάπτισμα μετανοίας εἰς ἄφεσιν ἁμαρῖῶν," in *Zeit und Geschichte: Dankesgabe an Rudolph Bultmann zum 80. Geburtstag,* ed. E. Dinkler (Tübingen, Germany: J. C. B. Mohr [Paul Siebeck], 1964), 98–99, who terms John's baptism "an eschatological sacrament that produces repentance and forgiveness" and adds that the hendiadys "repentance and forgiveness" "describes nothing less than endtime salvation."

36. In Böcher's view, these passages are a "spiritualization" of Old Testament water rites, whose function was to remove unclean spirits, presumably through the action of God's Spirit; he also notes the association between water and wind/Spirit (רוח) in Gen. 1:1–2; Dan. 7:2; and various New Testament passages such as Matt. 7:25–27.

37. See especially 1QS 4:21: "to cleanse him by a Holy Spirit from all acts of wickedness and to sprinkle upon him a Spirit of Truth like waters of purification" (my trans.).

38. Representative early Christian texts include 1 Cor. 6:11, 12:13, Eph. 4:4–6, Tit. 3:5, and John 3:5.

39. The reasoning here is similar to Dale Allison's argument that John the Baptist's theology was apocalyptic and so was that of the early church; it therefore makes more sense to assume that Jesus, the middle term between the two, was also apocalyptic in orientation than that Jesus deapocalypticized and then the church reapocalypticized; see introd., n. 13 (p.162).

40. Cf. the biblical idiom "to pour out the Spirit" (Isa. 32:15, 44:3; Ezek. 39:29; Joel 2:28 [LXX 3:1]; Zech. 12:10), which turns up both at Qumran (4QDibHam[a] [4Q504] 18:16–17) and in the New Testament (Acts 2:16; Tit 3:5–6); cf. Dunn, *Baptism in the Holy Spirit,* 12–13. Cf. also the allusions to sprinkling with the Spirit in 1QH[a] 15:6–7 and to "drinking the Spirit" in 1 Cor. 10:4 and 12:13. A liquid-like conception of the Spirit is also found in the pagan world; see, for example, Longinus, *Subl.* 13.2, which describes the πνεῦμα as a divine semen that impregnates the Pythia; cf. Eduard Schweizer et al., "Pneuma, Pneumatikos," in *Theological Dictionary of the New Testament,* edited by Gerhard Kittel and Gerhard Friedrich (Grand Rapids, Mich.: Eerdmans, 1968), 3:346, 350. For other references, see Volker Rabens, *The Holy Spirit and Ethics in Paul: Transformation and Empowering for Religious-Ethical Life,* WUNT 2.283 (Tübingen, Germany: Mohr Siebeck, 2010), index of subjects under "fluid," "liquid," "pouring," and "water."

41. The Jewish Publication Society and New Revised Standard Version translations obscure this point, since they translate מי חטאת (lit. "waters of sin") here as "water of purification." RSV, "water of expiation," is better.

42. See Webb, *John the Baptizer*, 96–105.

43. See, for example, Philo, *Unchangeable* 7, and *Spec. Laws* 1.257–60, cited by Webb, *John the Baptizer*, 111.

44. Similarly, Böhlemann, *Jesus und der Täufer*, 69–70 cites some of the Qumran texts referred to above but only to argue that pneumatological motifs were present in John's proclamation and that he thought his water baptism *anticipated* a future baptism in the Spirit.

45. This actually is what Josephus says about John's baptism, but it is probably not a completely accurate picture of the latter; see the sections above on "The Gospels and Josephus on John's Baptism," "Josephus on John's Baptism," and "John's Baptism as a Sacrament."

46. Here Dunn cites Deut. 30:6, Ps. 51, Isa. 1:10–18, and Joel 2:12–14.

47. Dunn, *Baptism in the Holy Spirit*, 15–17, 22.

48. Cf. Ferda, "John the Baptist," 170. On other links between John's ministry and the larger context of Isaiah 40, see Ferda, "John the Baptist," 174–86.

49. מי נדה means literally "waters of impurity" or "waters of uncleanness," but the sense is waters for removing impurity or uncleanness; see Clines, *Dictionary of Classical Hebrew*, 5:623.

50. See above, n. 13.

51. Cf. Acts 5:31, in which Luke recycles phrases from Luke 3:3//Mark 1:4 (τοῦ δοῦναι μετάνοιαν τῷ Ἰσραὴλ καὶ ἄφεσιν ἁμαρτιῶν) but associates repentance and forgiveness of sins with Jesus, the pioneer and savior (ἀρχηγὸν καὶ σωτῆρα), rather than with John.

52. Cf. Ferda, "John the Baptist," 169–70n36. The idea that John's baptism was intended to convey forgiveness of sins was also inconvenient for early Christians because Jesus himself had received baptism, which impugned the doctrine of his sinlessness. Struggles with this problem are visible in passages such as Luke 3:21a; Matt. 3:13–15; Justin, *Dialogue* 88.4; *Gospel of the Nazoreans* 13 (Jerome, *Dialogues against the Pelagians* 3.2 [Migne, *PL* 23.597B–598A; J. K. Elliott, *The Apocryphal New Testament: A Collection of Apocryphal Christian Literature in an English Translation* (Oxford: Clarendon Press, 1993), 24]). Cf. Böcher, "Ass Johannes der Täufer," 203; John Dominic Crossan, *In Parables: The Challenge of the Historical Jesus* (New York: Harper & Row, 1973), 233; John Dominic Crossan, *The Historical Jesus: The Life of a Mediterranean Jewish Peasant* (San Francisco: Harper, 1991), 233.

53. Trans. Evans. The passage continues: "What was intended then was a baptism of repentance, as a kind of applicant for the remission and sanctification which in Christ was soon to follow *(quasi candidatus remissionis et sanctificarionis in Christo subsecuturae)*. For that which we read, 'He preached a baptism of repentance unto remission of sins' [cf. Mark 1:4], was an announcement made in view of a remission which was to be *(in futuram remissionem enuntiatum est);* for repentance comes first, and remission follows, and this is the meaning of preparing the way. But one who prepares a thing does not himself perform it, but provides for its performance by someone else" (Evans trans. alt.).

Cf. Aphrahat, *Demonstrations* 12.10: "Be aware, my friend, that the baptism of John does not bring about forgiveness of sins, but [only] repentance"; Aphrahat goes on to cite the story in Acts 19 as a proof text. Translation from Adam Lehto, *The Demonstrations of Aphrahat, the Persian Sage*, Gorgias Eastern Christian Studies 27 (Piscataway, N.J.: Gorgias Press, 2010).

54. προοίμιον . . . τοῦ εὐαγγελίου τῆς χάριτος; Pseudo-Justin Martyr, *Questions and Answers to the Orthodox* 37 (PG 6.1284 [455]), cited in Innitzer, *Johannes der Täufer,* 208, 209n5.

55. See, for example, Gregory the Great, *Homilies on the Gospels* 1.20 (PL 76.1160D [1516–17]), cited in Innitzer, *Johannes der Täufer,* 209–10n6; cf. Bede, *Homily* 1.1 (on Mark 1:4–8). Gregory may be exploiting the similarity between the verb the Vulgate uses, *praedicare* ("to announce"), and *praedicere* ("to foretell"); the former sometimes appears with the meaning of the latter, as for example in Tertullian, *Flight in Persecution* 6 (Charlton T. Lewis and Charles Short, *A Latin Dictionary* [Oxford: Clarendon Press, 1879], 1416 [1. *praedico* II).

56. Lawrence T. Martin, trans. and ed., *The Venerable Bede: Commentary on the Acts of the Apostles,* Cisterian Studies 117 (Kalamazoo, Mich.: Cisterian Publications, 1989), 153.

57. *Bapt. Jo. non erat per se sacramentum, sed quasi quoddam sacramentale disponens ad baptisma Christi;* cf. Innitzer, *Johannes der Täufer,* 310n2. The Fourth Gospel may already be pointing in a similar direction in 3:25–30, where it moves from a discussion of καθαρισμός to a comparison between Jesus's baptism and John's to the latter's statement that he is not ὁ Χριστός, but only the friend of the bridegroom. The implication may be that John's baptism does not purify from sin, but Jesus's does, because he is the one who anoints with the Spirit.

58. *in futuram remissionem quae esset postea per sanctificationem Christi subsecutura.*

59. *quia nulli hominum sine Spiritu sancto peccata dimittuntur.*

60. *quid amplius in Christi baptismate consequamur.*

61. *perfectum autem baptisma, nisi quod in cruce et in resurrectione Christi est, non potest dici.*

62. *dum servi baptismo plus quam habuit tribuis.*

63. *dominicum destruis, cui amplius nihil relinquis.*

64. On the possibility that the Benedictus, along with the other passages that center on John in Luke 1, goes back to Baptist circles, see app. 4 on John's priestly background.

65. This translation reflects the aorist ἐπισκέψατο, which is read by A, C, D, and the Koine text-tradition, as well as most versions. Some interpreters, such as Fitzmyer, *Gospel According to Luke,* 1:388, prefer the future ἐπισκέψεται ("will visit"), which is read by p[4], B, ℵ, W, Θ, and so on, and is thus better attested. As Raymond E. Brown, *The Birth of the Messiah: A Commentary on the Infancy Narratives in Matthew and Luke,* Anchor Bible Reference Library (New York: Doubleday, 1979), 373 points out, however, "The aorist is the more difficult reading (since in the chronology of the infancy narrative Jesus has not yet 'visited us')." Brown acknowleges that the aorist could be an assimilation to the aorist of the same verb in 1:68, but he points out that it is also possible to see the future as an assimilation to the two future-tense verbs in the immediate vicinity (1:76). In any event, even if we accept the future in 1:78 as original, this just means that the salvific event is future from the point of view of Zechariah. It could therefore be a reference to his son's future ministry, like the futures in 1:76, rather than to Jesus's ministry.

66. See the section "John's Baptism as Sacrament."

67. Dibelius never quite says this, though many of his arguments point in this direction, for instance that possession of the Spirit became a shibboleth in the early church's competition with Baptist circles. Dibelius's main concern, however, is not to get back to "the historical Baptist" but to explore the way in which later Christian concerns have shaped the New Testament portraits of John.

68. See, for example, Dibelius, *Die urchristliche Überlieferung*, 139–40. On Dibelius's tendency to characterize John in an anti-Judaic fashion, see Meier, *Marginal Jew*, 2:82n95, and cf. the treatment of Dibelius in Gerdmar, *Roots of Theological Anti-Semitism*, 347–72. The contrast between John, the ascetic proclaimer of judgment, whose judgmentalism is sometimes linked with his Jewishness or his commitment to the Law, and Jesus, the joyous, forgiving liberator and proclaimer of the dominion of God, has been a staple of the "scientific" scholarship of the past two centuries and is still with us; see, for example, Strauss, *New Life of Jesus*, 1:265–66; Ernest Renan, *The Life of Jesus*, (1863; Eng. trans., Great Minds Series; Amherst, N.Y.: Prometheus Books, 1991), 69–76; Adolf Harnack, *What is Christianity?* (1900; repr., Gloucester, Mass.: Peter Smith, 1978), 38–52; Joachim Jeremias, *New Testament Theology*, pt. 1, *The Proclamation of Jesus* (New York: Scribner's, 1971), 1:148–49; W. Barnes Tatum, *John the Baptist and Jesus: A Report of the Jesus Seminar* (Sonoma, Calif.: Polebridge Press, 1994), 157. For more examples, and a good refutation, see Allison, *Constructing Jesus*, 204–20.

69. See Böcher, "Wasser," 203.

70. I therefore disagree with Ernst, *Johannes der Täufer* (1989), 355–56, who asserts that the association of John with joy in Luke 1:14 conflicts with the tenor of his ministry.

71. Cf. Jeremias, *Parables of Jesus*, 169–80, on the theme of "Das drohende Zuspät" ("the threatening 'too late'") in Jesus's eschatological parables. The association of the Davidic Messiah with fire is rare, but it does occur; see, for example, 4 Ezra 13:10, and cf. the "king from the sun" in Sib. Or. 3:652, right after the reference to "the flame of the fire" in 3.651. In general terms, the Messiah is often associated with destruction; see, for example, Isa. 11:4; Pss. Sol. 17:21–24; 1 En. 45:6; 55:3–4; 65:1–12; 4Q285.

My reconstruction of John's message is in line with chap. 3, in which I argue that John saw himself as Elijah. In Mal. 4:1–5, Elijah will return *before* the "great and terrible day of the Lord," which will burn like an oven, to avert the threatened curse from the land of Israel. (Though if the Elijah of 4:5 is identical with the "messenger of the covenant" who prepares the Lord's way in 3:1, the continuation of the latter passage associates the messenger himself with fire [3:2–3].)

72. Taylor, *Immerser*, 49–100; Klawans, *Impurity and Sin*, 138–43. A precursor to Klawans is Webb, *John the Baptizer*, 196, though he does not argue in as much detail as Klawans.

73. See, for example, Lev. 14–16 and Num. 19; 2 Sam. 11:2–4 (Bathsheba); 2 Kgs. 5:14 (Naaman). The exceptions are passages such as Ps. 51:7, which may be metaphorical rather than a description of an actual ritual, and Ezek. 36:25, which may have Levitical as well as moral impurity in view. See Taylor, *Immerser*, 59–60; Klawans, *Impurity and Sin;* Hayah Katz, "'He Shall Bathe in Water; Then He Shall Be Pure': Ancient Immersion Practice in the Light of Archaeological Evidence," *Vetus Testamentum* 63 (2012): 369–80; Jodi Magness, *Stone and Dung, Oil and Spit: Jewish Daily Life in the Time of Jesus* (Grand Rapids, Mich.: Eerdmans, 2011), 16. See also the excellent survey in Harrington, *Purity Texts.*

74. Taylor, *Immerser*, 63.

75. Taylor, *Immerser*, 97–98 can only reconcile her reconstruction with Mark 1:4 by a tricky sort of retroversion into Aramaic and then an appeal to the vagueness of the retroverted Aramaic. Her description does, however, cohere with Josephus's description of John's baptism in *Ant.* 18.117 and is paralleled by 1QS 3:7–9 and New Testament passages such as 1 Pet. 3:21 and Heb. 9:13–14, 10:22—overlaps that have been partly acknowledged above (see, for example, the section "Josephus on John's Baptism").

76. On Mandean baptismal practices, see the section "The Mandean Literature" in chap. 1.

77. See chap. 2, n. 55 (p. 178). The closest thing to a counterexample comes in the Pseudo-Clementine *Homilies* 2.23, which describes John as a "Day-Baptist" (ἡμεροβαπτιστής); see app. 7, where I argue that the identification is unhistorical.

78. See Sanders, *Paul and Palestinian Judaism,* passim, who includes both the rabbis and the Qumran community, among others, in this judgment. Some of the subheadings in the entry under "Sin" in Sanders's subject index are instructive: "always characteristic of man *vis-à-vis* God," "universality of," "unwitting sins of the pious," "in IV Ezra as inescapable, but still punishable transgression which damns."

79. See app. 10 on apocalyptic belief and perfectionism.

80. Klawans, *Impurity and Sin,* 140–41, considers but rejects the possibility that John shared the Qumran view that sin was ritually defiling.

81. The metaphor pictures a preliminary act of laying the root bare and placing the ax on it in preparation for the chops that will immediately hew it down; see Ernst, *Johannes der Täufer* (1989), 302.

82. On sanctifying the people for holy war, see Deut. 23:10–14; Josh. 3:5, 7:13; 1 Sam. 21:4–5; 2 Sam. 11:11; 1QMilhamah 7:4–7; cf. Robert G. Boling and G. Ernest Wright, *Joshua: A New Translation with Introduction and Commentary,* AB 6 (Garden City, N.Y.: Doubleday, 1982), 163; Hengel, *Zealots,* 278n263; Susan Niditch, *War in the Hebrew Bible: A Study in the Ethics of Violence* (New York: Oxford University Press, 1993), 88. The sanctification ritual explicitly includes washing, that is, immersion, in Deut. 23:11, and probably immersion is implied by קדש and התקדש in passages such as Josh. 3:5, 7:13, as well; see also Joel 3:9 (MT 4:9), Jer. 6:4, 51:27–28, and Patrick D. Miller, *The Divine Warrior in Early Israel,* Harvard Semitic Monographs 5 (Cambridge, Mass.: Harvard University Press, 1973), 157.

83. Purity issues also seem to be connected with John's baptism in the reference in the Syriac version of the Pseudo-Clementine *Recognitions* 1.54.6–8, which seems to conflate "the scribes and Pharisees, who were baptized by John" with "the pure disciples of John" (ܬܠܡܝܕܘܗܝ ܕܟܝܐ, ܐܠܡܝܕܘܗܝ) who "separated themselves greatly from the people."

84. For background on the *Didascalia,* see Marcus, "*Testaments of the Twelve Patriarchs* and the *Didascalia Apostolorum,*" 600–602. Thanks to Lucas Van Rompay for his help on this section, especially with the Syriac texts and translations.

85. The *Homilies* insist that Christians not only abstain from certain meats but also wash after having sexual intercourse "and that the women on their part should keep the law of menstruation" (ἄφεδρον φυλάσσειν)—a law that involved bathing (*Hom.* 7.8.2, Ante-Nicene Fathers trans. alt.; cf. Lev. 15:19–22). Wehnert, "Taufvorstellungen in den Pseudoklementinen," 2:1078–79, locates this passage in the Peter-Simon novella, which he dates to the end of the second or the beginning of the third century CE.

86. Hebrews lumps "various baptisms" (διάφοροι βαπτισμοί) together with regulations about food and drink as aspects of the old order that have now been swept away along with the whole Temple system (Heb. 9:8–10).

87. In addition to the passages below, see also *Didascalia* 26 (247.27–248.2/230.5–7 and 260.25–261.13/243.9–21). Unless otherwise noted, all *Didascalia* citations are from the edition of Arthur Vööbus, *The Didascalia Apostolorum in Syriac,* Corpus Scriptorum Christianorum Orientalium 175–76, 179–80 (Leuven, Belgium: Secrétariat du Corpus-SCO, 1979); they are listed by chapter and Syriac page number plus line numbers/English page number plus line numbers. It is striking that *Didascalia* 26 (260.2–7/242.14–20)

takes up two of the same issues treated in the Qumran halakhic document 4QMMT, the impurity that results from contact with hides and from stepping on a bone.

88. I wish to thank my research assistant in the Duke Graduate Program in Religion, Joseph Longarino, for his help with this section.

89. Jonathan Klawans, "Notions of Gentile Impurity in Ancient Judaism," *AJS Review* 20 (1995): 286n6, points out that the notion of Gentile impurity necessitates proselyte immersion, though proselyte immersion does not necessarily imply Gentile impurity. Hayes, *Gentile Impurities and Jewish Identities*, 107–44, like Klawans, argues against the view of Gedaliah Alon, "The Levitical Uncleanness of Gentiles," in *Jews, Judaism and the Classical World: Studies in Jewish History in the Times of the Second Temple and Talmud* (Jerusalem: Magnes Press, 1977), 146–89, that the idea of the ritual impurity of Gentiles was an ancient halakhic tradition dating from First Temple times and generally accepted in the Second Temple period. Both acknowledge, however, that it is assumed in certain rulings in the Mishnah (for example, m. Mak. 2:3) and unambiguous in the Tosefta (t. Zabim 2:1), and in the view of Hayes at least, it was instituted by early tannaitic authorities. Klawans (p. 312) dates its "authoritative formulation" a little later: "Gentile ritual impurity indeed emerged in the first century, and only gradually took root until its authoritative formulation in the Tosefta and Talmudim."

His assumption of the lateness of the Toseftan formulation, however, may need to be revised in light of a tendency in some recent rabbinic scholarship to date Toseftan traditions earlier than corresponding Mishnaic ones; see, for example, Judith Hauptman, "How Old is the Haggadah?" *Judaism* 51 (2001): 5–18. Also, the meaning of terms such as "instituted" (Hayes) and "authoritative formulation" need more precise definition; in the history of liturgy, rites can become widespread without being "authoritatively formulated" or "instituted" by strong centralized authorities; see Joel Marcus, "*Birkat Ha-Minim* Revisited," *NTS* 55 (2009): 523–51; Joel Marcus, "Passover and Last Supper Revisited," *NTS* 59 (2013): 303–24.

90. Solomon Zeitlin, "The Halaka in the Gospels and Its Relation to the Jewish Law at the Time of Jesus," *Hebrew Union College Annual* 1 (1924): 357–63; cf. Klawans, "Notions of Gentile Impurity," 286n6. Despite Klawans's qualifications cited in the previous note, he prounces Zeitlin's view "in some ways compelling."

91. This contrasts with the certainty about the Levitical impurity of Gentiles of many scholars a generation ago, so influentially Alon, "Levitical Uncleanness of Gentiles," (see above, n. 89). On proselyte baptism, see Joachim Jeremias, *Infant Baptism in the First Four Centuries* (1958; Eng. trans., London: SCM, 1960), 24–29, who says that "nearly all scholars who in the last sixty years have concerned themselves with the date of the introduction of proselyte baptism have come to the conclusion that it came into practice in pre-Christian times" (28–29).

92. I do not consider T. Levi 14:6, which speaks of cleansing "the daughters of Gentiles . . . with an unlawful cleansing," as early evidence for proselyte baptism, since I regard the Testaments of the Twelve Patriarchs as a late-second-century Jewish-Christian document, not a pre-Christian Jewish one (see Marcus, "*Testaments of the Twelve Patriarchs* and the *Didascalia Apostolorum*"). Neither do I include Sib. Or. 4:162–170 (from around 80 CE), which combines an exhortation to repent with one to "wash your whole bodies in perennial rivers," since it is unclear to me that it refers to proselyte baptism. I do think, however, that Joseph and Aseneth 14:12, 15, which describes Aseneth washing her face in "living water" as she converts to Judaism, may reflect proselyte baptism. The

objection of Ferguson, *Baptism in the Early Church*, 77, that Aseneth washes only her face, not her whole body, ignores the allegorical nature of the narrative and its fictive setting in a time before the promulgation of the Torah. On the dating of Joseph and Aseneth, see Jill Hicks-Keeton, "Rewritten Gentiles: Conversion to 'the Living God' in Ancient Judaism and Christianity" (Ph.D. diss., Duke University, 2014), chap. 4: the Egyptian Jewish author was familiar with the Septuagint, so the work was probably written after 100 BCE, and he seems to reflect a thriving Jewish community in Egypt, so it was probably written before the Diaspora Revolt of 115–117 CE wiped out Alexandrian Jewry.

93. Cf. Klawans, "Notions of Gentile Impurity," 302n87, who points to m. Yoma 3:3, "which obligates all Jews—even those not impure—to immerse before entering the Temple court for service."

94. Shaye J. D. Cohen, "Is 'Proselyte Baptism' Mentioned in the Mishnah? The Interpretation of M. Pesahim 8.8," in *The Significance of Yavneh and Other Essays in Jewish Hellenism* (1994; repr., Tübingen, Germany: Mohr Siebeck, 2010), 328: "However, even if I have explained the Mishnah incorrectly, even if the Shammaites, in fact, are referring to 'proselyte baptism,' we must not exaggerate the evidentiary value of M. Pesahim 8:8."

95. See Taylor, *Immerser*, 69, who calls the evidence for it inconclusive.

96. Although the point is made here that Gentiles cannot contract the same sort of impurity that Jews do through flux, they are nevertheless "unclean like Zabs [people with fluxes] in every respect"—that is, they have an intrinsic uncleanness.

97. Klawans, "Notions of Gentile Impurity," 298n67, citing 11QTemple 40:6 and 4QFlor 1:4, says that at Qumran "proselytes . . . are excluded from the Temple but are not otherwise considered to be impure. The exclusion of proselytes results from their inherent profaneness: so inherent is this profaneness that it endures even after conversion." Note, however, the conflation of "common" (κοινόν) and "unclean" (ἀκάθαρτον) in Acts 10:28; Klawans does not note the conflation of the terms in this passage, either in "Notions of Gentile Impurity" or in *Impurity and Sin*.

98. With regard to Acts 10:28, Klawans ("Notions of Gentile Impurity," 300–302) also points out that κολλᾶσθαι can suggest sexual intercourse, so it is unclear that this passage forbids simple contact with Gentiles, and cites the Acts reports about "god-fearing" Gentiles attending synagogues: "Had Gentiles really been considered to be inherently impure (ritually or morally), Gentiles would not have been invited to the synagogues, and the class of God-fearers would not have existed."

99. Webb, *John the Baptizer*, 129n120, and Sänger, "Ist er heraufgestiegen," 1:293–94, both acknowlege that this is a good question, though neither of them recognizes proselyte baptism in the Second Temple period. Webb speculates that the answer may be that Gentile women signified conversion to Judaism by performing sacrifice or by the sort of repentance shown by Aseneth in Joseph and Aseneth 10–14.

100. See Cohen, *Beginnings of Jewishness*, on this transition.

101. See Thiessen, *Contesting Conversion*.

....

CHAPTER FIVE   Jesus

1. On this problem, see chap. 4, n. 52 (p. 201).

2. This reconstruction basically follows Matthew, who probably represents the Q version better than Luke in this case (ὁ ὀπίσω μου ἐρχόμενος, which is supported by John, vs. ἔρχεται ὁ ἰσχυρότερός μου, which Luke gets from Mark); see Robinson, Hoffmann, and Kloppenborg, *Critical Edition of Q*, 14. In any event, there is not much

difference between the Markan form and the Q form. On the omission of "[he will baptize you] with the Spirit" from my reconstruction, see chap. 4, end of the section "The Gospels on John's Baptism."

3. See Davies and Allison, *Matthew*, 1:314–15. Several of these texts ascribe the Spirit to the coming figure, but for the reasons I have outlined in the previous chapter, I do not think that John spoke of a coming baptism in the Spirit in the original form of Matt. 3:11//Luke 3:16. The association, however, probably helps explain why a reference to the Spirit was added at a later stage in the development of the logion, and early enough to have influenced the Gospel forms of it.

4. See chap. 3, n. 7 (p. 188).

5. Cf. Acts 19:4, which the Revised Standard Version renders, "John baptized with the baptism of repentance, telling the people to believe in the one who was to come after him, that is Jesus." But it is not clear from this (and even less clear in the Greek) whether Luke is ascribing to John the belief that Jesus was the Messiah or whether that is Luke's own confession of faith; cf. Barrett, *Acts*, 2:897.

6. Already in Psalm 2:2, 7, the anointed Davidic king is referred to by God as his son. This expectation has definitely become eschatological by the time we reach 4QFlor (4Q174) 1:10–13, where the oracle about God's son in 2 Sam. 7:13–14 is interpreted as a reference to the "Shoot of David" (cf. Isa. 11:1). 4Q246 speaks of a king who will be called "Son of God" and "Son of the Most High" (cf. Luke 1:32); this also is probably a reference to the Davidic Messiah (see John J. Collins, *The Scepter and the Star: The Messiahs of the Dead Sea Scrolls and Other Ancient Literature*, Anchor Bible Reference Library [New York: Doubleday, 1995], 154–69).

7. See Frank W. Beare, *The Earliest Records of Jesus: A Companion to the Synopsis of the First Three Gospels by Albert Huck* (New York: Abingdon, 1962), 40–42; Marcus, *Mark*, 1:163–64.

8. On the linkages between Matt. 11:2–6//Luke 7:18–23 and 4Q521, see Allison, *Intertextual Jesus*, 109–14.

9. For the basic argument here, see Dibelius, *Die urchristliche Überlieferung*, 18, though not, of course, the references to 4Q521. See also Sanders, *Historical Figure of Jesus*, 94.

10. Kraeling, *John the Baptist*, 128–31, as summarized by Wink, *John the Baptist*, 23.

11. See Wink, *John the Baptist*, 24: "The absence of a further response by John merely indicates what parties on both sides knew to be fact, that John did *not* accept Jesus as the Coming One."

12. On the (mostly indirect) links between miracle-working and messianic traditions, see Marcus, *Mark*, 1:499. Those who wish to affirm that John believed in Jesus from the time of Jesus's baptism have sometimes harmonized this belief with Matt. 11:2–6//Luke 7:18–23 by saying that the latter records the beginning of John's *doubt* about Jesus, which was linked perhaps with the depressing circumstances of his imprisonment or his disappointment with the nonpolitical nature of Jesus' ministry. See, for example, Edersheim, *Life and Times of Jesus*, 1:666–69, who speaks melodramatically of John's "day of darkness and terrible questioning." As Steve Mason, *Josephus and the New Testament* (Peabody, Mass.: Hendrickson Publishers, 2003), 221 points out, however, the story seems to imply not the beginning of John's doubt but the beginning of his interest in the possibility of Jesus being the Messiah, which has been piqued by miracle reports. On the history of the interpretation of this problem, see Joel Marcus, "John the Baptist and Jesus," in *When Judaism and Christianity Began: Essays in Memory of*

Anthony J. Saldarini, ed. A. J. Avery-Peck, D. Harrington, and J. Neusner, Supplements to the Journal for the Study of Judaism 85 (Leiden, the Netherlands: Brill, 2004), 185–87.

13. On the textual question about *Ant.* 18.63–64, see app. 2, n. 2 (p. 223).

14. See app. 1 on the chronology of John's ministry.

15. Mason, *Josephus and the New Testament,* 214.

16. In Mark 6:14, 16, Herod Antipas is recorded as thinking that Jesus is John the Baptist raised from the dead, and in 8:28 some of the Jewish populace is said to share this opinion. It is probable that some sort of historical memory of popular beliefs underlies these reports; they do not serve Christian interests, and the passage in which they occur is concerned to refute them.

17. See Mason, *Josephus and the New Testament,* 213–25, who concludes that Josephus does not see John as a "figure in the Christian tradition" (217) and appositely asks "whether it is more likely that Josephus has taken a figure who was a herald of Jesus and, erasing his Christian connection, made him into a famous Jewish preacher, or whether the early Christian tradition has coopted a famous Jewish preacher as an ally and subordinate of Jesus" (219). As Mason comments, "The answer seems clear."

18. On the Slavonic Josephus, see app. 9.

19. ὁ ὀπίσω μου ἐρχόμενος ἔμπροσθέν μου γέγονεν, ὅτι πρῶτός μου ἦν.

20. Cf. discussion of the priority issue in the section on the Fourth Gospel in chap. 1.

21. See for example Mark 1:17//Matt. 4:19, Mark 8:34//Matt. 16:24//Luke 9:23, Matt. 10:38//Luke 14:27. Cf. also John 12:1; Acts 5:37 (Judas the Galilean), 20:30 (false pastors). For an extra–New Testament parallel, see 1 Macc. 2:27–28 (Mattathias at the beginning of the Maccabean Revolt calls "all who are zealous for the Law" to come after him [εξελθέτω ὀπίσω μου]). Rabbis do not usually call pupils to come after them (the pupil seeks out the *rav,* not the other way around), but they do "go after" the rabbi, following at a respectful distance; see for example b. ʿErub. 30a; b. Ketub. 66b; and Martin Hengel, *The Charismatic Leader and His Followers,* Studies of the New Testament and its World (1968; Eng. trans, New York: Crossroad, 1981), 52.

22. Dibelius, *Die urchristliche Überlieferung,* 111–13; cf. Wink, *John the Baptist,* 94–95, though Wink prescinds from the historical question of whether or not Jesus had a baptismal ministry.

23. Dodd, *Historical Tradition in the Fourth Gospel,* 285–86. Dodd rightly asserts that 4:2 probably comes from a subsequent editor rather than the author of the Gospel: "It is difficult to believe that any writer would have made a statement and contradicted it in the same breath, to the hopeless ruin of his sentence."

24. Meier, *Marginal Jew,* 2:122. According to Meier, the picture of Jesus baptizing is included in the Gospel because "it was too deeply rooted in the Johannine tradition and too widely known to friend and foe alike simply to be omitted."

25. Early Christian commentators are aware of the problem; see, for example, Augustine, in his *Homilies on John* 15.3: "It may perplex you, perhaps, to be told that Jesus baptized more than John, and then immediately after, that Jesus himself did not baptize. What? Is there a mistake made, and then corrected?" (trans. alt. from Saint Thomas Aquinas, *Catena Aurea: Commentary on the Four Gospels Collected Out of the Works of the Fathers* [Oxford: Parker, 1842]). Tertullian, *Baptism* 11, has avoided of the difficulty by interpreting John 4:1 as a reference to Jesus getting others to baptize, an "ordinary and general way" of speaking, similar to saying, "The emperor has posted an edict" or "The governor beat him with rods." In contrast, to take John 3:26 and 4:1 literally would be unfitting: "For unto whom could he baptize? Unto repentance? Then what need had

he of a forerunner? Unto remission of sins? But he granted that with a word. Unto himself? But in humility he used to keep himself hidden. Unto the Holy Spirit? But he had not yet ascended to the Father." Trans. from Evans, *Tertullian's Homily on Baptism*, 25. Cf. the discussion of Tertullian in the section "Forgiveness and the Spirit" in chap. 4.

26. For more discussion of Mark 11:27–33, see below in the section "John and Jesus: Elijah and Elisha?"

27. ὁ ἐλθὼν δι' ὕδατος καὶ αἵματος . . . οὐκ ἐν τῷ ὕδατι μόνον ἀλλ' ἐν τῷ ὕδατι καὶ ἐν τῷ αἵματι.

28. Martinus C. de Boer, "Jesus the Baptizer: 1 John 5:5–8 and the Gospel of John," *JBL* 107 (1988): 87–106. Translation of 1 John 5:6 above is from this article, p. 89.

29. Not a reference to his own baptism by John, which is the way it is usually taken.

30. Crucial to this argument is de Boer's observation that the only other mention of blood in 1 John is in 1:7, where the reference is to Jesus's own blood, the active agent that cleanses from sin.

31. De Boer precinds from the question of whether or not Jesus actually had a baptismal ministry; see de Boer, "Jesus the Baptizer," 95n25. But I believe we can use his arguments about 1 John to strengthen the case that he did.

32. Cf. the discussions above of Matthew's displacement of "unto the forgiveness of sins" from the account of John's baptism to the account of Jesus's death: chap. 4, section on "Forgiveness and the Spirit," and the opening of the present chapter.

33. As Meier, *Marginal Jew*, 2:167 points out, John 2:18 is an independent witness to the fact that Jesus was questioned about his authority soon after the Temple cleansing.

34. The passage also has many Semitisms; see Marcus, "John the Baptist and Jesus," 180n2.

35. The key clause here is "Why then did you not believe him?" in Mark 11:31. This, the Jewish leaders think, will be Jesus's response if they deny the authority of John's baptism. Although the historicity of this description might be questioned because of its claim to give insight into a private conversation among Jesus's opponents, the basic line of thought could be reconstructed from their failure to answer. For a consideration of and argument against alternate interpretations of the clause, see Marcus, "John the Baptist and Jesus," 181–83.

36. This is probably because Elisha's death is reported in the Old Testament (2 Kgs. 13:20), whereas Elijah's is not; instead, Elijah is taken up to heaven alive (2 Kgs. 2:11–12). See Marcus, "John the Baptist and Jesus," 193n51.

37. See Morton Smith, "What Is Implied by the Variety of Messianic Figures?" *JBL* 78 (1959): 66–72; M. de Jonge, "The Use of the Word 'Anointed' in the Time of Jesus," *Novum Testamentum* 8 (1966): 132–48.

38. See Raymond E. Brown, "Jesus and Elisha," *Perspective* 12 (1971): 85–104.

39. According to the Fourth Gospel, "John did no sign [= miracle]" (John 10:41), but Jesus did many.

40. From the Hebrew text of Sir. 48:12: "When Elijah was enveloped in the whirlwind, Elisha was filled with his spirit. Twice as many signs he wrought, and marvels with every utterance of his mouth" (trans. from Patrick W. Skehan and Alexander A. Di Lella, *The Wisdom of Ben Sira: A New Translation with Notes, Introduction, and Commentary*, AB 39 [New York: Doubleday, 1987], 530). Rabbinic traditions sometimes enumerate the miracles of Elijah and Elisha to prove the point; see, for example, b. Sanh. 47a and b. Ḥul. 7b.

41. In the section entitled "Doubts" above, I argued that the messianic prophecy in Mark 1:7–8//Matt. 3:11–12//Luke 3:15–18 did not originally refer to Jesus; here I am saying that elements of this prophecy originally were not messianic but did refer to Jesus as an Elisha-like figure. What I am positing, then, is that the passage may mix different elements, including various statements of the Baptist, perhaps uttered at different times and having to do with different though interrelated subjects, and all edited by later Christians. It is noteworthy that in John 1:15, 27 (cf. 1:30) the Baptist uses ὁ ὀπίσω μου ἐρχόμενος without a messianic nuance. That could reflect Johannine theology, but it could also reflect a memory about John's use of the phrase.

42. "Coming after" denotes a follower, disciple, or petitioner in Matt. 4:19//Mark 1:17; Matt. 10:38//Luke 14:27; Matt. 16:24//Mark 8:34//Luke 9:23; Mark 1:20; Luke 19:14, 21:8; John 12:19. Cf. also Acts 5:37, 20:30. "Coming after" denotes something besides being a follower in Matt. 16:23//Mark 8:33; Mark 1:17; John 1:15, 27, 30. For "going after" as a term for following into battle, see 1 Macc. 2:27–28 and cf. Marcus, *Mark*, 1:184.

43. וילך אחרי אליהו וישרתהו; καὶ ἐπορεύθη ὀπίσω Ηλιου καὶ ἐλειτούργει αὐτῷ.

44. The Targum reads תחותך, which reproduces the Hebrew, and could mean either "under you" or "in your place"; cf. Marcus Jastrow, *A Dictionary of the Targumim, the Talmud Babli and Yerushalmi, and the Midrashic Literature* (1886–1903; repr., New York: Judaica, 1982), 1661.

45. See David T. Lamb, "'A Prophet Instead of You' (1 Kings 19.16): Elijah, Elisha, and Prophetic Succession," in *Prophecy and Prophets in Ancient Israel: Proceedings of the Oxford Old Testament Seminar,* ed. John Day, Library of Hebrew Bible/Old Testament Studies 531 (New York: T&T Clark, 2010), 182–83, who notes that this is a unique case of prophetic succession in the Old Testament.

46. Skehan and Di Lella, *Ben Sira,* 534.

47. Meier, *Marginal Jew,* 2:141–42 is skeptical that Matt. 11:10//Luke 7:27 goes back to the historical Jesus. His observations about "the formal, scribal tone" of the allusion to Mal. 3:1, which also weaves in Exod. 23:20, are well taken, but there is probably still be a kernel of truth here. If, as I argue in chap. 3, John did present himself as Elijah, it would not be surprising for his onetime associate to apply Mal. 3:1 to him. Compare and contrast Robinson, "Elijah, John and Jesus," who thinks that John did not identify himself as Elijah but that Jesus did.

48. There are minor variations between the Matthean and Lukan forms of this Q saying. Luke does not have the "Amen" at the beginning, a locution that Luke seems to disfavor, eliminating it from seven of the ten instances he takes over from Mark. He also does not have "has arisen," another verb he seems to dislike, eliminating it from seven of the ten instances he takes over from Mark; on the other hand, this verb is a favorite of Matthew, so it is also possible that Matthew has added it. Luke lacks "the Baptist" as a modifier of John's name and he has "dominion of God" rather than Matthew's Jewish circumlocution "dominion of heaven," which probably reproduces Jesus' speech pattern. None of these differences affects the meaning of the passage substantially.

49. For Jesus's disciples as the citizens of the kingdom, see Mark 4:11 pars.; Matt. 5:3–11//Luke 6:20–22; Matt. 5:19–20; Matt. 16:18–19, 20:20–23; Luke 12:31–32; Luke 18:28–30; Luke 22:28–30. Though not all of these passages can be confidently assigned to the historical Jesus, many or most of them probably go back to him.

50. Dibelius, *Die urchristliche Überlieferung,* 13. Crossan, *Historical Jesus,* 237–38, also thinks the tension between the two halves is intense but ascribes both to the

historical Jesus, "and that leaves only one conclusion, namely, that between those twin assertions Jesus changed his view about John's mission and message."

51. Davies and Allison, *Matthew*, 2:251–52. Davies and Allison do not, however, unequivocally endorse the futuristic interpretation.

52. See Jacques Schlosser, *Le règne de Dieu dans les dits de Jesus*, Etudes bibliques (Paris: J. Gabalda, 1980), 1:163.

53. Cf. Clement of Alexandria, *Stromata* 1.21.136, who says that John prophesied "until the baptism of salvation" (μέχρι τοῦ σωτηρίου βαπτίσματος). As the Ante-Nicene Fathers editor observes, this is a reference to "the baptism of Jesus as distinguished from the baptism of repentance. John is clearly recognized, here, as of the old dispensation."

54. See Harold Bloom, *The Anxiety of Influence: A Theory of Poetry* (New York: Oxford University Press, 1973), esp. Bloom's statement of his argument's central principle on p. 30: "Poetic Influence—when it involves two strong, authentic poets,—always proceeds by a misreading of the prior poet, an act of creative correction that is actually and necessarily a misinterpretation."

55. For examples of precursor and successor movements, see Allison, *Jesus of Nazareth*, 93–94. See also Bat-Zion Eraqi Klorman, "The Messiah Shukr Kuḥayl II (1868–75) and His Tithe *(Ma'aśer)*: Ideology and Practice as a Means to Hasten Redemption," in *Essential Papers on Messianic Movements and Personalities in Jewish History*, ed. Marc Saperstein (New York: New York University Press, 1992), 457–58, 469: the messianic movement of Shukr Kuḥayl II was the continuation of the messianic movement of Shukr Kuḥayl I, and Shukr Kuḥayl II claimed to be Shukr Kuḥayl I raised from the dead (cf. Mark 6:14–16, 8:28).

56. See Max Weber, *The Sociology of Religion*, (1922; Eng. trans., Boston: Beacon Press, 1963), 60–61, 77–79.

57. Denis Martin MacEoin, *The Messiah of Shiraz: Studies in Early and Middle Babism*, Iran Studies 3 (Leiden, the Netherlands: Brill, 2009), 11, 15.

58. Margrit Eichler, "Charismatic Prophets and Charismatic Saviors," *Mennonite Quarterly Review* 55 (1981): 45–61. The two leaders she is referring to are Jan Matthys, who understood himself to be Enoch, the Second Witness from Rev. 11:1–12, and was killed at the end of 1533 "during a sortie that he undertook by divine inspiration with only a few men," and Jan van Leyden, who understood himself to be the savior, replaced the city council of Münster with twelve elders, had himself crowned as king, and was executed when the city fell to the authorities in 1535. There was also an earlier figure, Melchior Hoffman, who was understood as Elijah, the first witness of Rev. 11:1–12, and was imprisoned in Strasbourg before Matthys rose to power.

59. Herman Ferguson, quoted in Manning Marable, *Malcolm X: A Life of Reinvention* (New York: Viking Press, 2011), 268. Marable makes Ferguson's phrase "he was developing too fast" into the title for the chapter in his biography that deals with Malcolm's split from Elijah Muhammad, which is the source of the present paragraph (235–68).

60. For background, see D. M. MacEoin, "Babism," in *Encyclopaedia Iranica* (1988; repr., 2011), http://www.iranicaonline.org/articles/babism-index; Juan Cole, "Bahā'-Allāh," in *Encyclopaedia Iranica* (1988; repr., 2011), http://www.iranicaonline.org/articles/baha-allah.

61. It is possible that some of these parallels reflect Christian influence on Bahā' Allāh and his followers, who were in touch with Christians from early on; see Christopher Buck, "A Unique Eschatological Interface: Bahá'u'lláh and Cross-Cultural Messianism," in *In Iran*, Studies in Bábí and Bahá'í History 3 (Los Angeles: Kalimát Press,

1986), 163–67. As we will see below, Bahā' Allāh explicitly "demoted" the Bāb to the status of a John the Baptist–type figure. On Bahā' Allāh's exegesis of the New Testament in his *Book of Certitude*, see Christopher Buck, *Symbol and Secret: Qur'an Commentary in Bahá'uláh's Kitáb-i Íqán*, Studies in the Bábí and Bahá'í Religions 7 (Los Angeles: Kalimát Press, 1995), 111–14. Despite this explicit influence, the comparison is still interesting: Bahā' Allāh certainly did not demote the Bāb in his later writing because of the John the Baptist example, but because of the dynamics of a successor needing to supersede his predecessor.

62. Moojan Momen, *Baha'u'llah: A Short Biography* (Oxford: Oneworld, 2007), 11.

63. William McElwee Miller, *The Baha'i Faith: Its History and Teachings* (South Pasadena, Calif.: William Carey Library, 1974), 51 (trans. slightly altered).

64. On the Islamic background of the Bāb's teaching, including his "manifestation" theory, see Miller, *Baha'i Faith*, 1–12.

65. For details and analysis, see Denis MacEoin, "The Babi Concept of Holy War," *Religion* 12 (1982): 93–129.

66. For the evidence that the Bāb designated Subh-i-Azal to succeed him (a point disputed by later Bahā'īs), see Denis MacEoin, "Divisions and Authority Claims in Babism (1850–1866)," *Studia Iranica* 18 (1989): 93–99.

67. Denis MacEoin, "From Babism to Baha'ism: Problems of Militancy, Quietism, and Conflation in the Construction of a Religion," *Religion* 13 (1983): 220–22.

68. See Miller, *Baha'i Faith*, 99.

69. For the details, see Miller, *Baha'i Faith*, 54–55; MacEoin, "Divisions and Authority"; MacEoin, "Babism to Baha'ism," 220–22. See esp. what MacEoin says in the latter article on p. 220: "Babism had been marked from the beginning by a rather diffuse charismatic authority vested in more than one individual, and, after the deaths of the main bearers of that authority, a period of semi-anarchy had ensued, during which competing and conflicting claims to some kind of inspiration were advanced by a large number of individuals."

70. Momen, *Baha'u'llah*, 31–33.

71. MacEoin, "Babism to Baha'ism," 221–22.

72. Momen, *Baha'u'llah*, 69.

73. MacEoin, "Babism to Baha'ism," 222–30.

74. Miller, *Baha'i Faith*, 100, 103, 139.

75. H. M. Balyuzi, *Edward Granville Browne and the Bahá'i Faith* (London: George Ronald, 1970), 39–40.

76. Muḥammad Afnán and William S. Hatcher, "Western Islamic Scholarship and Bahá'í Origins," *Religion* 15 (1985): 39–40.

77. Bahā'ī writers frequently accuse non-Bahā'ī scholars of obscuring this "truth." Balyuzi's book is a polemical assault on the scholarship of Edward Granville Browne, whose admiration for the Bāb was great and who, as described below, objected to the way his image had been subordinated to that of Bahā' Allāh. As for Afnán and Hatcher, on pp. 49–50n48, they accuse Denis MacEoin of perpetrating "a gross distortion and misrepresentation of the Báb's teachings" by his "systematic omission of the very focal point and central concern of the *Bayān*, namely the imminent advent of 'The-One-Whom-God-Will-Make-Manifest.'" Such assertions illustrate MacEoin's point about the dogmatic heavy-handedness that has prevented the emergence within the ranks of Bahā'īs of true scholarship on the history of their movement (MacEoin, *Messiah of Shiraz*, xvii).

78. Cf. Kenneth Cragg, *Jesus and the Muslim: An Exploration* (London: Allen & Unwin, 1985), 24, 38n4, 52–53; Marshall, "Christianity in the Qur'ān," 14–15; David Marshall, "Heavenly Religion or Unbelief? Muslim Perspectives on Christianity," *Anvil* 23 (2006): 90. The translation of the Qur'ānic passage is from Cragg. See also Lupieri, *Giovanni Battista fra storia e leggenda*, 393–94, who mentions not only the relativizing of Jesus in Islam but also his relativizing in the Unification Church of Sun Myung Moon; on the latter, see George D. Chryssides, *The Advent of Sun Myung Moon: The Origins, Beliefs, and Practices of the Unification Church* (New York: St. Martin's Press, 1991), 108–30,

79. On Browne's frustration with the Bāhā'īs, see Moojan Momen, ed., *The Bábí and Bahá'í Religions 1844–1944: Some Contemporary Western Accounts* (Oxford: G. Ronald, 1981), 32–36. Cf. L. P. Elwell Sutton, review of *Edward Granville Brown and the Bahá'í Faith*, by H. M. Balyuzi, *Journal of the Royal Asiatic Society*, n.s., 104 (1972): 70–71, who implies that Browne's use of the term Bābī, even when speaking of the movement as it developed after the recognition of Bahā' Allāh, reveals Browne's blindness to the way in which Bahā' Allāh had eclipsed the Bāb within the movement.

80. On the 1865 work of Joseph A. de Gobineau, *Les Religions et les Philosophies dans l'Asie Centrale*, and its great influence, see Momen, *Bábí and Bahá'í Religions*, 17–26.

81. Edward Granville Browne, *A Year Amongst the Persians: Impressions as to the Life, Character, & Thought of the People of Persia Received During Twelve Months' Residence in the Country in the Years 1887–1888* (1893; repr., New York: Macmillan; Cambridge: Cambridge University Press, 1926), 328–29.

82. Edward Granville Browne, "The Bábís of Persia," *Journal of the Royal Asiatic Society* 3 (1889): 505.

83. It would be great if an ancient historian had taken the sort of interest in the Baptist (or, for that matter, Jesus) movement that Gobineau and Browne took in the Bāb. Lacking such sources, except for Josephus's short paragraph, we are left in a situation analogous to that of a future historian trying to piece together the "historical Bāb" from the slanted portrayal of him in Bahā'ī literature.

84. Cf. the quotation of Bultmann at the end of the section "Friendly Competition?" in chap. 1.

85. See above in the section "John and Jesus: Elijah and Elisha?"

86. See Joel Marcus, "The Beelzebul Controversy and the Eschatologies of Jesus," in *Authenticating the Activities of Jesus*, ed. B. Chilton and C. A. Evans (Leiden, the Netherlands: Brill, 1999), 247–77, for the hypothesis that Jesus was already a charismatic healer before his baptism by John; what he gained from joining John's movement was an apocalyptic interpretation of his healings.

··························

CHAPTER SIX   Herod Antipas

1. The Fourth Gospel prescinds from describing John's imprisonment and death, perhaps out of a concern that John not compete with Jesus in martyrdom. Luke 3:19–20 mentions John's imprisonment but not his martyrdom, leaving out both the Markan narrative of the latter (Mark 6:17–29//Matt. 14:3–12) and the allusion to it in the discussion about Elijah in Mark 9:11–13//Matt. 17:10–13. Luke does, however, have Antipas mention it in 9:9. Perhaps Luke, like John, wants to avoid competition from the Baptist in the matter of martyrdom, but Luke does omit a great deal of Markan material (cf. the "Great Omission" of Mark 6:45–8:10). For more speculation about this Lukan omission, see Ernst, *Johannes der Täufer* (1989), 111–12; Michael Hartmann, *Der Tod Johannes' des Täufers: eine exegetische und rezeptionsgeschichtliche Studie auf dem Hintergrund*

narrativer, intertextueller und kulturanthropologischer Zugänge, Stuttgarter Biblische Beiträge (Stuttgart: Verlag Katholisches Bibelwerk, 2001), 252–53.

2. Luke does not suggest a motivation; in 9:9 he just has Antipas mention the fact that he had John decapitated.

3. On the halakhic issues involved in the question of whether or not it actually was incestuous, see chap. 3, section on "John as an Eschatological Decider and Enforcer."

4. The original text of Mark 6:22 probably names the girl Herodias, like her mother, but this seems to be a mistake, since Josephus, *Ant.* 18.136 calls her Salome, and Josephus was probably better informed about Herodian names than Mark; cf. Marcus, *Mark,* 1:396.

5. The manuscripts read στάσει, which Louis H. Feldman translates as "sedition." Eusebius attests ἀποστάσει, which Feldman translates as "revolt." Feldman (Loeb Classical Library Josephus 9.83 n. f) rightly says that, whichever reading is chosen, a political insurrection is implied.

6. Clare K. Rothschild, "'Echo of a Whisper': The Uncertain Authenticity of Josephus' Witness to John the Baptist," in *Ablution, Initiation, and Baptism,* ed. David Hellholm et al., BZNW 176 (Berlin: De Gruyter, 2011), 1:263 says that βαπτισμῷ συνιέναι suggests group baptism. It may, however, suggest something slightly different: coming together in a group in order to be baptized individually. It is hard to imagine how group baptism would work with only one baptizer.

7. Feldman translates χρωμένοις βαπτισμῷ συνιέναι as simply "to participate in baptism." That would be a good translation for χρᾶσθαι βαπτισμῷ or συγχρᾶσθαι βαπτισμῷ, but it does not take adequate account of συνιέναι. That word, when it does not mean "to understand," frequently has a hostile or militaristic sense (see Henry George Liddell, Robert Scott, and Henry Stuart Jones, *A Greek-English Lexicon with a Supplement* [Oxford: Clarendon Press, 1968] 1718 [I]), which would fit the overall context here.

The picture of John is even more explicitly revolutionary in the Slavonic Josephus, where he summons the Jews to freedom, proclaiming that he will show them the way of the Law whereby they may free themselves from the holders of power, so that no mortal but only God rules over them. On this reworking of Josephus, see app. 9.

8. Ernst Lohmeyer, *Das Urchristentum,* 1:111.

9. Yet Matthew retains the Markan report that Antipas was distressed when manipulated into killing John; this is an example of Matthean "editorial fatigue" in redacting Mark. On the phenomenon, see Mark Goodacre, "Fatigue in the Synoptics," *NTS* 44 (1998): 45–58.

10. On Pilate's ruthlessness, see Josephus, *J.W.* 2.169–177; *Ant.* 18.60–62, 85–87; Philo, *Embassy* 299–305; Luke 13:1; Marcus, *Mark,* 2:1026–27.

11. For other echoes of the Esther story in Mark's account of John's beheading, see Marcus, *Mark,* 1:96–97.

12. Cf. Crossan, *Historical Jesus,* 231–32, who concludes, "Whatever John's intentions may have been, Antipas was not paranoid to consider a conjunction of prophet and crowds, desert and Jordan, dangerously volatile."

13. See the sections on "The Qumran Attitude toward Gentiles" and "Revising the Jewish/Gentile Antinomy" in chap. 2.

14. Norman Cohn, *The Pursuit of the Millennium: Revolutionary Millenarians and Mystical Anarchists of the Middle Ages,* rev. ed. (New York: Oxford University Press, 1970), 47–50.

15. Ibid., 95–96.

16. Ibid., 128–29.

17. Ibid., 137–38.

18. Apart from Antipas's basic attitude and possibly the name of Herodias's daughter, the location of the execution differs: Josephus has it taking place at Machaerus, Antipas's fortress on the eastern shore of the Dead Sea in southern Perea, whereas Mark, through the presence of Galilean gentry, implies that it took place in Antipas's official palace in Tiberias in Galilee.

19. Both also, and probably coincidentally, describe the story of Antipas, Herodias, and the execution of John in a flashback, out of historical sequence; see Sanders, *Historical Figure of Jesus,* 289. As for the fact that both link John's death with Antipas's marriage to Herodias but in different ways, this is to be expected when later writers develop a common body of tradition in their own way.

20. See Harold W. Hoehner, *Herod Antipas,* Society for New Testament Studies Monograph Series 17 (Cambridge: Cambridge University Press, 1972), 144–45, who claims that the order of events in *Ant.* 18.109–119 "makes it possible for the reader to suppose that the unlawful marriage was the effective cause of Antipas' fear of a popular uprising." McDonald, "What Did You Go Out to See?," 63 makes a similar linkage.

21. On the Herodians' search for religious legitimacy, see Menachem Stern, "The House of Herod and the Roman Empire After the Death of Herod [Hebrew]," in *Studies in Jewish History: The Second Temple Period* (Jerusalem: Yad Ishak Ben-Zvi, 1991), 232–45.

22. Morten Horning Jensen, *Herod Antipas in Galilee: The Literary and Archaeological Sources on the Reign of Herod Antipas and Its Socio-Economic Impact on Galilee,* WUNT 2.125 (Tübingen, Germany: Mohr Siebeck, 2006), 106 points out that of the five surviving sons of Herod's original ten, only Antipas and Philip held political office, and of all the sons "Antipas had the highest rank ruling over the most important Jewish area next to Judea," which was under direct Roman control (ibid., 107–8). On the golden shields incident, see Brown, *Death of the Messiah,* 1:701–3, who says the date of the incident is uncertain but perhaps after 31 CE.

23. Brown, *Death of the Messiah,* 1:777 concludes, "The paucity of historical data means that we cannot verify either the enmity or the subsequent friendship, but neither is implausible."

24. E. Mary Smallwood, *The Jews under Roman Rule: From Pompey to Diocletian,* Studies in Judaism in Late Antiquity 20 (Leiden, the Netherlands: Brill, 1976), 184; see also 163–66.

25. Jensen, *Herod Antipas in Galilee,* 235–36; see already Smallwood, *Jews under Roman Rule,* 184.

26. Morten Horning Jensen, "Message and Minting: The Coins of Herod Antipas in the Second Temple Context as a Source for Understanding the Religio-Political and Socio-Economic Dynamics of Early First Century Galilee," in *Religion, Ethnicity, and Identity in Ancient Galilee: A Region in Transition,* ed. Jürgen Zangenberg, Harold W. Attridge, and Dale B. Martin (Tübingen, Germany: Mohr Siebeck, 2007), 312. For a similar view, see Monika Bernett, "Roman Imperial Cult in the Galilee: Structures, Functions, and Dynamics," in *Religion, Ethnicity, and Identity,* ed. Zangenberg, Attridge, and Martin, 344–48. In contrast, see Richard A. Horsley and Neil Asher Silberman, *The Message and the Kingdom: How Jesus and Paul Ignited a Revolution and Transformed the Ancient World* (Minneapolis: Fortress, 1997), 22, who characterize Antipas's coinage

as provocative, giving symbolic expression to his political ambitions and messianic dreams.

27. Bernett, "Roman Imperial Cult," 344, drawing on Manfred Lämmer, "Griechische Wettkämpfe in Galiläa unter der Herrschaft des Herodes Antipas," *Kölner Beiträge zur Sportwissenschaft* 5 (1976): 37–67. Bernett (n. 24) contrasts Agrippa's putatively conservative games with the provocative action of his father, Herod the Great, who "faced a riot in Jerusalem during the preparations of the first games for Caesar (Augustus) in 28 BCE owing to the image-like trophies that had been set up around the theater (Josephus, *Ant.* 15.268–79)." Lämmer points to y. Erub. 5:1 (22b), in which R. Simeon mentions the Tiberian stadium without condemning it.

28. Jensen, *Herod Antipas in Galilee,* 144–45, supplemented by a private communication of May 2, 2014: Bernett "is probably right that the spectacles and games performed in these places [Tiberias and Taricheae] came with some form of imperial honor. We just don't know how and to what extent. Therefore it seems farfetched to conclude that (a) Antipas established games, and (b) created games that did not conflict with central demands of the Torah."

29. On Josephus's bias against Herod the Great and Herod Antipas, see Jensen, *Herod Antipas in Galilee,* 229–30. Josephus appears to censure Antipas for the marriage when he says that "falling in love with Herodias, . . . he brazenly broached to her the subject of marriage" (ἐρασθεὶς δὲ Ἡρωδιάδος . . . τολμᾷ λόγων ἅπτεσθαι περὶ γάμου). But it is actually Herodias and not Antipas whom he charges with impiety: "Herodias, taking it into her head to flout the way of our fathers, married Herod, her husband's brother by the same father, who was tetrarch of Galilee; to do this she parted from a living husband" (*Ant.* 18.136).

30. εἰδὼς παράνομον τὸν οἰκισμὸν καὶ ἀπὸ τοῦ Ἰουδαίοις πατρίου, *Ant.* 18.38 (Loeb Classical Library trans. alt.).

31. Lee Levine, "R. Simeon B. Yoḥai and the Purification of Tiberias: History and Tradition," *Hebrew Union College Annual* 49 (1974): 168.

32. Cf. b. Šabb. 33b–34a: "[R. Simeon said to the inhabitants of Tiberias], 'Is there anything here that requires amending?' They said, 'There is a place of doubtful uncleanliness, and priests have to take the trouble of going around it'" (my trans.). As Levine points out, this suggests that the problem was localized and affected only priests.

33. Mark 6:18//Matt. 14:4 gives no indication as to whether John's denunciation of Antipas's marriage took place in public or in private. It is possible that it took place in private and that it was initiated by Antipas's curiosity or fear concerning the new prophet who had arisen in his realm (on curiosity as a possible motivation, cf. Luke 23:8). But it is also possible that John shouted out a denunciation in public when Antipas was touring near John's sphere of activity. Or perhaps we should imagine John sending a message to Antipas through intermediaries, as Jesus does in Luke 13:31–33.

34. Steven Runciman, *The Byzantine Theocracy* (Cambridge: Cambridge University Press, 1977), 34–35.

35. J. B. Bury, *History of the Later Roman Empire from the Death of Theodosius I to the Death of Justinian* (London: Macmillan, 1923), 1:157–58.

36. Stuart Airlie, "Private Bodies and the Body Politic in the Divorce Case of Lothar II," *Past and Present* 161 (1998): 7.

37. Ibid.

38. Ibid., 33.

39. See Marcus, *Mark,* 1:398–99.

40. Airlie, "Private Bodies and the Body Politic," 36.

41. For short summaries of John and Isabella, see Henry A. Myers and Herwig Wolfram, *Medieval Kingship* (Chicago: Nelson-Hall, 1982), 157–58; James Holt, "John. King of England," in *Encyclopaedia Britannica,* online ed., https://www.britannica.com/biography/John-king-of-England, accessed May 26, 2018. For a splendid, in-depth study, see Nicholas Vincent, "Isabella of Angoulême: John's Jezebel," in *King John: New Interpretations,* ed. S. D. Church (Woodbridge, U.K.: Boydell Press, 1999), 165–219.

42. See Vincent, "Isabella of Angoulême," 174–75, who says that John went out of his way to obtain letters from many bishops testifying that his marriage to Isabella was legitimate—an example of protesting too much. "The suspicion remains that his bride was a pre-pubescent child in 1200, and that the king stepped in where Hugh de Lusignan, Isabella's betrothed husband, had believed it indecent to tread."

43. For the charge that the new wife was "more Jezebel than Isabel," see Matthew Paris, who in his mid-thirteenth-century *Chronica Majora* (4.253) attributes this opinion to many in France; see Vincent, "Isabella of Angoulême," 165. On the rumors of Isabella's sexual escapades, see Vincent, "Isabella of Angoulême," 200–204.

44. See W. G. van Emden, "Kingship in the Old French Epic of Revolt," in *Kings and Kingship in Medieval Europe,* ed. Anne J. Duggan, King's College London Medieval Studies 10 (London: King's College London Centre for Late Antique and Medieval Studies, 1993), 332–33.

45. See James A. Brundage, "Matrimonial Politics in Thirteenth-Century Aragon: Moncado v. Urgel," in *Sex, Law and Marriage in the Middle Ages,* Collected Studies Series CS397 (1980; repr., Aldershot, U.K.: Ashgate, 1993), 281.

46. Ibid., 275.

47. Ibid., 282.

48. See Alison Weir, *The Six Wives of Henry VIII* (New York: Grove Weidenfeld, 1992), 246–47, 251–52, 264–65.

49. See K. J. Kesselring, *The Northern Rebellion of 1569: Faith, Politics and Protest in Elizabethan England* (New York: Palgrave Macmillan, 2007), 25.

50. See chap. 3, section on "John as an Eschatological Halakhic Decider and Enforcer."

51. On the ethnic identity of Herod's realms of Galilee and Perea, see Hoehner, *Herod Antipas,* 53–55; Jürgen Zangenberg, Harold W. Attridge, and Dale B. Martin, eds., *Religion, Ethnicity, and Identity in Ancient Galilee: A Region in Transition* (Tübingen, Germany: Mohr Siebeck, 2007). Both areas were predominantly Jewish, but there were some Gentile residents; for Galilee, see Strabo, *Geography* 16.2.34, and Josephus, *Life* 67. As for Perea, Josephus (*Ant.* 20.2) describes a dispute between "the Jewish inhabitants of Perea" (τοὺς τὴν Περαίαν κατοικοῦντας Ἰουδαίους) and the inhabitants of Philadelphia; this could either speak of the Jewish subset of the Perean population or of the population as a whole as Jewish.

52. Contrary to Josephus (*Ant.* 18.110), Antipas's repudiation of Aretas's daughter and marriage to Herodias may have been based not only on infatuation but also on a desire to placate Jewish opinion, which had been outraged by his marriage to a foreign wife.

53. On the chronology of events here, see app. 1.

54. Kraeling, *John the Baptist,* 90–91.

55. On the problems this war raises for the chronology of John's life, see app. 1.

56. See, for example, Schlosser, *Le règne de Dieu,* 2:515; Ernst, *Johannes der Täufer* (1989), 169; Davies and Allison, *Matthew,* 2:153.

57. See Luz, *Matthew*, 2:141. Luz also mentions Jesus's follower Judas Iscariot, whose surname may refer to the Sicarii ("dagger-men"), a militant anti-collaborationist Palestinian Jewish party. See Josephus, *J.W.* 2.254–257; Marcus, *Mark*, 1:264.

58. Compare the section in the previous chapter on the Bābī/Bahā'ī parallel: Bahā' Allāh dropped the Bāb's emphasis on literal holy war, instead proclaiming that nonviolent proselytizing was the true *jīhād*.

"Since the days of" in Matt. 11:12 may be an apocalyptic trope; "in those days" refers to the end-time in the Old Testament prophetic books (for example, Jer. 31:33; Joel 3:1; Zech. 8:23) and the first two Gospels (for example, Matt. 7:22, 9:15; Mark 13:17, 19, 24; cf. Davies and Allison, *Matthew*, 1:288).

59. On the date of the War Scroll, see below, n. 62.

60. David Flusser, *Judaism of the Second Temple Period* (Grand Rapids, Mich.: Eerdmans; Jerusalem: Hebrew University Magnes Press, 2007–9), 333. On conditional pacifism, see Gordon M. Zerbe, *Non-Retaliation in Early Jewish and New Testament Texts: Ethical Themes in Social Contexts,* Journal for the Study of Pseudepigrapha Supplement Series 13 (Sheffield, U.K.: JSOT Press, 1993).

61. Flusser, *Judaism of the Second Temple Period*, 10–16.

62. On the War Scroll, see Philip R. Davies, "War of the Sons of Light Against the Sons of Darkness," in Schiffman and VanderKam, *Encyclopedia of the Dead Sea Scrolls*, 2:967: the composition of the scroll should probably be assigned to the late first century BCE or the early first century CE, a view supported by the Herodian script and the prominent role of the Kittim (Romans). "Such a period," Davies writes, "makes plausible the view of a final war that would have to involve a confrontation with the Romans, against whom a hostile attitude is now expressed (unlike, for example, the attitude of the Habakkuk commentary, where they are not treated as enemies but agents of divine punishment on a corrupt Jewish leadership." On the date of the other scrolls, see the articles in the same work on the Habakkuk Pesher (Moshe J. Bernstein, 2:649: first half of the first century BCE), the Hodayot (Émile Puech, 1:367: second half of the second century BCE), and the Community Rule (Michael A. Knibb, 2:793-97: second half of the second century BCE). Also against the thesis of pacifist Essenes at Qumran are the archaeological remains of weapons; see Jodi Magness's article on weapons in the same work, 2:970–73.

63. Flusser, *Judaism of the Second Temple Period*, 1:333.

64. Bovon, *Luke*, 1:124: "In contrast to the later church, there are at this point no forbidden occupations."

65. Bovon, *Luke*, 1:123 wonders whether it is "Christian parenesis from the Hellenistic congregation placed in the Baptist's mouth, or was it even composed by Luke himself?" He cites Bultmann, *History of the Synoptic Tradition*, 145, who says: "This is a catechism-like section, naively put into the Baptist's mouth, as though soldiers had gone on a pilgrimage to John. There is one thing that makes it improbable that we are here dealing with a product of the primitive Church—that the profession of a soldier is taken for granted. Neither does the passage appear to be Jewish. It is perhaps a relatively late Hellenistic product, developed (by Luke himself) out of the saying from the tradition in v 11 (ὁ ἔχων δύο χιτῶνας κτλ ['the one who has two tunics,' etc.]." Although he disputes the thesis that the passage was created by Luke, Ernst, *Johannes der Täufer* (1989), 94–96, also doubts that it reflects John's own thought; rather, he attributes it to circles of John's disciples who were trying to make his teaching relevant for a later time by ethicizing and deapocalypticizing it.

....

Conclusion

1. Cf. Marcus, "Modern and Ancient Jewish Apocalypticism," 19, and Marcus, "Once and Future Messiah," 392, for examples from the modern Chabad movement.

2. This, at least, seems to be the implication of Matt. 3:16–17//Luke 3:22//John 1:32–34. Mark 1:10–11, the earliest canonical account, is more cautious: only Jesus sees the Spirit descend and hears the heavenly voice acclaiming him as God's son. See Marcus, *Mark,* 1:163–64, on the history of the tradition.

3. See Matt. 3:14–15 and Luke 3:21, and cf. *Gospel of the Nazareans* (Jerome, *Pelag.* 3.2): "Behold, the mother of the Lord and his brothers said to him, 'John the Baptist baptizes for the remission of sins; let us go and be baptized by him.' But he said, 'What have I committed, that I should be baptized of him, unless it be that I am saying this in ignorance?'" See also above, chap. 4, n. 52 (p. 201).

4. "Sich realisierende Eschatologie"; see Jeremias, *Parables of Jesus,* 229n3, who says that he owes this expression to a letter from Ernst Haenchen.

5. See, for example, Charles Harold Dodd, *The Parables of the Kingdom* (1935; repr., London: Nisbet, 1948), 50; Theissen and Merz, *The Historical Jesus,* 252, 256. This contrast is popular with Christian scholars but not limited to them. See, for example, David Flusser and R. Steven Notley, *Jesus* (1997; repr., Jerusalem: Hebrew University Magnes Press, 2001), 110: "This, then, is the 'realized eschatology' of Jesus. He is the only Jew of ancient times known to us who preached not only that people were on the threshold of the end of time, but that the new age of salvation had already begun."

6. On realized eschatology at Qumran, see chap. 2, n. 20 (p. 174); on realized eschatology in the book of Jubilees, see Todd R. Hanneken, *The Subversion of the Apocalypses in the Book of Jubilees,* Society of Biblical Literature Early Judaism and Its Literature 34 (Leiden, the Netherlands: Brill, 2012), 148.

7. Jeremias, *New Testament Theology,* 49.

8. Dunn, *Baptism in the Holy Spirit,* 14.

9. See James L. Kugel, *How to Read the Bible: A Guide to Scripture, Then and Now* (New York: Free Press, 2007), 15, 32; John Sandys-Wunsch, *What Have They Done to the Bible? A History of Modern Biblical Interpretation* (Collegeville, Minn.: Liturgical Press, 2005), 16–17, 23, 55–57, 63, 87, 105, 152, 157–58.

For the role played by biblical contradictions in Spinoza's thought on the Bible, see Benedict Spinoza, *Theological-Political Treatise,* Cambridge Texts in the History of Philosophy (Cambridge: Cambridge University Press, 2007), chap. 2, "On the Prophets" passim; also p. 100.

10. On reinterpretation of Old Testament traditions within the Old Testament, Second Temple Judaism, and early Christianity, see P. R. Ackroyd and C. F. Evans, eds., *The Cambridge History of the Bible,* vol. 1, *From the Beginnings to Jerome* (Cambridge: Cambridge University Press, 1970); Michael Fishbane, *Biblical Interpretation in Ancient Israel* (Oxford: Clarendon Press, 1985); Martin Jay Mulder, ed., *Mikra: Text, Translation, and Reading and Interpretation of the Hebrew Bible in Ancient Judaism and Early Christianity,* Corpus Rerum Iudaicarum ad Novum Testamentum (Philadelphia: Fortress, 1988); Magne Sæbø, ed., *Hebrew Bible/Old Testament: The History of Its Interpretation,* vol. 1, *From the Beginnings to the Middle Ages (Until 1300);* pt. 1, *Antiquity* (Göttingen, Germany: Vandenhoeck & Ruprecht, 1996).

11. See S. Vernon McCasland, "Matthew Twists the Scriptures," *JBL* 80 (1961): 143–48.

12. On Jewish-Christian disputations in the Middle Ages, see Hyam Maccoby, *Judaism on Trial: Jewish-Christian Disputations in the Middle Ages,* Littman Library of Jewish Civilization (Rutherford, N.J.: Fairleigh Dickinson University Press; London: Associated University Presses, 1982). On Muslim polemics about Christian and Jewish interpretations of the Bible, see Sidney H. Griffith, *The Bible in Arabic: The Scriptures of the "People of the Book" in the Language of Islam,* Jews, Christians, and Muslims from the Ancient to the Modern World (Princeton, N.J.: Princeton University Press, 2013).

13. See Richard B. Hays, *Echoes of Scripture in the Letters of Paul* (New Haven, Conn.: Yale University Press, 1989), 154–56; Marcus, *Way of the Lord,* 202–3.

14. There is a similar but less radical form of this idea in 1 Pet. 1:11: the prophets "inquired what person or time was indicated by Spirit of Christ within them when predicting the sufferings of Christ and the subsequent glory." The next verse says that it was subsequently revealed to them that their prophecies concerned not their own time but the later era in which the author's addressees live.

15. William Blake, *The Marriage of Heaven and Hell,* in *The Complete Poetry and Prose of William Blake: Newly Revised Edition,* ed. D. V. Erdman (New York: Anchor Books, 1988), 35.

16. T. S. Eliot, similarly, commends several commentators for bringing out aspects of his verse of which he himself had been unaware; see Christopher Ricks and Jim McCue, eds., *The Poems of T. S. Eliot,* vol. 1, *Collected and Uncollected Poems* (Baltimore: Johns Hopkins University Press, 2015), 1574–76. An example is Eliot's comment to Thomas McGreevy in 1931, concerning McGreevy's *T. S. Eliot: A Study:* "Your *explication de texte* of *The Waste Land* interested me very much. I can say without irony that it is extremely acute; but I must add that the author was not nearly so acute or learned as the critic. You have told me, in fact, much that I did not know; and I feel that I understand the poem much better after reading your explanation of it. Well! I supposed that I was merely working off a grouch against life while passing the time in a Swiss sanatorium; but apparently I meant something by it." Similarly, in a letter to Philip Mairet in 1956, he writes: "The fact that a poem can mean different things to different persons . . . must, however paradoxically, be reconciled with the assertion that it has an absolute and unalterable meaning. At the same time, the author, it must be remembered, regarding his own work after it is completed, is hardly more than one reader amongst others, and while the poem is being written, he must be too busy to be fully conscious of what the poem means."

17. Bloom, *Anxiety of Influence,* 30.

18. See also Samuel Beckett's letter of November 6, 1962, to Arland Ussher after the latter had sent Beckett a few pages from his journal about Beckett's *Waiting for Godot:* "I have read your meditations with great pleasure. I wish I had something intelligent to offer in return. But . . . I have nothing wherewith either to agree or disagree with what you say about my work, with which my unique relation—and it is a tenuous one—is the making relation. I am with it a little in the dark and fumbling of making, as long as that lasts, then no more. I have no light to throw on it myself and it seems a stranger in the light that others throw." From Martha Dow Fehsenfeld and Lois More Overbeck, eds., *The Letters of Samuel Beckett,* vol. 3, *1956–1965* (Cambridge: Cambridge University Press, 2014), 511.

19. *In Our Time,* April 22, 2010.

20. This is the thesis of Luke Timothy Johnson, *The Real Jesus: The Misguided Quest for the Historical Jesus and the Truth of the Traditional Gospels* (San Francisco:

HarperSanFrancisco, 1996), following in the footsteps of Martin Kähler, *The So-Called Historical Jesus and the Historic Biblical Christ* (1892; Eng. trans., Philadelphia: Fortress, 1964).

21. Letter of April 5, 1882, trans. Rudolf Smend, "Julius Wellhausen and His Prolegomena to the History of Israel," *Semeia* 25 (1982): 6. The German original is in Julius Wellhausen, *Briefe*, ed. Rudolf Smend (Tübingen, Germany: Mohr Siebeck, 2013), 98.

22. Karl Barth, *The Word of God and the Word of Man* (1928; repr., New York: Harper, 1957), 28–50.

23. See "The Yavneh Legend of the Stammaim," chap. 7 of Boyarin, *Border Lines*, 151–201.

24. See Brown, *Introduction to New Testament Christology.*

25. See Willard M. Swartley, *Slavery, Sabbath, War, and Women: Case Issues in Biblical Interpretation*, Conrad Grebel Lectures (Scottdale, Pa.: Herald Press, 1983). Swartley shows that in the antebellum years the defenders of slavery usually had the more detailed exegetical arguments, whereas abolitionists tended to appeal to generalities such as the love of Jesus.

26. On the constructive nature of memory but also the limits to such constructivity, see Barry Schwartz, *Abraham Lincoln and the Forge of National Memory* (Chicago: University of Chicago Press, 2000).

27. On the importance of Luke 2:52 in patristic and medieval debates about the humanity of Jesus, see Jaroslav Pelikan, *The Christian Tradition: A History of the Development of Doctrine*, 5 vols. (Chicago: University of Chicago Press, 1971–91), 1:251.

······························

Appendix 1: The Chronology of John's Life

1. Brown, *Birth of the Messiah*, 413.

2. See Brown, *Birth of the Messiah*, 241–43, 250–52.

3. See Brown, *Birth of the Messiah*, 166–67. A more recent study, Paul D. Maier, "The Date of the Nativity and the Chronology of Jesus' Life," in *Chronis, Kairos, Christos: Nativity and Chronological Studies Presented to Jack Finegan*, ed. Jerry Vardaman and Edwin M. Yamauchi (Winona Lake, Ind.: Eisenbrauns, 1989), 113–30, opts for 5 BCE. Jerry Vardaman, "Jesus' Life: A New Chronology," in *Chronos, Kairos, Christos*, ed. Vardaman and Yamauchi, 55–82 argues that Jesus was born in 12 BCE. This ignores the linkage that Matthew's Gospel makes with the death of Herod the Great, which occurred in 4 BCE (Matt. 2:19), and Luke 3:1, which locates the beginning of John the Baptist's ministry in the fifteenth year of the reign of Tiberius (= 28–29 CE [see below]; Vardaman thinks this may be the result of a textual error) in combination with Luke 3:23, which has Jesus being about thirty years old when he begins his ministry shortly after his baptism by John.

4. Fitzmyer, *Gospel According to Luke*, 1:455.

5. Brown, *Death of the Messiah*, 2:1373–76, relays the results of Blinzler's survey of about one hundred scholars: "None whom he lists has opted for AD 34 or 35, while between one and three respectively have opted for the years 26, 27, 28, 31, 32, and 36. Thirteen opted for AD 29, fifty-three for 30, and twenty-four for 33." Brown himself concludes that the most probable dates for Jesus's death are April 7, 30, CE and April 3, 33, CE (the two times in the time range 26–36 CE, when Passover Eve fell on a Friday, thus corresponding to the Johannine dating of Jesus's crucifixion to the day before Passover [John 19:14, 31, 42]). Helen Bond, "Dating the Death of Jesus: Memory and the

Religious Imagination," *NTS* 59 (2013): 461–75 stretches this range somewhat by arguing that all we can know is that Jesus died somewhere around Passover (perhaps a week or so before it) between 29 and 34 CE. I am not as skeptical as she is, however, about a closer link with the festival, since a pilgrimage to Jerusalem during Passover week is a plausible motivation for one of Jesus's rare visits (or sole visit) to the city.

6. The uncertainty results from the fact that the Greek manuscripts of *Ant.* 18.106 read εἰκοστῷ, but the Latin reads *vicesimo secundo.*

7. Kirsopp Lake, "The Date of Herod's Marriage with Herodias and the Chronology of the Gospels," *Expositor* 4 (1912): 465–66.

8. See Brown, *Death of the Messiah,* 2:1373. Caiaphas's high priesthood ended about the same time, in 36/37 CE.

9. See Colin J. Humphreys and W. G. Waddington, "The Jewish Calendar, a Lunar Eclipse and the Date of Christ's Crucifixion," *Tyndale Bulletin* 43 (1992): 335. According to Humphreys and Waddington, the only years between 26 and 36 CE in which 14 Nisan fell on a Thursday or Friday were 27 (Thursday), 30 (Friday), and 33 (Friday).

10. See, however, Nikos Kokkinos, "Crucifixion in A.D. 36: The Keystone for Dating the Birth of Jesus," in *Chronis, Kairos, Christos,* ed. Vardaman and Yamauchi, 134, who places Herod's marriage to Herodias in 33 or 34, John's death in 35, the war of Aretas in 36, and Jesus's crucifixion in the same year.

11. Johannes Tromp, "John the Baptist According to Flavius Josephus, and His Incorporation in the Christian Tradition," in Empsychoi Logoi—*Religious Innovations in Antiquity: Studies in Honour of Pieter Willem Van der Horst,* ed. Alberdkina Houtman, Albert de Jong, and Magda Misset-van de Weg (Leiden, the Netherlands: Brill, 2008), 135–49.

12. This assumes that the *Testimonium Flavianum,* or some version of it, was actually written by Josephus; see the sources addressing this question listed in app. 2, n. 2 (p. 223).

13. On the implication of John's superiority, see the section "Luke-Acts, Matthew" in chap. 1; on the implication of Jesus's sinfulness, see the section "Forgiveness and the Spirit" in chap. 4; on both, see the introduction to chap. 5. Tromp's only response to this point is to say (147n44) that "oral tradition, the eventual source of the Gospels, is capable of forgetting inconvenient elements." But the real issue is whether either oral or written Christian sources are likely to have *invented* inconvenient elements.

14. See the section on the Gospel of John in chap. 1.

15. Some modern historians adopt a similar procedure when faced with a similar challenge. For example, Shelby Foote, *The Civil War: A Narrative,* 3 vols. (New York: Random House, 1958–74), typically ends the story of a Civil War campaign in one region before moving to another region, for which he has to go backwards in time a considerable way.

16. See Sanders, *Historical Figure of Jesus,* 289. It is a curious coincidence that the Gospels, too, relate the story about Herodias's marriage and John's execution in a flashback (Mark 6:17–29//Matt. 14:3–12).

17. As Sanders, *Historical Figure of Jesus,* 289 puts it, "Josephus wrote that Aretas's daughter 'reached her father and told him what Herod [Antipas] planned to do. Aretas made this the beginning of hostility over boundaries in the district of Gamala.' 'Made this the beginning of' is not necessarily 'as soon as'; on the contrary, one supposes that some time elapsed between the divorce and the war." It should also be noted that ἀρχή can mean "source" or "first principle," perhaps even "pretext," as well as chronological beginning (see Liddell, Scott, and Jones, *Greek-English Lexicon.* 252), and indeed this

nuance is in line with Josephus's exact syntax, ὁ δὲ ἀρχὴν ἔχθρας ταύτην ποιησάμενος περί τε ὅρων ἐν γῇ Γαβαλίτιδι ("having made this [Antipas's repudiation of his daughter] a pretext for hostility concerning boundaries in the district of Gabalis"). This suggests that the real casus belli was not Antipas's marital behavior but a long-simmering border dispute. When Aretas finally attacked, however, he shrewdly invoked Antipas's scandalous divorce and remarriage as a pretext rather than the crass political dispute over boundaries. The Romans apparently saw through this charade and punished Aretas for it.

18. See Hoehner, *Herod Antipas,* 125–26.

....

Appendix 2: Is Josephus's Account of John a Christian Interpolation?

1. Nir, "Josephus' Account of John the Baptist." Rothschild, "'Echo of a Whisper,'" 1:255–90, also raises questions about the authenticity of Josephus's account, but she does not find strong reasons for doubting it; her essay seems chiefly designed to raise heuristic questions. As she seems to recognize, however, this sort of questioning could equally well deconstruct just about any other ancient account of a historical personage. See her confusingly stated conclusion: "This is not to say with strict historicists that no history can be proven such that, for example, we cannot attribute Josephus' works to him. It is only impossible to make a definitive claim about a single brief passage" (283).

2. For the two sides of the debate, see John P. Meier, "Jesus in Josephus: A Modest Proposal," *CBQ* 52 (1990): 76–103 (for authenticity), and Ken Olson, "A Eusebian Reading of the *Testimonium Flavianum,*" in *Eusebius of Caesarea: Tradition and Innovations,* ed. Aaron Johnson and Jeremy Schott (Cambridge, Mass.: Harvard University Press, 2013), 97–114 (against). In Olson's view, Eusebius, who is the first author to show knowledge of the *Testimonium,* is also its author. If so, however, it is strange that Eusebius speaks about the *Testimonium Flavianum* coming after Josephus's notice about John (see *Ecclesiastical History* 1.11.7), thus affirming the New Testament presentation of John as Jesus's precursor but contradicting the order that occurs in actual manuscripts of Josephus. Cf. Rothschild, "'Echo of a Whisper,'" 1:281: "It would not have been in Eusebius' best interest either to place his forged fragment about Jesus prior to the narrative about John the Baptist, or to refer to it in this way, or to dissemble about its placement."

3. See Dibelius, *Die urchristliche Überlieferung,* 124.

4. Mason, *Josephus and the New Testament,* 153, citing *Ant.* 7.338, 341, 356, 374, 384, 9.236, 16.42; *J.W.* 2.139. On the use of the "double commandment" in Second Temple Judaism in general, see Zerbe, *Non-Retaliation,* 139–160; Dale C. Allison, *Resurrecting Jesus: The Earliest Christian Tradition and Its Interpreters* (New York: T&T Clark, 2005), 152–60.

5. See Klausner, *Jesus of Nazareth,* 240–41; Ernst, *Johannes der Täufer* (1989), 254n5.

6. See Hengel, *Zealots,* index under "Josephus"; David M. Rhoads, *Israel in Revolution 6–74 CE: A Political History Based on the Writings of Josephus* (Philadelphia: Fortress, 1976), 159–73; Ernst, *Johannes der Täufer* (1989), 254–55. A prime example is the reference in *J.W.* 6.312–313 to the biblical oracle that sparked the war against the Romans by prophesying that "at that time" (the time of the outbreak of the Jewish revolt against Rome), one from the Jews' country would become the ruler of the world. Josephus reinterprets this messianic oracle as a reference to Vespasian's assumption of emperorship.

7. See Ernst, *Johannes der Täufer* (1989), 254–56, who also notes other discrepancies from the Gospel accounts such as the place of John's execution (Machaerus in Transjordan rather than Galilee) and the name of Herodias's first husband (Herod rather than

Philip). Cf. Mason, *Josephus and the New Testament*, 151: "It is a mark of Josephus' complete isolation from the early Christian world of thought that he devotes significantly more space to John the Baptist than to Jesus—even if we admit his account of Jesus as it stands." For a similar argument, see Meier, *Marginal Jew*, 2:19–20.

8. Heinrich Graetz, *Geschichte der Juden von den ältesten Zeit bis auf die Gegenwart*, 11 vols. (Leipzig, Germany: Leiner, 1853–68), 3:277n3.

9. As summarized by Nir, "Josephus' Account of John the Baptist," 34–35.

10. Étienne Nodet, "Jésus et Jean-Baptiste selon Josephe," *Revue biblique* 82 (1985): 326 argues that the passage fits well in its context and that its final phrase takes up its first one; it is therefore not an interpolation but a typical Josephan excursus.

11. See, for example, the long retelling of the Daniel story in *Ant.* 10.186–281.

12. See, for example, the Essenes who refuse to swear an oath of allegiance to Herod the Great in *Ant.* 15.371–379; also the Pharisees Pollion and Samaias, who are mentioned in the same context.

13. See, for example, Daniel, who offends Nebuchadnezzar and is thrown into the fiery furnace because he refuses to worship the king's image (*Ant.* 10.212–215); also Josephus's positive attitude toward the "scholars" responsible for tearing down the golden eagle placed on the gate of the Temple by Herod the Great (*Ant.* 17.149–167). The latter passage is similar to the one about Herod Antipas executing John, since in both cases Josephus goes on to emphasize that God rightly judged the Herodian ruler responsible for the execution (*Ant.* 17.168, 18.119). Cf. Mason, *Josephus and the New Testament*, 152: "In keeping with the thesis of *Antiquities*, Antipas was quickly punished by God for his misdeeds."

14. See Mason, *Josephus and the New Testament*, 153: Josephus's Baptist "is a persecuted philosopher of the sort familiar to Josephus' readers, condemned by an unjust ruler for his fearless virtue." Besides the examples given in the previous note, see also Josephus's description of the fate of Socrates in *Ag. Ap.* 2.262–268. I am indebted to correspondence with Mason for his help with this paragraph.

15. Among the Mandeans, true baptism *(maṣbuta)*, which is performed by a priest, is distinguished from other immersions that are self-administered; see Drower, *Mandaeans*, 101–2. For the relation between the Mandeans and John the Baptist, see the section on the Mandeans in chap. 1.

16. Nir, "Josephus' Account of John the Baptist," 51, 62.

17. For discussion of Moore's term "normative Judaism," see Jacob Neusner, "Judaism in Late Antiquity," *Judaism* 15 (1966): 230–40; Sanders, *Paul and Palestinian Judaism*, 34; Wayne A. Meeks, "Judaism, Hellenism, and the Birth of Christianity," in *Paul Beyond the Judaism/Hellenism Divide*, ed. Troels Engberg-Pedersen (Louisville, Ky.: Westminster John Knox Press, 2001), 22–23.

18. Nir, "Josephus' Account of John the Baptist," 45.

19. For Josephus's spiritual experimentation with the Essenes, of whom the Qumran sectarians were probably a part, as well as with the Pharisees and Sadducees, see his *Life* 10–11. Such experimentation is a philosophical trope (cf. Justin, *Dialogue* 1–8 and see Philip A. Harland, "Journeys in Pursuit of Wisdom: Thessalos and Other Seekers," in *Travel and Religion in Antiquity*, ed. Philip A. Harland, Studies in Christianity and Judaism [Waterloo, Ontario: Wilfred Laurier University Press, 2011], 123–40), but Josephus does seem to know a lot about the Essenes (see *J.W.* 2.119–161; *Ant.* 18.18–22).

....

Appendix 4: Was John from a Priestly Background?

1. For nine other points of overlap, see Joseph A. Fitzmyer, *Luke the Theologian: Aspects of His Teaching* (New York: Paulist Press, 1989), 35–36; cf. already Brown, *Birth of the Messiah,* 38–39.

2. See Meier, *Marginal Jew,* 216.

3. See Fitzmyer, *Gospel According to Luke,* 1:357.

4. Bultmann, *History of the Synoptic Tradition,* 294–95.

5. Dibelius, *From Tradition to Gospel,* 123–24.

6. For others with similar views, see Brown, *Birth of the Messiah,* 245n34; Ernst, *Johannes der Täufer* (1989), 270–71. Fitzmyer, *Gospel According to Luke,* 1:309, reckons with a Baptist source in Luke 1:5–25, 57–66b. This is identical to the source discerned by Martin Dibelius, "Jungfrauensohn und Krippenkind: Untersuchungen zur Geburtsgeschichte Jesu im Lukas-Evangelium," in *Botschaft und Geschichte: Gesammelte Aufsätze: Erster Band—Zur Evangelienforschung* (1932; repr., Tübingen, Germany: J. C. B. Mohr [Paul Siebeck], 1953), 3, though Dibelius calls the end of the source 1:66a; it is evident from p. 3, n. 5, however, that he means only to exclude the last clause, "For the hand of the Lord was with him," so that (as for Fitzmyer) the source ends with the significant question, "What then will this child be?"

7. Brown, *Birth of the Messiah,* 266. See also Ernst, *Johannes der Täufer* (1989), 270–72; Bovon, *Luke,* 1:32: "Luke transmits the Jewish context and the details of Jewish ceremonies almost flawlessly."

8. Betz, "Was John the Baptist an Essene?" 23. See also Brownlee, "John the Baptist," 35–37; Ferguson, *Baptism in the Early Church,* 87.

9. Lawrence, *Washing in Water,* 104; cf. pp. 30–31 (on priestly washing in the Old Testament) and 52–56 (on priestly washing in Second Temple literature). The references include Exod. 29:4, 30:18–21, 40:30–32; Num. 8:4–22; Lev. 16:4, 24, 22:6; 2 Chr. 4:6; Josephus, *Ant.* 3.258; 8.85–87; Philo, *Spec. Laws,* 1.117–119.

10. Cf. Hans-Josef Klauck, "Die Frage der Sündenvergebung in der Perikope von der Heilung des Gelähmten (Mk 2,1–12 parr.)," *Biblische Zeitschrift* N.F. 25 (1981): 236–37.

11. See Shaver, "Prophet Elijah in the Literature of the Second Temple Period," 195.

12. T. Ps.-J. Deut. 33:11 makes the connection between Elijah's priesthood and his sacrifice on Mount Carmel: "May you accept with goodwill the sacrifice from the hands of Elijah the priest on Mount Carmel" (my trans.).

13. On the tradition of the priesthood of Elijah, see Ginzberg, *Legends of the Jews,* 6:316n3. On the date of LAB, see Daniel Harrington in *Old Testament Pseudepigrapha* 2:299, who argues for a pre-70 CE dating, and Howard Jacobson, *A Commentary on Pseudo-Philo's Liber Antiquitatum Biblicarum,* 1:199–210, who argues for a post-70 CE dating, perhaps as late as the aftermath of the Bar Kochba Revolt.

Later instances of the equation of Elijah with Phinehas include Num. Rab. 21:3; Pirqe R. El. (ed. Friedlander) 29 (p. 213; see n. 9) and 47 (p. 371); T. Ps-J. Exod. 6:18; Num. 25:11–12; Deut. 30:4. On Elijah as a priest without reference to Phinehas, see T. Ps.-J. Deut. 30:4, 33:11 (see previous note); b. B. Meṣ 114a-b; Aphrahat, *Demonstrations* 15.5; Epiphanius, *Panarion* 55 [*Against the Melchizedekians* 33].3.5.

. . . .
Appendix 5: The "Others" in Josephus, *Antiquities* 18.118

1. Meier, *Marginal Jew*, 2:58; on the question of the authenticity of the *Testimonium Flavianum*, see app. 2, n. 2 (p. 223).

2. Meier, *Marginal Jew*, 2:58.

3. Loeb Classical Library Josephus, vol. 9, p. 82, note c.

4. Roland Schütz, *Johannes der Täufer*, Abhandlungen zur Theologie des Alten und Neuen Testaments 50 (Zürich: Zwingli, 1967), 24.

5. Even less likely is the interpretation of Rothschild, "'Echo of a Whisper,'" 1:260, who suggests, on the basis of Luke 3:10–14, that John's original audience was tax collectors and soldiers, so "the others" were people outside those circles. But there is no hint of such an original audience in Josephus's own report about John, and the Lukan notice is likely unhistorical; see the section "Challenges to the Thesis of John's Militancy" in chap. 6.

6. See Webb, *John the Baptizer*, 36, who notes that "others" suggests an expansion beyond those identified in 18.117 as "the Jews."

7. A variation on this thesis is provided by Kirsopp Lake in his note to his Loeb Classical Library translation of Eusebius, *Hist. eccl.* 1.11: "It would seem to mean that John was preaching to ascetics and suggested baptism as a final act of perfection. This explains the reference to 'when the rest collected.' So long as John preached to ascetics Herod did not mind but was disturbed when the rest of the public manifested interest." But nothing in the Josephan contexts suggests the asceticism of the addressees, only their virtue.

8. For example, κελεύοντα τοῖς Ἰουδαίοις τοῖς ἀρετὴν ἐπασκοῦσιν καὶ τοῖς τὰ πρὸς ἀλλήλους δικαιοσύνῃ καὶ πρὸς τὸν θεὸν εὐσεβείᾳ χρωμένοις βαπτισμῷ συνιέναι ("commanding those Jews who were exercising virtue and practicing justice toward one another and piety toward God, to come together by means of baptism").

9. Private communication, September 11, 2015.

10. Winger's interpretation would be more likely if Josephus's phrase τῶν ἄλλων had lacked the anaphoric (see glossary) definite article.

11. Webb, *John the Baptizer*, 36.

12. Ibid., 369n44.

13. Samuel Tobias Lachs, "John the Baptist and His Audience," *Gratz College Annual of Jewish Studies* 4 (1975): 29; cf. Webb, *John the Baptizer*, 369n44. On the meaning of ἡ περίχωρος τοῦ Ἰορδάνου, see Davies and Allison, *Matthew*, 1:297.

14. For example, *Ant.* 1.15, 155, 192, 4.137, 8.262, 12.241, 13.245, 247, 14.186, 16.37, 19.290; *J.W.* 2.397; *Apion* 1.59, 60, 211, 2.117, 138, 189, 234, 271, 280, 287.

15. Some scholars have argued that the soldiers who approached John for advice in Luke 3:14 may have included Gentiles; see, for example, Marshall, *Gospel of Luke*, 143: "They were not Roman soldiers, but the forces of Herod Antipas, stationed in Peraea (possibly including non-Jews, like his father's army, Jos. *Ant.* 17.198f.)." As shown in the section "Challenges to the Thesis of John's Militancy" in chap. 6, however, this passage is probably unhistorical; Luke 3:14, therefore, cannot be used as additional backup for the idea that the "others" in *Ant.* 18.118 are Gentiles.
. . . .
Appendix 6: Knut Backhaus's Interpretation of Acts 19:1–7

1. Backhaus, *Die "Jüngerkreise" des Täufers Johannes*, 190–213.

2. Backhaus, *Die "Jüngerkreise" des Täufers Johannes*, 212 asserts that there were

other "semi-Christian" groups oriented to the historical Jesus and his proclamation but without access to the Easter proclamation; however, he cites no examples (he rejects in n. 580 the assertion that the Q community was one such group). His closest analogy is the individual and groups described in Matt. 7:22–23//Luke 13:25–27, Mark 9:38–41// Luke 9:49–50; Acts 19:13–16, who cast out demons in Jesus's name but lack a deeper connection to the Jesus movement. But these exorcists for hire are scarcely disciples of Jesus in the way Backhaus is positing of those described in Acts 19:1–6.

3. Backhaus, Die "Jüngerkreise" des Täufers Johannes, 208, himself notes the discrepancy that although the Ephesian "disciples" are called "believers" (πιστεύσαντες) in 19:2, they are implicitly exhorted to believe in Jesus in 19:4 (ἵνα πιστεύσωσιν . . . εἰς τὸν Ἰησοῦν). See Käsemann, "Disciples of John the Baptist," 136: "It is not easy to understand why men who have already 'come over' [to Christianity] should have to have explained to them the role of the Baptist as the forerunner of Jesus, and the significance of his baptism as merely a baptism of repentance; this would seem necessary only for those who were still disciples of the Baptist."

4. For Backhaus, Die "Jüngerkreise" des Täufers Johannes, 207, this immediate baptism is evidence that the Ephesian "disciples" have a previous history of adherence to Jesus, since the proclamation about him in 19:4 is so short, in contrast to missionary proclamations elsewhere in Acts (2:14–36, 3:12–26, 4:8–12, 10:34–43, 13:16–41). But the Phillipian jailer is converted after hearing only the exhortation, "Believe in the Lord Jesus, and you will be saved, you and your household" (Acts 16:31), and the Ethiopian eunuch is converted in a similarly quick manner (8:35–38). Such conversions may not be psychologically plausible, but they fit Luke's narrative style.

5. See Käsemann, "Disciples of John the Baptist," 141, who speaks of "an overpainting by Luke of the tradition he had to hand." Backhaus, Die "Jüngerkreise" des Täufers Johannes, 196 acknowledges that Käsemann has convinced the majority of scholars of the correctness of this view.

There is a certain analogy between Luke's nontechnical use of the "disciples"/"believing" vocabulary for adherents of the Baptist and the nontechnical use of the term "believers" for Christians in an early Meccan sura of the Qur'ān (85:4–8; see Marshall, "Christianity in the Qur'ān," 8, and cf. the discussion of the Qur'ānic analogy in chap. 1).
....

Appendix 7: The "Day-Baptists"

1. On this passage, see the section on the Pseudo-Clementine literature in chap. 1; on its date, see n. 53 in that chapter (pp. 167–68).

2. Kurt Rudolph, Antike Baptisten: Zu den Überlieferungen über frühjüdische und -christliche Taufsekten, Sitzungsberichte der Sächsischen Akademie der Wissenschaften zu Leipzig, Philologisch-Historische Klasse 121.4 (Berlin: Akademie-Verlag, 1981), 8; on Mandean baptismal terminology, see the section "The Mandean Literature" in chap. 1.

3. ἔφασκον δὲ μηδένα ζωῆς τυγχάνειν αἰωνίου, εἰ μή τι ἂν καθ' ἑκάστην βαπτίζοιτο τις ἐν ὕδατι, ἀπολουόμενός τε καὶ ἁγνιζόμενος ἀπὸ πάσης αἰτίας. Trans. from Frank Williams, The Panarion of Epiphanius of Salamis: Book I (Sects 1–46), Nag Hammadi and Manicaean Studies 63 (Leiden, the Netherlands: Brill, 2009), 45.

4. On the relation between the Tosefta passage about the "Dawn Immersers" and the reports from the Church Fathers about "Day-Baptists," see S. Krauss, "The Jews in the Works of the Church Fathers," Jewish Quarterly Review 5 (1892): 127n2; Saul Lieberman, Tosefeth Rishonim: A Commentary Based on Manuscripts of the Tosefta and Works of the Rishonim and Midrashim in Manuscripts and Rare Editions (1936–38; repr., New

York: Jewish Theological Seminary, 1999), 4:160; Rudolph, *Antike Baptisten,* 9; Ferguson, *Baptism in the Early Church,* 72–73.

5. Liddell, Scott, and Jones, *Greek-English Lexicon,* 770 (I).

6. On the manuscripts and editions of the Tosefta, see Günter Stemberger, *Introduction to the Talmud and Midrash,* 2nd ed. (Edinburgh: T&T Clark, 1996), 158–61.

7. See, for example, m. Yad. 4:6–8.

8. As suggested in private correspondence by Shamma Friedman (July 11, 2013) and Aaron Amit (March 3, 2016). See already Lieberman, *Tosefeth Rishonim,* 4:160.

9. The sort of impurities that may have worried such constant bathers is suggested by b. Ber. 22a, where the "Dawn Immersers" are concerned with nocturnal emissions, which render a man ritually unclean.

10. The Pharisees' response in the Vienna text implies that it is impossible for anyone—even the rigorist Dawn Immersers—to rid their body of all impurity. My thanks to Aaron Amit (see above, n. 8) for helping me understand this form of the text.

11. The rabbinic sources speak of self-immersion (טבל; cf. Jastrow, *Dictionary of the Targumim,* 517). The Christian sources use a compound with βαπτιστής, a noun that is related to the verb βαπτίζειν. In the Pseudo-Clementines this verb in the active or passive voice signifies a one-time rite administered by another, but in the middle voice it signifies a self-administered washing to restore ritual purity after contamination; see Jürgen Wehnert, "Taufvorstellungen in den Pseudoklementinen," 2:1078.

12. See Anders Hultgård, "The Mandean Water Ritual in Late Antiquity," in *Ablution, Initiation, and Baptism,* ed. David Hellholm et al., BZNW 176 (Berlin: De Gruyter, 2011), 1:69–70.

13. See the section "The Mandean Literature" in chap. 1.

14. See Wehnert, "Taufvorstellungen in den Pseudoklementinen," 2:1082–84.

. . . .

Appendix 8: John the Baptist's Use of Isaiah 40:3

1. For the texts, see Marcus, *Way of the Lord,* 12–17.

2. For other Mark/Q overlaps, see Marcus, *Mark,* 1:51–53, and subject index under "Q."

3. Cf. Morna D. Hooker, "Isaiah in Mark," in *Isaiah in the New Testament,* ed. Steve Moyise and Maarten J. J. Menken, The New Testament and the Scriptures of Israel (London: T&T Clark, 2005), 35–36.

4. See Dodd, *Historical Tradition in the Fourth Gospel;* Brown, *Gospel According to John;* Martin Hengel, *The Johannine Question* (London: SCM; Philadelphia: Trinity Press International, 1989); Richard Bauckham, *The Testimony of the Beloved Disciple: Narrative, History, and Theology in the Gospel of John* (Grand Rapids, Mich.: Baker Academic, 2007).

5. See Dodd, *Historical Tradition in the Fourth Gospel,* 252–53.

6. On the programmatic nature of Mark 1:1–3, see Marcus, *Way of the Lord,* 12–47.

7. M. J. J. Menken, "The Quotation from Isa. 40,3 in John 1,23," *Biblica* 66 (1985): 190–205 is probably correct in his surmise that this is why the Evangelist substitutes the second imperative in Isa. 40:3, "make straight" (εὐθύνατε), for the first one, "prepare" (ἑτοιμάσατε): "prepare" too easily invokes Elijah.

8. See the section "The Returning Elijah as a Legal Arbitrator" in chap. 3 and the section "Jesus as Sole Spirit Bestower" in chap. 4 for Elijah's association with the Jordan River (2 Kgs. 2), which is in the Judean wilderness. For another famous passage about Elijah in the wilderness, see 1 Kgs. 19.

9. Dodd, *Historical Tradition in the Fourth Gospel,* 253.

10. See app. 4, and cf. Stegemann, *The Library of Qumran,* 216.

11. See chap. 4, "Jesus as Sole Spirit Bestower."

12. See 1QS 8:13–16: "They shall separate from the session of perverse men to go to the wilderness, there to prepare the way of the LORD, as it is written, 'In the wilderness prepare the way of the Lord, make straight in the desert a highway for our God.' This means the study of the Law, which God commanded by means of Moses [for them] to do according to everything that has been revealed from age to age, and as the prophets have revealed by His holy spirit" (*Dead Sea Scrolls Electronic Library* trans. alt.); cf. 1QS 9:19–21.

13. See Bultmann, *History of the Synoptic Tradition,* 246; Willi Marxsen, *Mark the Evangelist* (Nashville: Abingdon, 1969), 34–38; Meier, *Marginal Jew,* 2:87–88n115; Taylor, *Immerser,* 20, 25–29; Klawans, *Impurity and Sin,* 141; Ferguson, *Baptism in the Early Church,* 87.

14. See Marcus, *Way of the Lord.*

15. See Taylor, *Immerser,* 27; Marjo C.A. Korpel and Johannes C. de Moor, *The Structure of Classical Hebrew Poetry: Isaiah 40–55,* Oudtestamentische Studiën 41 (Leiden, the Netherlands: Brill, 1998), 24; Eugene Ulrich and Peter W. Flint, *Qumran Cave 1.II—The Isaiah Scrolls: Part 2, Introductions, Commentary, and Textual Variants,* Discoveries in the Judaean Desert 32 (Oxford: Clarendon Press, 2010), 110.

16. See, for example, Lam. Rab. 1.2.23; Pesiq. Rab. [Braude] 29/30 B.4; Kallah Rab. 5:3; cf. Charlesworth, "John the Baptizer," 357: "Many Jews, as did Jesus and his followers, most likely interpreted the text to mean that the Voice is in the wilderness."

17. The only difference is that in John 1:23 the abbreviated citation is prefaced by the single word ἐγώ ("I am"): ἐγὼ φωνὴ βοῶντος ἐν τῇ ἐρήμῳ· εὐθύνατε τὴν ὁδὸν κυρίου.

18. Meier, *Marginal Jew,* 2:87–88 drives too sharp a wedge between John and his predecessors when he says that if John did apply Isa. 40:3 to himself as "the voice crying in the wilderness," then "on this one point he stands with the New Testament tradition over against both the MT and the self-understanding of Qumran."

· ·

Appendix 9: The Baptist in the Slavonic Version of Josephus's *Jewish War*

1. See also Louis H. Feldman, "Flavius Josephus Revisited: The Man, His Writings, and His Significance," in *Aufstieg und Niedergang der römischen Welt: Geschichte und Kultur Roms im Spiegel der neueren Forschung,* Teil 2, Principat, Band 21, Halbband 2, *Religion* (Berlin: De Gruyter, 1984), 771–72.

2. Cf. 1QS 6:6–8: "In any place where is gathered the ten-man quorum, someone must always be engaged in study of the Law, day and night, continually, each one taking his turn. The general membership will be diligent together for the first third of every night of the year, reading aloud from the Book, interpreting Scripture and praying together."

· ·

Appendix 10: Apocalyptic Belief and Perfectionism

1. John Bogart, *Orthodox and Heretical Perfectionism in the Johannine Community as Evident in the First Epistle of John,* Society of Biblical Literature Dissertation Series 33 (Missoula, Mont.: Scholars Press, 1977), 104–6.

2. Ibid., 144.

3. It does not seem to me that all the examples of Christian perfectionism cited in R. Newton Flew, *The Idea of Perfection in Christian Theology: An Historical Study of*

the Christian Ideal for the Present Life (Oxford: Clarendon Press, 1968) are catalyzed by burning eschatology.

4. See Stanley M. Burgess, "Montanist and Patristic Perfectionism," in *Reaching Beyond: Chapters in the History of Perfectionism*, ed. Stanley M. Burgess (Peabody, Mass.: Hendrickson Publishers, 1986), 119–25.

5. See Cohn, *Pursuit of the Millennium*, 174–76.

6. See Richard T. Hughes, "Christian Primitivism as Perfectionism: From Anabaptists to Pentecostals," in *Reaching Beyond*, ed. Burgess, 230–31; Edith L. Blumhofer, "Purity and Preparation: A Study in the Pentecostal Perfectionist Heritage," in *Reaching Beyond*, ed. Burgess, 257–59; Catherine Wessinger, ed., *The Oxford Handbook of Millennialism* (New York: Oxford University Press, 2011), 496–97.

7. Schweitzer, *Quest of the Historical Jesus*, 323.

8. Gershom G. Scholem, *Major Trends in Jewish Mysticism* (1941; repr., New York: Schocken, 1961), 318–19. Cf. Scholem's more extended treatment of this linkage in the chapter "Redemption Through Sin" in Gershom Scholem, *The Messianic Idea in Judaism and Other Essays on Jewish Spirituality* (London: Allen & Unwin, 1971), 78–141, esp. 110.

9. See Aviezer Ravitzky, *Messianism, Zionism, and Jewish Religious Radicalism*, Chicago Studies in the History of Judaism (Chicago: University of Chicago Press, 1996), 184–88.

10. See Ada Rapoport-Albert, "God and the Zaddik as the Two Focal Points of Hasidic Worship," in *Essential Papers on Hasidism: Origins to Present*, ed. Gershon David Hundert, Essential Papers on Jewish Studies (1977; repr. New York: New York University Press, 1991), 299–329.

11. Bryan Wilson, *Magic and the Millennium* (New York: Harper & Row, 1973), 211, 214, 232, 307, 447n113.

12. See Robert Jay Lifton, *Destroying the World to Save It: Aum Shinrikyō, Apocalyptic Violence, and the New Global Terrorism* (New York: Henry Holt, 1999), 25, 124, 204–5, 240, 253, 267, 323.

. . . .

Appendix 11: The Meaning of "Purification" in John 3:25

1. See above, chap. 2, n. 30 (pp. 175–76), for the localization of Aenon.

2. I am not necessarily treating John's account of the dispute as historical; I am asking what sense the Fourth Evangelist makes of it.

3. Backhaus, *Die "Jüngerkreise" des Täufers Johannes*, 256.

4. Brown, *Gospel According to John*, 1:151–52.

5. See, for example, John 13:10–11, 15:3; 1 John 1:7–9; Eph. 5:26; Tit. 2:14; Heb. 1:3, 9:14, 22–24; 2 Pet. 1:9; cf. Rudolf Schnackenburg, *The Gospel According to St. John* (New York: Crossroad, 1968–82), 1:414; Backhaus, *Die "Jüngerkreise" des Täufers Johannes*, 258.

6. See the survey in Harrington, *Purity Texts*.

7. See the chart "*Kathar* Words in the Septuagint" at the end of this appendix; this sorts the nuances of these words into four categories: Levitical impurity, moral impurity, idolatry, and neutral/ambiguous. The largest of these categories is Levitical impurity. Unlike Klawans, *Impurity and Sin*, 26–28, I do not regard the impurity caused by idolatry as a subset of moral impurity; it seems to me that it falls somewhere midway between Klawans's categories of "ritual" and "moral," and indeed points up the somewhat artificial nature of the division.

8. See chap. 4, n 73 (p. 203).

9. See the halakhic topics listed in Qimron and Strugnell, *Qumran Cave 4*, 147; they include the purity of those who slaughter the red heifer, the purity of hides, the purity

of liquid streams, the impurity of the leper at various stages of the healing process, and the impurity of those who touch human bones. The positions on these questions espoused by the "we" group, perhaps the Zadokites, who were the germ of the Qumran community, are counterposed to those espoused by two other groups, apparently the Hasmonean priests ("you") and the Pharisees ("they"; ibid., 175).

10. Here the issues discussed are whether a jar of olives needs to be opened "to let out the moisture that exudes from the fruit, lest the moisture 'render it susceptible to uncleanness'" (Lev. 11:34, 38; cf. Herbert Danby, *The Mishnah: Translated from the Hebrew with Introduction and Brief Explanatory Notes* [Oxford: Oxford University Press, 1933], 429n4) and how long the uncleanness of anointing oil lasts (the oil may be impure because of contact with Gentiles; cf. Joseph M. Baumgarten, "The Essene Avoidance of Oil and the Laws of Purity," in *Studies in Qumran Law* [Leiden, the Netherlands: Brill, 1977], 88–97).

11. The issues addressed include whether or not the priest who slaughters the red heifer (Num. 19:1–4) must be in a state of ritual purity, whether or not the scriptures render the hands unclean, whether or not an unbroken stream of liquid is clean, and whether or not a master is responsible for an injury committed by his slave.

12. The issues addressed concern the circumstances in which an unclean person communicates his impurity to others and whether or not certain objects are susceptible to uncleanness.

The Mandaeans, an Aramaic-speaking, baptizing sect that traces its teaching back to John (see the section "The Mandean Literature" in chap. 1), differ from Jews in their view of what causes ritual impurity. See Drower, *Mandaeans*: among the things that can cause pollution are standing water (p. 50), urine (pp. 42, 56–57), and even breath (p. 31); cf. Lupieri, *Mandaeans*, 15–16, 19–22.

13. See Shaye J. D. Cohen, "Menstruants and the Sacred in Judaism and Christianity," in *The Significance of Yavneh and Other Essays in Jewish Hellenism* (1991; repr., Tübingen, Germany: Mohr Siebeck, 2010), 410–14; Charlotte Elisheva Fonrobert, *Menstrual Purity: Rabbinic and Christian Reconstructions of Biblical Gender*, Contraversions (Stanford, Calif.: Stanford University Press, 2000), 172–209.

14. On these categories, see above, n. 7.

GLOSSARY

Anaphoric Relating to something previously referred to.

Baraita An "extraneous" rabbinic tradition, that is, one not found in the Mishnah, but supposed to be Tannaitic and quoted anonymously in the Talmud.

BCE "Before the Common (or Christian) Era"; corresponds to old-style BC ("Before Christ").

CE "Common (or Christian) Era"; corresponds to old-style AD (*Anno Domini* = "in the year of the Lord").

Gentile Non-Jewish; a non-Jew.

Gezerah shavah Literally "equal category" (Hebrew); the rabbinic interpretative rule whereby two biblical passages that contain identical or similar expressions are regarded as treating the same topic.

Halakhic Having to do with the observance of Jewish law.

Josephus Palestinian Jewish historian who fought against the Romans in the revolt of 66–73 CE and then went over to their side, ending his days as a guest of the ruling Flavian dynasty (hence sometimes called "Flavius Josephus") in Rome, where he wrote an account of the war *(Jewish War)* and a history of the Jews from the beginning to his own era *(Jewish Antiquities)* as well as an autobiography (*Life*).

Ketiv Literally "written," that is, how a word is written in the MT (see below), as opposed to *Qere,* how it is read. The latter is a device for suggesting scribal emendations.

LXX The Septuagint, the Greek translation of the Old Testament.

Miqveh Jewish ritual bath.

Mishnah Authoritative compilation of Jewish law, promulgated under the authority of R. Judah the Prince at the beginning of the third century CE.

MT Masoretic Text, the traditional form of the original Hebrew and Aramaic text of the Old Testament.

Parablepsis An eyeskip, that is, the eye of a scribe jumping to a later place in a text being copied. Frequent cause of scribal error.

Pericope A self-contained unit within the scripture; from the Greek for "cut around."

Q Hypothetical source for the material shared by Matthew and Luke but not present in Mark.

Qere See *Ketiv* above.

Qumran Site in the Judaean Desert, near the Dead Sea, where the Dead Sea Scrolls were found; home of a dualistic Jewish sect identical to or related to the Essenes.

Supersessionism, supersessionist The belief that the church has replaced (superseded) Israel as the people of God, and one who holds that belief.

Synecdoche A figure of speech in which the part stands for the whole or vice versa, for example, "thirty head of cattle" or "the city was sleeping."

Synoptic Gospels   Matthew, Mark, and Luke, the first three Gospels in the New Testament; so-called because they can be laid out easily in parallel columns and read synoptically ("with one eye").

Talmud   Literally "learning"; commentary on the Mishnah that appeared in two forms, the Palestinian (or Jerusalem) Talmud (fifth century CE) and the Babylonian (major redaction in the eighth century CE).

Tanna, Tannaitic   "Repeater" of traditions; a rabbinic teacher from the time of Hillel and Shammai (early first century CE) to R. Judah the Prince and his contemporaries at the beginning of the third century CE. The opinions of the Tannaim (plural of Tanna) are compiled in the Mishnah. "Tannaitic" = pertaining to the Tannaim.

Tosefta   Literally "addition," that is, to the Mishnah: a collection of Tannaitic sayings not included in the Mishnah.

Two-Source Theory   The theory, accepted by the majority of scholars on the Synoptic Gospels, that Mark was the earliest Gospel and the major source for Matthew and Luke, who also had available to them another source, Q.

BIBLIOGRAPHY

Abegg, Martin, Peter Flint, and Eugene Ulrich. *The Dead Sea Scrolls Bible: The Oldest Known Bible*. San Francisco: HarperSanFrancisco, 1999.

Ackroyd, P. R., and C. F. Evans, eds. *The Cambridge History of the Bible*. Vol. 1, *From the Beginnings to Jerome*. Cambridge: Cambridge University Press, 1970.

Afnán, Muḥammad, and William S. Hatcher. "Western Islamic Scholarship and Bahá'í Origins." *Religion* 15 (1985): 29–51.

Airlie, Stuart. "Private Bodies and the Body Politic in the Divorce Case of Lothar II." *Past and Present* 161 (1998): 3–38.

Alexander, Philip S. "'In the Beginning': Rabbinic and Patristic Exegesis of Genesis 1:1." In *The Exegetical Encounter Between Jews and Christians in Late Antiquity*, edited by Emmanouela Grypeou and Helen Spurling, 1–29. Jewish and Christian Perspective Series 18. Leiden, the Netherlands: Brill, 2009.

——. "Jewish Believers in Early Rabbinic Literature (2d to 5th Centuries)." In *Jewish Believers in Jesus: The Early Centuries*, edited by Oskar Skarsaune and Reidar Hvalvik, 659–709. Peabody, Mass.: Hendrickson Publishers, 2007.

——. "'The Parting of the Ways' from the Perspective of Rabbinic Judaism." In *Jews and Christians: The Parting of the Ways A.D. 70 to 135: The Second Durham-Tübingen Research Symposium on Earliest Christianity and Judaism (Durham, September 1989)*, edited by J. D. G. Dunn, 1–25. WUNT 66. Tübingen, Germany: J. C. B. Mohr (Paul Siebeck); Grand Rapids, Mich.: Eerdmans, 1992.

Allison, Dale C. "'Elijah Must Come First.'" *JBL* 103 (1984): 256–58.

——. *Constructing Jesus: Memory, Imagination, and History*. Grand Rapids, Mich.: Baker Academic Press, 2010.

——. *The Intertextual Jesus: Scripture in Q*. Valley Forge, Pa.: Trinity Press International, 2000.

——. "Jesus and the Covenant: A Response to E. P. Sanders." *Journal for the Study of the New Testament* 29 (1987): 57–78.

——. *Jesus of Nazareth: Millenarian Prophet*. Minneapolis: Fortress, 1998.

——. *The New Moses: A Matthean Typology*. Edinburgh: T&T Clark, 1993.

——. "A Plea for Thoroughgoing Eschatology." *JBL* 113 (1994): 651–68.

——. *Resurrecting Jesus: The Earliest Christian Tradition and Its Interpreters*. New York: T&T Clark, 2005.

Alon, Gedaliah. "The Levitical Uncleanness of Gentiles." In *Jews, Judaism and the Classical World: Studies in Jewish History in the Times of the Second Temple and Talmud*, 46–89. Jerusalem: Magnes Press, 1977.

Anderson, A. A. *2 Samuel*. Word Biblical Commentary 11. Dallas: Word Books, 1989.

Arberry, Arthur J. *The Koran Interpreted*. New York: Macmillan, 1955.

Aune, David Edward. *The Cultic Setting of Realized Eschatology in Early Christianity.* Novum Testamentum Supplements 28. Leiden, the Netherlands: Brill, 1972.

Backhaus, Knut. "Echoes from the Wilderness: The Historical John the Baptist." In *Handbook for the Study of the Historical Jesus,* vol. 1, *How to Study the Historical Jesus,* edited by Tom Holmén and Stanley E. Porter, 1747–85. Leiden, the Netherlands: Brill, 2011.

———. *Die "Jüngerkreise" des Täufers Johannes: eine Studie zu den religionsgeschichtlichen Ursprüngen des Christentums.* Paderborner Theologische Studien 19. Paderborn, Germany: Ferdinand Schöningh, 1991.

Baldensperger, Wilhelm. *Der Prolog des vierten Evangeliums: sein polemisch-apologetischer Zweck.* Freiburg, Germany: J. C. B. Mohr (Paul Siebeck), 1898.

Balyuzi, H. M. *Edward Granville Browne and the Bahá'í Faith.* London: George Ronald, 1970.

Bamberger, Bernard J. *Proselytism in the Talmudic Period.* 1939. Reprint, New York: KTAV Publishing House, 1968.

Bammel, Ernst. "The Farewell Discourse of the Evangelist John and Its Jewish Heritage." *Tyndale Bulletin* 44 (1993): 103–16.

———. Review of *Die "Jüngerkreise" des Täufers Johannes,* by Klaus Backhaus. *Journal of Theological Studies* 43 (1992): 583–84.

Barclay, John. "Apologetics in the Jewish Diaspora." In *Jews in the Hellenistic and Roman Cities,* edited by John R. Bartlett, 129–48. London: Routledge, 2002.

Barclay, John M. G. *Against Apion.* Flavius Josephus, Translation and Commentary 10. Leiden, the Netherlands: Brill, 2007.

———. *Jews in the Mediterranean Diaspora from Alexander to Trajan (323 BCE–117 CE).* Edinburgh: T&T Clark, 1996.

———. *Paul and the Gift.* Grand Rapids, Mich.: Eerdmans, 2015.

Barrera, Julio Trebolle. "Elijah." In *Encyclopedia of the Dead Sea Scrolls,* edited by Lawrence H. Schiffman and James C. VanderKam, 1:246. New York: Oxford University Press, 2000.

Barrett, C. K. *A Critical and Exegetical Commentary on the Acts of the Apostles.* International Critical Commentary. 2 vols. Edinburgh: T&T Clark, 1994–98.

———. *The Gospel According to St John: An Introduction with Commentary and Notes on the Greek Text.* London: S.P.C.K., 1962.

Barth, Karl. *The Word of God and the Word of Man.* 1928. Reprint, New York: Harper, 1957.

Bauckham, Richard. *The Testimony of the Beloved Disciple: Narrative, History, and Theology in the Gospel of John.* Grand Rapids, Mich.: Baker Academic, 2007.

Bauer, Walter. *Das Johannesevangelium.* Handbuch zum Neuen Testament 6. Tübingen, Germany: J. C. B. Mohr (Paul Siebeck), 1925.

———. *Orthodoxy and Heresy in Earliest Christianity.* 1934. English translation, Philadelphia: Fortress, 1971.

———. *Rechtgläubigkeit und Ketzerei im ältesten Christentum.* 1934. Reprint, Beiträge zur historischen Theologie 10. Tübingen, Germany: Mohr, 1964.

Bauer, Walter; William F. Arndt; F. Wilbur Gingrich; and Frederick W. Danker. *A Greek-English Lexicon of the New Testament and Other Early Christian Literature.* 2nd ed. Chicago and London: University of Chicago Press, 1979.

Baumgarten, Joseph M. "The Essene Avoidance of Oil and the Laws of Purity." In *Studies in Qumran Law,* 88–97. Leiden, the Netherlands: Brill, 1977.

——. "The Exclusion of *Netinim* and Proselytes in 4Q Florilegium." In *Studies in Qumran Law*, 75–87. Leiden, the Netherlands: Brill, 1977.

——. "Gentiles." In *Encyclopedia of the Dead Sea Scrolls*, edited by Lawrence H. Schiffman and James C. VanderKam, 1:304–6. New York: Oxford University Press, 2000.

——. "Proselytes." In *Encyclopedia of the Dead Sea Scrolls*, edited by Lawrence H. Schiffman and James C. VanderKam, 2:700–701. New York: Oxford University Press, 2000.

——. "4Q500 and the Ancient Conception of the Lord's Vineyard." *Journal of Jewish Studies* 40 (1989): 1–6.

Baur, Ferdinand Christian. *Paul the Apostle of Jesus Christ: His Life, Works, His Epistles and Teaching.* 1875–76. Reprint, Peabody, Mass.: Hendrickson Publishers, 2003. Originally published in German 1845.

Beare, Frank W. *The Earliest Records of Jesus: A Companion to the Synopsis of the First Three Gospels by Albert Huck.* New York: Abingdon, 1962.

Beck, Edmund, ed. *Des heiligen Ephraem des Syrers Hymnen contra haereses.* Corpus scriptorum christianorum orientalium 169–170/Scriptores Syri 76–77. Leuven, Belgium: Imprimerie Orientaliste L. Durbecq, 1957.

Becker, Eve-Marie. "'Kamelhaare . . . und wilder Honig.'" In *Die bleibende Gegenwart des Evangeliums: Festschrift für Otto Merk zum 70.Geburtstag,* edited by Roland Gebauer and Martin Meiser, 13–28. Marburg, Germany: N. G. Elwert, 2003.

Berg, Shane A. "An Elite Group within the *Yahad:* Revisiting 1QS 8–9." In *Qumran Studies: New Approaches, New Questions,* edited by Michael Thomas Davis and Brent A. Strawn, 161–77. Grand Rapids, Mich.: Eerdmans, 2007.

Bernett, Monika. "Roman Imperial Cult in the Galilee: Structures, Functions, and Dynamics." In *Religion, Ethnicity, and Identity in Ancient Galilee: A Region in Transition,* edited by Jürgen Zangenberg, Harold W. Attridge, and Dale B. Martin, 337–56. Tübingen, Germany: Mohr Siebeck, 2007.

Bernstein, Moshe J. "Pesher Habakkuk." In *Encyclopedia of the Dead Sea Scrolls,* edited by Lawrence H. Schiffman and James C. VanderKam, 2.647-650. New York: Oxford University Press, 2000.

Betz, Otto. "Was John the Baptist an Essene?" *Bible Review* 6, no. 6 (1990): 18–25.

Blake, William. *The Marriage of Heaven and Hell.* In *The Complete Poetry and Prose of William Blake,* newly rev. ed., edited by D. V. Erdman, 33–44. New York: Anchor Books, 1988.

Bloom, Harold. *The Anxiety of Influence: A Theory of Poetry.* New York: Oxford University Press, 1973.

Blumhofer, Edith L. "Purity and Preparation: A Study in the Pentecostal Perfectionist Heritage." In *Reaching Beyond: Chapters in the History of Perfectionism,* edited by Stanley M. Burgess, 257–82. Peabody, Mass.: Hendrickson Publishers, 1986.

Böcher, Otto. "Ass Johannes der Täufer kein Brot (Luk. vii. 33)?" *NTS* (1971–72): 90–92.

——. "Wasser und Geist." In *Verborum Veritas: Festschrift für Gustav Stählin zum 70. Geburtstag,* edited by Otto Böcher and Klaus Haacker, 197–209. Wuppertal, Germany: Theologischer Verlag Rolf Brockhaus, 1970.

Bogart, John. *Orthodox and Heretical Perfectionism in the Johannine Community as Evident in the First Epistle of John.* Society of Biblical Literature Dissertation Series 33. Missoula, Mont.: Scholars Press, 1977.

Böhlemann, Peter. *Jesus und der Täufer: Schlüssel zur Theologie und Ethik des Lukas.*

Society for New Testament Studies Monograph Series 99. Cambridge: Cambridge University Press, 1997.

Boling, Robert G., and G. Ernest Wright. *Joshua: A New Translation with Introduction and Commentary.* AB 6. Garden City, N.Y.: Doubleday, 1982.

Bond, Helen. "Dating the Death of Jesus: Memory and the Religious Imagination." *NTS* 59 (2013): 461–75.

Boulluec, Alain Le. *La notion d'hérésie dans la littérature grecque, IIe-IIIe siècles.* Paris: Etudes Augustiniennes, 1985.

Bovon, François. *Luke.* Hermeneia. 3 vols. Minneapolis: Fortress, 2002–12.

Boyarin, Daniel. *Border Lines: The Partition of Judaeo-Christianity.* Divinations. Philadelphia: University of Pennsylvania Press, 2004.

Braun, Herbert. *Qumran und das Neue Testament.* 2 vols. Tübingen, Germany: J. C. B. Mohr (Paul Siebeck), 1966.

Briggs, Charles Augustus. *The Messiah of the Gospels.* New York: Scribner's, 1894.

Brooke, George J. *4Q Florilegium in the Context of Early Jewish Exegetical Method.* Journal for the Study of the Old Testament: Supplement Series 2. Sheffield, U.K.: JSOT Press, 1985.

Broshi, Magen. "Qumran: Archaeology." In *Encyclopedia of the Dead Sea Scrolls,* edited by Lawrence H. Schiffman and James C. VanderKam, 733–39. New York: Oxford University Press, 2000.

Brown, Raymond E. *The Birth of the Messiah: A Commentary on the Infancy Narratives in Matthew and Luke.* Anchor Bible Reference Library. New York: Doubleday, 1979.

———. *The Death of the Messiah: From Gethsemane to the Grave; A Commentary on the Passion Narratives in the Four Gospels.* Anchor Bible Reference Library. New York: Doubleday, 1994.

———. *The Gospel According to John.* AB 29 and 29A. Garden City, N.Y.: Doubleday, 1966–70.

———. *An Introduction to New Testament Christology.* New York: Paulist Press, 1994.

———. "Jesus and Elisha." *Perspective* 12 (1971): 85–104.

———. "Three Quotations from John the Baptist in the Gospel of John." *CBQ* 22 (1960): 292–98.

Browne, Edward Granville. "The Bábís of Persia." *Journal of the Royal Asiatic Society* 3 (1889): 485–526, 881–1009.

———. *A Year Amongst the Persians: Impressions as to the Life, Character, & Thought of the People of Persia Received During Twelve Months' Residence in the Country in the Years 1887–1888.* 1893. Reprint, New York: Macmillan; Cambridge: Cambridge University Press, 1926.

Brownlee, W. H. "John the Baptist in the New Light of Ancient Scrolls." In *The Scrolls and the New Testament,* edited by Krister Stendahl, 33–53. London: SCM, 1957.

Brundage, James A. "Matrimonial Politics in Thirteenth-Century Aragon: Moncada v. Urgel." 1980. Reprint, in *Sex, Law and Marriage in the Middle Ages,* 271–82. Collected Studies Series CS397. Aldershot, U.K.: Ashgate, 1993.

Buber, Martin. *The Prophetic Faith.* New York: Macmillan, 1949.

Buck, Christopher. *Symbol and Secret: Qur'an Commentary in Bahá'u'láh's Kitáb-i Íqán.* Studies in the Bábí and Bahá'í Religions 7. Los Angeles: Kalimát Press, 1995.

———. "A Unique Eschatological Interface: Bahá'u'lláh and Cross-Cultural Messianism." In *In Iran,* 157–79. Studies in Bábí and Bahá'í History 3. Los Angeles: Kalimát Press, 1986.

Buckley, Jorunn Jacobsen, and Ezio Abrile. "Mandaean Religion." In *Encyclopedia of*

Religion, edited by Lindsey Jones, 8:5634–40. Detroit: Macmillan Reference USA, 2005.

Bultmann, Rudolf. "Die Bedeutung der neuerschlossenen mandäischen und manichäischen Quellen für das Verständnis des Johannesevangeliums." *Zeitschrift für die neutestamentliche Wissenschaft und die Kunde der älteren Kirche* 24 (1925): 100–146.

———. *The Gospel of John: A Commentary.* 1941. English translation, Philadelphia: Westminster, 1971.

———. *History of the Synoptic Tradition.* 1921. English translation, New York: Harper & Row, 1963.

———. "Der religionsgeschichtliche Hintergrund des Prologs zum Johannes-Evangelium." In *Eucharistērion: Studien zur Religion und Literatur des Alten und Neuen Testaments; Hermann Gunkel zum 60. Geburtstage, dem 23. Mai 1922 dargebracht von seinen Schülern und Freunden,* 2 Teil, *Zur Religion und Literatur des Neuen Testaments,* 1–26. Forschungen zur Religion und Literatur des Alten und Neuen Testaments 36.2//N.F. 19.2. Göttingen, Germany: Vandenhoeck & Ruprecht, 1923.

———. *Theology of the New Testament.* 2 vols. in 1. New York: Scribner's, 1951–55.

Burgess, Stanley M. "Montanist and Patristic Perfectionism." In *Reaching Beyond: Chapters in the History of Perfectionism,* edited by Stanley M. Burgess, 119–46. Peabody, Mass.: Hendrickson Publishers, 1986.

Bury, J. B. *History of the Later Roman Empire from the Death of Theodosius I to the Death of Justinian.* London: Macmillan, 1923.

Charlesworth, James H. "John the Baptizer and Qumran Barriers in the Light of the *Rule of the Community.*" In *The Provo International Conference on the Dead Sea Scrolls: Technological Innovations, New Texts, and Reformulated Issues,* edited by Donald W. Parry and Eugene Ulrich, 353–75. Studies on the Texts of the Desert of Judah 30. Leiden, the Netherlands: Brill, 1999.

———. "Les Odes de Salomon et les manuscrits de la mer morte." *Revue biblique* 77 (1970): 522–49.

———, ed. *The Odes of Solomon: The Syriac Texts.* Society of Biblical Literature Texts and Translations 13/SBL Pseudepigrapha Series 7. Chico, Calif.: Scholars Press, 1977.

———, ed. *The Old Testament Pseudepigrapha.* 2 vols. Garden City, N.Y.: Doubleday, 1983.

Chaves, Mark. *Congregations in America.* Cambridge, Mass.: Harvard University Press, 2004.

Childs, Brevard S. *Isaiah.* Old Testament Library. Louisville: Westminster John Knox Press, 2001.

———. *The Struggle to Understand Isaiah as Christian Scripture.* Grand Rapids, Mich.: Eerdmans, 2004.

Chryssides, George D. *The Advent of Sun Myung Moon: The Origins, Beliefs, and Practices of the Unification Church.* New York: St. Martin's Press, 1991.

Clines, David, ed. *The Dictionary of Classical Hebrew.* 8 vols. Sheffield, U.K.: Sheffield Academic Press, 1993–2011.

Cogan, Mordechai, and Hayim Tadmor. *II Kings: A New Translation with Introduction and Commentary.* AB 11. New York: Doubleday, 1988.

Cohen, Shaye J. D. *The Beginnings of Jewishness: Boundaries, Varieties, Uncertainties.* Berkeley: University of California Press, 1999.

———. "Is 'Proselyte Baptism' Mentioned in the Mishnah? The Interpretation of M. Pesahim 8.8." 1994. Reprint, in *The Significance of Yavneh and Other Essays in Jewish Hellenism,* 316–28. Tübingen, Germany: Mohr Siebeck, 2010.

———. "Menstruants and the Sacred in Judaism and Christianity." 1991. Reprint, in *The*

Significance of Yavneh and Other Essays in Jewish Hellenism, 393–415. Tübingen, Germany: Mohr Siebeck, 2010. Essay originally published 1991.

——. "Were Pharisees and Rabbis the Leaders of Communal Prayer and Torah Study in Antiquity? The Evidence of the New Testament, Josephus, and the Early Church Fathers." In *Evolution of the Synagogue: Problems and Progress,* edited by Howard Clark Kee and Lynn H. Cohick, 89–105. Harrisburg, Pa.: Trinity Press International, 1999.

Cohn, Norman. *The Pursuit of the Millennium: Revolutionary Millenarians and Mystical Anarchists of the Middle Ages.* Rev. ed. New York: Oxford University Press, 1970.

Cole, J. R. I. "Bahā' Allāh." In *Encyclopaedia Iranica.* 1988. Reprint, 2011. Available online at http://www.iranicaonline.org/articles/baha-allah.

Collins, Billie Jean, ed. *The SBL Handbook of Style.* 2nd ed. Atlanta: SBL Press, 2014.

Collins, John J. *Daniel: A Commentary on the Book of Daniel.* Hermeneia. Minneapolis: Fortress, 1993.

——. *The Scepter and the Star: The Messiahs of the Dead Sea Scrolls and Other Ancient Literature.* Anchor Bible Reference Library. New York: Doubleday, 1995.

Cotton, Hannah M., and Ada Yardeni. *Aramaic, Hebrew and Greek Documentary Texts from Naḥal Ḥever and Other Sites: With an Appendix Containing Alleged Qumran Texts (the Seiyâl Collection II).* Discoveries in the Judaean Desert 27. Oxford: Clarendon Press, 1997.

Cragg, Kenneth. *Jesus and the Muslim: An Exploration.* London: Allen & Unwin, 1985.

Crandall, Keith A. "Convergent and Parallel Evolution." In *Encyclopedia of Evolution,* edited by Mark Pagel, 1:201–5. Oxford: Oxford University Press, 2002.

Crossan, John Dominic. *The Historical Jesus: The Life of a Mediterranean Jewish Peasant.* San Francisco: Harper, 1991.

——. *In Parables: The Challenge of the Historical Jesus.* New York: Harper & Row, 1973.

Cullmann, Oscar. *The Johannine Circle.* Philadelphia: Fortress; London: SPCK, 1976.

——. "Die literarischen und historischen Probleme des pseudoklementinischen Romans." In *Vorträge und Aufsätze 1925–1962,* edited by Karlfried Fröhlich, 225–31. Tübingen, Germany: J. C. B. Mohr, 1966.

——. *Le problème littéraire et historique du roman pseudo-clémentin: Étude sur le rapport entre le Gnosticisme et le Judéo-Christianisme.* Etudes d'Histoire et de Philosophie Religieuses 23. Paris: Libraire Félix Alcan, 1930.

——. "Samaria and the Origins of the Christian Mission." In *The Early Church: Studies in Early Christian History and Theology,* edited by A. J. B. Higgins, 185–92. 1953–54. English translation, Philadelphia: Westminster, 1956.

——. "Ὁ ὀπίσω μου ἐρχόμενος." In *The Early Church: Studies in Early Christian History and Theology,* edited by A. J. B. Higgins, 177–82. 1947. English translation, Philadelphia: Westminster, 1956.

Danby, Herbert. *The Mishnah: Translated from the Hebrew with Introduction and Brief Explanatory Notes.* Oxford: Oxford University Press, 1933.

Darwin, Charles. *The Annotated Origin: A Facsimile of the First Edition of* On the Origin of Species. 1859. Reprint, Cambridge, Mass.: Belknap Press of Harvard University Press, 2009.

Davies, Philip R. "War of the Sons of Light Against the Sons of Darkness." In *Encyclopedia of the Dead Sea Scrolls,* edited by Lawrence H. Schiffman and James C. VanderKam, 2:965–68. New York: Oxford University Press, 2000.

Davies, W. D., and Dale C. Allison. *A Critical and Exegetical Commentary on the Gospel*

According to Saint Matthew. International Critical Commentary. 3 vols. Edinburgh: T&T Clark, 1988–97.

de Boer, Martinus C. "Jesus the Baptizer: 1 John 5:5–8 and the Gospel of John." *JBL* 107 (1988): 87–106.

de Jonge, M. "The Use of the Word 'Anointed' in the Time of Jesus." *Novum Testamentum* 8 (1966): 132–48.

deSilva, David A. *Introducing the Apocrypha.* Grand Rapids, Mich.: Baker Academic, 2002.

De Vries, Simon J. *Prophet Against Prophet: The Role of the Micaiah Narrative (I Kings 22) in the Development of Early Prophetic Tradition.* Grand Rapids, Mich.: Eerdmans, 1978.

Dibelius, Martin. *From Tradition to Gospel.* 1933. English translation, Cambridge: James Clarke, 1971.

——. "Jungfrauensohn und Krippenkind: Untersuchungen zur Geburtsgeschichte Jesu im Lukas-Evangelium." In *Botschaft und Geschichte: Gesammelte Aufsätze: Erster Band—Zur Evangelienforschung,* 1–78. 1932. Reprint, Tübingen, Germany: J. C .B. Mohr (Paul Siebeck), 1953.

——. *Die urchristliche Überlieferung von Johannes der Täufer.* Forschungen zur Religion und Literatur des Alten und Neuen Testaments 15. Göttingen, Germany: Vandenhoeck & Ruprecht, 1911.

Dodd, C. H. *Historical Tradition in the Fourth Gospel.* Cambridge: Cambridge University Press, 1963.

Dodd, Charles Harold. *The Parables of the Kingdom.* 1935. Reprint, London: Nisbet, 1948.

Donaldson, Terence L. *Judaism and the Gentiles: Jewish Patterns of Universalism (to 135 CE).* Waco, Tex.: Baylor University Press, 2007.

Drawnel, Henryk. *An Aramaic Wisdom Text from Qumran: A New Interpretation of the Levi Document.* Journal for the Study of Judaism: Supplement Series 86. Leiden, the Netherlands: Brill, 2004.

Drijvers, Hans. "Syrian Christianity and Judaism." In *Jews Among Pagans and Christians in the Roman Empire,* edited by Judith Lieu, John North, and Tessa Rajak, 124–46. London: Routledge, 1994.

Drower, E. S. *The Mandaeans of Iraq and Iran: Their Cults, Customs, Magic, Legends, and Folklore.* Leiden, the Netherlands: Brill, 1962.

Dunn, James D. G. *Baptism in the Holy Spirit.* London: SCM, 1970.

Edersheim, Alfred. *The Life and Times of Jesus the Messiah.* 1883. Reprint, Grand Rapids, Mich.: Eerdmans, 1971.

Edsman, Carl-Martin. *Le baptême du feu.* Acta seminarii neotestamentici upsaliensis 9. Leipzig, Germany: Alfred Lorentz; Uppsala, Sweden: A.-B. Lundequistska Bokhandeln, 1940.

Edwards, Douglas E. "Dress and Ornamentation." In *Anchor Bible Dictionary,* 2:232–38. New York: Doubleday, 1992.

Ehrlich, Arnold Bogumil. *Randglossen zur hebräischen Bibel.* 1914. Reprint, Hildesheim, Germany: G. Olms, 1968.

Ehrman, Bart D. *The Orthodox Corruption of Scripture: The Effect of Early Christological Controversies on the Text of the New Testament.* New York: Oxford University Press, 1993.

Eichler, Margrit. "Charismatic Prophets and Charismatic Saviors." *Mennonite Quarterly Review* 55 (1981): 45–61.

Elliott, J. K. *The Apocryphal New Testament: A Collection of Apocryphal Christian Literature in an English Translation.* Oxford: Clarendon Press, 1993.

Enslin, Morton. "Once Again: John the Baptist." *Religion in Life* 27 (1958): 557–66.

Epstein, Isadore, ed. *Hebrew-English edition of the Babylonian Talmud.* 30 vols. London: Soncino Press, 1990.

Ernst, Josef. *Johannes der Täufer, der Lehrer Jesu?* Biblische Bücher 2. Freiburg, Germany: Herder, 1994.

———. *Johannes der Täufer: Interpretation–Geschichte–Wirkungsgeschichte.* BZNW 53. Berlin: De Gruyter, 1989.

Evans, C. F. *Saint Luke.* New Testament Commentaries. London: SCM; Philadelphia: Trinity Press International, 1990.

Evans, Ernest. *Tertullian's Homily on Baptism.* London: S.P.C.K., 1964.

Fehsenfeld, Martha Dow, and Lois More Overbeck, eds. *The Letters of Samuel Beckett.* Vol. 3, *1956–1965.* Cambridge: Cambridge University Press, 2014.

Feldman, Louis H. "Flavius Josephus Revisited: The Man, His Writings, and His Significance." In *Aufstieg und Niedergang der römischen Welt: Geschichte und Kultur Roms im Spiegel der neueren Forschung.* Teil 2, Principat, Band 21, Halbband 2, *Religion,* edited by Hildegard Temporini and Wolfgang Haase, 763–862. Berlin: De Gruyter, 1984.

Ferda, Tucker S. "John the Baptist, Isaiah 40, and the Ingathering of the Exiles." *Journal for the Study of the Historical Jesus* 10 (2012): 154–88.

Ferguson, Everett. *Baptism in the Early Church: History, Theology, and Liturgy in the First Five Centuries.* Grand Rapids, Mich.: Eerdmans, 2009.

Fields, Weston W. *The Dead Sea Scrolls: A Full History.* Vol. 1, *1947–1960.* Leiden, the Netherlands: Brill, 2009.

Fishbane, Michael. *Biblical Interpretation in Ancient Israel.* Oxford: Clarendon Press, 1985.

Fitzmyer, Joseph A. *The Gospel According to Luke.* AB 28 and 28A. New York: Doubleday, 1981–85.

———. *Luke the Theologian: Aspects of His Teaching.* New York: Paulist Press, 1989.

Flew, R. Newton. *The Idea of Perfection in Christian Theology: An Historical Study of the Christian Ideal for the Present Life.* Oxford: Clarendon Press, 1968.

Flusser, David. "The Baptism of John and the Dead Sea Sect [Hebrew]." In *Essays on the Dead Sea Scrolls in Memory of E. L. Sukenik,* 209–38. Tel Aviv: Hekhal Ha-Sefer, 1961.

———. *Judaism of the Second Temple Period.* 2 vols. Grand Rapids, Mich.: Eerdmans; Jerusalem: Hebrew University Magnes Press, 2007–09.

Flusser, David, and R. Steven Notley. *Jesus.* 1997. Reprint, Jerusalem: Hebrew University Magnes Press, 2001.

Fonrobert, Charlotte Elisheva. *Menstrual Purity: Rabbinic and Christian Reconstructions of Biblical Gender.* Contraversions. Stanford, Calif.: Stanford University Press, 2000.

Foote, Shelby. *The Civil War: A Narrative.* 3 vols. New York: Random House, 1958–74.

Franklin, R. W., ed. *The Poems of Emily Dickinson: Reading Edition.* Cambridge, Mass.: Belknap Press of Harvard University Press, 1999.

Franzmann, Majella. "Mandaeism." In *Religion Past and Present,* edited by Betz, Hans Dieter; Don S. Browning; Bernd Janowski; and Eberhard Jüngel. 8:21–22. 1998. Reprint, Leiden, the Netherlands: Brill, 2010.

Frey, Jörg. *Die johanneische Eschatologie.* WUNT 96. 3 vols. Tübingen, Germany: J. C. B. Mohr (Paul Siebeck), 1997–2000.

Fujita, Shozo. "The Metaphor of Plant in Jewish Literature of the Intertestamental Period." *Journal for the Study of Judaism in the Persian, Hellenistic, and Roman Periods* 7 (1976): 30–45.

Fuller, Reginald H. *The Foundations of New Testament Christology.* New York: Scribner's, 1965.

García Martínez, Florentino. *The Dead Sea Scrolls Translated: The Qumran Texts in English.* Leiden, the Netherlands: Brill, 1994.

Gerdmar, Anders. *Roots of Theological Anti-Semitism: German Biblical Interpretation and the Jews, from Herder and Semler to Kittel and Bultmann.* Studies in Jewish History and Culture 20. Leiden, the Netherlands: Brill, 2009.

Gibson, Shimon, and Joan E. Taylor. "Roads and Passes Round Qumran." *Palestine Exploration Quarterly* 140 (2008): 225–27.

Ginsburg, Christian D. *The Essenes: Their History and Doctrines; The Kabbalah: Its Doctrines, Development, and Literature.* 1864. Reprint, London: Routledge & Kegan Paul, 1955.

Ginzberg, Louis. *The Legends of the Jews.* 7 vols. Philadelphia: Jewish Publication Society, 1909–38.

———. *An Unknown Jewish Sect.* 1922. English translation, Moreshet Series 1. New York: Jewish Theological Seminary, 1976.

Gnilka, Joachim. "Die essenischen Tauchbäder und die Johannestaufe." *Revue de Qumran* 3 (1961): 184–207.

Goodacre, Mark. *The Case Against Q: Studies in Markan Priority and the Synoptic Problem.* Harrisburg, Pa.: Trinity Press International, 2002.

———. "Fatigue in the Synoptics." *NTS* 44 (1998): 45–58.

Goodman, Martin. *The Ruling Class of Judaea: The Origins of the Jewish Revolt Against Rome A.D. 66–70.* Cambridge: Cambridge University Press, 1987.

Goodman, Martin, and Geza Vermes. *The Essenes According to the Classical Sources.* Oxford Centre Textbooks 1. Sheffield, U.K.: JSOT Press, 1989.

Grabbe, Lester L. "The Pharisees: A Response to Steve Mason." In *Judaism in Late Antiquity,* edited by Alan J. Avery-Peck and Jacob Neusner, 34–47. Handbook of Oriental Studies. Section 1: The Near and Middle East. Vol. 53. Leiden, the Netherlands: Brill, 2000.

Graetz, Heinrich. *Geschichte der Juden von den ältesten Zeiten bis auf die Gegenwart.* 11 vols. Leipzig, Germany: Leiner, 1853–68.

———. *History of the Jews.* Vol. 2. 1863. English translation, Philadelphia: Jewish Publication Society, 1893.

Grant, Frederick C. *Hellenistic Religions: The Age of Syncretism.* Library of Liberal Arts. New York: Liberal Arts Press, 1953.

Gray, John. *I & II Kings.* 1964. Reprint, Old Testament Library. London: SCM, 1977.

Greenfield, Jonas C., Michael E. Stone, and Esther Eshel. *The Aramaic Levi Document: Edition, Translation, Commentary.* Studia in Veteris Testamenti pseudepigraphica 19. Leiden, the Netherlands: Brill, 2004.

Griffith, Sidney H. *The Bible in Arabic: The Scriptures of the "People of the Book" in the Language of Islam.* Jews, Christians, and Muslims from the Ancient to the Modern World. Princeton, N.J.: Princeton University Press, 2013.

Hammond, Philip C. *The Nabateans—Their History, Culture and Archaeology.* Studies in Mediterranean Archaeology 37. Gothenburg, Sweden: P. Åströms Förlag, 1973.

Hanneken, Todd R. *The Subversion of the Apocalypses in the Book of Jubilees.* Society of Biblical Literature Early Judaism and Its Literature 34. Leiden, the Netherlands: Brill, 2012.

Harland, Philip A. "Journeys in Pursuit of Wisdom: Thessalos and Other Seekers." In

Travel and Religion in Antiquity, edited by Philip A. Harland, 123–40. Studies in Christianity and Judaism. Waterloo, Ontario: Wilfrid Laurier University Press, 2011.

Harnack, Adolf. *What is Christianity?* 1900. Reprint. Gloucester, Mass.: Peter Smith, 1978.

Harrington, Hannah K. *The Purity Texts.* Companion to the Qumran Scrolls. London: T&T Clark, 2004.

Hartmann, Michael. *Der Tod Johannes des Täufers: eine exegetische und rezeptionsgeschichtliche Studie auf dem Hintergrund narrativer, intertextueller und kulturanthropologischer Zugänge.* Stuttgarter Biblische Beiträge. Stuttgart: Verlag Katholisches Bibelwerk, 2001.

Hauptman, Judith. "How Old Is the Haggadah?" *Judaism* 51 (2001): 5–18.

Hayes, Christine E. *Gentile Impurities and Jewish Identities: Intermarriage and Conversion from the Bible to the Talmud.* New York: Oxford University Press, 2002.

Hays, Richard B. *Echoes of Scripture in the Letters of Paul.* New Haven, Conn.: Yale University Press, 1989.

Heilman, Samuel C., and Menachem M. Friedman. *The Rebbe: The Life and Afterlife of Menachem Mendel Schneerson.* Princeton, N.J.: Princeton University Press, 2010.

Hengel, Martin. *The Charismatic Leader and His Followers.* 1968. English translation, SNTW. New York: Crossroad, 1981.

——. *The Johannine Question.* London: SCM; Philadelphia: Trinity Press International, 1989.

——. *The Zealots: Investigations Into the Jewish Freedom Movement in the Period from Herod I Until 70 A.D.* 1961. English translation, Edinburgh: T&T Clark, 1989.

Hicks-Keeton, Jill. "Rewritten Gentiles: Conversion to 'the Living God' in Ancient Judaism and Christianity." Ph.D. diss., Duke University, 2014.

Hill, Andrew E. *Malachi: A New Translation with Introduction and Commentary.* AB 25D. New York: Doubleday, 1998.

Hobbs, T. R. *2 Kings.* Word Biblical Commentary 13. Waco, Tex.: Word Books, 1985.

Hoehner, Harold W. *Herod Antipas.* Society for New Testament Studies Monograph Series 17. Cambridge: Cambridge University Press, 1972.

Hoffmann, Paul. *Studien zur Theologie der Logienquelle.* Neutestamentliche Abhandlungen 8. Münster (Westphalia), Germany: Aschendorff, 1975.

Holmén, Tom. "Doubts About Double Dissimilarity: Restructuring the Main Criterion of Jesus-of-History Research." In *Authenticating the Words of Jesus,* ed. Bruce Chilton and Craig A. Evans, 47–80. New Testament Studies and Tools 28.1. Leiden, the Netherlands: Brill, 1999.

Holt, James. "John. King of England." *Encyclopaedia Britannica.* Online ed. https://www.britannica.com/biography/John-king-of-England. Accessed May 26, 2018.

Hooker, Morna D. "Isaiah in Mark." In *Isaiah in the New Testament,* edited by Steve Moyise and Maarten J. J. Menken, 35–49. The New Testament and the Scriptures of Israel. London: T&T Clark, 2005.

Horsley, Richard A., and Neil Asher Silberman. *The Message and the Kingdom: How Jesus and Paul Ignited a Revolution and Transformed the Ancient World.* Minneapolis: Fortress, 1997.

Hughes, Richard T. "Christian Primitivism as Perfectionism: From Anabaptists to Pentecostals." In *Reaching Beyond: Chapters in the History of Perfectionism,* edited by Stanley M. Burgess, 213–55. Peabody, Mass.: Hendrickson Publishers, 1986.

Hultgård, Anders. "The Mandean Water Ritual in Late Antiquity." In *Ablution, Initiation, and Baptism,* edited by David Hellholm, Tor Vegge, Øyvind Norderval, and Christer Hellholm, 1:69–99. BZNW 176. Berlin: De Gruyter, 2011.

Humphreys, Colin J., and W. G. Waddington. "The Jewish Calendar, a Lunar Eclipse and the Date of Christ's Crucifixion." *Tyndale Bulletin* 43 (1992): 331–51.

Hyman, Aaron. *Torah Haketubah Vehamessurah.* Tel Aviv: Dvir, 1979.

Innitzer, Theodor. *Johannes der Täufer nach der heiligen Schrift und der Tradition.* Vienna: Verlag von Mayer, 1908.

Jacobson, Howard. *A Commentary on Pseudo-Philo's* Liber Antiquitatum Biblicarum *with Latin Text and English Translation.* Arbeiten zur Geschichte des antiken Judentums und des Urchristentums 31. Leiden, the Netherlands: Brill, 1996.

Jassen, Alex P. *Mediating the Divine: Prophecy and Revelation in the Dead Sea Scrolls and Second Temple Judaism.* Studies on the Texts of the Desert of Judah, 68. Leiden, the Netherlands: Brill, 2007.

Jastrow, Marcus. *A Dictionary of the Targumim, the Talmud Babli and Yerushalmi, and the Midrashic Literature.* 1886–1903. Reprint, New York: Judaica, 1982.

Jensen, Morten Horning. *Herod Antipas in Galilee: The Literary and Archaeological Sources on the Reign of Herod Antipas and Its Socio-Economic Impact on Galilee.* WUNT, 2.215. Tübingen, Germany: Mohr Siebeck, 2006.

———. "Message and Minting: The Coins of Herod Antipas in the Second Temple Context as a Source for Understanding the Religio-Political and Socio-Economic Dynamics of Early First Century Galilee." In *Religion, Ethnicity, and Identity in Ancient Galilee: A Region in Transition,* edited by Jürgen Zangenberg, Harold W. Attridge, and Dale B. Martin, 277–313. Tübingen, Germany: Mohr Siebeck, 2007.

Jeremias, Joachim. *Infant Baptism in the First Four Centuries.* 1958. English translation, London: SCM, 1960.

———. *New Testament Theology.* Part 1, *The Proclamation of Jesus.* New York: Scribner's, 1971.

———. *The Parables of Jesus.* 2nd rev. ed., New York: Scribner's, 1972.

Johnson, Luke Timothy. "The New Testament's Anti-Jewish Slander and the Conventions of Ancient Polemic." *JBL* 108 (1989): 419–41.

———. *The Real Jesus: The Misguided Quest for the Historical Jesus and the Truth of the Traditional Gospels.* San Francisco: HarperSanFrancisco, 1996.

Jones, F. Stanley. *An Ancient Jewish Christian Source on the History of Christianity: Pseudo-Clementine Recognitions 1.27–71.* Texts and Translations 37. Atlanta: Scholars Press, 1995.

Käsemann, Ernst. "The Disciples of John the Baptist in Ephesus." In *Essays on New Testament Themes,* 136–48. The New Testament Library. Philadelphia: Fortress, 1964.

Kähler, Martin. *The So-Called Historical Jesus and the Historic Biblical Christ.* 1892. English translation, Philadelphia: Fortress, 1964.

Kaplan, Steven. *The Beta Israel (Falasha) in Ethiopia: From Earliest Times to the Twentieth Century.* New York: New York University Press, 1992.

Katz, Hayah. "'He Shall Bathe in Water; Then He Shall Be Pure': Ancient Immersion Practice in the Light of Archaeological Evidence." *Vetus Testamentum* 63 (2012): 369–80.

Kazmierski, Carl R. "The Stones of Abraham: John the Baptist and the End of Torah (Matt. 3,7–10 par. Luke 3,7–9)." *Biblica* 68 (1987): 22–40.

Keith, Chris, and Anthony Le Donne, eds. *Jesus, Criteria, and the Demise of Authenticity.* London: T&T Clark, 2012.

Kelhoffer, James A. *The Diet of John the Baptist: "Locusts and Wild Honey" in Synoptic and Patristic Interpretation.* WUNT 176. Tübingen, Germany: Mohr Siebeck, 2005.

Kesselring, K. J. *The Northern Rebellion of 1569: Faith, Politics and Protest in Elizabethan England*. New York: Palgrave Macmillan, 2007.

Klauck, Hans-Josef. "Die Frage der Sündenvergebung in der Perikope von der Heilung des Gelähmten (Mk 2,1–12 parr.)." *Biblische Zeitschrift* N.F. 25 (1981): 223–48.

Klausner, Joseph. *Jesus of Nazareth: His Life, Times, and Teaching*. 1925. English translation, New York: Macmillan, 1929.

——. *The Messianic Idea in Israel: From Its Beginning to the Completion of the Mishnah*. New York: Macmillan, 1955.

Klawans, Jonathan. *Impurity and Sin in Ancient Judaism*. New York: Oxford University Press, 2000.

——. "Notions of Gentile Impurity in Ancient Judaism." *AJS Review* 20 (1995): 285–312.

Kloppenborg, John S. "On Dispensing with Q? Goodacre on the Relation of Luke to Matthew." *NTS* 49 (2003): 210–36.

Klorman, Bat-Zion Eraqi. "The Messiah Shukr Kuḥayl II (1868–75) and His Tithe (*Maʿaśer*): Ideology and Practice as a Means to Hasten Redemption," in *Essential Papers on Messianic Movements and Personalities in Jewish History*, ed. Marc Saperstein, 456–72. New York: New York University Press, 1992.

Knibb, Michael A. *The Qumran Community*. Cambridge Commentaries on Writings of the Jewish and Christian World, 200 BC to AD 200. Vol. 2. Cambridge: Cambridge University Press, 1987.

——. "Rule of the Community." In *Encyclopedia of the Dead Sea Scrolls*, edited by Lawrence H. Schiffman and James VanderKam, 2.793-97. New York: Oxford University Press, 2000.

Koehler, Ludwig, and Walter Baumgartner. *The Hebrew and Aramaic Lexicon of the Old Testament: Study Edition*. Leiden, the Netherlands: Brill, 2001.

Kokkinos, Nikos. "Crucifixion in A.D. 36: The Keystone for Dating the Birth of Jesus." In *Chronis, Kairos, Christos: Nativity and Chronological Studies Presented to Jack Finegan*, edited by Jerry Vardaman and Edwin M. Yamauchi, 133–63. Winona Lake, Ind.: Eisenbrauns, 1989.

Korpel, Marjo C. A., and Johannes C. de Moor. *The Structure of Classical Hebrew Poetry: Isaiah 40–55*. Oudtestamentische Studiën 41. Leiden, the Netherlands: Brill, 1998.

Kraeling, Carl H. *John the Baptist*. New York: Scribner's, 1951.

Krauss, S. "The Jews in the Works of the Church Fathers." *Jewish Quarterly Review* 5–6 (1892–94): 122–57, 82–89, 225–61.

Kugel, James L. *How to Read the Bible: A Guide to Scripture, Then and Now*. New York: Free Press, 2007.

——. *Traditions of the Bible: A Guide to the Bible as It Was at the Start of the Common Era*. Cambridge, Mass.: Harvard University Press, 1998.

Kuhn, Heinz-Wolfgang. *Enderwartung und gegenwärtiges Heil: Untersuchungen zu den Gemeindeliedern von Qumran mit einem Anhang über Eschatologie und Gegenwart in der Verkündigung Jesu*. Studien zur Umwelt des Neuen Testaments 4. Göttingen, Germany: Vandenhoeck & Ruprecht, 1966.

Kunin, Seth D. *Juggling Identities: Identity and Authenticity Among the Crypto-Jews*. New York: Columbia University Press, 2009.

Labahn, Antje. "Aus dem Wasser kommt das Leben: Waschungen und Reinigungsriten in früjüdischen Texten." In *Ablution, Initiation, and Baptism*, edited by David Hellholm, Tor Vegge, Øyvind Norderval, and Christer Hellholm, 1:157–219. BZNW 176. Berlin: De Gruyter, 2011.

Lachs, Samuel Tobias. "John the Baptist and His Audience." *Gratz College Annual of Jewish Studies* 4 (1975): 28–32.

Lake, Kirsopp. "The Date of Herod's Marriage with Herodias and the Chronology of the Gospels." *Expositor* 4 (1912): 462–77.

Lamb, David T. "'A Prophet Instead of You' (1 Kings 19.16): Elijah, Elisha, and Prophetic Succession." In *Prophecy and Prophets in Ancient Israel. Proceedings of the Oxford Old Testament Seminar,* edited by John Day, 172–87. Library of Hebrew Bible/Old Testament Studies 531. New York: T&T Clark, 2010.

Lämmer, Manfred. "Griechische Wettkämpfe in Galiläa unter der Herrschaft des Herodes Antipas." *Kölner Beiträge zur Sportwissenschaft* 5 (1976): 37–67.

Lange, Armin, and Matthias Weigold. *Biblical Quotations and Allusions in Second Temple Jewish Literature.* Journal of Ancient Judaism: Supplement Series 5. Göttingen: Vandenhoeck & Ruprecht, 2011.

Lapide, Cornelius à. *S. Matthew's Gospel—Chaps. I. to IX.* Vol. 1 of *The Great Commentary.* London: John Hodges, 1893.

Laufen, Rudolf. *Die Doppelüberlieferungen der Logienquelle und des Markusevangeliums.* Bonner biblische Beiträge 54. Bonn, Germany: Peter Hanstein Verlag, 1980.

Lauterbach, Jacob Z. "The Sadducees and Pharisees." 1913. Reprint, in *Rabbinic Essays,* 23–48. Cincinnati: Hebrew Union College Press, 1951.

Lawrence, Jonathan David. *Washing in Water: Trajectories of Ritual Bathing in the Hebrew Bible and Second Temple Literature.* Academia Biblica 23. Atlanta: Society of Biblical Literature, 2006.

Lee, Yongbom. *Paul, Scribe of Old and New: Intertextual Insights for the Jesus-Paul Debate.* Library of New Testament Studies 512. London: Bloomsbury–T&T Clark, 2015.

Leeming, H., and K. Leeming, eds. *Josephus' Jewish War and Its Slavonic Version: A Synoptic Comparison of the English Translation by H. St. Thackeray with the Critical Edition by N. A. Meščerskij of the Slavonic Version in the Vilna Manuscript Translated into English by H. Leeming and L. Osinkina.* Arbeiten zur Geschichte des antiken Judentums und des Urchristentums 46. Leiden, the Netherlands: Brill, 2003.

Lehto, Adam. *The Demonstrations of Aphrahat, the Persian Sage.* Gorgias Eastern Christian Studies 27. Piscataway, NJ: Gorgias Press, 2010.

Lenowitz, Harris. *The Jewish Messiahs: From the Galilee to Crown Heights.* New York: Oxford University Press, 1998.

Levenson, Jon D. *Inheriting Abraham: The Legacy of the Patriarch in Judaism, Christianity, and Islam.* Princeton, N.J.: Princeton University Press, 2012.

———. *Resurrection and the Restoration of Israel: The Ultimate Victory of the God of Life.* New Haven, Conn.: Yale University Press, 2006.

Levine, Amy-Jill, and Marc Zvi Brettler, eds. *The Jewish Annotated New Testament: New Revised Standard Version Bible Translation.* Oxford: Oxford University Press, 2011.

Levine, Lee. "R. Simeon B. Yohai and the Purification of Tiberias: History and Tradition." *Hebrew Union College Annual* 49 (1974): 134–85.

Levy, David M. "The Hostile Act." *Psychological Review* 48 (1941): 356–61.

Lewis, Charlton D. and Charles Short, *A Latin Dictionary.* Oxford: Clarendon Press, 1879.

Liddell, Henry George; Robert Scott; and Henry Stuart Jones, *A Greek-English Lexicon With a Supplement.* Oxford: Clarendon Press, 1968.

Lidzbarski, Mark. *Das Johannesbuch der Mandäer.* Berlin: A. Töpelmann, 1915.

Lieberman, Saul. *Tosefeth Rishonim: A Commentary Based on Manuscripts of the Tosefta* and Works of the Rishonim and Midrashim in Manuscripts and Rare Editions. 1936–38. Reprint, New York: Jewish Theological Seminary, 1999.

Lietzmann, Hans. "Ein Beitrag zur Mandäerfrage." In *Kleine Schriften I: Studien zur spätantiken Religionsgeschichte,* 124–40. Texte und Untersuchungen 67. Berlin: Akademie-Verlag, 1958.

Lifton, Robert Jay. *Destroying the World to Save It: Aum Shinrikyō, Apocalyptic Violence, and the New Global Terrorism.* New York: Henry Holt, 1999.

Lightfoot, J. B. *St. Paul's Epistle to the Galatians: With Introductions, Notes and Dissertations.* 1875. Reprint, Lynn, Mass.: Hendrickson Publishers, 1981.

Loader, William. *Sexuality and the Jesus Tradition.* Grand Rapids, Mich.: Eerdmans, 2005.

Lohmeyer, Ernst. *Das Evangelium des Markus.* 1937. Reprint, Kritisch-exegetischer Kommentar über das Neue Testament (Meyer-Kommentar) 1.2. Göttingen, Germany: Vandenhoeck & Ruprecht, 1951.

——. *Das Urchristentum.* Vol. 1, *Johannes der Täufer.* Göttingen, Germany: Vandenhoeck & Ruprecht, 1932.

Loisy, Alfred. *Le Mandéisme et les origines chrétiennes.* Paris: Émile Nourry, 1934.

Lupieri, Edmondo. *Giovanni Battista fra storia e leggenda.* Biblioteca di Cultura Religiosa. Brescia, Italy: Paideia, 1988.

——. "Johannes der Täufer." In *Religion in Geschichte und Gegenwart,* 4:514–18, Tübingen: Mohr Siebeck, 1998.

——. *The Mandaeans: The Last Gnostics.* Italian Texts and Studies on Religion and Society. Grand Rapids, Mich.: Eerdmans, 2002.

Luz, Ulrich. *Matthew: A Commentary.* Hermeneia. 3 vols. Minneapolis: Fortress, 1989–2005.

Lüdemann, Gerd. *Early Christianity According to the Traditions in Acts: A Commentary.* London: SCM, 1989.

Maccoby, Hyam. *Judaism on Trial: Jewish-Christian Disputations in the Middle Ages.* Littman Library of Jewish Civilization. Rutherford, N.J.: Fairleigh Dickinson University Press; London: Associated University Presses, 1982.

MacEoin, Denis. "The Babi Concept of Holy War." *Religion* 12 (1982): 93–129.

——. "Divisions and Authority Claims in Babism (1850–1866)." *Studia Iranica* 18 (1989): 93–129.

——. "From Babism to Baha'ism: Problems of Militancy, Quietism, and Conflation in the Construction of a Religion." *Religion* 13 (1983): 219–55.

MacEoin, Denis Martin. *The Messiah of Shiraz: Studies in Early and Middle Babism.* Iran Studies 3. Leiden, the Netherlands: Brill, 2009.

MacEoin, D. M. "Babism." In *Encyclopaedia Iranica.* 1988. Reprint, 2011. http://www .iranicaonline.org/articles/babism-index.

Magness, Jodi. *The Archaeology of Qumran and the Dead Sea Scrolls.* Studies in the Dead Sea Scrolls and Related Literature. Grand Rapids, Mich.: Eerdmans, 2002.

——. "The Community at Qumran in Light of Its Pottery." In *Methods of Investigation of the Dead Sea Scrolls and the Khirbet Qumran Site: Present Realities and Future Prospects,* edited by Michael O Wise, Norman Golb, John J. Collins, and Dennis G. Pardee, 39–50. Annals of the New York Academy of Sciences 722. New York: New York Academy of Sciences, 1994.

——. *Stone and Dung, Oil and Spit: Jewish Daily Life in the Time of Jesus.* Grand Rapids, Mich.: Eerdmans, 2011.

——. "Weapons." In *Encyclopedia of the Dead Sea Scrolls,* edited by Lawrence H. Schiffman and James C. VanderKam, 2:970–73. New York: Oxford University Press, 2000.

Maier, Paul D. "The Date of the Nativity and the Chronology of Jesus' Life." In *Chronis, Kairos, Christos: Nativity and Chronological Studies Presented to Jack Finegan,* edited by Jerry Vardaman and Edwin M. Yamauchi, 113–30. Winona Lake, Ind.: Eisenbrauns, 1989.

Manson, T. W. *The Sayings of Jesus as Recorded in the Gospels According to St. Matthew and St. Luke with Introduction and Commentary.* 1937. Reprint, London: SCM, 1957.

Marable, Manning. *Malcolm X: A Life of Reinvention.* New York: Viking, 2011.

Marcus, Joel. "The Beelzebul Controversy and the Eschatologies of Jesus." In *Authenticating the Activities of Jesus,* edited by B. Chilton and C. A. Evans, 247–77. Leiden, the Netherlands: Brill, 1999.

——. "*Birkat Ha-Minim* Revisited." *NTS* 55 (2009): 523–51.

——. "The Circumcision and the Uncircumcision in Rome." *NTS* 35 (1989): 67–81.

——. "The Intertextual Polemic of the Markan Vineyard Parable." In *Tolerance and Intolerance in Early Judaism and Christianity,* edited by Graham N. Stanton and Guy G. Stroumsa, 211–27. Cambridge: Cambridge University Press, 1998.

——. "John the Baptist and Jesus." In *When Judaism and Christianity Began: Essays in Memory of Anthony J. Saldarini,* edited by A. J. Avery-Peck, D. Harrington, and J. Neusner, 1:179–97. Supplements to the Journal for the Study of Judaism 85. Leiden, the Netherlands: Brill, 2004.

——. *Mark: A New Translation with Introduction and Commentary.* Anchor Yale Bible 27 and 27A. New Haven, Conn.: Yale University Press, 2000–2009.

——. "Mark 9,11–13: As It Has Been Written." *Zeitschrift für die neutestamentliche Wissenschaft und die Kunde der älteren Kirche* 80 (1989): 42–63.

——. "Modern and Ancient Jewish Apocalypticism." *Journal of Religion* 76 (1996): 1–27.

——. "The Once and Future Messiah in Early Christianity and Chabad." *NTS* 47 (2001): 381–401.

——. "Passover and Last Supper Revisited." *NTS* 59 (2013): 303–24.

——. "The *Testaments of the Twelve Patriarchs* and the *Didascalia Apostolorum:* A Common Jewish-Christian Milieu?" *Journal of Theological Studies* 61 (2010): 596–626.

——. *The Way of the Lord: Christological Exegesis of the Old Testament in the Gospel of Mark.* Louisville, Ky.: Westminster–John Knox; Edinburgh: T&T Clark, 1992.

Marshall, David. "Christianity in the Qur'ān." In *Islamic Interpretations of Christianity,* edited by Lloyd Ridgeon, 3–29. New York: St. Martin's Press, 2001.

——. "Heavenly Religion or Unbelief? Muslim Perspectives on Christianity." *Anvil* 23 (2006): 89–100.

——. *God, Muhammad and the Unbelievers: A Qur'anic Study.* Richmond, U.K.: Curzon Press, 1999.

Marshall, I. Howard. *The Gospel of Luke: A Commentary on the Greek Text.* New International Greek Testament Commentary. Exeter, U.K.: Paternoster; Grand Rapids, Mich.: Eerdmans, 1978.

Martin, Lawrence T., trans. and ed. *The Venerable Bede: Commentary on the Acts of the Apostles.* Cisterian Studies 117. Kalamazoo, Mich.: Cisterian Publications, 1989.

Marxsen, Willi. *Mark the Evangelist.* Nashville: Abingdon, 1969.

Mason, Steve. "Fire, Water and Spirit: John the Baptist and the Tyranny of Canon." *Studies in Religion* 21 (1992): 163–80.

——. *Flavius Josephus on the Pharisees: A Composition-Critical Study.* Studia Post-Biblica 39. Leiden, the Netherlands: Brill, 1991.

———. *Josephus and the New Testament.* Peabody, Mass.: Hendrickson Publishers, 2003.

McCasland, S. Vernon. "Matthew Twists the Scriptures." *JBL* 80 (1961): 143–48.

McDonald, J. Ian H. "What Did You Go Out to See? John the Baptist, the Scrolls, and Late Second Temple Judaism." In *The Dead Sea Scrolls in Their Historical Context,* edited by Timothy H. Lim, 53–64. Edinburgh: T&T Clark, 2000.

McLean, Bradley H. *Citations and Allusions to Jewish Scripture in Early Christian and Jewish Writings Through 180 C.E.* Lewiston, N.Y.: Edwin Mellen Press, 1992.

Meeks, Wayne A. "Simon Magus in Recent Research." *Religious Studies Review* 3 (1977): 137–42.

———. "Judaism, Hellenism, and the Birth of Christianity." In *Paul Beyond the Judaism/ Hellenism Divide,* edited by Troels Engberg-Pedersen, 17–27. Louisville, Ky.: Westminster John Knox Press, 2001.

Meier, John P. "Jesus in Josephus: A Modest Proposal." *CBQ* 52 (1990): 76–103.

———. *A Marginal Jew: Rethinking the Historical Jesus.* Anchor Bible Reference Library. 5 vols. New Haven, Conn.: Yale University Press, 1991–2016.

Menken, M. J. J. "The Quotation from Isa. 40,3 in John 1,23." *Biblica* 66 (1985): 190–205.

Meyers, Carol L., and Eric M. Meyers. *Zechariah 9–14: A New Translation with Introduction and Commentary.* AB 25C. New York: Doubleday, 1993.

Meyers, Eric M. "Khirbet Qumran and Its Environs." In *The Oxford Handbook of the Dead Sea Scrolls,* edited by Timothy H. Lim and John J. Collins, 21–45. Oxford Handbooks in Religion and Theology. Oxford: Oxford University Press, 2010.

Milgrom, Jacob. *Leviticus: A New Translation with Introduction and Commentary.* AB 3. 3 vols. New York: Doubleday, 1991–2001.

Milik, J. T. *The Books of Enoch.* Oxford: Clarendon Press, 1976.

Miller, Patrick D. *The Divine Warrior in Early Israel.* Harvard Semitic Monographs 5. Cambridge, Mass.: Harvard University Press, 1973.

Miller, William McElwee. *The Baha'i Faith: Its History and Teachings.* South Pasadena, Calif.: William Carey Library, 1974.

Moen, Ingrid Johanne. "Marriage and Divorce in the Herodian Family: A Case Study of Diversity in Late Second Temple Judaism." Ph.D. diss., Duke University, 2009.

Moesinger, Georg, ed. *Evangelii concordantis expositio facta a sancto Ephraemo doctore syro.* Venice: Libraria PP. Mechitaristarum in Monasterio S. Lazari, 1876.

Molin, Georg. "Elijahu: Der Prophet und sein Weiterleben in den Hoffnungen des Judentums und der Christenheit." *Judaica* 8 (1953): 65–94.

Momen, Moojan, ed. *The Bábí and Bahá'í Religions 1844–1944: Some Contemporary Western Accounts.* Oxford: G. Ronald, 1981.

———. *Baha'u'llah: A Short Biography.* Oxford: Oneworld, 2007.

Moule, C. F. D. *An Idiom Book of New Testament Greek.* 2nd ed. Cambridge: Cambridge University Press, 1959.

Mulder, Martin Jay, ed. *Mikra: Text, Translation, and Reading and Interpretation of the Hebrew Bible in Ancient Judaism and Early Christianity.* Corpus Rerum Iudaicarum ad Novum Testamentum. Philadelphia: Fortress, 1988.

Muraoka, T. *A Greek-English Lexicon of the Septuagint.* Leuven, Belgium: Peeters, 2009.

Murphy, Catherine M. *Wealth in the Dead Sea Scrolls and in the Qumran Community.* Studies on the Texts of the Desert of Judah 40. Leiden, the Netherlands: Brill, 2002.

Murphy-O'Connor, J. "John the Baptist and Jesus: History and Hypotheses." *NTS* 36 (1990): 359–74.

Myers, Henry A., and Herwig Wolfram. *Medieval Kingship.* Chicago: Nelson-Hall, 1982.

Neusner, Jacob. "'Judaism' After Moore: A Programmatic Statement." *Journal of Jewish Studies* 31 (1980): 141–56.

——. "Judaism in Late Antiquity." *Judaism* 15 (1966): 230–40.

——. *The Tosefta: Translated from the Hebrew with a New Introduction.* 2 vols. Peabody, Mass.: Hendrickson Publishers, 2002.

Newsom, Carol. "Constructing 'We, You, and the Others' Through Non-Polemical Discourse." In *Defining Identities: We, You, and the Other in the Dead Sea Scrolls*, edited by Florentino García Martínez and Mladen Popović, 13–21. Proceedings of the Fifth Meeting of the IOQS in Groningen. Leiden, the Netherlands: Brill, 2008.

Nickelsburg, George W. E. *Resurrection, Immortality, and Eternal Life in Intertestamental Judaism.* Harvard Theological Studies 26. Cambridge, Mass.: Harvard University Press, 1972.

——. *1 Enoch 1.* Hermeneia. Minneapolis: Fortress, 2001.

Niditch, Susan. *My Brother Esau Is a Hairy Man: Hair and Identity in Ancient Israel.* New York: Oxford University Press, 2008.

——. *War in the Hebrew Bible: A Study in the Ethics of Violence.* New York: Oxford University Press, 1993.

Nikiprowetzky, Valentin. "Réflexions sur quelques problèmes du quatrième et du cinquième livre des Oracles Sibyllins." *Hebrew Union College Annual* 43 (1972): 29–76.

Nir, Rivka. "Josephus' Account of John the Baptist: A Christian Interpolation?" *Journal for the Study of the Historical Jesus* 10 (2012): 32–62.

Nitzan, Bilhah. "302. 4QpapAdmonitory Parable." In *Qumran Cave 4.XV: Sapiential Texts, Part I*, 125–49. Discoveries in the Judaean Desert 20. Oxford: Clarendon Press, 1997.

Nodet, Étienne. "Jésus et Jean-Baptiste selon Josephe." *Revue biblique* 82 (1985): 321–48, 497–524.

Olson, Ken. "A Eusebian Reading of the *Testimonium Flavianum*." In *Eusebius of Caesarea: Tradition and Innovations*, edited by Aaron Johnson and Jeremy Schott, 97–114. Cambridge, Mass.: Harvard University Press, 2013.

Origen. *Homilies on Luke; Fragments on Luke.* Trans. Joseph T. Lienhard. Fathers of the Church 94 Washinton, D.C.: Catholic University Press of America, 1996.

Pattengale, Jerry A. "Aenon." In *Anchor Bible Dictionary*, 1:87. New York: Doubleday, 1992.

Pelikan, Jaroslav. *The Christian Tradition: A History of the Development of Doctrine.* 5 vols. Chicago: University of Chicago Press, 1971–91.

Peretti, Aurelio. "Echi di dottrine esseniche negli Oracoli Sibillini giudaici." *La parola del passato* 17 (1962): 247–95.

Petersen, David L. *Late Israelite Prophecy: Studies in Deutero-Prophetic Literature and in Chronicles.* Society of Biblical Literature Monograph Series. Missoula, Mont.: Scholars Press, 1977.

Pietersma, Albert, and Benjamin G. Wright, eds. *A New English Translation of the Septuagint.* New York: Oxford University Press, 2007.

Piovanelli, Pierluigi. "The *Toledot Yeshu* and Christian Apocryphal Literature: The Formative Years." In *Toledot Yeshu ("The Life Story of Jesus") Revisited: A Princeton Conference*, edited by Peter Schäfer, Michael Meerson, and Yaacov Deutch, 89–100. Tübingen, Germany: Mohr Siebeck, 2011.

Plisch, Uwe-Karsten. *The Gospel of Thomas: Original Text with Commentary.* Freiburg, Germany: Deutsche Bibelgesellschaft, 2008.

Pritchard, James B., ed. *Ancient Near Eastern Texts Relating to the Old Testament,* 3rd ed. Princeton, N.J.: Princeton University Press, 1969.

Puech, Émile. "Hodayot." In *Encyclopedia of the Dead Sea Scrolls,* edited by Lawrence H. Schiffman and James VanderKam, l. 365-69. New York: Oxford University Press, 2000.

Qimron, Elisha, and John Strugnell. *Qumran Cave 4.V: Miqṣat Maʿaśe Ha-Torah.* Discoveries in the Judaean Desert 10. Oxford: Clarendon Press, 1994.

Rabens, Volker. *The Holy Spirit and Ethics in Paul: Transformation and Empowering for Religious-Ethical Life.* WUNT 2.283. Tübingen, Germany: Mohr Siebeck, 2010.

Rapoport-Albert, Ada. "God and the Zaddik as the Two Focal Points of Hasidic Worship." 1977. Reprint, in *Essential Papers on Hasidism: Origins to Present,* edited by Gershon David Hundert, 299–329. Essential Papers on Jewish Studies. New York: New York University Press, 1991.

Rappaport, Roy A. *Ritual and Religion in the Making of Humanity.* Cambridge Studies in Social and Cultural Anthropology. Cambridge: Cambridge University Press, 1999.

Ravitzky, Aviezer. *Messianism, Zionism, and Jewish Religious Radicalism.* Chicago Studies in the History of Judaism. Chicago: University of Chicago Press, 1996.

Reed, Annette Yoshiko. "'Jewish Christianity' After the 'Parting of the Ways': Approaches to Historiography and Self-Definition in the Pseudo-Clementines." In *The Ways That Never Parted: Jews and Christians in Late Antiquity and the Early Middle Ages,* edited by Adam H. Becker and Annette Yoshiko Reed, 189–231. Texte und Studien zum antiken Judentum 95. Tübingen, Germany: Mohr Siebeck, 2003.

Reinhartz, Adele. *Befriending the Beloved Disciple: A Jewish Reading of the Gospel of John.* New York; London: Continuum, 2001.

Renan, Ernest. *The Life of Jesus.* 1863. English translation, Great Minds Series. Amherst, N.Y.: Prometheus Books, 1991.

Reumann, John. "The Quest for the Historical John the Baptist." In *Understanding the Sacred Text: Essays in Honor of Morton S. Enslin on the Hebrew Bible and Christian Beginnings,* edited by John Reumann, 182–99. Valley Forge, Pa.: Judson Press, 1972.

Rhoads, David M. *Israel in Revolution 6–74 C.E.: A Political History Based on the Writings of Josephus.* Philadelphia: Fortress, 1976.

Ricks, Christopher, and Jim McCue, eds. *The Poems of T. S. Eliot.* Vol. 1, *Collected and Uncollected Poems.* Baltimore: Johns Hopkins University Press, 2015.

Rindoš, Jaroslav. *He of Whom It Is Written: John the Baptist and Elijah in Luke.* Österreichische biblische Studien 38. Frankfurt: P. Lang, 2010.

Rishell, C. W. "Baldensperger's Theory of the Origin of the Fourth Gospel." *JBL* 20 (1901): 38–49.

Robinson, James M., Paul Hoffmann, and John S. Kloppenborg, eds. *The Critical Edition of Q: Synopsis Including the Gospels of Matthew and Luke, Mark and Thomas with English, German, and French Translations of Q and Thomas.* Hermeneia. Minneapolis: Fortress; Leuven, Belgium: Peeters, 2000.

Robinson, John A. T. "Elijah, John and Jesus: An Essay in Detection." *NTS* 4 (1958): 263–81.

———. "The 'Others' of John 4.38: A Test of Exegetical Method." 1959. Reprint in *Twelve New Testament Studies,* 61–66. Studies in Biblical Theology. Naperville, Ill.: Alec R. Allenson, 1962.

Römer, Thomas C. *The So-Called Deuteronomistic History: A Sociological, Historical and Literary Introduction.* London: T&T Clark, 2005.

Rothschild, Clare K. *Baptist Traditions and Q.* WUNT 190. Tübingen, Germany: Mohr Siebeck, 2005.

——. "'Echo of a Whisper': The Uncertain Authenticity of Josephus' Witness to John the Baptist." In *Ablution, Initiation, and Baptism,* edited by David Hellholm, Tor Vegge, Øyvind Norderval, and Christer Hellholm, 1:255–90. BZNW 176. Berlin: De Gruyter, 2011.

Royse, James R. *Scribal Habits in Early Greek New Testament Papyri.* New Testament Tools, Studies and Documents 36. Leiden, the Netherlands: Brill, 2008.

Rudolph, Kurt. *Antike Baptisten: Zu den Überlieferungen über frühjüdische und -christliche Taufsekten.* Sitzungsberichte der Sächsischen Akademie der Wissenschaften zu Leipzig. Philologisch-Historische Klasse 121.4. Berlin: Akademie-Verlag, 1981.

——. *Die Mandäer.* Forschungen zur Religion und Literatur des Alten und Neuen Testaments 74. N.F. 56. Göttingen, Germany: Vandenhoeck & Ruprecht, 1960.

Runciman, Steven. *The Byzantine Theocracy.* Cambridge: Cambridge University Press, 1977.

Sæbø, Magne, ed. *Hebrew Bible/Old Testament: The History of Its Interpretation.* Vol. 1, *From the Beginnings to the Middle Ages (Until 1300).* Pt. 1, *Antiquity.* Göttingen, Germany: Vandenhoeck & Ruprecht, 1996.

Sanders, E. P. *The Historical Figure of Jesus.* London: Penguin Press, 1993.

——. *Jesus and Judaism.* Philadelphia: Fortress, 1985.

——. *Judaism: Practice and Belief 63 BCE–66 CE.* London: SCM; Philadelphia: Trinity Press International, 1992.

——. *Paul and Palestinian Judaism: A Comparison of Patterns of Religion.* Philadelphia: Fortress, 1977.

——. *The Tendencies of the Synoptic Tradition.* Society for New Testament Studies Monograph Series 9. Cambridge: Cambridge University Press, 1969.

Sandys-Wunsch, John. *What Have They Done to the Bible? A History of Modern Biblical Interpretation.* Collegeville, Minn.: Liturgical Press, 2005.

Sänger, Dieter. "'Ist er heraufgestiegen, gilt er in jeder Hinsicht als ein Israelit' (bYev 47b). Das Proselytentauchbad im frühen Judentum," in *Ablution, Initiation, and Baptism,* edited by David Hellholm, Tor Vegge, Øyvind Norderval, and Christer Hellholm, 1:291–334. BZNW 176. Berlin: De Gruyter, 2011.

Satlow, Michael L. *Jewish Marriage in Antiquity.* Princeton, N.J.: Princeton University Press, 2001.

Schlatter, Adolf. *Johannes der Täufer.* 1880. Reprint, Basel, Switzerland: Verlag Friedrich Reinhardt AG., 1956.

Schlosser, Jacques. *Le règne de Dieu dans les dits de Jesus.* Etudes bibliques. Paris: J. Gabalda, 1980.

Schnackenburg, Rudolf. *The Gospel According to St. John.* New York: Crossroad, 1968–82.

Schoeps, Hans-Joachim. *Theologie und Geschichte des Judenchristentums.* Tübingen, Germany: J. C. B. Mohr (Paul Siebeck), 1949.

Scholem, Gershom. *The Messianic Idea in Judaism and Other Essays on Jewish Spirituality.* London: Allen & Unwin, 1971.

Scholem, Gershom G. *Major Trends in Jewish Mysticism.* 1941. Reprint, New York: Schocken, 1961.

Schütz, Roland. *Johannes der Täufer.* Abhandlungen zur Theologie des Alten und Neuen Testaments 50. Zürich: Zwingli, 1967.

Schwartz, Barry. *Abraham Lincoln and the Forge of National Memory.* Chicago: University of Chicago Press, 2000.

Schwartz, Daniel R. "On Pharisaic Opposition to the Hasmonean Monarchy," 1983. Reprint, in *Studies in the Jewish Background of Christianity.* WUNT 60. Tübingen, Germany: J. C. B. Mohr (Paul Siebeck), 1992.

Schwartz, Seth. Review of *Flavius Josephus on the Pharisees: A Composition-Critical Study* by Steve Mason. *AJS Review* 19 (1994): 83–88.

Schweitzer, Albert. *The Quest of the Historical Jesus: First Complete Edition.* 1913. English trans., Minneapolis: Fortress, 2001.

Schweizer, Eduard; Hermann Kleinknecht; Friedrich Baugärtel; Werner Bieder; and Erik Sjöberg. "Pneuma, Pneumatikos." In *Theological Dictionary of the New Testament,* edited by Gerhard Kittel and Gerhard Friedrich, 6:332–454. Grand Rapids, Mich.: Eerdmans, 1968..

Scobie, C. H. H. *John the Baptist.* London: SCM, 1964.

Sekki, Arthur Everett. *The Meaning of Ruah at Qumran.* Society of Biblical Literature Dissertation Series 110. Atlanta: Scholars Press, 1989.

Shaked, Shaul. "Qumran and Iran: Further Considerations." *Israel Oriental Studies* 2 (1972): 433–46.

Shauf, Scott. *Theology as History, History as Theology: Paul in Ephesus in Acts 19.* BZNW 133. Berlin: Walter de Gruyter, 2005.

Shaver, Brenda J. "The Prophet Elijah in the Literature of the Second Temple Period: The Growth of a Tradition." Ph.D. diss., University of Chicago, 2001.

Skehan, Patrick W., and Alexander A. Di Lella. *The Wisdom of Ben Sira: A New Translation with Notes, Introduction, and Commentary.* AB 39. New York: Doubleday, 1987.

Smallwood, E. Mary. *The Jews under Roman Rule: From Pompey to Diocletian.* Studies in Judaism in Late Antiquity 20. Leiden, the Netherlands: Brill, 1976.

Smend, Rudolf. "Julius Wellhausen and His Prolegomena to the History of Israel." *Semeia* 25 (1982): 1–20.

Smith, Morton. "The Account of Simon Magus in Acts 8." In *Harry Austryn Wolfson Jubilee Volume: On the Occasion of His Seventy-Fifth Birthday; English Section,* 2:735–49. Jerusalem: American Academy for Jewish Research, 1965.

———. "What Is Implied by the Variety of Messianic Figures?" *JBL* 78 (1959): 66–72.

Smyth, Herbert Weir. *Greek Grammar.* 1920. Reprint, Cambridge, Mass.: Harvard University Press, 1956.

Sommer, Benjamin D. Review of *Resurrection and the Restoration of Israel,* by Jon D. Levenson. *Journal of Religion* 90 (2010): 554–56.

Sotomayor, Manuel. "Los grandes centros de la expansión del cristianismo." In *Historia del cristianismo: I. El mundo antiguo,* edited by Manuel Sotomayor and José Fernández Ubiña, 189–226. Madrid: Universidad de Granada, 2006.

Spinoza, Benedict. *Theological-Political Treatise.* Cambridge Texts in the History of Philosophy. Cambridge: Cambridge University Press, 2007.

Stegemann, Hartmut. *The Library of Qumran: On the Essenes, Qumran, John the Baptist, and Jesus.* Leiden, the Netherlands: Brill; Grand Rapids, Mich.: Eerdmans, 1998.

Steinmann, Jean. *Saint John the Baptist and the Desert Tradition.* New York: Harper, 1958.

Stemberger, Günter. *Introduction to the Talmud and Midrash.* 2nd ed. Edinburgh: T&T Clark, 1996.

Stern, Menachem. "The House of Herod and the Roman Empire After the Death of Herod [Hebrew]." In *Studies in Jewish History: The Second Temple Period,* 232–45. Jerusalem: Yad Ishak Ben-Zvi, 1991.

Stone, Michael Edward. *Fourth Ezra: A Commentary on the Book of Fourth Ezra.* Hermeneia. Minneapolis: Fortress, 1990.

Strauss, David Friedrich. *A New Life of Jesus.* London: Williams and Norgate, 1865.

Strecker, Georg. *Das Judenchristentum in den Pseudoklementinen.* Texte und Untersuchungen 70. Berlin: Akadmie-Verlag, 1981.

Streeter, Burnett Hillman. *The Four Gospels: A Study of Origins.* London: Macmillan, 1924.

Stuckenbruck, Loren T. *1 Enoch 91–108.* Commentaries on Early Jewish Literature. Berlin: Walter de Gruyter, 2007.

Sutton, L. P. Elwell. Review of *Edward Granville Brown and the Bahá'í Faith,* by H. M. Balyuzi. *Journal of the Royal Asiatic Society,* n.s., 104 (1972): 70–71.

Swartley, Willard M. *Slavery, Sabbath, War, and Women: Case Issues in Biblical Interpretation.* Conrad Grebel Lectures. Scottdale, Pa.: Herald Press, 1983.

Tatum, W. Barnes. *John the Baptist and Jesus: A Report of the Jesus Seminar.* Sonoma, Calif.: Polebridge Press, 1994.

Taylor, Joan E. *The Immerser: John the Baptist within Second Temple Judaism.* Grand Rapids, Mich.: Eerdmans, 1997.

ter Haar Romeny, Bas. "Hypotheses on the Development of Judaism and Christianity in Syria in the Period After 70 CE." In *Matthew and the Didache: Two Documents from the Same Jewish-Christian Milieu?,* edited by Huub van de Sandt, 13–33. Assen, the Netherlands: Royal Van Gorcum; Minneapolis: Fortress, 2004.

Theissen, Gerd, and Antoinette Merz. *The Historical Jesus: A Comprehensive Guide.* London: SCM, 1998.

Theobald, Michael. *Das Evangelium nach Johannes: Kapitel 1–12.* Regensburger Neues Testament. Regensburg, Germany: Friedrich Pustet, 2009.

Thiessen, Matthew. *Contesting Conversion: Genealogy, Circumcision, and Identity in Ancient Judaism and Christianity.* New York: Oxford University Press, 2011.

Thomas Aquinas, Saint. *Catena Aurea: Commentary on the Four Gospels Collected Out of the Works of the Fathers.* Oxford: Parker, 1842.

Thomas, Joseph. *Le mouvement baptiste en Palestine et Syrie (150 av. J.-C.-300 ap. J.-C.).* Universitas Catholica Lovaniensis. Dissertationes ad gradum magistri in Facultate Theologica vel in Facultate Iuris Canonici Consequendum Conscriptae 2.58. Gembloux, Belgium: J. Duculot, 1935.

Thyen, Hartwig. "Βάπτισμα μετανοίας εἰς ἄφεσιν ἁμαρίῶν." In *Zeit und Geschichte. Dankesgabe an Rudolph Bultmann zum 80. Geburtstag,* edited by E. Dinkler, 97–125. Tübingen, Germany: J. C. B. Mohr (Paul Siebeck), 1964.

Tiller, Patrick A. "The 'Eternal Planting' in the Dead Sea Scrolls." *Dead Sea Discoveries* 4 (1997): 312–35.

Tilly, Michael. *Johannes der Täufer und die Biographie der Propheten: die synoptische Täuferüberlieferung und das jüdische Prophetenbild zur Zeit des Täufers.* Beiträge zur Wissenschaft vom Alten und Neuen Testament, 7th Series 17 [137]. Stuttgart: Verlag W. Kohlhammer, 1994.

Tov, Emmanuel, ed. *The Dead Sea Scrolls Electronic Library.* Leiden, the Netherlands: Brill; Provo, Utah: Brigham Young University, 2006. CD-ROM, produced by Noel B. Reynolds.

Trombley, Frank. "Overview: The Geographical Spread of Christianity." In *The Cambridge History of Christianity,* vol. 1, *Origins to Constantine,* edited by M. Mitchell and F. Young, 302–13. Cambridge: Cambridge University Press, 2006.

Tromp, Johannes. "John the Baptist According to Flavius Josephus, and His Incorporation in the Christian Tradition." In Empsychoi Logoi—*Religious Innovations in Antiquity: Studies in Honour of Pieter Willem Van der Horst,* edited by Alberdkina Houtman, Albert de Jong, and Magda Misset-van de Weg, 135–49. Leiden, the Netherlands: Brill, 2008.

Tuckett, Christopher M. "The Current State of the Synoptic Problem." In *New Studies in the Synoptic Problem: Oxford Conference, April 2008; Essays in Honour of Christopher M. Tuckett,* edited by Paul Foster, Andrew Gregory, John S. Kloppenborg, and Joseph Verheyden, 9–50. Bibliotheca Ephemeridum Theologicarum Lovaniensium 239. Leuven, Belgium: Peeters, 2011.

Ulrich, Eugene, and Peter W. Flint. *Qumran Cave 1.II—The Isaiah Scrolls: Part 2, Introductions, Commentary, and Textual Variants.* Discoveries in the Judaean Desert 32. Oxford: Clarendon Press, 2010.

van Emden, W. G. "Kingship in the Old French Epic of Revolt." In *Kings and Kingship in Medieval Europe,* edited by Anne J. Duggan, 305–50. King's College London Medieval Studies 10. London: King's College London Centre for Late Antique and Medieval Studies, 1993.

Van Voorst, Robert E. *The Ascents of James: History and Theology of a Jewish-Christian Community.* Society of Biblical Literature Dissertation Series 112. Atlanta: Scholars Press, 1989.

VanderKam, James C. *The Dead Sea Scrolls Today.* Grand Rapids, Mich.: Eerdmans; London: SPCK, 1994.

———. "Jubilees, Book of." In *Encyclopedia of the Dead Sea Scrolls,* edited by Lawrence H. Schiffman and James C. VanderKam, 1:434–38. New York: Oxford University Press, 2000.

Vardaman, Jerry. "Jesus' Life: A New Chronology." In *Chronos, Kairos, Christos: Nativity and Chronological Studies Presented to Jack Finegan,* edited by Jerry Vardaman and Edwin M. Yamauchi, 55–82. Winona Lake, Ind.: Eisenbrauns, 1989.

Venturini, Karl Heinrich Georg. *Natürliche Geschichte des grossen Propheten von Nazareth.* Copenhagen: Bethlehem, 1806.

Vianès, Laurence, ed. *Malachie.* La Bible d'Alexandrie 23.12. Paris: Les Éditions du Cerf, 2011.

Vielhauer, Philipp. "Das Benedictus des Zacharias (Luk 1,68–79)." In *Aufsätze zum Neuen Testament,* 28–46. Theologische Bücherei: Neudrucke und Berichte aus dem 20. Jahrhundert 31. Munich: Chr. Kaiser Verlag, 1965.

———. "Tracht und Speise Johannes der Täufers." In *Aufsätze zum Neuen Testament,* 47–54. Theologische Bücherei: Neudrucke und Berichte aus dem 20. Jahrhundert 31. Munich: Chr. Kaiser Verlag, 1965.

Vincent, Nicholas. "Isabella of Angoulême: John's Jezebel." In *King John: New Interpretations,* edited by S. D. Church, 165–219. Woodbridge, U.K.: Boydell Press, 1999.

Vogel, Manuel. "Jesusgemeinden und Täufergruppen zwischen Abgrenzung und Wertschätzung—eine Skizze." In *Juden und Christen unter römischer Herrschaft. Selbstwahrnehmung und Fremdwahrnehmung in den ersten beiden Jahrhunderten n.Chr.*, edited by Niclas Förster and Jacobus Cornelis de Vos, 74–84. Göttingen: Vandenhoeck & Ruprecht, 2015.

von Dobbeler, Stephanie. *Das Gericht und das Erbarmen Gottes: Die Botschaft Johannes des Täufers und ihre Rezeption bei den Johannesjüngern im Rahmen der Theologiegeschichte des Frühjudentums.* Bonner Biblische Beiträge 70. Frankfurt: Athenäum, 1988.

Vööbus, Arthur. *The Didascalia Apostolorum in Syriac.* Corpus scriptorum christianorum orientalium 175–76, 179–80. Leuven, Belgium: Secrétariat du Corpus SCO, 1979.

Vuong, Lily C. *Gender and Purity in the Protevangelium of James.* WUNT 2.358. Tübingen, Germany: Mohr Siebeck, 2013.

Wallace, Daniel B. *Greek Grammar Beyond the Basics: An Exegetical Syntax of the New Testament.* Grand Rapids, Mich.: Zondervan, 1996.

Webb, Robert L. "Jesus' Baptism: Its Historicity and Implications." *Bulletin for Biblical Research* 10 (2000): 261–309.

——. *John the Baptizer and Prophet: A Socio-Historical Study.* Journal for the Study of the New Testament: Supplement Series 62. Sheffield, U.K.: JSOT Press, 1991.

Weber, Max. *The Sociology of Religion.* 1922. English translation, Boston: Beacon Press, 1963.

Wehnert, Jürgen. "Taufvorstellungen in den Pseudoklementinen." In *Ablution, Initiation, and Baptism*, edited by David Hellholm, Tor Vegge, Øyvind Norderval, and Christer Hellholm, 2:1071–1114. BZNW 176. Berlin: De Gruyter, 2011.

Weir, Alison. *The Six Wives of Henry VIII.* New York: Grove Weidenfeld, 1992.

Wernberg-Møller, P. *The Manual of Discipline.* Studies on the Texts of the Desert of Judah 1. Grand Rapids, Mich.: Eerdmans, 1957.

Wessinger, Catherine, ed. *The Oxford Handbook of Millennialism.* New York: Oxford University Press, 2011.

Williams, Frank. *The Panarion of Epiphanius of Salamis: Book I (Sects 1–46).* Nag Hammadi and Manicaean Studies 63. Leiden, the Netherlands: Brill, 2009.

Wilson, Bryan. *Magic and the Millennium.* New York: Harper & Row, 1973.

Wink, Walter. *John the Baptist in the Gospel Tradition.* Society for New Testament Studies Monograph Series 7. Cambridge: Cambridge University Press, 1968.

Wirgin, Wolf. "Simon Maccabaeus and the *Prophetes Pistos*." *Palestine Exploration Quarterly* 103 (1971): 35–41.

Wise, Michael O., Martin G. Abegg Jr., and Edward M. Cook. *The Dead Sea Scrolls: A New Translation.* San Francisco: HarperSanFrancisco, 2005.

Wolfson, Elliott R. *Open Secret: Postmessianic Messianism and the Mystical Revision of Menaḥem Mendel Schneerson.* New York: Columbia University Press, 2009.

Yadin, Y. *The Temple Scroll.* 2 vols. Jerusalem: Israel Exploration Society, 1977-1983.

Zangenberg, Jürgen. "Opening up Our View: Khirbet Qumran in a Regional Perspective," in *Religion and Society in Roman Palestine: Old Questions, New Approaches*, edited by Douglas R. Edwards, 170–87. New York: Routledge, 2004.

Zangenberg, Jürgen, Harold W. Attridge, and Dale B. Martin, eds. *Religion, Ethnicity, and Identity in Ancient Galilee: A Region in Transition.* Tübingen, Germany: Mohr Siebeck, 2007.

Zeitlin, Solomon. "The Halaka in the Gospels and Its Relation to the Jewish Law at the Time of Jesus." *Hebrew Union College Annual* 1 (1924): 357–73.

Zerbe, Gordon M. *Non-Retaliation in Early Jewish and New Testament Texts: Ethical Themes in Social Contexts.* Journal for the Study of Pseudepigrapha Supplement Series 13. Sheffield, U.K.: JSOT Press, 1993.

INDEX OF MODERN AUTHORS

INDEX OF ANCIENT SOURCES